Y0-BFY-260

The President Makers

THE CULTURE OF POLITICS AND LEADERSHIP

IN AN AGE OF ENLIGHTENMENT

1896-1919

BY MATTHEW JOSEPHSON

973.9
J77

HARCOURT, BRACE AND COMPANY, NEW YORK

COPYRIGHT, 1940, BY
MATTHEW JOSEPHSON

All rights reserved, including the right to reproduce this book or portions thereof in any form.

first edition

Typography by Robert Josephy

PRINTED IN THE UNITED STATES OF AMERICA
BY QUINN & BODEN COMPANY, INC., RAHWAY, N. J.

CONTENTS

448686

Foreword v

BOOK ONE

I. The Golden Years of McKinley and Hanna 3
II. The Scholars in Politics 29
III. A "Splendid Little War"; and the Making of a President 65
IV. Toward National Political Leadership 111
V. Toward Leadership: "Rooseveltiana" 139
VI. Principally World-Wandering 175
VII. The Politics of Reform 210
VIII. The Politics of Depression 246

BOOK TWO

IX. An Attempted "Restoration" 285
X. The Ballinger Case: An American Affaire Dreyfus 306
XI. "Doctor Wilson" 330
XII. Colonel House's Vision 364
XIII. The Menace of La Follette 397
XIV. "Armageddon" 422

xv. "The New Freedom": Climax of the Liberal Revolution 460

xvi. Leadership Through War 496

xvii. The Martyrdom of Dr. Wilson 533

Sources 567

Index 573

FOREWORD

For a hundred years our country was so rich and lucky, it has been said, that political thought was largely unnecessary. However, there is no mistaking the fact that toward the beginning of this century Americans were doing a heap of thinking—as they are also doing at the present time.

For the generation of 1896 to 1919, the central events and issues assumed a political form. Man was more than ever the political animal, and the political leader was more the key figure than he had been since the 1860's. The period itself appeals to us, in retrospect, as far more cultivated and social-minded than that of the preceding generation, of the "robber barons" and the spoilsmen. It produced a very noteworthy political culture. It produced a whole gallery of remarkable and diverse leading characters; and even boasted a technique for reproducing them: President Making. In our present troubled days, we think almost with envy of the time of the earlier Rooseveltians and the Wilsonians; of its hope and promise; we think of it as an Age of Enlightenment.

Here was a generation that was certainly bent on discovering the "promise of American life," to use the phrase of one of its ablest spokesmen, the late Herbert Croly. Intellectually it welcomed change; it set off vigorously in search of new methods, new ideas of leadership, a new equilibrium for political democracy.

Casting off the prejudice against public life then entertained in educated circles, men of "talent and wealth" determinedly entered politics and prepared themselves carefully for their future parts. In their various ways the new type of political leaders set out to "save" the country from some dimly imagined, but to them, always imminent peril. They sang and they debated; they organized and fought; until public opinion was deeply aroused.

One thing must be said for the characteristic leaders of the party of progress; they always asked a great deal of their followers. Both Theodore Roosevelt and Woodrow Wilson, for example, demanded on the part of the rich capitalists who so often supported their campaigns both self-denial and self-control. Meanwhile the leaders who were closer, in line of real interest or sympathy, to the plain people, also showed at this time a characteristic tendency to ask a great deal of them. Men like the elder La Follette or Mr. Justice Brandeis held that democracy was essentially a "process of education." Their progressive programs favored neither an overruling capitalism nor an all-embracing state socialism, but a purer, more extended form of political democracy. Therefore, they required of the citizens an alert public conscience, a growing knowledge of public affairs, and readiness to intervene intelligently at almost every point of the governing process, local or national, parliamentary or administrative (and technical).

Thus political democracy, as shown by the raging discussions and controversies of the time, was carried to a highly advanced zone. It demanded almost too much of the people, some believed, although in this itself its chief glory resided.

It represented if you wish the "harder" way. Many serious reverses were suffered. In the end the political democracy of the earlier Rooseveltian era reached the walls of its own limitations, so to speak; it fell back, failing to solve the dilemmas it had created, the problems of economic democracy. Most of its gains were quickly undone by a hostile Supreme Court and a triumphant opposition party. But whatever the failings of the system and period—and democracy at its best always seems more talkative and less "orderly" than the sullenly boastful tyrannies of today—whatever the failings, they were not those of people who abdicate and leave all decisions to some soldier of fortune, some master of the gangs in the street, some self-styled band of the "elite." To the totalitarians, who now say: Think no more; trouble your minds no more. We will think for you; we will rule for you.

In the earlier Rooseveltian period, then, we may examine democracy under most favorable conditions. We may note its failures, drawing lessons also from the remarkable historical parallels between the earlier cycle of reform and that which began again after 1929. For example, to understand the New Deal, its pattern of thought, its experiments, we must recall that most of the men who furnished its plans were educated under the Square Deal or the New Freedom. Before the "Brains Trust" so-called, there was the "Tennis Cabinet" of Theodore Roosevelt; or, whenever he cared to heed them, there were the council of "best minds" and secret Presidential advisers of Dr. Wilson. We perceive the continuity of tactics and doctrine in the New Deal policies which mainly represent, after all, a resurgence of 1912 ideas, though at a later, far more difficult stage of development for American society. The decade of Harding, Coolidge and Hoover seems but a miscarried "Restoration," interrupting only briefly the longer cycle of political change and meliorism.

Historical parallels may be vastly instructive, though they must be used with caution. For example, early in the second term of President Franklin D. Roosevelt, toward 1938, the movement of progress showed signs of reaching its natural limits, halting before apparently insurmountable obstacles, in a manner nearly identical with the stoppage of President Wilson's New Freedom program. The forward movement under Wilson, had it continued at its swift, initial pace, would have confronted quickly the tormenting problem of economic inequality. There are now clear enough signs that the Wilsonian movement, at first so immensely promising, halted *before* the first World War was upon us, rather than because of the coming of war.

So under the second Roosevelt, in a later phase of our economic development, very imposing social gains had been registered. We were, by 1937, the time of the President's contest to "liberalize" the Supreme Court, farther along the road of social progress than ever before. We had departed boldly enough, as a government, from the policy of laissez-faire so that one out of every six Americans was supported by government aid. Some constructive ideas were in the air; new methods were being mastered, beginnings were being made at the management of giant public projects by devoted and patriotic young public servants of a new type. There was bustle and hope again, and a new *human* prosperity. We could see the new towns of the future, solidly constructed according to modern blueprints, rising beside, or in the midst of, the old, grimy, tumble-down cities of yesterday; the husk of the old life being thrown off by the new.

Then, very markedly, the advancing movement, which hoped to conserve and increase human and natural wealth alike, came to a halt. Once more, by a historical "coincidence," in the midst of domestic crisis, unfinished and unsolved, we turn as a nation to confront the world's wars, the dangers and the opportunities they offer. (At such times, there are always wars on hand.) Soon the country's energy, treasure and credit may all be diverted to investments wholly different from the peaceful constructive enterprises of yesterday. The clock can be turned back; the large social gains abandoned, as decaying monuments to forgotten victories of peacetime.

Yet the thoughtful reader, who knows something of history, need feel little surprise at such "coincidence" or historical recurrence. He is familiar with the smell of blood and the sight of violence in the pages of the past—yet he is also mindful that all the pirates and plunderers of the ages would have starved, would have had nothing to steal, if man had not been in the long run given chiefly to building, creating, husbanding. To him barbarism both at home and abroad is not something whose existence is to be denied—but a challenge. He is neither unduly frightened, nor driven to lose faith in his own reason.

Even in the period of our history partially described in this work, one of the most enlightened and humane we know of, our free republic was involved in two important wars. Our "age of enlightenment" opens with one brief "lightning-war" against a weaker power; it closes with a larger, heavier engagement, in which the United States participates wholeheartedly in a great conflict of the European powers, for the declared purpose of spreading peace, justice and free, popular government throughout the world.

MATTHEW JOSEPHSON

BOOK ONE

I. THE GOLDEN YEARS OF McKINLEY AND HANNA

THE DECISIVE victory of the conservative Republicans over the Democrats and Populists, upon the clear issue of money inflation, seemed to bring at last, in the fall of 1896, release from an intolerable burden of anxiety that had oppressed many good men. While the citizens of the predominantly rural West and South were deeply cast down, those of the typically industrial and commercial regions, the North Central and Northeastern states, were loudly exuberant. They exulted because "anarchy" and "repudiation" were beaten; because "Danton, Robespierre, and Marat" (Bryan, Altgeld, and Tillman) and all the others who, in the phrase of the young Theodore Roosevelt, "made war on the elegancies and decencies of life" were hurled down to defeat.

"God's in his Heaven, all's right with the world!" Mark Hanna had telegraphed to McKinley on the night of November 3, 1896. In his bedroom in Canton, Ohio, Mr. McKinley knelt and prayed for joy. In Union League Clubs sedate old men danced in each other's arms. The golden years had begun; the golden years of those whom the Jacobins of 1896 called Gold-bugs.

"Recent events may well cause those who represent business interests to rejoice on their escape from threatened perils," wrote the outgoing President, Grover Cleveland, with statesmanlike moderation.[1] In truth, the McKinley administration seemed to open an era of sunlit hope and promise for those whom we may

[1] Grover Cleveland, *Letters,* Nov. 16, 1896, p. 461.

call the party of business. It was as consummation and reward after long, arduous struggle. Compliments were showered as often upon Mark Hanna, the national chairman of the Republican party, as upon the successful candidate; for it was Hanna's aggressive generalship in the campaign, and especially the "scare" he threw into the country, that seemed the largest factor in defeating Bryan. Now Hanna, the "triumphant business man in politics," was widely expected to play a very large part in the new government. This gave assurance that the ruling party—though its President had sometimes in the past been a wavering politician—would rule frankly in the name of business interests.

McKinley was aware of the distress among the people. Depression in business and popular distress would be his chief concern, he promised in his first inaugural address. To bring recovery and the "full dinner pail" he would urge two principal measures: the enactment of a higher tariff; the defense of the gold standard.

And what could be better, from the point of view of large business interests? Their owners earnestly believed that if the government could but safeguard their capital by sound financial laws, and increase their profits by favoring tariff acts, a portion of their prosperity would not fail to circulate or seep downward to the masses of laborers and farmers. They asked for aid and encouragement, and where this could not be given they asked only to be "let alone." Such were the concepts of policy embraced by the most eminent capitalists at the end of the last century. Such they are now.

The Republican party, which, we must remember, was founded by men like Lincoln, and as recently as 1890 favored currency inflation, now in 1896 seemed more firmly wedded to big business interests than ever before. Moreover, the McKinley-Hanna partnership seemed to be the strongest political combination known by this party since the Civil War. It was also, in many ways, the final flower of our professional politics as cultivated for a generation past.

William McKinley himself was a finished product of the old professional school. John Hay, who knew him well, sometimes likened him to a medieval Cardinal of Mother Church. With Congressmen, whose ways he knew deeply, he dealt with a fine, Italian hand. He knew and enjoyed the arts of combination and conciliation; he distributed the patronage with a light touch. McKinley was effusively sentimental in his personal relations, and in public sometimes concealed his ignorance under an air of gravity and excessive virtue which could be unwittingly funny. His very pompous speeches, according to Edwin L. Godkin, were utterly devoid of meaning and showed that the Republican party had reached limits of "intellectual poverty and moral weakness" in choosing its standard-bearer.[2]

But under McKinley not only were relations between the White House and Congress harmonious, but the executive departments also were managed by an imposing group of like-minded financiers and Republican elders, who functioned with ease and authority. The Cabinet members and the leading diplomatic appointees had been chosen from among the representatives and friends of large business interests. Several of them had even belonged to the well-known McKinley "syndicate" which, under Mark Hanna's initiative, had rescued McKinley from bankruptcy in '93 and financed his subsequent campaign for the Presidency. John Hay, one of the generous subscribers, an experienced diplomat, a distinguished writer, and a man of fortune by marriage, was named Ambassador to Great Britain, and would soon replace the aged party leader, John Sherman, as Secretary of State. General Russell Alger, the lumber baron and political boss of Michigan, was made Secretary of War; Lyman Gage, president of the First National Bank of Chicago, Secretary of the Treasury; Cornelius Bliss, also a banker, from New York, Secretary of the Interior.

Then, at the President's side there stood always the formidable Hanna, a truly national boss, who had rebuilt the party organization and subdued the great regional bosses under his command. Under Hanna, the relationship of the Republican party with big business was more intimate and effective than ever before. Under

[2] Godkin, *Problems of Democracy*, p. 267.

Hanna, the great corporations expected that "protection against hostile legislation" for whose cost regular taxes had been assessed against them. Under Hanna, the Republican party itself now displayed a gratifying financial responsibility like that of a great commercial corporation.

Thus the road lay open, straight ahead. A business men's government, dreamed of in the days of the spoilsmen Politicos, had come at last.

After the panic of 1893, a strong movement of consolidation, mainly led by J. Pierpont Morgan, New York's leading investment banker, steadily eliminated the quarrelsome "robber barons" in both the railroad and the industrial field. Judging, after November 3, 1896, that all signs were propitious, Morgan boldly extended his operations beyond the railroad world that had been his special province hitherto. In one great industry after another he brought about "community of interests" by throwing together the leading corporations into great, centralized holding companies or trusts. McKinley's inauguration marked the beginning of the greatest movement of consolidation in American business. In 1897 alone, while the government looked on tolerantly, new incorporations were established with a total nominal capital of 3.5 billions of dollars. Within the several years that followed, the nation's dominant trusts in the copper, sugar, tobacco, oil, marine, smelting, and steel industries were formed—the steel trust being the biggest of all holding companies, and the seven together having an aggregate capital of 2.5 billions of dollars.

With the launching of the great trusts and of their new securities (chiefly under the sponsorship of the Morgan and Rockefeller banks), there came a tremendous financial boom. Mr. Morgan was widely recognized as the "hero" of the great boom, which appeared to reach its climax between 1899 and 1901. In the wake of the giant consolidations there followed hundreds of smaller promotions and speculative coups; and soon the newly made nabobs of coal, coke, and barbed wire, along with their relatives, servants, and even their favorite ministers, flung themselves upon the market places in a frenzy of speculation. Into the fashionable centers of metropolitan cities they crowded; to the watering places they bustled, to join in an orgy of conspicuous expenditure, with their fine clothes, their glittering carriages, and their jingling pockets.

The prosperity of 1899, after the quick war with Spain, made it a year of "miracles." John Hay spoke with wonder and apprehension of the "insolent prosperity" of the United States. Men of gentle breeding and social pretension found their exclusive social world invaded by new-rich vulgarity in every form. These were the days of stupendous "international marriages"—when American heiresses purchased foreign titles at stupendous prices—of "$5,000 breakfasts," "$10,000 luncheons," and "$15,000 suppers," social functions which the popular press now qualified only according to the sums of money expended for them. The popular press, typified by Pulitzer's New York *World* and Hearst's New York *Journal*, in terms of pretended moral censure, gave fulsome reports of the Lucullan feasts of the new grandees, reports calculated to arouse lustful envy among the people.

These were the golden years of McKinley and Hanna.

"Almost every morning paper was filled with accounts of the . . . new railroad and industrial combinations. The relations between this process of business consolidation and the existing Republican supremacy was unmistakable." Thus the authorized biographer of Mark Hanna drew the implications of the McKinley-Hanna program.[3] Instead of professing a decent abhorrence of the new financial monsters, as political men usually did in public, Mark Hanna placed the trust boom directly to the credit of his party. "Mr. Hanna did not fear or hesitate to come out frankly in favor of these combinations," Croly relates. Despite the Sherman Anti-Trust Law and the common law, the government stood squarely behind the movement of financial concentration.

At this period Henry Adams, descendant of Presidents and patricians, and (as he described himself) the inveterate "stable companion" of statesmen, resided permanently in Washington,

[3] Herbert Croly, *Marcus Alonzo Hanna*, p. 296.

watching events as one absorbed in the great game of history. His own family fortunes had been linked with two revolutionary periods in American history, and this gave him an added perspective, a strong sense of the past. From his devoted friend John Hay, who was high in the inner circle of the ruling party, he gathered not a little inside stuff about the present. Thus armed, Henry Adams was enabled to make interesting judgments concerning the political-social upheavals of the 1890's. They marked, he concluded, one of those decisive epochs in the nation's history; their outcome was to be not merely "the final surrender of the country to capitalism," but a surrender to capitalism in its higher phase, that of great finance capitalists and investment bankers, centralizing and ruling virtually all industry. Adams' prophecies were written down in letters of the time (1896), as well as in his *Education*, several years later.

With the victory of 1896, Adams judged, the bankers had become "the greatest single power in the country, and infallibly control the drift of events." He himself pretended to an old-fashioned dislike of bankers and capitalistic society. But, as he wrote afterward in *The Education*, "All one's friends, all one's best citizens, reformers, churches, colleges, educated classes, had joined to force submission to capitalism." It had come; and, as a dividend-receiver, Adams resigned himself with cheerful cynicism. For, if such a society were to run at all, it must be run by capital. ". . . Nothing could surpass the nonsensity of trying to run so complex and so concentrated a machine by Southern and Western farmers in grotesque alliance with city day-laborers. . . ."[4]

Then, in passages full of insight, Adams sketches the flowering of America's imperial age. A favorable trend of commercial exchanges was causing the accumulation here of colossal bank deposits and gold, making the United States independent of European capital and herself one of the great creditor nations of the world, driven, in turn, to seek new outlets, new markets, new investment opportunities for her mountains of capital and expanded

[4] Henry Adams, *Letters*, Vol. II, p. 96.

productive energies. These momentous developments determined the politics of "McKinleyism"—for this was the name that Adams and later historians gave to the program to which McKinley himself may have contributed unconsciously only a part.

"McKinleyism," in essence, was "the system of combinations, consolidations, trusts, realized at home, realizable abroad." To the President—or perhaps, rather, to the silent partner, Hanna—this meant "the pooling of interests . . . in a general trust into which every interest should be taken, more or less at its own valuation, and whose mass should, under his management, create efficiency." [5]

At home "McKinleyism" required that the rival party bosses, as well as the competing captains of industry, were to be merged into a grand alliance, a kind of super-trust. Abroad, beyond the water's edge, the chance of combining the growing world force of America with that of nations which held the balance of power on earth, would offer itself ostensibly as the task of imperial diplomacy. This was the task to which the subtle John Hay, as Ambassador to England, and as Secretary of State, set himself for the decade after 1896. "Having looked with such a benevolent eye upon the merger of railroads and . . . industrial combinations, McKinley permitted Hay to see what he could do in the way of bringing the Powers abroad into a grand concert of agreement upon their common world-wide interests." [6]

It was a bold concept, worthy of those crowded hours when the stern, lonely, ill-favored Morgan labored like a titan to cement his vast "community of interests," when the crass, bullet-headed Hanna bestrode the land like a national boss.

McKinley and his partners, thought Henry Adams, in furthering trusts and combinations at home and abroad, "achieved very remarkable results." But, he added reflectively: "How much they cost was another matter."

[5] Adams, *The Education of Henry Adams*, p. 373.

[6] Dennett, *John Hay*, pp. 328, 330.

2

Under McKinley, the political government appeared very strong, in contrast with preceding administrations. Its high councils were filled mainly with rough-handed men of the "practical" type, probably the strongest men of professional politics and business in their generation. To be sure, Edwin L. Godkin, a sort of Gloomy Dean of the period, characterized them as being "mostly ignorant and completely secluded from foreign influences and without knowledge of any other state of society, with great contempt for history and experience. . . ." This political character would have its dangers. Yet accustomed as they were to handling large ventures in a large way, they worked to fulfill Hamilton's old dream of centralized, authoritative rule by "talents and wealth" —with the qualification that deficiency of talent was to be offset by mass of wealth.

The passion for order, for consolidation, pervaded even Congress. Much had been done in recent years toward co-ordinating the old "bear garden" that was the House of Representatives; while, in the Senate, new arrivals found the power of Nelson Aldrich, of Rhode Island, by his control of party caucus and Senate committees, little less than that of a dictator. Within a few minutes of a caucus meeting the program of a whole session of Congress might be dispatched. The Dingley Tariff Act, with its hundreds of complex schedules, was passed in the early weeks of the McKinley administration with almost no discussion worth the name. Opportunities for public hearings on this measure were negligible. Louis D. Brandeis, then a young Boston lawyer, presented himself before Representative Dingley's committee in behalf of a recently formed association favoring low tariff rates. "I desire to speak," he said, "on behalf of those, who, I believe, form a far larger part of the people of this country than any who have found representation here. . . . The consumers. . . ." He was greeted with jeering laughter.[7]

[7] Lief, *Brandeis*, p. 49.

But behind the executive and legislative organs of the government there stood always the supporting party institution, with its army of "workers," the men who managed primary conventions and gathered votes. Here in the party institution, more vital than at any time since Andrew Jackson's reign, there was (on the Republican side), an unheard-of regimentation and discipline under one man: Mark Hanna.

The Ohio coal and iron magnate was one of those key figures of the period who typified, for the caustic Godkin, contempt for learning, ignorance of the ways of other civilized society, indifference to the lessons of history. Certainly he was a new kind of political hero. Though John Hay thought him "a born general in politics," he ruled not among crowds, by eloquence, but from a desk in a private office.

His dictatorial temper, his blunt epithets, his shocking candor about the use of money, made men fear him, as they feared the red-nosed Morgan. Men of gentle feeling, at sight of the paunchy figure, the jowled face, the heavy mouth and piercing eye of the Ohio boss, would be taken aback. He seemed feudal, warlike; a man who would crush out or buy all those who stood in his way. In time, more credit would be given to the "benevolence" which underlay Hanna's feudalism; and to the shrewd wisdom with which he read the forces of his time. A peculiar glory adhered to him for having "made" a President, not by chance, but by long planning; many rich, ambitious Americans suddenly desired to imitate him, and become President Makers in their own right.

Entering politics late in life, Hanna had discovered nothing, invented nothing. He had taken the tools that were at hand, the machinery for gathering "voting cattle," and improved them. The alliance between large corporate business and political parties had long existed; Hanna perfected it, regularizing the tax laid upon business. It was his boast that money entrusted to him suffered little waste; that he and his lieutenants could be counted on to "use every cent of it right."

Washington, as a capital, often strikes one as a façade, ornate of marble, hollow-sounding. There you may see the President, like the polished figure in bronze of a typical politician, shaking people's hands, making conventional speech. Or the legislators on Capitol Hill performing their parts in a well-rehearsed play. The realities of political power are often to be felt elsewhere: in the field, at the grass roots.

Hurrying away to the banks of the Ohio River or of Lake Erie, we may glimpse the President Maker arduously at work, at the battle front itself. There is a state election campaign on, and Mr. Hanna, besides being national chairman of the Republican party, is, in his own right, boss of the Ohio suzerainty, and must oversee its action in person. With a retinue of Congressmen, aides, and "distinguished Ohioans," as well as baggage containing goodly store of cash, the great man journeys upon a tour of his state in a private train, stopping at hotels in small cities, conferring everywhere with county chairmen and district leaders, counting noses, distributing money.

In the papers of William C. Beer, a lawyer who acted as political liaison agent and lobbyist for a great insurance company of New York, there has been preserved for us a most graphic and candid picture of Mark Hanna in action at the front, in the summer of 1899, two years after McKinley's inauguration. Here we see, to our surprise, that there is great concern in inner circles over the results of the election. For Ohio is a "pivotal" state, and renewed success in the national elections will depend greatly upon the outcome here.

The first thing that surprises us is the strain, the difficulty, the apprehension everyone shows. Evidently the "protecting" of business from hostile legislation is a far less simple or easy affair than one would have assumed. McKinley himself, as Beer who has just visited him in Washington reports, is highly anxious about the results of the local Ohio elections.

"He has d—— good reason to be!" explodes Hanna. And he adds: "Please tell Pres. McCall [of the New York Life Insurance

Company] that I have had a very hard fight. . . . It has been hard work and has nearly worn me out." [8]

Then Hanna relates, for the benefit of the insurance company, how he himself has gone through the smaller towns and cities calling together the leaders, and "personally given out the necessary funds, one hundred dollars here, one hundred dollars there, and so on."

That night from Hanna's hotel room in Lima, Ohio, letters giving reports of the current situation and appealing urgently for funds go forth to Mr. J. Pierpont Morgan, to the heads of the Pennsylvania railroad and other railroads.

"I wrote by hand for Hanna," notes Beer in his memorandum, "twenty-two letters to railroad presidents, general managers and superintendents, and to Senator [Thomas C.] Platt and other prominent express officials." These letters urged the "extreme necessity" upon the large employers, "to get out every vote among their employees and shop-men on election day." By all this expenditure, by laborious preparation, by constant vigilance, Hanna hoped they could carry Ohio by a narrow, but safe, plurality.[9]

Why the "extreme necessity"? Why was it necessary that the leader of the victorious party work night and day in order to influence the voice of the electorate in the desired sense? Were not the Boy Orator and the Free Silver agitators defeated for good and all? Was the country not safely surrendered to high capitalism, as Henry Adams surmised? The actual picture in Ohio, then the most boss-ridden and "corrupted" of states, was utterly different from the expected one.

After two years of orthodox Republican leadership, in both peace and war, the old Western Reserve, including the large cities of Cleveland and Toledo, was aflame with opposition. That year, an opponent of Hanna's regular machine was to be elected Mayor of Cleveland; and soon afterward another opponent, Tom L. Johnson, formerly a public-utility magnate himself, and now converted to radical Single Tax doctrines, was to capture Hanna's

[8] Beer, *Hanna*, appendix, p. 306.
[9] *Ibid.*, pp. 307-308.

own city, Cleveland, and reign over it for long years. In nearby Toledo, also, another singular character, Samuel Jones—called "Golden Rule" Jones—had arisen to challenge the regulars in 1897. A prosperous small manufacturer, Jones had made himself loved and celebrated for his profit-sharing enterprises. Entering local politics, he quickly won over his townspeople, preaching to them in language so simple that even the foreign-born workers could understand the most deeply radical of doctrines: those of the Golden Rule, of the Declaration of Independence, of Thomas Jefferson. The newspapers of both parties, combining to slander him, accomplished nothing in a series of elections.

Though Mark Hanna controlled the national party machine, the state and its legislature, local revolt of surprising vigor and dangerous scope threatened him repeatedly. In 1899 Mayor Jones planned to run for the Governorship itself as an independent candidate, using the same picturesque methods that had succeeded so well in smaller contests. The anxiety Hanna showed in the nocturnal interview with Mr. Beer, and his decision to go himself to Toledo by a morning train, to checkmate the enemy, becomes explicable.

> I have quietly summoned all our leaders there . . . and am going to follow the same tactics I used to beat Jones in the Convention—to get the delegation—you remember? They sent word a few days ago that if they had five thousand they could buy up all of Jones's lieutenants—his head men. Those fellows understand perfectly well that Jones can't be elected Governor, that there will be no offices, and they are not in this for their health. They convinced me as to the scheme, and I sent them a thousand dollars yesterday, and will give them the rest tomorrow.[10]

Thus bribery—oh, unpleasant word!—as ancient as the arts of assassination, seems clearly to have been used in completing the "educational" program in Ohio. Nor was money spared in hiring carriages to transport the voters of the countryside. "It is quite easy to see where 25,000 votes were changed . . . within the

[10] Beer, *Hanna,* appendix, pp. 307-308.

week before election day," runs Beer's secret memorandum to his employers. Money was well expended, since the added votes brought exactly the narrow margin of victory that year.

Yet it was like holding a dike against the ceaselessly pounding, invading sea. Local revolt would be overcome in Ohio; but it made new breaches and broke through at other points. It was at this very period, when national party organization came into such strong hands, that political unrest assumed a specially local or municipal shape. Now was the heyday of city reformers and Single Taxers who hoped to establish their experiments in taxation or Good Government in a local frame. And everywhere in these localities one could hear expressions similar to those reported in Ohio: "The people are sick of Hanna. . . . They have all they want of Hannaism." [11]

In Illinois, for example, where Governor John P. Altgeld had gone down to defeat in 1896, the Republican machine had installed a more complaisant Governor, approved by Charles T. Yerkes, Chicago's baron of street-cars. Preparations were then made to revive those "eternal monopoly bills" that Altgeld had vetoed; and the legislature at Springfield was known to be ready to pass them. But in Chicago the masses of Mr. Yerkes' "straphangers," forewarned by Altgeld's men, were roused to a fever suggesting renewed mob violence. Delegations of citizens marched on Springfield; and at their approach the Illinois legislators yielded in panic.

Then a few weeks later, when the excitement had abated, the utility ring planned a sudden thrust by which measures favoring the purpose of Yerkes' corporations were to be rushed, this time through the Chicago City Council. But the citizens rose again; some of them came with rope in their hands, showed it to the Aldermen, saying that it was intended for them if the street-car franchise bills were passed. They were not passed.[12]

Thus it was an unending struggle; and the fight must be carried over and over again to many points of the system. The Presi-

[11] *Ibid.*, pp. 310-311.
[12] Lloyd, *H. D. Lloyd*, Vol. II, p. 283.

dent Maker was, in reality, a harassed ruler, increasingly apprehensive of an opposition that mounted even among the educated middle class. The very prominence given to Mr. Hanna's methods at the hour of his triumphs aroused fear as to the effect of such methods on public morals and even public safety. The very measures taken by the large business interests (that he represented) to protect themselves by an alliance with corrupt professional politics "served only to inflame the irritation."[13]

What would become—a young New York reformer, John Jay Chapman, asked at this time—of a people who for long years lived, as a community, completely under boss rule? What would their habits be after a generation or so? What views could we expect to find in their hearts? "The masses will have been controlled by bribery and terrorism. . . . Money and place will have been corrupting them. A conviction will spread throughout the community that nothing can be done without a friend in court; that honesty does not pay and probably never has paid in the history of the world."

Yet the business leaders, believing that that system which enabled them to make money was "the only safe government," resisted all change and "clung to abuses as to a life-preserver." Reform, they argued, was expensive and served but "to excite the poor against the rich." To put honest politicians in office was something they feared, lest these might prove unable "to bribe the thieves not to steal from them!"[14]

Contemporary with the Mugwumps, rising in the Eastern cities of Boston and New York, were the Single Taxers and municipal reformers of Ohio, who were roused to intense activity by Hanna's ruthlessness. Here the followers of Tom L. Johnson and Golden Rule Jones strove to apply the Single Tax doctrines of Henry George to the local situation. As latter-day Christians in politics they reacted strongly against the extremes of poverty and squalor and vulgar wealth which their cities displayed. They hoped that the Single Tax, by eliminating ground rent, would transform their

[13] Croly, *op. cit.*, p. 326.
[14] Chapman, *Causes and Consequences*, pp. 28 ff.

towns into happy and beautiful places, with the artisan and mechanic rendered eternally prosperous. They too labored "to free the cities from privilege and partisanship" which retarded progress and battened on poverty. They trusted that they would bring about "the free city of today, which is the hope of democracy; tomorrow . . . the triumph of democracy."[15] They too, like the Eastern Mugwumps, or civil service reformers, centered their attack upon the groundwork of local government on which the whole national party system was based. In time the current of their agitation would merge also with the broader stream of democratic resurgence in the rural West.

3

Had anything truly been settled by the contest of 1896? How real was the victory of "McKinleyism"? No sooner had the battle ended than the victors realized that they had won only a truce, a temporary respite. For the warning that Edwin L. Godkin, the Cassandra of American journalism, had given them in 1894 still held true:

> . . . *The politics of the world are becoming more and more a controversy between rich and poor.* The influential and the rich men are taking the place of the feudal baron and the absolute monarch as objects of popular attack. . . .[16]

And Godkin, though he had not the slightest desire that the rich should give way to their inferiors, was independent enough to reproach the men of business themselves for having brought disaster nearer by their own follies. Had they not for years, by their demand for a protective tariff, made the government a partner in their enterprises and made every Presidential election "an affair of the pocket"? Had not the capitalists themselves spread the notion that the government owed assistance to individuals in carrying on business and making a livelihood?

[15] Brand Whitlock, *Letters,* pp. 84, 97.

[16] E. L. Godkin in *The Forum,* Mar., 1894; italics mine.

Another cultivated member of the conservative upper class, Theodore Roosevelt, was also convinced, like Godkin, that the victory of the Gold-bugs had brought little more than a temporary halt in hostilities. The young author, sportsman, clubman, and amateur of politics had given active help to his party from the stump in 1896. At the height of the panic over Bryan, he had written privately of his surprise at the "savage hatred of the unprosperous for the prosperous" that clearly underlay the whole silver movement. Here was the greatest crisis in our history, he felt, saving only that of the Civil War. "It is a semi-socialistic, agrarian movement, with free silver as a mere incident. . . ." Organized labor and all the other "ugly forces that seethe beneath the social crust," and feed "on class and sectional hatred," had supported Bryan. Though these were "the very people one would wish to help"—there was nothing to be done but to beat them back.[17]

Weeks passed after the election victory, and Theodore Roosevelt would still confide to his friend and fellow-Republican, Henry Cabot Lodge, his fears that Bryanism was still "too real and ugly a danger . . . and our hold on the forces that won the victory for us by no means too well assured."[18]

For what reply had the Gold Standard Republicans given to the insistent demands raised on behalf of the masses of people in great sections of the country? Complaint was made of the scarcity of money and credit; the winning party responded by reaffirming and defending the gold standard. Millions of farmers protested at the high cost of manufactured or consumer goods in relation to the price of grains; the conservative Republicans answered by raising the protective schedules higher than ever before. Labor had pressed for the right to collective bargaining, the eight-hour day, and a living wage, making bitter cry against the Federal courts that outlawed their strikes and imprisoned their leaders. The ruling party had simply proclaimed the sacredness of Court and Constitution. The average small man had shown a most vehement

[17] Cowles, *Letters from Theodore Roosevelt*, pp. 192-194; Sept. 27, 1896.

[18] Lodge, *Correspondence*, Vol. I, p. 240.

dislike for the new railroad and industrial trusts; he had petitioned for control of them by the government. The party in power answered by doing nothing, abandoning nearly all pending trust suits. Popular anxiety at the increasing, machinelike subjection of the political government to secret controls had been aired; many had urged that party nominations and elections be made more directly responsive to the popular will. Yet they had come to see the party machine transformed into the terrible Steam Roller; they had seen money and intimidation used more openly than ever before.

Truly they might say, as Bryan had said at Chicago: "We have petitioned, and our petitions have been scorned; we have entreated and our entreaties have been disregarded; we have begged, and they have mocked. . . ."

In short, none of the genuine social and "sectional" issues of the time had been fairly dealt with; and the regime of practical men seemed bent on forgetting or avoiding them as far as possible.

Beyond the Mississippi, Bryan still spoke from the Chautauqua platform, as a beloved leader of the West, and vowed that it was only "the first battle" that was ended. Yet, though the same profoundly democratic and "Jacobin" impulses still ruled the people of the Valley of Democracy, they turned away, nowadays, from the simpler nostrums of the Populist and Free Silver parties. Gold was more plentiful now; and farmers were relatively more prosperous after 1897. In the decade that followed they were to turn to solutions other than that of currency inflation.

Responding to the proposals of the more intelligent and inventive of the new sectional leaders, such as William S. U'Ren of Oregon, and Robert M. La Follette of Wisconsin, they began to consider the procedure of democracy itself and the possibilities of purifying it. The old equalitarian tendencies showed themselves again in demands that political government, local and Federal, be rescued from "invisible," machine control. The hope of more "direct democracy" was what U'Ren fostered when he succeeded in introducing the popular referendum, a device borrowed from the plebiscite of the Swiss. By this means the power of a hated public-utility corporation was suddenly broken in Oregon.

Meanwhile in Wisconsin, La Follette, another champion of the plain people, made persistent, vigorous agitation for the direct primary system of party nominations. Thus he hoped to wrest control of the state's dominant party organization from its old, corrupt masters, so that a just system of taxation, control of the private monopolies, and enlightened social laws might follow.

Banished from public life in 1891, after his rupture with the Republican machine, La Follette knew that it would require a struggle of many years to win over the party for his own independent faction. Sometimes he wondered seriously if the game were worth the candle for himself and his friends.

> But there was the good State of Wisconsin ruled by a handful of men, who had destroyed every vestige of democracy in the Commonwealth. They settled in private conference practically all nominations for . . . offices, controlled conventions, dictated legislation, and . . . even sought to lay corrupt hands on the courts of justice.[19]

To revive democracy, to rescue it from corrupt machine control and make it once more the instrument of popular will—these, rather than the economic cure-all of currency inflation, were the objects of the new Western leaders, still obscure in a national sense at the turn of the century.

In a speech of 1897, before students of the University of Chicago, La Follette both challenged the reigning Mark Hannas and, in characteristic fashion, addressed an appeal to youth. "Abolish the caucus," he cried. "Go back to the first principles of democracy; go back to the people."[20]

The Jacksonian temper still lived in the West and especially in its middle border. In spite of defeat, there was no want of determination and faith. Many hands were at work.

But even in the "plutocratic" East, in the bosom of the ruling party itself, there was an ambitious, adventurous faction of

[19] La Follette, *Autobiography*, p. 172.
[20] *Ibid.*, p. 197.

younger men who held their own ideas of policy and leadership, and dreamed of supplanting the old chieftains.

4

All things after March 4, 1897, seemed perfectly ordered for a millennial age of business prosperity. Yet why was it that when one looked a little under the surface, or listened to the talk of leading personages in Washington or New York society, one received an impression of abiding gloom, of brooding apprehension for the future?

The seed of opinion, ideas, talents, of history and civilization, often flourished best in small, homogeneous social groups. These favoring conditions were often to be found in compact England or France, and were less discernible in sprawling America. Yet during the '90's there did exist for a time, in Washington, a few such "centers of culture," circles of men and women of charm and wit, ever engaged in the discussion of human affairs, to be met usually at the luxurious mansion of John Hay or at the equally fastidious home of Henry Cabot Lodge, the young Senator from Massachusetts, called "the Scholar in Politics." Here were to be seen not only literary notables and visiting foreign celebrities, but also those native public figures who embodied such talent as the new Hamiltonian dynasty of wealth contained. Here, as the French would say, was *un monde*, a definite little social microcosm, with its members drawn from the wealthy class, or men of influence and office who enjoyed the social graces. Speaker Thomas B. Reed, the cynical, witty elder statesman, was one of the circle, but not Mark Hanna; the corporation lawyer and Cabinet member, Elihu Root, but not Edward Harriman; Theodore Roosevelt and Albert Beveridge, but not Matt Quay.

Here the news of the day was studied, the political reverberations of events throughout the world were avidly discussed; ideas were born and plots laid; and men and women departed to lobby, to cajole Senators or Cabinet Secretaries to take some new "line";

or even to intrigue for somebody's Presidential boom; or bring on a war.

It was these people whom James Bryce saw much of during his visit to the United States, and whom he had in mind when he remarked, in *The American Commonwealth*, upon the prevailing "apathy among the luxurious classes and fastidious minds, who . . . are disgusted by the superficial vulgarities of public life." America's educated and wealthy class, he said, "find no smooth and easy path lying before them. Since the masses do not look to them for guidance, they do not come forward to give it. If they wish for office, they must struggle for it, avoiding the least presuming upon their social position."

Another English observer, Cecil Spring Rice, then Secretary of Legation at Washington, also wrote home similar intimate impressions of Hay, Adams, Lodge, Roosevelt, and other American luminaries. He too said of these cultivated men that in their talk "there was something melancholy." On political questions those who were in politics would make "open profession of partisanship and bitterness, with an open contempt of any of the ordinary considerations of honor or honesty or high feeling." Others who were not in politics, when touching on public questions, spoke with "a sort of bitter despair in their minds which is hard to describe and not pleasant to listen to. . . ."[21]

John Jay Chapman, who also knew well these men of leisure and education, said of them with a flash of insight: "Though they may think they are not affected by commercialism, their attitude of mind is precisely that of a lettered class living under a tyranny."[22]

For they did not conceal their misgivings concerning the supposedly strong but ignorant men who ruled our government. John Hay often and again lamented the "corruption, the self-seeking, the cowardice," that filled our official life ever since the days when he served as Lincoln's private secretary. While, next door, Henry Adams would look out from his library window across LaFayette

[21] Gwynn, *Sir Cecil Spring Rice*, Vol. I, pp. 64-65, 102.
[22] Chapman, *op. cit.*, p. 40.

Square toward the White House, and ponder upon "democracy's neglect of the well-born and intelligent." [23] But most of all these men of culture, who thought often of the lessons of history, suffered from a fear of "the mob" which, though expressed constantly in the form of jests, remained nevertheless their deepest obsession.

To the young Theodore Roosevelt, a Governor Altgeld was a "demagogue," a Benedict Arnold. The dispatch of Federal troops to Chicago during the general railway strike of 1894 had saved us from "a repetition of what occurred during the Paris Communes!" [24]

"I know the Populists and the laboring men well and their faults . . ." he had written in a letter of December, 1894. "I like to see a mob handled by the regulars, or by good State-Guards, not overscrupulous about bloodshed." [25] The election of 1896, he felt, had "raised the evil spirit of revolution. . . ." The legend persisted that in his youthful spirits he had thought of issuing armed challenges to the radical adversaries; that he had said they should be suppressed "as the Communes of Paris were suppressed by taking ten or a dozen of their leaders out, by standing ten or a dozen of them against a wall and shooting them dead!" [26]

But while fear of the mob animated the young leaders, they also expressed in private a deep disgust for that "unholy alliance" of corrupt professional politics and big business that stood over them. Quietly they deplored "Dollar Mark" Hanna, and longed for the coming of civil-service reform, which would halt jobbing and thievery in public office. McKinley they rated an "infirm" man, who would be unequal to gigantic labor riots, they feared, or to the danger of a foreign conflict. Of the business men's government that McKinley had established, Henry Cabot Lodge, himself a millionaire by inheritance, spoke with unconcealed scorn, saying that "the business man dealing with a large political question is

[23] Dennett, *Hay*, p. 164.
[24] T. Roosevelt in *The Forum*, Feb., 1895.
[25] *Matthews Papers*, to Brander Matthews.
[26] Willis J. Abbot in the New York *Journal*, Oct. 29, 1896.

really a painful sight."[27] And Roosevelt, amid the tumult of labor uprising, reminded himself also that the banker and merchant too needed "education and sound chastisement." He inveighed against those men who deified "success through financial trickery," who had but "the imagination of a green-grocer," and to whom trade and property were more sacred than honor or national glory. Could the values of justice, humanity, and culture be propagated by such as these? he questioned.[28]

Though placed within the Hamiltonian party, as the epoch of "McKinleyism" opened, the faction of conservative upper-class intellectuals, typified by Lodge and Roosevelt, was already embarked upon a search for new doctrines, for a new ideology of leadership. They had premonitions of the gravity of the real situation and of historic opportunities as well. These "scholars in politics" were convinced that McKinley, Hanna, and their associates were ignorant and without insight into the forces of history; their ideas, like those of the typical "Old Guard" Republicans, dated from the Civil War, and would have to be changed one day. Hence they, the new men, already pressed forward impatiently to shoulder them aside.

In truth, the apparently invincible Old Guard and the businessmen-in-politics, who now headed a movement that seemed so powerful, were nearly all to be scattered and decimated in a surprisingly short time. In how few years illness, age, or electoral misfortune would overtake nearly all of them!—while the less "sound," younger men rushed into their offices as with the effect of a palace revolution.

Nor was the concern with the future pattern of political leadership limited to the conservative intellectuals only in the one party. In August, 1897, at Richmond, Virginia, shortly after McKinley and Hanna took over the reins of government, we find Professor Woodrow Wilson of Princeton University, a Southern Democrat,

[27] Cowles, *op. cit.*, pp. 182-183.

[28] *Matthews Papers*, T. R. to Brander Matthews, Dec., 1894; *Forum*, Feb., 1895.

delivering an address significantly entitled "Leaderless Government," whose line of thought paralleled most remarkably that of Lodge and Roosevelt.

There was much unrest, much "vague radicalism" abroad, he said.

> The nation is made—its mode of action is determined; what we now want to know is: what is it going to do with its life, its material resources and its spiritual strength? How is it to gain and keep a common purpose in the midst of complex affairs . . . ? How is the nation to get definite leadership and form steady, effective parties? . . . How shall we settle questions of economic policy? Who is to reconcile our interests . . . ?

Who, in short, would provide "wisdom in action"? Only, he asked as if in deep doubt, "our men of affairs"? [29] Wilson, for his part, would continue to doubt them, and in the pages of his private letters to confide his own long-cherished hopes for a role in public life.

It was at this time, while new tactics of leadership and new ideologies were being sought in the circles I have described, that the very curious American philosopher of history, Brooks Adams, turned up, almost providentially, with his prophetic study of historical trends, *The Law of Civilization and Decay*, published in December, 1895, and widely read and discussed by the literati in the years that followed, then unjustly forgotten. The younger brother of Henry Adams, himself eccentric enough, had shifted suddenly from the practice of law and the pursuit of reform in Massachusetts politics to furnishing historical theories for the younger statesmen, such as Lodge (to whom he was related) and Roosevelt, his friend, whom he strongly influenced.

Brooks Adams resembled the Italian philosopher Vico, as he foreshadowed the German Spengler, in his ingenious use of historical parallels and "cycles of culture." His own cycles—differing from the biological cycles of Henry Adams—were based on the

[29] W. Wilson, *Public Papers*, Vol. I, pp. 338, 339.

shiftings of the great trade routes of the world and the rise and fall of commercial empires. The United States, he held, now dominated the main trade routes of the modern world, running from the Atlantic to the Pacific, as Rome had once dominated Mediterranean commerce. Although here "the conventions of popular government were still preserved," he argued, the country was already falling subject to an aristocracy of money-lenders as absolute as that of Rome. Soon our commercial civilization, with its love of gain and usury, would grow less energetic, less warlike, less "heroic." Ultimately its rulers would be unequal to the mastery of fearfully complex social problems; and, using copious illustrations from past history, Brooks Adams forecast inevitable revolutions and catastrophes to come in a comparatively early future. The very weaknesses and default of the ruling class, as in the French Revolution, would contribute to the debacle.

However doubtful in validity these theories may have appeared to most men at the time, we find that they gained currency with Roosevelt, with Lodge, and evidently with the young Beveridge. We find the terms of Brooks Adams occurring constantly in Roosevelt's early speeches and writings, as in Lodge's. They provide an orientation toward a reviving nationalism, toward the "soldierly virtues," which Roosevelt nowadays admired, and seem to rationalize the increasingly critical spirit (among the new Hamiltonians) toward the crass commercialism of the age. Greed and demagogy, both disturbing and dividing our society, must be struck down, and a virile, fraternal sentiment for the glory of the nation made to rule in their place.

Albert Beveridge, who shone as a stump speaker for the Republicans in 1896, attacked those who fomented sectional and clan conflict—in terms that might have been borrowed from Brooks Adams. "Today the issue is national life," he said. "Are the American people a nation, or are they an aggregation of localities? Is the Stars and Stripes the flag of a vital nation . . . of an invincible people?"[30]

[30] Bowers, *Beveridge*, p. 63.

At the time of the Venezuela crisis, in the winter of 1895-1896, both Lodge and Roosevelt brimmed over with war fever, the latter expressing the most fervent hope that our government would now adopt a more "spirited" foreign policy. Brooks Adams meanwhile wrote to Roosevelt in dark tones that the crisis with England seemed to offer a possible way of escape or regeneration. "The whole world seems to be rotting, rotting. The one hope for us, the one chance to escape from our slavery, even for a year, is war, war which shall bring down the British Empire." [31]

Even after the momentary danger of war with England had passed, Roosevelt and Lodge continued to search for war and preach foreign adventure and annexation. The moral and historical arguments with which each adorned his purpose resembled strongly those of Brooks Adams. Let men cease to hold trade and manufacture sacred and set above them "national honor and glory . . . courage and daring and loyalty and unselfishness," wrote the young Theodore Roosevelt. He prayed that this rich nation might not, by growing timid and slothful, fall an easy prey to those people who embodied "those most valuable of all qualities, the soldierly virtues." [32]

Sometimes Roosevelt hoped for a war on grounds of "humanity and self-interest" combined. At others he admitted that he desired it for the sake of "the benefit done to our people by giving them something to think of which isn't material gain. . . ." [33] He reproached our trade-unionists for thinking too much of material gain; and regarded with ill-concealed dislike the barons of the bag, typified by the former grocer Hanna, who "owned" the administration in 1897 and seemed resolved to direct it only toward the paths of peaceful commerce.

On the whole the conservative intellectuals, typified by Roosevelt and Lodge, when the Golden Years of McKinley and Hanna opened, were discontented and restless. They conceived of no large, constructive, domestic projects to occupy their own ener-

[31] *T. R. Papers,* Brooks Adams to T. R., Feb. 25, 1896.

[32] Speech of Jun. 2, 1897.

[33] *T. R. Papers,* T. R. to Commander W. W. Kimball, Nov. 19, 1897.

gies and appeal to the aspirations of the people. Within their party, their hidden opposition to the reigning leaders resolved itself into a persistent, intriguing agitation for a war, any war that would yield those thrills of generous emotion, those pulse-throbbings that gave to statesmen and to patriots, to warriors and to poets, as Roosevelt said, their grandest opportunities.

The temper and historical circumstances of the late 1890's are an extraordinary parallel to those of America exactly a century before. Then too the Federalists, the party of talents and wealth, held power, though with increasing difficulty. Meanwhile the anti-Federalists, championing that "ever-increasing class which labor under the hardships of life," as Madison said, by their hunger for equality offered a certain threat to the "gentry." The mood of the latter, who still ruled the republic firmly, grew both pessimistic and cynical. Though the Federalist leaders coldly defied popular opinion, they constantly feared a democratic upheaval, and groped for ways to outflank it. One of them, the dour Yankee, Fisher Ames, even went so far as to lament the fortunate geographical position of our country which made the possibility of war with a foreign power so remote that no threat from this direction served to check domestic political strife. Would, he said, that there were some formidable neighbor close at hand, whose threat might for a time at least "inspire stronger fears than demagogues can inspire." [34] For in those days, too, they who attacked the rule of the "gentry" were but demagogues.

[34] Ford, *Rise and Growth of American Politics*, p. 71.

II. THE SCHOLARS IN POLITICS

On a Friday evening of November, 1894, Theodore Roosevelt, then a mere Civil Service Commissioner, stood before a large gathering of the Harvard Civil Service Reform Club, at Cambridge, making a thumping speech on the need for governmental reform and the still more burning need of educated young men to carry this out.

Decent people, he said, wanted decent politics. But corruption was organized—by office-holding mercenaries—while decency was unorganized. "The only way to break up this organization is by taking away from the political leaders the offices by which they pay themselves." Our political government must be salvaged by a concerted drive for civil service reform. And Harvard men, cried the thick-set, energetic, bespectacled alumnus in ringing tones, must take an increasingly active part in this effort; they must recall that they had "special duties as well as special privileges."

But, he went on to warn them, they must be prepared to change their methods and manners. They must be active in politics not from a theoretical "collegian" point of view, but from a "practical" one. They must proceed not merely as "good men" but as "manly" men. "Away with mere feebleness," he cried, "this is a rough, work-a-day, practical world." Too often had people of the better sort turned with mingled scorn and discouragement from contact with the lower ranks of politics and party life. But what a sad and evil thing it would be if men of culture and social position, men possessed of a moral sense and "devotion to what is right," should show themselves lacking in the energy and manliness necessary to impose their will. We must make our blows against evil count and not let those rude, unlettered elements who stand for evil alone "have all the virile qualities." The new crusaders must be, above all, virile; they must, he would exclaim, baring his teeth, be ready even to be "tough."[1]

The speech which Theodore Roosevelt gave when he was thirty-five was true in type to those he would be giving twenty years later. Its message, its spirit, was deeply characteristic of the conservative élite which pushed itself vigorously into American public life at the turn of the century, and which was to play so bold and brilliant a part in the politics of the new century.

Here, necessarily, there will be much to say of Theodore Roosevelt and his career. Of the new men in politics he becomes easily, by his many-sided, tireless activities, by the high gifts of his temperament, his infectious example and influence, the central or key figure. He was unmistakably a man of his time, and the Zeitgeist was lusty in him. All that happened to him from beginning to end seems, in afterthought, in the highest degree symptomatic rather than accidental.

That he was a man of "average" mental attainments, as he himself sometimes admitted, rather than one of unusual intellectual powers, is all the more helpful to our plan of studying the pattern of political leadership as it took shape in the beginning of the present century. He sprang, to be sure, from the bosom of the upper class; but with passing time he would learn to swallow many of his inherited prejudices and speak for the aspirations of much larger groups.

He reflected intensely the ideas and interests of his epoch; indeed he echoed, or responded to, the pulsations of popular feeling with remarkable sensitiveness, becoming himself an instrument of public opinion, a sort of "sounding board" for *vox populi*, as he said. While responding, he also, as the embodiment of changing popular sentiment, stimulated and provoked even better than

[1] *Harvard Crimson*, Dec., 1894, No. 41, Vol. XXVI; also J. E. Spingarn to author.

he knew. Decisive measures of law, sweeping reforms from which he himself shrank, were to be enacted by others, thanks to the momentum he had helped to generate.

Most important of all, he introduced a new note, a breath of fresh air into our public life, after thirty years of degraded spoils politics, of uncritical and complacent drifting. His eloquent public utterances sounded more forcefully than any others the new political attitude, at once more critical toward the social canons of the preceding generation and more enlightened and refined in its approach to the massive social questions that had been accumulating under those who had gone before him.

Theodore Roosevelt was to mount to the highest office probably as the first man in forty years who, in that sanctified place, actually questioned or dreamed of questioning the accepted standards of respectability of his predecessors. Perhaps most of all he himself would have liked to be remembered as a moral motive force, one who turned himself and other men of his time to "higher things" than thoughts of "factories and railways," or "piled-up riches," or "roaring, clanging industrialism." [2]

For nearly forty years American public life had been degraded; Presidents and Senators and Governors had been puppets of the great overlords of industry and finance who held real power after the industrial revolution. But with Roosevelt the Political Man, *homo politicus*, was to be revived. The era of Enlightenment that came in with him—both enlightened and repentant in contrast with the age of the "robber barons" and the spoilsmen—was in effect an American counterpart of the Liberal or Social Democratic movements that ruled western Europe also at the end of the nineteenth century. The era was stamped so deeply with the first Roosevelt's virtues and defects (which linger to our own day) that in all justice we are disposed to call it "Rooseveltian."

But—to return to Theodore Roosevelt's speech at Harvard in 1894—his Macedonian appeal to men of his university and social

[2] *T. R. Papers*, T. R. to Frédéric Mistral, Dec. 15, 1904.

class to come and rescue our politics represented in one sense nothing new in itself. It was, indeed, an old Mugwump or Non-Partisan idea. The Mugwump leaders, Carl Schurz, George William Curtis, Godkin, who with the various members of the Adams family initiated the first civil service reform organizations, were the mentors of Roosevelt's youth. Since the days of the Tweed Ring and the Crédit Mobilier affair they had been distressed by the accumulated public scandal and shame, and frightened at the very costs of partisan, spoils politics. Their hope of elevating the tone of our government service resided in introducing honest, educated, and able men into the administrative corps. To this end they attempted to stimulate an enlightened public opinion and summon up an independent bloc of voters controlling the balance of power between the two corrupt parties.

In short, the older reformers strove to force their influence upon the party institution "from above." They called indignation meetings of good citizens, organized state and even "national" conventions, while ministers from the pulpit, university presidents, and the independent press supported them. Not a few wealthy capitalists who had been gouged by the politicos came to their aid.[3]

Yet while scheming to name Presidents and pull wires on a grand scale, they developed at no time any hold upon the masses of voters. The net results of their crusades were ludicrous; one fiasco followed another, and many of the original Mugwump leaders deserted the reform movement. Bitter with disappointment, Henry Adams in 1881 had warned his young colleague and pupil at Harvard, Henry Cabot Lodge, to shun politics; saying,

[3] For many years the long-range objectives of the Independent group had been to break down the narrow walls of partisan loyalties, attached to some leader who headed a "Blaine Legion," or aroused by the waving of "the bloody shirt," yet actually grounded in the lust among the lower ranks for the spoils of office. Men like Edwin L. Godkin believed that, if we were to arrive at good government, the unpledged or Independent vote in large states such as New York and Massachusetts must be increased and carefully wielded in the balance of election contests; the bonds of party discipline must be relaxed, and "the expression of open dissent from party programmes" made "respectable." (Godkin, *op. cit.*, pp. 211-212.)

"I have never known a young man to go into politics who was not the worse for it." [4]

But the procedure of Roosevelt and of his friend Lodge, as well, in one sense did represent a departure from that of the older men, those whom the arrogant boss Roscoe Conkling had called the "man-milliners," the "carpet-knights" of reform. Roosevelt in his Harvard speech urged that educated and well-bred men should no longer shrink from the "rough, work-a-day" side of politics; they must establish contact with the plain people; they must be ready to undergo apprenticeship among the lowest ranks of party "workers."

This was precisely what Roosevelt himself had done, upon being graduated from Harvard and returning to New York. He had applied for membership and had been admitted—after overcoming some natural suspicions—to his district Republican club, which met in a room above a corner saloon. He had stubbornly refused the advice—or the solemn warnings—of his family and his family's friends; and his determination to enter politics at the bottom of the ladder had seemed as scandalous to them as if he had decided to devote himself to poetry or the theater. They told him that politics were "low," that local party organizations were not the place for "gentlemen" but were run rather by saloon-keepers and horse-car conductors, who would be brutal and unpleasant to deal with. He answered that if this were true, then the people he had been frequenting did not belong to the governing class, "whereas the horse-car conductors and their like plainly did"; and that he for his part "intended to be one of the governing class." [5]

The young man's unconventional behavior suggests already that clairvoyance that leads to veritable discoveries or innovations. He showed qualities of intense curiosity, the desire to learn for himself of the realities of political life and power; he showed independence of mind in judging that those who passed for "gentlemen" should begin among the rank and file the work of elevat-

[4] Adams, *Letters*, Vol. I, p. 331.

[5] Roosevelt, *An Autobiography*, pp. 55-56.

ing our public life. Thus there began for Roosevelt twenty years of apprenticeship, a long period of training, marked with many painful contretemps, a preparation for his later climb to the political heights which was so erroneously considered "meteoric" or even "accidental."

The decision of a young man of "old Knickerbocker" family and independent means to enter politics—rather than railroading or banking—appeared without rhyme or reason at the time, in view of the low estate to which political life had sunk in the 1880's. Probably the love of literature and history that Roosevelt had absorbed during his Cambridge years was not unrelated to this decision. No doubt he pictured to himself a world filled with William Pitts, Edmund Burkes, and Wellingtons rather than the humbler members of the "Jake Hess Republican Club" of the Twenty-first District of New York, who were his first colleagues.

The impulse to public life, and especially to reform activities such as now gripped the cultivated and wealthy circles in Boston, frequented at this time by Roosevelt, in itself suggested the beginning of a higher stage in our great economic revolution after the Civil War. Leisure-class ideals of literary-political glory, such as the eighteenth-century Americans had known, were spreading again, if slowly. The plundering of the public treasury, winked at during the more frenzied phases of wealth-getting, was now strongly deplored in good company.

Lodge, when Roosevelt met him at Harvard, was divided in his mind between the choice of a career in literature and one in politics. This son of New England patricians, who had a local reputation for industry and talent, had been counseled by Henry Adams to turn his steps toward the "historico-literary line," as a career that could be made to pay well in money, reputation, and other solid values. In their most respectable town of Boston, Adams observed: "No one has done better and won more in any business or pursuit, than has been acquired by men like Prescott, Motley, Frank Parkman, Bancroft and so on in historical writing. . . ." Yet none of these had been men of extraordinary gifts; and now that they were passing, Boston was "running dry of literary authorities." By his ability Lodge might with ease "enthrone himself as a species of literary lion. . . . With it comes social dignity, European reputation, and a foreign mission to close." [6]

Lodge had decided, however, to combine from the beginning both the "historico-literary" and the political career. His wealth, which rumor traced to a great "rum-and-nigger" fortune, and his cultured background disposed him to the effort. His boyhood memories were filled with the eloquence of great men such as Daniel Webster, Charles Sumner, and Emerson, who used to call upon his father and discourse upon the state of the world. Inspired with their example he prepared himself, it is said, to become a master of languages and of letters, a poised speaker at the dinner table or from the public rostrum. One of his friends, John T. Morse, recalls that even from earliest years Lodge "always had himself well in hand." He bore himself with almost too much measure and pride; and his popularity among his Massachusetts neighbors was never "strictly personal." [7]

When he came of age and inherited his fortune, Lodge gave great dinners at his home, and with the aid of a cellar of famous old Madeira maintained a high level of talk. To a Roosevelt, Lodge was the cultured young man of letters, "writing brilliant books in his handsome library in the forenoon and entertaining agreeable company at his hospitable mahogany in the evenings." Roosevelt heard much from his friend, eight years his senior, of the need for "philosophic statesmanship" and for "introducing education, training, character" into our public life.[8]

Often among the company were those other young Mugwumps, such as Moorfield Storey, who had been the secretary and protégé of Sumner, and Brooks Adams, with whose aid Lodge launched the Commonwealth Club, devoted to the "purification of politics." [9]

From 1880 on, Lodge made serious efforts to play a part in local politics; he sought to become a delegate to national Repub-

[6] Adams, *Letters,* Vol. I, p. 228.

448686

[7] *Harvard Graduates' Magazine,* Mar., 1925.

[8] *H. C. Lodge Papers,* Harvard College, Lodge to Goss.

[9] Howe, *Moorfield Storey,* pp. 141-142.

lican conventions. Though Henry Adams scolded him, he continued his efforts, despite some disappointments. Mornings he continued to work at his historical literature: the biographies of his Federalist ancestor, George Cabot, and George Cabot's famous friend, Alexander Hamilton. Afternoons, he repaired to South Boston, seeking out the local professionals of politics, through whom he hoped to secure his election to Congress.

This Boston swell "had always got what he wanted," as his friend Morse relates. But in some manner the partisans of reform, and Lodge, their active local leader, begot for themselves by 1884 a certain ill-repute during their struggle with the dreadful spoilsman General Ben Butler. In fact rumors of Lodge's Jekyll-and-Hyde character, circulating even at this time, had it that Butler's own shady methods had been turned against him; a hired "rowdy element" seemed to have become uppermost in the respectable faction itself. Those rumors Lodge indignantly denied as miserable calumnies, against which he set the record of his past life, his position, his education, his character.[10]

Roosevelt at Harvard has been pictured as both bookish and passionately fond of sports, an indifferent student and yet full of impetuous curiosity for all things. He became a member of fashionable clubs; he was fastidious, even a little showy in dress, with a touch of the exhibitionism that often clings to men who love public life. He had also a serious side that led him to direct a Sunday school class every week.[11]

His social connections with Boston deepened when he met Alice Lee, who became his first wife. She was the daughter of George Cabot Lee, one of Boston's leading bankers, and like his partner, Higginson, a convinced Mugwump. The fervor for civil service reform so strong in Boston at this time now swept up the young Roosevelt.[12]

[10] *H. C. Lodge Papers*, letter of Oct. 22, 1884.

[11] Pringle, *Roosevelt*, pp. 32-33.

[12] Not long before, the fierce political strife of the "Dreadful Decades" in New York, with its Democratic Tweeds and Republican Conklings, had pene-

In childhood Theodore Roosevelt evidently received a firm, Christian upbringing from his father, whom he pictures as just and wise, "the best man I ever knew." One might almost say that he inherited from him a disposition to political reform. It was Lodge, however, who evidently imparted to him the twin ambitions of becoming a great tribune and a great man of letters. Roosevelt thought Lodge, who possessed already a literary reputation, one of the most brilliant and forceful men he had ever met; and his friend was to gain over him an empire which another contemporary at Harvard, Owen Wister, rated as that of an "evil genius." But those who knew Cabot Lodge only as a cold and scheming man were ignorant of the hidden side of him which brought tears to his eyes when he read poetry to a friend.

Roosevelt too was soon deep in the historico-literary line. At the age of twenty-two he set to work on his long chronicle, *The Naval War of 1812*. Thereafter biographies and historical studies, essays on travel and political subjects, flowed from his pen.

In his early twenties he pictured himself, in his letters, as living an intense life of the mind; he described his joy at visiting a literary club, "a kind of Boston 'Century,'" where he met writers like Henry James and Edward Everett Hale. Dreams possessed him of a life more cultured, more filled with large events, in short, *less boresome*, than that of most others in his class. He looked forward to that "far distant salon, wherein we are to gather

trated to the very home of the Roosevelt family. The worthy Theodore Roosevelt, Sr., widely known in New York as a rich merchant and public-spirited citizen, had been "interested in every social reform" movement of the time, working with the Citizens' Committee which fought the Tweed Ring, and with the moderate Republicans who opposed the "Stalwart" machine. Thus President Hayes, in a sudden movement against Senator Roscoe Conkling, in 1877 nominated the elder Roosevelt for Collector of the Port of New York, a tremendous patronage job, overseeing half the customhouse business of the country—a business long in the hands of the machine, and a nest of corruption. But the "courtesy of the Senate" invoked by Conkling for two years blocked confirmation of Roosevelt, Sr., who died suddenly in 1878. Thus the public career he had been ready to embrace at a sacrifice was killed in the bud. Although the incident has not been noticed much, the younger Roosevelt could not have failed to associate the spoilsmen's opposition to his father with sorrow at his early death.

society men who take part in politics, literature and art, and politicians, authors and artists, whose bringing up and personal habits do not disqualify them for society." For the paramount thing was to escape from the desperately dull life that most of his friends appeared to lead. He continues: "The ——s are two fine-looking fellows of excellent family and faultless breeding, with a fine old country-place, four-in-hands, tandems, a yacht, and so on; but, oh, the decorous hopelessness of their lives!"[13]

The ideals of a Lodge and Roosevelt thus corresponded to those of many members of the leisure class in England. Literature, history, the arts, good society, were the ornaments of a good life; to stand for Parliament, to play a leading part in politics, both dispatched a duty and made life fuller still. But in America things were vastly different; and to pass directly from Harvard College to the Senate was no easy matter.

2

Fifteen years of political apprenticeship had passed for Theodore Roosevelt, the "silk stocking dude," before the critical year of 1896. He held minor public offices almost constantly, being elected Assemblyman from his district for three years, 1881 to 1884; running unsuccessfully for Mayor of New York in 1886; and being appointed a United States Civil Service Commissioner under President Harrison in 1889, President of the New York City Police Board in 1895, and finally, Assistant Secretary of the Navy in 1897, following McKinley's election. It was a record of varied experience and service, not lacking in distinction, yet on the whole unsatisfying, and certainly less brilliant than that of William Howard Taft, who also as a young reformer of respectable upper-class connections entered Ohio local politics at the same time and rose to be a Solicitor General and Federal judge while still in his early thirties. Nor did Roosevelt, like another contemporary, that strange young Texan of independent fortune and

[13] Cowles, *op. cit.*, pp. 77-78.

literary tastes, Edward M. House, become one of the "powers behind the throne" in the party organization of a great state. Nor did his record show that admirable consistency and zeal in pursuit of reform that distinguished certain of his acquaintances, such as the Bostonian Moorfield Storey, who despite high abilities was nearly all his life excluded from political office.

Imbued in the beginning with the Mugwump's belief in the primacy of "righteousness" above "partisanship," Roosevelt's early career could be summed up as a series of strategic retreats from such ideals—retreats, however, which brought him ever closer to the conquest of power.

In his *Autobiography*, often very pertinent and revealing, though disingenuous with its glaring omissions, Roosevelt has given a colorful picture of his early days in the lower ranks of his trade. The party, which he formally joined after providing suitable credentials, he describes as having still some of the character of a "private corporation," made up of a network of local district sub-organizations or clubs. The fiction of free and secret balloting in a democracy was dissolved for him soon after he joined the "Jake Hess Club," named after one of Republican boss Platt's city henchmen. Meetings were held once or twice a month in a large, dismal, barnlike room over a saloon, having the usual dingy benches, spittoons, and dais, and also the usual picture of General Grant on the wall. Here the real soldiers of democracy plied their trade. Under the command of Jake Hess and his "heelers," primaries were "managed," nominations were "arranged," and election campaigns were "organized." Here Roosevelt, the thin, blond, bespectacled, overdressed young man, after overcoming the hostility of his rough comrades—much to his credit, and thanks to the human warmth, charm, and high spirits he always had under his "dude's" dress—came at last to feel himself one of the "governing class," one of the nation-wide guild of political workers to whom public affairs were a constant rather than a spasmodic object of interest.

Owing to dissensions within the Republican party in New York the chance of being nominated for Assemblyman came early; and with the aid of prominent residents of his "silk stocking" district, such as Joseph H. Choate and Elihu Root, he was elected to the State Legislature in November, 1881. At Albany other myths concerning "government by discussion" and parliamentary action were dispelled. Laws were enacted not by juristic debate but by the pressure of powerful interests standing behind the local politicians. "There was no real party division. . . ." [14] The notorious Black Horse Cavalry, who alternately accepted bribes and extorted blackmail money in return for passing or obstructing certain legislative acts, drew their members from the Republican as well as the Tammany side. "Probably a third" of the legislators were crooked, Roosevelt estimated, and the rest were more or less helpless.

After a time Roosevelt, as an outsider, began open and vigorous attacks upon one of the most generally hated of the "special interests" who ruled the local parliament from behind the scenes: Mr. Jay Gould himself. He succeeded in carrying through one day a resolution for the investigation of various stock-jobbing scandals touching elevated railway finance, and charging the sinister Gould with the corruption of a New York Supreme Court judge. Nothing came of the affair beyond the investigation and its report; yet the metropolitan newspapers that were not then owned by Jay Gould applauded the youthful Assemblyman as one, at least, who "called men and things by their right name," which took no little courage "in these days of subserviency to the robber-barons of the Street." "There is a splendid career open for a young man of position, character, and independence like Mr. Roosevelt who can denounce the legalized robbery of Gould and his allies without descending to the turgid abuse of the demagogue, and without . . . the cowardly caution of the politician." [15]

Soon the dude was hailed by the spokesmen of reform, especially by Godkin in the *Post* and in the *Nation*, as a shining model to all his fellow society men. A banquet was given in his honor at Delmonico's by eminent Goo-Goos; and it was said that

[14] Roosevelt, *An Autobiography*, p. 64.

[15] The New York *Times*, Apr. 6, 1882; Bishop, *Roosevelt*, Vol. I, p. 12.

his example was sufficient "to shame thousands who complain that politics are so dirty no decent gentleman can engage in them."[16]

At the beginning of his second year in the Albany Legislature he had been honored by being given the minority vote of his party for Speaker. But the following year, when the Republicans regained the majority in both houses of the Legislature, he resolved to be Speaker in more than an honorary sense. Unabashed, he ran about everywhere and canvassed several up-state counties, soliciting support in the autumn of 1883. But now that actual control of the Legislature was located in the post of the Speaker, the Republican managers ended their dissensions and, in caucus, elected a "regular" Speaker over Roosevelt by a very heavy vote. It was a stinging lesson in party discipline. Roosevelt had counted decidedly upon his advancement in New York State politics; and he attributed this crushing reverse, which left him standing alone and without prospects for the future, to his frequent independence, his voting without paying heed to "teamwork" or to the views of his party.

At this period also another deep lesson was administered to the young statesman. An old family friend and prominent lawyer had invited him to lunch, and, in a heart-to-heart chat, attempted to open his artless mind to the realities of politics and business. He both liked young Roosevelt and was sorry for him. The "reform play" in the Legislature, the airing of the Westbrook-Gould scandal, was all very well; Roosevelt had acquitted himself creditably in the Legislature and shown that he could make himself useful in the right kind of law firm or business concern. But he had gone far enough and must not overplay his hand. It was time, his friend advised, "to leave politics and identify [himself] with the right kind of people, the people who would always in the long run control others and obtain the real rewards which were worth having." Did that, Roosevelt asked, mean yielding to "the ring" in politics? The lawyer answered impatiently that talk of "rings" was all poppycock. The real "ring," the inner circle, was made up

[16] Bishop, *op. cit.*, Vol. I, p. 29.

in actuality of "certain big business men, and the politicians, lawyers and judges who were in alliance with and to a certain extent dependent upon them." The successful man, whether in business, law, or politics, had to win his success by the backing of those same forces—or go down to failure.[17]

Here, he recalls in his memoirs, he received his "first glimpse of that combination between business and politics which I was in after years so often to oppose."

Meanwhile his friend Cabot Lodge, whose constant advice and aid counted for so much both in literary and political enterprises, began to make rapid progress in mastering the intricacies of Massachusetts politics, receiving the Republican nomination for Congress and becoming state chairman of his party in 1884. It was not through his personal charm, according to common report, that the wealthy scholar won the electoral support of the Lynn shoemakers and the Charlestown Navy Yard workers.

That year the two friends went together as delegates to the Republican national convention, and shared an experience that was decisive for Lodge and that tried the soul of Roosevelt. Still playing the reformer, Lodge was the active head of the group of New England Mugwumps who fought to oppose the nomination of the immitigable James G. Blaine. The candidate supported by Lodge, Schurz, Moorfield Storey, Charles W. Eliot, Josiah Quincy, and other Massachusetts Independents was the able but colorless Senator George F. Edmunds, Vermont's Favorite Son, who had the advantage of never having been touched either by recent public scandal or factious strife. To their cause Roosevelt was able to bring over a small, Independent minority of the New York delegation as well.

Because the real race lay between President Arthur and Blaine,

[17] Roosevelt, *An Autobiography*, pp. 76, 77, 85.

That Roosevelt did not weakly and unreflectingly accept the counsel of the lawyer speaks for his own originality, force of will, and desire for *innovation*, which make his career so noteworthy. Otherwise we should not be writing of him today.

leaders of the two rival factions in the Republican party, our earnest reformers hoped for a long deadlock out of which their candidate would be chosen as a compromise figure. Thus the two young politicians, Lodge and Roosevelt, filled with excitement at the prospect of "making a President," worked day and night to win over doubtful state delegations.

The struggle was brief. At the proper moment the "stampede" for the immensely popular Blaine, idol of the professionals, overwhelmed them as with the force of an avalanche. *"Blaine! Blaine! James G. Blaine!"* thundered the exultant followers of the Plumed Knight whose plumes were besmirched by scandal.

Of all men in politics at that time none aroused more revulsion in Independent breasts than James G. Blaine. Henry Cabot Lodge has related that during a private conference in May, 1884, he and Roosevelt had agreed to remain "regular" and abide loyally by the majority decision of the party convention.[18] But whatever private pledges Theodore Roosevelt may have given Lodge, he felt himself placed in a terrible quandary. His whole purpose in entering politics as a moral venture had been to contend against such an example of official corruption as Blaine was reputed to be. Meanwhile, all of his closest friends and fellow reformers both in New York and Boston, all the men whose good opinion he had earned, were preparing to "bolt." That is, they were organizing as a group to influence public opinion in favor of the expected reform candidate whom the Democrats would offer that season, Governor Grover Cleveland. By all his lights, Roosevelt too should have "switched" to Cleveland. That Roosevelt was racked by doubts, that he felt his position most critical, is all too clear. He made several contradictory statements: early reports reflected his extreme disillusionment, and indicated that he expected to join the "bolt" against Blaine. But these were promptly denied by him, although in private he wrote to his sister, Mrs. Cowles, of his bitter sense of betrayal, of the betrayal of "all the men of the broadest culture and highest character" in his party.[19]

[18] Lodge, *op. cit.*, Vol. I, pp. 13-14.
[19] Cowles, *op. cit.*, pp. 54-55.

Meanwhile he took sudden flight to the cattle ranch which he had acquired the year before in Dakota Territory, and remained there silent, alone, wrestling with his soul during several weeks. One alternative that was always left to him, one that the educated man of wealth always held, was that of quitting politics entirely. Certainly he might choose to be silent, abstaining from any active canvassing for Mr. Blaine.

But his "alter ego" of those days, Cabot Lodge, would leave him no rest. Lodge had come to the parting of the ways with his more discriminating Mugwump friends. He was already heavily committed to Massachusetts organization politics, even in a pecuniary sense; and he proposed now to continue along that line. To Carl Schurz (whom he, like so many other intellectuals of the period, admired as one of the nobler types in American politics, and who now pleaded with Lodge to "obey a noble impulse," to "bolt") he defended his decision to remain "regular" as the only feasible course for him. "By staying in the party I can be of some use. By going out, I destroy all the influence and power for good I possess." [20]

It was in these terms that he must have appealed to the sulking Roosevelt, who, during a hurried trip East shortly before July 19, 1884, saw Lodge and was won over by him.

In his well-known biography of Alexander Hamilton, published two years before, Lodge had written some meaningful passages concerning Hamilton's decision to vote for the adoption of the Constitution despite his own dislike for many of its provisions. These sentences tell us much concerning the author's outlook on life:

> Had he been an agitator or a sentimentalist of muddy morals and high purposes, a visionary and an idealist, he would have stood up and howled against this constitution. . . . As he was none of these things, but a patriotic man of clear and practical mind, he knew that the *first rule of successful and beneficial statesmanship was not to sulk because one cannot have just what one wants, but to take the best thing obtainable, and sustain it to the uttermost.*[21]

[20] Fuess, *Schurz,* p. 288.

[21] Italics mine.

"Sentimentalist" and "agitator"—such may have been the reproaches with which Lodge tackled his younger friend's *crise de conscience*. Meanwhile the fate of their whole grandiose Hamiltonian design for the future conquest of Congress, Senate, Cabinet, or even the White House turned upon accepting "the best thing obtainable," following the party line and observing party discipline. For, in a close election, even the "bolting" of young minor leaders would have its weight for independent voters—and would be neither forgotten nor forgiven. Roosevelt resisted no more that day. There is a telling phrase which occurs at this period in his intimate correspondence with his sister: "Cabot has felt that I was a brand snatched from the burning. . . ." [22]

How often in those early years the sagacious Cabot was to snatch him from danger and carry him off safely for the Republican party! For Cabot recognized high qualities in the young Roosevelt, fed his boundless ambitions, and sustained him when others doubted. From this moment in 1884—when Roosevelt issued to the New York press his prepared statement that after mature consideration he had decided to vote for Blaine—from this moment dates the period of closest political collaboration between the two friends, and the long ascendancy of Lodge's will and direction over Roosevelt. His words were almost identical with those Lodge had used in writing to Schurz: "Whatever good I have been able to accomplish in public life has been accomplished through the Republican party." He could not, he declared, act at the same time as a "guerilla chief," outside the party, and as a "colonel in the regular army." [23]

The "treason" of the reformer Lodge caused a tempest in Boston. Lifelong friendships were broken at this time. Moorfield Storey never spoke to Lodge for forty years after, though both served together as Overseers at Harvard. Roosevelt, who came to Boston in October to stump for Lodge in the Congressional campaign, was also bitterly condemned by his Boston friends, espe-

[22] Cowles, *op. cit.*, p. 149.
[23] Bishop, *op. cit.*, Vol. I, p. 36.

cially when the exposure of the famous "Mulligan Letters" appeared to blacken Mr. Blaine's public reputation beyond repair. Roosevelt is alleged to have said: "I hope to God he [Blaine] will be defeated." The reasons he and Lodge gave for their conduct appeared to be a mixture of personal ambition and hope of promotion through the elimination of rivals who "bolted." [24]

In New York, censure of Roosevelt was also frequently heard. Edwin L. Godkin appeared all the more disappointed in him, inasmuch as he had formerly praised him, and now delivered some merciless drubbings. "Jack in the Box" and "ranting young humbug [who] made the very term reform redolent of hypocrisy" were some of the epithets reserved for Roosevelt after 1884 in the independent press.[25]

"I have been called a reformer, but I am a Republican," Roosevelt was reported to have said by a Boston newspaper. This interview he repudiated in part.[26]

Censure that stung only hardened the young man's resolve. By October he took to the stump, speaking in behalf of the party if not noticeably of the candidate. He guarded thereafter a bitter dislike for his reformist friends, which they cordially returned, whereas he now found unexpected beauties of character in his professional associates. They at least were "men of action." "They are not always polished, but they are strong, and as a whole I think them pretty good fellows," he wrote somewhat later to one of his

[24] "Diary of Storey" in Howe, *op. cit.*, pp. 154-155.

[25] H. C. Lodge, *op. cit.*, Vol. I, p. 121, citing the New York *World*.

[26] In a somewhat indiscreet speech at Boston in October, 1884, Theodore Roosevelt attributed the nomination of Mr. Blaine ("against the wishes of many of us, against my wishes and votes") to the stupidity of the masses. Blaine was nominated "because those whom Abraham Lincoln in one of those quaint remarks of his called 'the plain people' wished to see him President. He was nominated against the wishes of the most intellectual men, the most virtuous and honorable men, but he was nominated fairly and honorably . . . and I for one am glad to abide by the judgment of the 'plain people.'" (Howe, *op cit.*, pp. 157-158, footnote.) Thus T. R. against his own inclinations appeared to be following a "popular" line for "practical" reasons. Moorfield Storey thought Roosevelt was "unprincipled" ever after. He would never support an unpopular cause because it was right. He would, however, support a cause that seemed "righteous" to him, if it were popular.

literary friends, Brander Matthews. "Oh, you Mugwumps!" he would exclaim resentfully. "The way you arrogate all virtue to yourself is enough to exasperate an humble party man like myself." [27]

Despite the somersaults of our Mugwump renegades, Blaine was defeated; in Boston, Lodge, who stood for Congress, was likewise defeated—although his "regularity" gained him the post of state chairman of his party. The party which could have rewarded Roosevelt was out of power for four years. These years in which he posed as "an humble party man" were not in any sense happy ones. Indeed, they represented a phase of extreme moral and intellectual confusion, during which the "practical" politician was somewhat prematurely and crudely superimposed upon his own better nature. In that same year, 1884, his gloom was deepened by the sudden death of his first wife, Alice Lee Roosevelt. In his autobiography he passes quickly over most of these events.

3

Do not think that Theodore Roosevelt in his mood of disillusionment relapsed wholly into the character of "an humble party man." He was to be no more faithful to orthodox Republicanism than to Mugwump reform. With the purely political man, loyalty to ideas and doctrines is relative rather than absolute. Even the dogmatic or "fanatical" type of political leader is found to pursue often a devious rather than a head-on march toward his objectives.

Roosevelt's apprentice years were compounded of irresolute waverings and contradictory impulses, reflecting well the contradictions within the middle-class republic and its institutions. In those years the amateur of politics—as Grover Cleveland, who observed him both at Albany and Washington, remarked—"was looking to a public career, studying political conditions with a care that I had never known any man to show." [28] The problem of developing a substantial following of voters, building a functional

[27] *Matthews Papers*. T. R. to Brander Matthews, Feb. 10, 1890; July 31, 1889.
[28] Josephson, *The Politicos*, p. 442.

strength of his own from the ground up, remained for a long time unsolved.

He preserved within him some pure white flower, sprung perhaps from his decent moral upbringing, his environment and inheritance, that made it less possible for him to enjoy downright dishonesty or skulduggery than it was for that other Harvard swell, Boies Penrose, who, beginning as a reformer in Philadelphia politics, turned wickedly and cheerfully into the henchman of boss Matt Quay. Roosevelt was not obviously a handy man of the party hierarchy at administering bribes or swinging "deals." Thus his sphere of usefulness seemed limited for a long time to "mere scavenging work," as he himself called it, or to ornamenting minor administrative posts, his very appointment representing something of a concession to those who demanded "good men in office."

His work as Civil Service Commissioner at Washington during the six years from 1889 to 1895 was also creditable, especially for vigorous attempts to enforce the new merit and examination system and for hounding criminal characters out of government offices. Yet here too he was to learn bitter lessons concerning the narrow limits of governmental reform. There were collisions with Senators and cabinet members, party bosses who vehemently opposed the elimination of their henchmen from government payrolls. Once more the newspapers spoke well of the vigorous and courageous civil service reformer in Washington. Then he was forgotten. He found that his usefulness was restricted; that he was expected to "cleanse the Augean Stables" only up to a point where he did no hurt to the larger interest of his party in the spoils of office. Mr. Harrison, "the little grey man in the White House," he reported privately, "treated him with a cold and hesitating disapproval." [29]

The label of the reformer clung to him, whether he chose it or not. As Civil Service Commissioner under Harrison and then for several years under Cleveland (who retained him with a worthy gesture), Roosevelt could be seen "battling the spoilsmen" with a

[29] Cowles, *op. cit.*, p. 113.

gusto that was native and a forthrightness that made his advancement in politics more interesting and more difficult at once.

Then when the more Machiavellian Lodge would come forward to caution him, warning him not to precipitate quarrels which would injure his party's election prospects, he would retreat for a time. He would promise to behave with a more "statesmanlike reserve" in the future.[30]

With the November, 1894, elections fresh opportunities for practical experience had come to Roosevelt just when he was growing bored with civil service reform. In his native city of New York, sensational exposures (by the Lexow Committee) of corruption in the police and street-cleaning departments had led to the defeat of the Tammany "rascals" and their replacement by a non-partisan or "Fusion" ticket, allied with the city's regular Republican minority. The Goo-Goos promptly bethought themselves of Theodore Roosevelt, and invited him in December, 1894, to become Street Cleaning Commissioner. It was an office that plainly needed his reforming hand.

With Lodge's advice this offer was refused as touching a position Roosevelt "could not afford to be identified with."[31] But a few weeks later there came the offer of membership in New York's Police Commission; and further—thanks to Lodge—the offer carried with it the promise that young Roosevelt would be named president of the board of four by an understanding with the new Mayor, William L. Strong. That he regarded the appointment as a career opportunity in which he intended to prove himself fit for higher stations is shown by his letter to Lodge written in May, 1895, shortly after he bustled into the damp, gloomy Mulberry Street headquarters: ". . . In a couple of years or less . . . the department will be in good running order. . . . I shall be quite ready . . . to take up a new job."

Opportunities and dangers were large as the youthful Commissioner at the age of thirty-six took over one of the most important

[30] Lodge, *op. cit.*, Vol. I, p. 82.

[31] Cowles, *op. cit.*, p. 149; Lodge, *op. cit.*, Vol. I, p. 142.

and difficult of offices. The police department of New York was very nearly at the heart of the system of political corruption then flourishing. For nearly three years the Rev. Charles H. Parkhurst had been fulminating from the pulpit of his Madison Square Church against the iniquities of Tammany and the organized trade in vice and gambling carried on by a Tammany-ruled police.

Then, in 1894, the probings of the Lexow Committee of the New York State Legislature had brought out facts more complete and more shocking still. The rank and file of the police were shown to be completely demoralized; appointments and promotions in the force were based frankly on cash payments. Throughout the metropolis, huge revenues, an unofficial tax or tithe, were regularly collected from the unlawful sale of liquor, the operation of gambling and brothel houses, and other indulgences. The illicit "licensing" activities by the New York City police were believed to yield more revenue than the legal licensing privileges exercised by the city or state governments themselves. Roosevelt, as an Assemblyman ten years ago, and member of the City Affairs Committee, had already glimpsed something of these conditions and even made a beginning toward exposing them. It was the partial knowledge of these conditions that had made him originally so strong for reform. The fact that the sale of police indulgences, gambling and liquor privileges, was but a minor department in the larger working alliance between the political rings and business interests does not seem to have dawned upon him at the time. What followed, as the eager Roosevelt leaped into the fray, took the pattern of a classical comedy which may be called "The Reform Wave."

The first act was an affair of popular revulsion and the turning out of the rascals by the Good Government men. Before the storm of public opinion Chief Croker, the master of Tammany Hall, retreated to Ireland for a temporary vacation, though muttering darkly as he left that he would soon return at the people's command.

Roosevelt, who now showed his flair for battle, began with a sudden, sharp thrust. He persuaded his fellow commissioners to dismiss the formidable and sinister Inspector Byrnes, one of those permanent officials who, because of long working relations with the criminal class, were considered more powerful than any mere commissioner. This bold move was followed up a few weeks later, on June 23, 1895, by an order to enforce the Sunday closing law for saloons throughout the metropolis. As Roosevelt said afterward: "The saloon was the chief source of the mischief. It was with the saloon that I had to deal, and there was only one way to deal with it. That was to enforce the law." [32]

On that Sunday morning when Roosevelt's bluecoats began closing up the public houses and making hundreds of arrests all over the city, there began the creation of a legend. A group of newspaper reporters who admired Roosevelt—among them Jacob Riis, the humanitarian author of *How the Other Half Lives;* Lincoln Steffens, then a police reporter; and Joseph Bucklin Bishop, afterward Roosevelt's biographer—all championed the commissioner with their pens. In addition, ministers of the pulpit and academic leaders helped to call favorable attention to this unique political figure, about whom a storm of mingled applause and denunciation henceforth raged.

Joseph B. Bishop thought him impulsive to the point of naïveté, with "essentially a boy's mind." Yet he said out loud the things that others knew but would not mention. He seemed to court head-on opposition. To those who warned him that in carrying out an unpopular blue law he should at least enforce it with some "discrimination," he replied bluntly that to do so would be "like believing in truthful mendacity." He would go on "enforcing honestly a law that has hitherto been enforced dishonestly." [33]

The second act is, thus, an exhilarating one. Amid high excitement the cleansing of the Augean Stables from basement to attic proceeded unremittingly. Honest men were in the saddle. The public rubbed its eyes at the unwonted sight of its officers actually enforcing the law. Indeed, it was a hopeful sign that many of the citizens of Gotham, not yet too lost in iniquity, responded warmly

[32] Roosevelt, *An Autobiography*, p. 191.
[33] Bishop, *op. cit.*, Vol. I, pp. 61, 63.

at first to the appeal of the devoted, strenuous official. His unconventional tours of inspection through the wicked city by night (he wore evening clothes covered with a long cloak), his tracking down of delinquent officers, his raids into dens of evil, became the talk of the town during the summer of 1895. "Teddy the Scorcher," a bellicose reformer ready to give blow for blow, in his cowboy costume, wearing pince-nez, and smiling with all his buck teeth, figured in newspaper story and cartoon until he became a colorful national celebrity.

The first enthusiasm over his law-enforcement campaign, as he reported modestly to Cabot Lodge, had made "the Good Government Club and their ilk regard me as a hero." [34] From Europe his faithful mentor, reading of Theodore's exploits in the London *Times* itself, sent warm compliments, happy that his anticipations for his pupil were being borne out. The Senator from Massachusetts—for he had recently attained this high station—now replied:

> I am glad that I have known you long and loved you well and that you are a person of loyal disposition, for you are rushing so rapidly to the front that the day is not distant when you will come into a large kingdom and by that time I shall be a back number and I shall expect you to give me a slice. . . . That Senatorship is getting well into sight, my dear boy.

But Lodge, who had a vision of his younger friend as a growing power in the practical politics of the Empire State, soon began to point out to him that being a hero to the Goo-Goos might prove an embarrassment. Theodore must indicate that his reformatory actions were aimed at the Democratic enemy and furthered a full-fledged, four-square Republicanism. He must even refuse to speak in public save at Republican gatherings.

To this line of advice Theodore shows himself fairly submissive, writing in answer: "This summer, I have, as you know, been careful to identify myself in every way with the Republicans. Hill has attacked me violently as a Republican. . . ." And again, sometime later, he writes, "During the two years I have been

[34] Lodge, *op. cit.*, Vol. I, p. 169, letter of Aug. 27, 1895.

here . . . I have in every way avoided any kind of attack upon the organization Republicans, and all I could legally do that they have asked me, I have done."

To such dutiful reports "Dear Cabot" would respond with praise and even flattery: Theodore was now doing "rightly, wisely and splendidly." He was showing good sense in avoiding any "personal quarrel with the machine." His work would "lead surely to even better things." But Theodore was so constituted that he suffered qualms, and sometimes exclaimed with disgust: "I feel all the time that very uncomfortable sensation of sailing under false colors." [35]

In the third act of the Reform Wave, popular enthusiasm flags, difficulties mount, the forward and uplift movement drags against an increasing resistance.

We must remark that the New York City Fusion administration of 1895-1897, of which Roosevelt was the most important officer after the Mayor, had a most superficial, an ephemeral, program. Goo-Goo reform, ignoring the deeper social evils of the day, changed in no sense those material conditions of poverty and hideously crowded, filthy housing which caused the proletarians to congregate in the saloons that were "poor men's clubs," or to seek excitement in gambling resorts, and submit on election days to the influence of the local heelers who were kindred to them and often befriended them in time of trouble. The characteristic measures of the civil service reformers, especially their more rigorous policing, seemed to strike directly at the few pleasures and liberties open to the masses.

Roosevelt, a typical upper-class product of Mugwump thought, never understood the working class well, and in his earlier phase concealed but little of his instinctive hostility to them. While in the State Legislature, as one of his later biographers, Henry Pringle, has shown, this aristocratic reformer considered no revolutionary changes within the pattern of his proposed improvements. He would support a bill to abolish sweatshop labor in tene-

[35] Lodge, *op. cit.*, Vol. I, pp. 169, 256.

ment houses, "as a measure of health." But when measures raising the wages of city laborers in Buffalo and New York to $2 a day, or fixing twelve hours as the maximum for street-car workers, were brought up, he denounced them as visionary, un-American, and "socialistic." [36] Any other line of action, in the view of reformers of comfortable means in his day, would be tantamount to "playing the demagogue."

At this period of his life Theodore Roosevelt's first-hand knowledge of the oppressed classes, the "other half," was extended somewhat, thanks to his friendship with Jacob Riis and Lincoln Steffens. With these two journalists he would sometimes wander upon slumming expeditions at night through the lower East Side, and would grow horrified at the things to be seen only a few minutes' walk from Gramercy Park or his own "silk stocking" district. He recalled vividly in his memoirs, long afterward, the hot, stinking, summer nights, the piles of refuse, the occasional dead horses lying in the streets, the incredible squalor and filth of the tenement quarters that made New York one of the world's hell-holes. To the influence of the tender-hearted Jacob Riis he attributed his own belated awareness of the cruelly contrasting extremes of showy wealth and wretched poverty to be seen everywhere in American cities. Yet nodding acquaintance with the slum-dwellers in no way changed his real prejudices.

Toward the labor movement, toward the rising trade-union organizations as a growing institution, eager to play its full-grown part within the social organism, he remained hostile. To be sure, these were "the very people one would wish to help," he would say paternally—they must never learn to help themselves! And he could still say, at the time when he was New York's police commissioner in 1896, that the remedy for our social troubles lay not in radical action, in "Popocracy," but in "inculcating higher ideals of citizenship and developing a nobler order of manhood." [37]

Thus Roosevelt's fear of the proletarians and of their rebellious instincts persisted strongly. That "organized labor," of which

[36] Pringle, *Roosevelt*, p. 78.

[37] New York *Journal*, Oct. 29, 1896.

he spoke often with contempt, might in its own behalf seek political instruments and directions of its own—as in turning to Mr. Bryan's party and free silver—was a development that he resented with every fiber of his nature. Addressing a trade-union audience on the East Side one night, he made a pleasing impression, and the union leaders proposed to him that he seek the endorsement of trade-unionists for some public office. Reporting this incident to Cabot, he relates how offended he was at the proposal, and how he thrust it away with scorn. And the working classes instinctively returned his suspicion and dislike, all through his career. With them the Reform Wave was not popular; and Roosevelt never developed a following among them comparable to that of the Tammany leaders who sometimes winked at the law for the sake of a trade-unionist in distress.

Moreover, the delicate, complex adjustments of the political parties, in relation to both large business interests and illicit commerce, were being disturbed by the reformers. The liquor dealers' associations were up in arms, and on them depended much of the vote-gathering in November. Their protests were joined with those of the lower classes, accustomed to taking their beer on Sundays, *en famille,* at the Viennese beer gardens of the Bowery. Soon the friends of the old order, noticing the changing tide, threw up cleverly contrived obstacles in the shape of obsolete blue laws, vexing local ordinances which their politicians ordered enforced and which caused spreading confusion and resentment. After a year in office, Commissioner Roosevelt found himself more and more exposed to blows from unseen hands, to flanking maneuvers.

He now felt himself in serious straits, with his popularity waning. Most embarrassing of all was the passage of the Raines Law by the State Legislature in April, 1896. While innocently pretending to be another liquor-control measure, it provided that hotels equipped to serve meals, and therefore permitted to serve liquor also on Sundays, could henceforth be located only in structures having ten rooms. ". . . The ten rooms required by law were used for prostitution in order to pay the overhead," records Henry Pringle in his often ironical biography of Roosevelt. This statute constituted, in concealed form, "the greatest boon to commercialized vice in the history of New York." [38] Hundreds upon hundreds of the new "hotels" were opened, and soon it was plain that the exertions of the reformers had produced but a greater outburst of general lechery.

The troubles of the Police Department, obliged to conduct raids in all directions, were multiplied rapidly. Its Board of Commissioners, two of whose four members submitted readily to machine orders, ceased to support Roosevelt. A hopeless deadlock ensued, and the bitter wranglings of the Board became known to the public in 1896.

To Roosevelt it was now plain that the leaders of his own Republican organization were combined "half-secretly" with the Tammany forces to undo him, as he hinted in several angry press interviews. Behind his increasing misfortunes, he suspected, was the cunning old hand of Thomas C. Platt, the so-called Easy Boss of New York Republicans, who was known to co-operate with the Tammany machine by a system of division of labor, the Democrats controlling the metropolitan spoils down-state while the Republicans managed the Albany Legislature up-state.

The young Police Commissioner now grew as despondent as he had been sanguine the season before. Hope of rising to grander offices, even of becoming President—such hope now lay always in the back of his mind, as Lincoln Steffens discovered—was dwindling fast. Even the respectable elements seemed weary of the uproar over the blue laws. Thus victory over the saloons seemed to leave him politically "without any opening." He lamented to Lodge: "It leads nowhere." [39] To another confidant he said: "I have offended so many powerful politicians that no political preferment in future will be possible for me. All the liquor interests . . . and all the party bosses will oppose me. . . . I realized this when I began my fight." [40]

But at this crisis "Dear Cabot" showered him with advice.

[38] Pringle, *op. cit.*, pp. 148-149.

[39] Lodge, *op. cit.*, Vol. I, pp. 168, 174-176, 181.

[40] Bishop, *op. cit.*, Vol. I, pp. 68-69.

Though hard pressed, Theodore could still strengthen his position in the party by sagacious conduct in the future. Above all, no outspoken accusations in the press. "Talk as little as possible," concluded Lodge, already aware of Theodore's weakness for publicity.

Theodore, however, replied in words that sounded as if he were girding himself to some desperate stroke, one that might throw his whole career into the balance but would at least save his honor as an independent in politics. Rumors came that the Republican party at its approaching state convention would, at Platt's bidding, pass resolutions which showed retreat on the question of Excise Law enforcement, thus repudiating Roosevelt's labors and mollifying the liquor dealers' association. The Commissioner felt himself betrayed, a martyr of the machine whose interests he had dared to oppose. Even Mayor Strong now seemed cowardly, and as for Platt, his conduct had been such "that a decent man must oppose him."[41]

These days he found himself "living in a welter of political intrigue of the meanest kind. . . ." With his own eyes he had witnessed electoral frauds that horrified him: a local primary election carried for his own party by 600 votes raised up from "vacant lots, from houses where [no one] lives, from houses of ill-fame and the like." And he is forced to remain silent, enduring the rebuffs of Platt's henchmen, "who intend to read me out of the party."[42] And yet none must know of the secret, inward torment devouringing the hero of the Goo-Goos, and which now speaks to us from page after page of his correspondence with "Dear Cabot." One might say that, as with Brutus, shame for his city and for himself was borne in upon him during sleepless nights. Perhaps, even, he heard voices calling: "*Speak, strike, redress!* Brutus, thou sleepest! Awake and see thyself. . . ."

Finally he bursts out to Lodge that he proposes to speak out, to attack the machine:

I have so far with no little self-command, refrained from hitting at any of the Republican people; but after the election is over, I am far

[41] Lodge, *op. cit.*, Vol. I, p. 142. [42] *Ibid.*, Vol. I, pp. 202, 212.

from certain that I shall keep my hands off them. However, if possible, I shall wait until I see you before taking action.[43]

When Lodge, who was then traveling overseas, received this letter some ten days later, he flew into a perfect panic. Theodore's whole future was at stake. He sat down and cabled from Paris a dispatch of solemn warning:

> You may be surprised to get a cable from me today [he wrote at the same time by letter] but one sentence in your letter of the 18th. troubled me and that was where you said that you might attack the Machine after the election. That I would not have you do for all the world. I know how trying it all is . . . but to come out and denounce Platt is simply playing Platt's own game.[44]

And once driven out of the party, where they wanted him, his hope of wresting leadership from the others would be ended.

As in similar crises, Roosevelt bowed once more before his mentor's will. When the cablegram from Paris had arrived, October 29, 1895, his wife Edith joined his friend in dissuading him from following the promptings of his heart, saying: "I do believe that dear Cabot cares more for you than anyone else in the world does." The reply to Cabot went forth: "All right! I won't attack anyone." [45]

Lodge preached regularity and discipline. Roosevelt must even force his attentions upon his fellow Republicans, whether they wanted him or not. "Do not fail to go on the stump—not through the city, where it is needless," Cabot counseled, "but through the State where . . . the masses of Republicans are with you. Make speeches for all the State Senators and Assemblymen that you can properly support, and . . . they must see you and get to know you. I regard this as of the utmost importance."

Finally "Dear Cabot" cheered on his protégé, tempting him with the strong wine of ambition: "I can judge of your standing and reputation better than you. . . . You have a great chance to take

[43] Lodge, *op. cit.*, Vol. I, p. 189, Oct. 18, 1895.
[44] *Ibid.*, Vol. I, p. 197, Oct. 30, 1895.
[45] *Ibid.*, Vol. I, p. 196.

the leadership of powerful and controlling elements of the party which can put you in the Senate. . . . I do not say you are to be President tomorrow. I do not say it will be—I am sure it may and can be."[46]

"During my two years as Police Commissioner," Roosevelt told his English friend, Cecil Spring Rice, "I may say I accomplished a great deal, but gradually things have so shaped themselves that I couldn't do anything more."[47]

He now turned to national affairs, bored with the local politics of cartage contracts and appointments for street-sweepers. Hand in hand with Lodge, his fellow conspirator, he continued to scheme for Senatorships or Presidencies. In the winter of 1896 the two devoted schemers had earnestly opposed the boom for McKinley, supporting instead Speaker Thomas B. Reed of Maine, a man of keen intellect, and breadth and force of character. For twenty years Reed had worn the collar of his party in Congress, though he knew how to laugh privately at himself and his colleagues. Yet in spite of the veteran Speaker's distinguished services, his claims to the nomination, supported by the "better element," were brushed aside by the all-powerful Mark Hanna. The elimination of the brilliant Reed, and his consequent decision to retire from public life, was a heartbreaking disappointment, whose meaning Roosevelt could scarcely miss. He sent the Speaker his condolences, and Reed answered in bitter vein that he was long used to "waiting for others to pass." He remarked: "Hanna's coarse ways are pretty hard to stand, especially when you appreciate that a great office can be retained by purchase as well as obtained by purchase."[48]

Yet Roosevelt, as did Lodge and Reed as well, labored with the habitual discipline of his calling for the success of McKinley that year.

At repeated intervals Theodore Roosevelt felt keenly the fickleness of crowd favor and the rebuffs of dominant party bosses.

[46] *Ibid.*, Vol. I, pp. 179-180.
[47] *T. R. Papers*, Apr. 28, 1897.
[48] *T. R. Papers*, Jul. 28, 1896.

Then the assault upon the heights of public power would appear but a slow, unrewarding progress—already extended over fifteen years by 1896—and he would reflect the gloom which visiting foreigners such as Viscount James Bryce noticed in circles of upper-class intellectuals.

In such moods the influence of the pessimistic philosopher of history, Brooks Adams, weighed upon him and was harder to throw off. Early in 1896 Roosevelt had read and written a review of Adams' *The Law of Civilization and Decay*. This writer's interpretation of the "natural laws of force and energy" determining the rise and fall of "concentrations" of civilization along the great trade routes of the world had a curious vogue. Roosevelt tended to thrust aside Adams' darker prophecies, refusing to believe that the American republic, abandoned to love of gain and usury, ruled by a purely money-lending class, was as inevitably doomed to collapse as the Roman republic. But Brooks Adams continued the debate between them firmly; he persisted in attaching himself to the young politician, in whom he, like Cabot Lodge, discerned high possibilities. The struggle over bimetallism, he argued, showed that the "producing classes," crushed under debt, were to be as subject slaves henceforth. Even the administrative leader or the military captain was but a paid official who must take his orders from the ruling class. Roosevelt's future turned upon his ability to submit to events with good grace, upon whether he fought or made his peace with the "system," the Machine.

Brooks Adams wrote him now:

> I have watched your career with deep interest. You may remember a year ago in Washington, *I told you to sell*. You may understand me better now. You are an adventurer and you have but one thing to sell—your sword. You can take your wages like Nelson and Clive, and fight where you are sent, just as every soldier must in a commercial age, or you can lie and rot. Capital will not employ you if you have a conscience, a heart, patriotism, honesty or self-respect.

But the earlier mercenary soldiers had still believed in the country and cause for which they fought. Today one must apparently fight only for "Wall Street," and "Wall Street is a harder master . . . wants men it can buy and own," concluded Adams bitterly—this descendant of Yankee Presidents and capitalists.

> I feared for you last year. I knew that courage and honesty would not help you. I hope, however, that you may still pull through and make your peace.
>
> In this world we must all live if we can—what is hardest is to be so made that you cannot sell. If you can sell, do. If you don't, others will. The world will be no better and you much the worse.[49]

A few weeks later Adams, having received, apparently, a despondent letter from his friend, returned to thc attack. He alluded to his own failures in fighting for a lost cause, civil service reform in Massachusetts. "What use?" he summed up. "Why not live and be hired by a force which masters you, rather than be crushed in a corner to no purpose?" The men of money would be willing to buy Roosevelt out, at almost his own price, for "Wall Street has desperate need of men like you." Let Roosevelt, who was "instinctively a fighter," hire out his sword as barbarian chieftains did for the Romans. "Why fall? Better to be Caesar in the chair of State, than the broken soldier in the arena." [50]

How much the subversive ideas of Brooks Adams ruled the mind of Roosevelt we cannot know. Certainly the terms in which his scholarly friend defined the dilemma of society, faced with the choice of violent proletarian revolution or social decadence eating at the top of the society, were always present in his writings and speeches. They run through his private thoughts like a thread which shows the figure in the carpet: the "weakening fibre" of latter-day Americans; the prospects of "race suicide," whereby the older Anglo-Saxon stock was to be submerged by the masses of alien immigrants; the preoccupation with the "strenuous life," the revival of "soldierly virtues," and reaction against the merely

[49] *T. R. Papers*, Brooks Adams to T. R., Feb. 25, 1896.

[50] *T. R. Papers*, B. Adams to T. R., Apr. 26, 1896.

Search of the Roosevelt Papers did not yield the letters written in reply to Brooks Adams at this period.

"commercial type of mind" in politics—haunted by these notions, Roosevelt, with Lodge and other intellectuals of the conservative class, searched for an alternative way out of the doom not seldom predicted for their world.

Brooks Adams' influence may perhaps be detected in the apparent heartiness with which Roosevelt at length "hired" his verbal sword to Mark Hanna for the fierce stump campaigns of '96; and in the swashbuckling violence with which he attacked the "anarchists" and "Popocrats," Bryan, Altgeld, and Debs, that season.

Little wonder that the restive masses of New York trusted not their city's Goo-Goos, and turned in large numbers not only to the party of Bryan but to Tammany afterward. For civil service reformers came and went, yet the inequalities existing under the constitutional law of the land, which Bryan challenged, remained unaltered. What did the Mayor Strongs or the Commissioner Roosevelts bring them but needless vexations—as in enforcing more rigorously laws that helped them not to slake their thirst and forget the wretchedness and weariness of summer nights in the slums? In 1897 the people turned once more to their old friends of Tammany Hall, those who had always remained close to them, who, while exploiting, had at least understood their misery, their inarticulate fears and wants.

When the fourth act of the comedy of reform was reached, and the full storm of local reaction broke upon the Good Government men in November, 1897, Theodore Roosevelt—fortunately for him—was already somewhere else, placed in a higher political post at the national capital and watching events as from a safe remove. (While suffering the loss of the city of New York, the Republican organization had worked successfully to win the nation for Republicanism; thus the Police Commissioner had found avenues open to him in Washington again.) "New York, as a whole, was glad to see him go. A small dose of reform, as practical politicians well know, lasts for years." [51]

[51] Pringle, *op. cit.*, p. 151.

The summer before, boss Richard Croker had hurried back from Ireland to take command of the Tammany revival, which he had predicted two years before. The people, he had said, would return to his camp after "an extravagant and hypocritical Republican reform administration."[52] Doubtless he knew also that Republican boss Tom Platt would hold hands with him this year, not for the first time so far as city affairs were concerned. That year the Citizens' Union, or non-partisan, reform candidate for Mayor, Seth Low, ran without grace of Republican fusion; though he made a strong demonstration in winning over 150,000 independent votes, the defection of the regular Republicans insured the sweeping victory of Tammany with nearly 234,000 votes.

Early on that Election Day, November 4, 1897, the huge city crowds gathered in the streets and squares to celebrate the expected outcome. The press reported:

TENDERLOIN MAKES MERRY

GOOD OLD DAYS ARE EXPECTED TO RETURN WITH THE TIGER—IT WILL BE "WIDE OPEN"

From six in the evening the dense crowds made Broadway, from Forty-second to Fourteenth Street, impassable; there was a sound of revelry, a fearful din of tin horns and rattles, of jovial crowds besieging bars and hotel corridors where "wine flowed in rivers." The bands played "Hard Times Come Again No More," and "Hot Time in the Old Town Tonight," and "Hear Dem Bells."

At eight o'clock, when the election returns were definitely known, New York seemed to go mad with joy. "The repression of years found vent in every description of boisterous license."[53] A Tammany leader cried to the crowds before the doors of Tammany Hall: "Do you think we'll sneak out the back way, this year?" "Never!" roared the crowd in answer. Tipsy men and women saluted the downfall of the hated Raines Law. Street-

[52] The New York *Times*, Nov. 4, 1897.

[53] The New York *World*, Nov. 4, 1897.

walkers proceeded everywhere, mocking at recent city police regulations.

In a large café at the Haymarket on Sixth Avenue a woman stood on a table tossing off one schooner of beer after another, whirling each one around her head and shouting: *"To hell with reform!"*

Banners were quickly produced bearing the same legend. Soon the cry seemed to be taken up all over the great city; and the thousands who had chafed at the bridle danced, sang, and shouted in refrain all that night: *"To hell with reform!"* [54]

[54] The New York *World*, Nov. 4, 1897.

III. A "SPLENDID LITTLE WAR"; AND THE MAKING OF A PRESIDENT

ONCE more Theodore Roosevelt was back in Washington; this time as Assistant Secretary of the Navy, an important post in the more or less brilliant McKinley administration. It had been no simple matter for Roosevelt's political friends, Cabot Lodge, the Senator for Massachusetts, and Speaker Reed and John Hay to overcome McKinley's misgivings about the Police Commissioner as a young hothead of some sort. Cabot had been forced to stretch the truth a little when he insisted that his protégé thought only to "push on the policies . . . in operation for the last two or three administrations."[1] More embarrassing still had been the preliminary requirement of winning the endorsement of New York's Republican boss, Senator Tom Platt. Roosevelt was virtually ordered to "step up and see him about the place," and must needs come hat in hand before the oily and cunning old man whom he detested, and who accorded assent rather than approval—"because Roosevelt would do less harm to the Organization," Platt thought, if removed from New York to Washington.[2]

Once more escaped from the "scavenging" labor and the dreary squabbles of local politics, Roosevelt could plunge himself into national, history-making affairs, as he had longed to do. Moreover, he was a figure again in those literary-political salons that made social life in the capital so much more amusing and stimulating in

[1] Lodge *op. cit.*, Vol. I, p. 241.

[2] Lodge, *op. cit.*, Vol. I, p. 264.

the '90's than in two or three preceding decades. There were good musicales at the discriminating and yet cosmopolitan homes of those two reigning hostesses, Mrs. Henry Cabot Lodge and Mrs. J. Donald Cameron, wives of wealthy Eastern Senators. There were distinguished men of letters to be met, a Rudyard Kipling observing his American admirers critically, a William Dean Howells; there were foreign diplomats and native financiers. There was good food and animated conversation with it, ranging in subject from the world of ideas and books to the Chinese curios of Henry Adams and the Botticelli purchased by John Hay. But above all there was talk of politics, now the very breath of life to Roosevelt, Lodge, and their circle of friends. At a *bal de début* given by the affluent Charles J. Bonapartes for their daughter, between the cotillions "they talked of civil service . . . even with the ladies." On vacations in the New Hampshire mountains "one nearly walked over a cliff talking politics." [3]

The political talk in influential circles close to the imperial McKinley regime embraced not only national affairs but, more than ever nowadays, international relations, the course of empire and trade, the acquisition and completion of the Isthmian canal, naval bases, expansion on the ocean to the south and the west, all the various moves in the game of world power politics, and America's part in them.

"You have a war on your hands," the outgoing President Cleveland said to McKinley on Inauguration Day. McKinley answered: ". . . If I can only go out of office . . . with the knowledge that I have done what lay in my power to avert this terrible calamity . . . I shall be the happiest man in the world." [4] But while McKinley hesitated, the whispers, the intriguing that foreshadowed an approaching conflict went on in the salons.

Ever since the Cuban insurrection had begun in 1895, agents of the revolutionary junta apparently had thronged Washington and held deep consultations with Republican leaders in the Senate such as Cameron of Pennsylvania, and Lodge. "I am kept here by

[3] John Hay, *Diaries*, Vol. II, p. 236.

[4] Rhodes, *op. cit.*, Vol. 18, p. 41.

Cuba, which I appear to be running . . ." is the curious phrase that occurs in a letter of Henry Adams to his brother Brooks. And again, to an English friend, not entirely in jest: "You had better sell all you have and buy with me in Cuba."[5]

Meanwhile, in high naval circles there was not only talk of a coming war but active preparation for it. Admiral Charles Henry Davis, the father-in-law of Lodge, learning that Theodore Roosevelt sought the office of Secretary of the Navy, wrote him: "There is a tremendous chance in that office," and expressed the earnest hope that the President would appoint him.[6] Roosevelt had been willing enough to take, as the best he could get, the subordinate post of Assistant Secretary in this strategic department.

2

Bored and disillusioned with reform politics, Roosevelt embraced the ideas of militant nationalism and "Americanism"; he dreamed of entering upon some great martial enterprise while thoughts of reform and "good citizenship" waned, not only in his mind, but in those of the other younger prophets in the ruling party. Their ambitions and frustrations, their fear of class-sectional divisions in the country, their "Hamiltonian" and distinctly anti-democratic views and historical concepts, their impatience with the McKinley-Hanna "politics of the cash-register," all disposed Roosevelt and his friends to join in the war-making of 1896-1898.

For more than a decade the orientation toward the cult .of "Americanism" had been apparent in Roosevelt's writings. Married again in 1886 to one whom he had known as a childhood friend, Edith Carow, he lived more happily; he resumed, especially at periods when he was out of office, the prolific writing of biographies and historical studies which had been held out to him and to Lodge as a path to public glory. Roosevelt's early writings contained many crudities, yet they were not wanting in talent and vigor; removed from public life he might have made his mark as

[5] Henry Adams, *Letters*, Vol. II, pp. 96, 99.

[6] *T. R. Papers*, C. H. Davis to T. R., Nov. 11, 1896.

a man of letters. But here it is the ideas in the early writings, *simpliste* or naïve though many of them were, that interest us most.

Very marked is the anti-democratic bias in Roosevelt, especially in the period of his career when he was under the influence of Cabot Lodge, the biographer of Alexander Hamilton. Lodge had written almost with nostalgia of the time when America was ruled by men who were "powerful by their talents if not by their numbers." He had written always of Jefferson as the villain in the piece—as that kindred soul, Beveridge, did later in his monumental *Life of John Marshall.* The followers of Jefferson were "worthless, noisy" persons, "given to useless agitation" and showing "anarchical tendencies." But for the earlier, "aristocratic" republic, dominated by Hamilton, Lodge could scarcely conceal his admiration, while condoning his hero's willingness at times to "accomplish a great right by doing a little wrong." Such tendencies, Lodge reflects, half-revealing his own faith, would never be wanting "to the champions of order, the saviours of society, the 'strong men' and the imperialists of this world." [7]

Similar principles are frankly expressed in Roosevelt's second published book, the rather amateurish, hastily written biography of Thomas Benton. Here too he shows a hearty dislike of the champions of thoroughgoing democracy, the "timid, shifty doctrinaire" Jefferson, the unruly Andrew Jackson who had brought on an explosion of "caste antagonism" in 1828. The author condemns all the "vague and senseless clamor" against a "supposititious aristocratic corruption" raised by "the mass of the ignorance of the country," and easily exploited by scheming demagogues to bring about that spoils system that Good Government men now contended against.[8]

But Thomas H. Benton, the long-winded Senator from Missouri, though an ally of Jackson in leading "the party of the multitude," possessed in the author's eyes the virtue of having sounded forth, perhaps earlier and more powerfully than all others, the call

[7] Lodge, *Alexander Hamilton,* p. 228; cf. also pp. 130, 184, 185.

[8] T. Roosevelt, *Thomas Benton,* pp. 72, 137.

to "Manifest Destiny." He aroused the "hardy and restless backwoodsmen," those American Vikings who had conquered wilderness and prairie, to move against their weaker neighbors and seize their territories. Benton embodied an "intense Americanism" that visioned the farthest expansion of the republic toward the Pacific and even to the mysterious Orient. And Roosevelt recalls with emotion those Texans of a "barbaric age," who raised the flag of the Lone Star State and precipitated a war of conquest with Mexico: "They were restless, brave and eager for adventure, excitement and plunder. . . . They had all the marks of a young and hardy race, flushed with the pride of strength and self-confidence."[9]

Thus the historical thinking of our latter-day Hamiltonians turned often with admiration to the earlier American pioneers who had overrun and conquered a whole vast continent. (It was, to be sure, a thinly populated, ill-defended continent.) Theodore Roosevelt, driven by some ill-defined "historic-literary" inspiration, had even gone to seek renewal of those experiences at first hand, when he traveled to the Far West in 1883 and acquired a part ownership in two cattle ranches. Was it a mere outburst of romanticism, whim of the eternal small boy in Roosevelt who, having once been sickly, attempted to brave hardships and live dangerously? Ranch owning was a fashionable speculation of the 1880's with their cattle booms, and brought then not a few titled Europeans to Western prairies in quest of adventure, big game, or quick wealth. Roosevelt's intuitions here led to financial loss, but to intangible gains.

He had escaped at last from the life of the Eastern cities, at once soft, confining, and unnatural. He would recall long afterward in his autobiography: "It was still the Wild West in those days. In that land we led a free and hardy life, with horse and rifle." He himself had been one of those "reckless riders who, unmoved, look in the eyes of life and death. We knew toil and hardship and hunger and thirst; and we saw men die. . . ."

[9] *Ibid.*, p. 178.

There was something of Lord Byron in the extravagantly costumed, slightly exhibitionist gentleman cowboy of 1883 to 1887. But there was also the instinct to leave his study and see things for himself, to renew contact with the land and the people, something which it was said most Americans of the wealthy class had already lost.

Afterward, back in his country house at Long Island, writing of the exploits of Meriwether and Clark, his convictions about the historic destiny of his people became crystallized. The Americans, he wrote, sprang fully into national life, became a distinct nation, *only at the moment when they began their work of conquest.*[10] He understood the deeds of the early border people all the better, and for him to write of them was "a labor of love," because he too had helped to settle the lonely cattle ranges of the Far West.

> For a number of years I spent most of my time on the frontier and lived and worked like any other frontiersman. . . . We guarded our herds of branded cattle and shaggy horses, hunted bear, bison, elk and deer, established civil government, and put down evil-doers, white and red, on the banks of the Little Missouri and . . . the Big Horn, exactly as did the pioneers who a hundred years previously had built their log-cabins beside the Kentucky or in the valleys of the Great Smokies. The men who have shared in the fast-vanishing frontier life of the present feel a peculiar sympathy with the already long-vanished frontier life of the past.[11]

Roosevelt, cherishing the American legend of the frontiersman, re-entered those experiences, embraced those memories, that he found most admirable in our history. All these epitomized for him the essence of "Americanism," the "great work" of conquest. Was it not time to return to "Americanism," to resume the "great work" of the early "conquering" Americans in new fields?

Thenceforth Roosevelt propounded "Americanism" in literature as well as in politics, almost with violence. "We must work according to our own ideas." [12]

[10] T. Roosevelt, *The Winning of the West*, Vol. I, p. 40.

[11] *Ibid.*, Preface, Vol. I, p. 16, written May, 1889, at Sagamore Hill.

[12] *Brander Matthews Papers*, letter of Jun. 29, 1894.

Meanwhile Henry Cabot Lodge was himself—though there was nothing of the cowboy in his exquisite composition—the most perfervid exponent of militant "Americanism" in Congress. Determined, ever since parting with his Mugwump friends, to essay the role of the "strong man" in politics, like the great Federalist statesman who was his chosen model, he shrank from nothing that would serve to extend his immediate power. David Graham Phillips, when he came some years later to investigate the Massachusetts political ring, found Lodge in absolute command of the state Republican organization, the ruthless machine boss under the robe of the scholar and man of letters. The old "Blaine gang" in Boston, entrenched in the Federal offices, had been taken over by him. Thenceforth, while still giving lip service to reform, he devoted himself unsleepingly for thirty years to securing offices and sinecures for his "boys." Every county, township and district in the state was carefully supervised by him personally. Does the southern Berkshire district appear doubtful? He dispatches agents capable of "organizing and arousing the district" in preparation for an election. The agent is told to visit the local committees and report accurately the condition of affairs. Sums of money are designated "to properly compensate" the agents in charge.[13] And combined with this organizing effort he makes appeals to the Irish masses of Boston by all sorts of oratorical somersaults and verbal "twists" of the lion's tail, narrow vindictive speeches against England in the best manner of James G. Blaine, so that Henry Adams who had known Lodge all his life, reading his anti-English speeches, rubbed his eyes and likened him to a cheap actor who "talks pure rot to order."[14]

On the other hand, J. T. Morse in his memoir of Lodge relates that the Senator admired the English intensely, envied especially their aptitude for imperial politics, and strove to emulate their aristocracy. It was simply that he had become convinced through negotiations with the English that they were successful

[13] *Lodge Papers* (Library of Congress), H. C. L. to Wellington Smith, Oct. 12, 1892.

[14] Adams, *Letters*, Vol. II, pp. 313, 267.

through being domineering and grasping. The United States, he argued, "must be as insolent and overbearing and ready to show fight as the others."[15] To Roosevelt, also, Lodge explained his pose of aggressiveness in similar terms. In the contests of international politics, he held, we must be more ruthless than the others; we must strike at them and strike hard if we would have them respect us and treat us well.

Through his post in the Senate Foreign Relations Committee, Lodge pressed the government toward a "spirited" foreign policy. In the magazine press he also conducted a shrill agitation for aggressive territorial expansion. "From the Rio Grande to the Arctic Ocean," he wrote, "there should be but one flag and one country. . . ." British dominion in Canada must be ended; likewise the strong places that Britain had fortified in the West Indies must be seized. With the Isthmian canal completed, Cuba would become necessary to us, and the Hawaiian Islands and Samoa no less. He concluded:

> We have a record of conquest, colonization and expansion unequalled by any people in the Nineteenth Century. We are not to be curbed now by the doctrines of the Manchester School which . . . as an importation are even more absurdly out of place than in their native land.[16]

To Lodge, as to Roosevelt, our people's conquests of Indian nomads and Mexican peasants represented the chief glory of our history. Would not this history repeat itself soon upon a grander stage?

The closing years of the nineteenth century were rendered dramatic by the world-wide race of the great powers to seize and colonize the remaining, undefended territories of Africa, Asia, and even Polynesia. England vibrated with the martial poetry of Rudyard Kipling and the speeches of "Joe" Chamberlain. In the African deserts columns of French free-booters collided danger-

[15] *Harvard Graduates' Magazine*, Mar., 1925.

[16] *Forum*, Mar., 1895.

ously with British forces. Germany, entering the world contest tardily, now roared and clanged with naval and marine construction, rivaling that taking place along the Clyde. Incidents of extreme international tension succeeded each other rapidly in the years after the financial depression of 1893, as accumulated capital and industrial surpluses in the older nations sought new markets and avenues for investment overseas.

In the summer of 1895, a stormy year in British politics, Cabot Lodge visited London and found himself lionized in a most agreeable manner. He spent whole days conferring with leading statesmen, such as Balfour, Curzon, and Joseph Chamberlain. His long letters reporting these meetings to Roosevelt, who followed his course with envious interest, show no signs of the anti-British sentiment assumed upon the American rostrum. Rather he appears infected with the imperial visions of the English politicians who, following Chamberlain's new lead, prepared to abandon their historic Free Trade doctrines and worked to strengthen the British Empire bonds. At this time some basis for an Anglo-American rapprochement may well have been laid.

Joseph Chamberlain too had been a reformer, concerned for twenty years as an enlightened captain of industry with all sorts of benevolent social legislation, "concessions" to labor in the shape of city parks, workers' homes, and municipal improvements. These, Chamberlain argued, were the "ransom" which industry "must pay to society for prosperity." But was it not plain now that the cycle of domestic reform and concession approached its limits? To a Cecil Rhodes, uneasy witness of large riots of the unemployed in London at this period, the paramount problem was to open up new provinces and markets, taking up the surplus population and goods "if only in order to preserve the forty million inhabitants of the United Kingdom from a murderous civil war." The need for new drives toward colonial trade obsessed even the Liberal statesmen; and Chamberlain perorated, on the eve of the Boer War: "Providence intended us to be a great governing power, conquering, yes, conquering, but only in order to civilize."

Cabot Lodge returned from England to witness episodes in

United States politics apparently no less alarming, as symptoms of unrest, than those of Europe. His own purposes were now more fully revealed to himself; his speeches were marked with the unmistakable accents of the British imperialists, those of belligerency justified in the light of an assumed humanitarian, "civilizing" mission.

Early in 1896, while tales of insurrection and the horrors of civil war in the Antilles agitated Americans, and proposals for formal recognition of the rebels occupied the Senate, Lodge had assumed the floor leadership of the faction that pressed for intervention. Our "pecuniary" interests in Cuba, he argued, were great, and our humane interests were likewise not to be denied.

> Free Cuba would mean a great market for the United States; it would mean an opportunity for American capital invited there by signal exemptions. . . . But we have a broader political interest in the fate of Cuba. She lies athwart the line which leads to the Nicaragua canal.
>
> . . . But, Mr. President, I am prepared to put our duty on a higher ground than either of these, and that is the broad ground of common humanity.[17]

The gospel of American imperialism was preached at this time even more eloquently by the still younger Republican prophet, Albert Beveridge of Indiana. The issue before the country, this disciple of the old Federalists now proclaimed constantly, was "national life." The conflicts and discontents of sections and classes must be resolved, under the one flag of the Stars and Stripes. On the eve of a war which he passionately courted he spoke in Boston in reverberant phrases: "*We are a conquering race. . . . We must obey our blood and occupy new markets, and if necessary new lands.*" For, were not our American factories and American soil already producing more than our people could consume? He added:

> Fate has written our policy for us; the trade of the world must and shall be ours. . . . We will cover the ocean with our merchant marines. We will build a navy to the measure of our greatness. Great col-

[17] Millis, *The Martial Spirit*, pp. 46-47.

onies governing themselves, flying our flag and trading with us, will grow about our posts of trade. . . . And American law, American order, American civilization, and the American flag will plant themselves on shores hitherto bloody and benighted, but by those agencies of God henceforth to be made beautiful and bright.[18]

Adding his own high-pitched voice to the growing chorus of the jingoes, Assistant Secretary of the Navy Roosevelt, in a speech on April 2, 1897, exhorted his fellow countrymen to abandon the timid leadership of the rich bankers and industrialists and to turn instead to the example of a Farragut. No nation could hold its place in the world unless it stood ready to "guard its rights with an armed hand." Liberty itself could be preserved only by men "willing to fight for an ideal." Then in an access of lyrical militarism, he cried:

No triumph of peace is quite so great as the supreme triumphs of war. The courage of the soldier, the courage of the statesman who has to meet storms which can only be quelled by soldierly virtues—this stands higher than any qualities called out merely in times of peace.

. . . No national life is worth having if the nation is not willing to stake everything on the supreme arbitrament of war, and to pour out its blood, its treasure, and tears like water rather than submit to the loss of honor and renown. . . .

The purpose was clear; the course was marked. It needed, however, the instruments and the materials for victorious warfare in modern times. Therefore Roosevelt said, in the same speech: "*We ask for a great navy. . . .*"

The sailor, with his rolling gait and flapping trousers, had replaced the bowlegged cowboy as a *beau idéal* in the mind of the adventurous dude in politics.

3

The seafaring and sea-fighting tradition of the Americans was an old and colorful one, with its high point probably the daring

[18] Bowers, *Beveridge*, p. 69 ff.

naval exploits of the war of 1812, which Roosevelt had chronicled. But it was Captain Alfred T. Mahan, a little-known American naval officer, and another of the strong historical thinkers working upon our later politics, who did most to define for the imperialist age the role and meaning of naval power and the program of the great navy. His book, *The Influence of Sea-Power upon History: 1660-1783*, published in 1890, became at once the most important work of military history and theory since Clausewitz in the early part of the nineteenth century, and was read and expounded by the statesmen and military leaders of all the great powers, from Britain to Japan.

Mahan had based his historical analysis on the peculiar effectiveness of British "control of the seas" ever since the seventeenth century, when the Dutch rivals had been crushed. From Britain's maritime dominance and her superior mobility in fighting landlocked enemies (including the French under Napoleon I) Mahan deduced his theory of the supremacy of the naval arm in modern warfare. Nations which would frankly pursue their "self-interest" (interchangeable with "extending foreign commerce"), he concluded, must devote themselves to a program for increasing their sea-power in systematic fashion: first, by strengthening armor and gun capacity, size and quantity of men-of-war; second, by acquiring naval stations, ports, and colonies helpful to the fueling and repair of the war vessels. Thus the acquisition of colonial territories overseas supported naval power, and naval power in turn helped to win greater territorial possessions and commercial expansion. The rightness of such expansion, such forcible pursuit of national self-interest, Mahan in his fatalistic vein (like Clausewitz or Machiavelli earlier) never seemed to question. Indeed, though a good, professing Christian in private life, he was one of the prophets of "total warfare," opposing nearly all those "sentimental" movements which tried to limit the increasing destructiveness and cruelty of modern arms by international agreements.

Mahan's ideas of sea-power were taken up with enthusiasm first abroad, and then found followers at home as well. From 1893 on, Mahan, by articles in the press and in magazines, urged a policy of a large navy and a small army for the United States, for like Britain we were an "island power" fronting on two great oceans. With a great navy we could "round out" our American empire, and dominate the Western Hemisphere, long regarded as the special province of United States commerce. Moreover, once the Isthmian canal were finished, our naval forces would stand athwart the new world-trade routes between Europe and the China Sea; and it must be our endeavor, he argued, to control the approaches to the canal in the Caribbean, as well as the strategic stations at its exit in the Pacific. Ever since 1880, when Lesseps had begun the building of the canal at the Isthmus of Panama, Captain Mahan had thought it imperative for American naval forces to dominate this position.

America had long repelled the notion of foreign entanglements. But "The canal at the Isthmus may bring our interests and those of foreign nations into collision," he surmised, "and in that case, which is for statesmen to forecast, we must without delay begin to build a navy which will at least equal that of England. . . ." Else, who would pay heed to the Monroe Doctrine? Our navy had long been neglected, Mahan pondered with the bitterness of a disappointed career officer. He dreamed for years of an "awakening." [19]

Toward 1893, both Roosevelt and Lodge became acquainted with Mahan, and turned into enthusiastic disciples of his great navy doctrine and his plans for the founding of a Naval College. Through the Senate Foreign Relations Committee and the Navy Department they acted later as his protectors and patrons.

With Mahan's aid, Roosevelt drew up programs of strategy and intensified naval preparation. Roosevelt's big-navy speech at Newport in April, 1897 (already quoted), made after receiving his new appointment, is stamped with Mahan's influence. Dreams of far-off naval conquests now possessed the ambitious young politician. His correspondence with Mahan in the spring of 1897 touched on the matter of secret preparations for strengthening the Pacific fleet and finding the most aggressive officer possible

[19] Puleston, *Mahan*, pp. 60, 131.

for its command. He confided to Mahan his feeling of dissatisfaction with his cautious superior, Secretary of the Navy John D. Long, whose restraining authority he sometimes attempted to override.[20]

President McKinley would have found his worst fears realized concerning Roosevelt's impetuous and headstrong spirit if he had known of Roosevelt's discussions with Mahan concerning provisions for the seizure of Hawaii, the dispatch of added munitions for the Pacific fleet, an attack upon the Philippines, and a possible brush with the Japanese.[21]

More and more, military reasoning replaced legal reasoning in Roosevelt's mind. Mahan in his letters admits that he knows no other reasoning. How should Hawaii be annexed, for instance? How was "the political problem" to be solved? He advised: "Do nothing unrighteous; but . . . *take the islands first and solve afterward.*"[22]

These plans were pushed rapidly after April, 1897, a year before war came. In September, 1897, the Assistant Secretary of the Navy told Lodge of dining with President McKinley and outlining to him the action to be taken in case of war with Spain. "I gave him a paper showing exactly where all our ships are." The disposition of the ships for a Cuban expedition was sketched in outline; and also, looking farther off in the Pacific, special arrangements were made to prevent the Japs from chipping in. To this end, "our Asiatic squadron should blockade, and if possible, take Manila."[23]

4

The Republican party in its platform resolutions of 1896 had promised to use its offices to bring peace and independence to Cuba, charging at the same time that the Spanish government

[20] *T. R. Papers,* T. R. to A. T. Mahan, May 1, May 6, 1897; Mahan to R., May 4, 1897.

[21] *Ibid.,* May 3, 1897, T. R. to Mahan.

[22] *Ibid.,* Mahan to T. R., May 6, 1897. Italics added.

[23] Lodge, *op. cit.,* Vol. I, p. 278, letter of Sept. 21, 1897.

showed itself unable to protect the property and lives of American citizens residing in her colony. But thereafter President McKinley had proceeded with a studied restraint, while constantly applying diplomatic pressure to the Spanish government. The horrors and atrocities of civil war (practiced by both sides), which agitated American opinion deeply, the herding of natives into concentration camps by the Spanish army authorities, the large destruction of property (fifty millions of it estimated as American-owned), would not be tolerated here for long. McKinley pressed the Spanish government to put an end to the Cuban warfare, and to grant some form of autonomy to the Cubans. Yet he accepted Spanish assurances, and showed a courteous patience, knowing like Cleveland that the Spanish would be unable to hold Cuba indefinitely, and that the island could be purchased by us eventually, if need be. Moreover, McKinley had set his heart upon restoring prosperity at home, and appeared remarkably sensitive to the financial shocks registered in our securities markets whenever the threat of war appeared.

"I do not think a war with Spain would be serious enough to cause much strain on the country or much interruption to the revival of prosperity . . ." Theodore Roosevelt had written to Lodge in December, 1896.[24] Here was the clear difference between the war party and the Big Business faction. Meanwhile McKinley drifted, as Walter Millis has pictured him in his detailed study of the Spanish-American war, *The Martial Spirit.* The President resisted the war-mongers, yet never shut the door against their agitation.

The Spanish ambassador, Dupuy de Lome, in a secret letter that became all too famous, characterized the President accurately enough as one who was "weak and a bidder for the admiration of the crowd, besides being a common politician who tries to leave a door open behind himself while keeping on good terms with the jingoes of his party."[25]

[24] Millis, *op. cit.*, p. 63.
[25] *Ibid.*, p. 98.

The exposure of this letter (as a result of theft) in a sensational New York newspaper on February 8, 1898, ended Dupuy de Lome's tenure of office here, and did much to bring war nearer. The mysterious explosion which destroyed the American battleship *Maine*, stationed in Havana harbor, occurred a week later and seemed to make hostilities inevitable.

For three years the drums of war had been sounding both on the political rostrum and in the sensational popular press, typified by Hearst's New York *Journal* and Pulitzer's *World*, both exploring or experimenting with the possible effects of war upon reader circulation. Accounts of beautiful spies, tragic martyrs, and unbelievably daring heroes among the Rebel cohorts had figured constantly in their front pages. With the destruction of the *Maine*, headlines of a size such as had never been seen before strengthened the hands of the war party.

Yet Mark Hanna, the man from the midlands, now in the Senate as the "fit representative" of business men, reflected their prevailing caution when he said, as late as the days following the *Maine* disaster, "I am not in favor of heedlessly precipitating the country into the horrors of war." He was also convinced that Spain would now "back down," yield autonomy to Cuba, or cede the island to us.[26] That the United States, just emerging from depression, and until now in dire need of foreign capital to develop its own immense resources, should suddenly seek to conquer backward territories in the sub-tropics seemed to him and to other hard-headed business men sheer madness.

Meanwhile the business groups interested in sugar and tobacco, and the light-waisted speculators who bought worthless bonds of the future "Cuban Republic" in the hope of their validation by a war, represented actually a small influence. An array of conservative politicians, including Aldrich's powerful clique in the Senate, and Speaker Reed in the House, struggled to bring calm to the country in February and March, and as late as the early days of April. They had the aid of a large, enlightened minority

[26] Rhodes, *op. cit.*, Vol. IX, p. 56.

of "anti-imperialists," typified by President Charles W. Eliot of Harvard and other academic and religious leaders.

But emotion rose throughout the country. Late in March a group of Senators headed by Redfield Proctor of Vermont told in the upper chamber a harrowing tale of horrors seen everywhere in Cuban cities, and of mass starvation in the camps of the *reconcentrados*. And Senator Thurston, a member of this delegation, whose wife had died of illness during the visit, cried out in a voice torn with passion, before crowded galleries, that the only people who now opposed a just war for the liberation of Cuba were the heartless financiers of Wall Street.[27]

In Congress, elements opposed to the McKinley administration, including the Western bloc of Republicans, the "radicals" of silver inflation, used the Cuban issue and the President's hesitant policy as a means of attack. In their mood of exasperation and discontent they pressed McKinley to end the interminable negotiations with Spain and to make a declaration of war. A secret caucus of forty or fifty Republican members of Congress sent a committee to him conveying the threat that they would introduce a resolution for war and vote with the Democrats to carry it through.[28] Even the formidable Bryan himself, national leader of the Democratic party, now at a great public dinner demanded that the Cubans be set free and that the United States recognize the Cuban "government."

Thus, fear that important Republican groups were at the point of revolting against party discipline, that the Western silver men might join with the hordes of Bryan in singing of a new "crown of thorns"—the failure to intervene in Cuba—now possessed McKinley and even Mark Hanna himself. General Russell Alger, the Michigan lumber baron who was Secretary of War, and Senator Cushman K. Davis, the strongly anti-labor Senator from Minnesota, both sent warning to McKinley that he must declare war soon. "He is in danger of ruining himself and the Republican

[27] *Congressional Record*, Mar. 23, 1898.
[28] Olcott, *McKinley*, Vol. II, p. 28.

party by standing in the way of the people's wishes. . . . He'll get run over and the party with him." [29]

War was inevitable. The young imperialists in the Government, such as Roosevelt, had been confident of the outcome since February 15, 1898, the day of the *Maine* disaster. "*Our internal political conditions will not permit its postponement*," ran one significant newspaper editorial comment. For if war were avoided, out of the frustration of the people, embittered by other vexations, there might come not only a political cyclone, but who knew what other political developments or legislation "ruinous to every sober interest in the country . . ."? [30]

Thus the war-makers were confident that for *internal political reasons*, despite the waverings of McKinley and his continued negotiations with Spain, war must come. This war would be "righteous," wrote another of the "literary fellows," John Hay, who now occupied the post of Ambassador to England and was possessed by new, glamorous ideas of imperial policy. "I have not for two years seen any other issue." [31]

The inner circle of conservative Republicans suddenly shifted to a position of leadership in the war movement, in the last days of March, 1898. Important financial figures now swung to the war party, men like John Jacob Astor, William Rockefeller, Thomas Fortune Ryan, and Stuyvesant Fish, making public statements on March 24, 1898, that they favored driving Spain from her last possessions in America.[32]

On March 27, 1898, the President sent to Madrid his ultimatum, which asked virtually the immediate abandonment of Cuba by Spain. From Madrid the zealous American ambassador, General Woodford, sent message after message urging delay. The Queen's government was yielding slowly; he reported then that Spain promised to suspend hostilities, to call a Cuban parliament and accord autonomy. The President (using sleeping powders)

[29] Olcott, *McKinley*, Vol. II, p. 28.
[30] Chicago *Times Herald*, cited by Millis, *op. cit.*, p. 124.
[31] Thayer, *John Hay*, Vol. II, p. 167.
[32] Beer, *Hanna*, pp. 199-200.

waited two weeks; then, as he was about to succeed by peaceful methods, professed himself dissatisfied with the Spanish replies and yielded suddenly to the war party, delivering to Congress on April 11, 1898, his message calling for war.

It proved to be a fortunate move. Six months later, with the successful election of November out of the way, Mark Hanna would be writing to McKinley of his contentment because the Western political ferment had been diverted or had died down. The "splendid little war" (as John Hay called it) had by then apparently closed the sectional divisions of the country, enabling the Republican party to hold in line the "silver states" west of the Missouri.[33] The baffled passions of a long period of depression, always ready to turn against a regime so profoundly conservative as that of the Gold-bug Republicans, had been safely channeled away.

The pulse of the country quickened to the excitement that warfare brings. The foreign devil drew attention from the domestic demons troubling the American family. Western cowboy and Eastern bourgeois, Yankee and Southerner, fought side by side. The "sense of common national feeling and interest, weakened after a generation of economic, sectional and class conflicts, was reawakened . . . in a sense favorable to the Administration."[34] The next Congress, the Fifty-sixth, would see the elimination of the Western bimetallists from Republican ranks, and the presence of a full and "regular" conservative majority. Thus the McKinley administration would proceed, in the afterglow of military triumph, to the enactment of the Gold Standard Act, which the politicians themselves had dreaded, postponing its passage for three years.

5

The Spanish-American war, the "splendid little war" in John Hay's apt words, had curious, unexpected overtones and by-products. One was the sudden thrust of the American naval force into the Far East, where Commodore Dewey with his Pacific squadron

[33] Stephenson, *Aldrich*, p. 448.

[34] Croly, *Hanna*, p. 279.

prevailed so brilliantly at Manila and added a generally unexpected, unknown imperial possession to the United States. The preparations for this move had been secretly ordered well in advance of the war, on February 25, 1898, by the high-handed Assistant Secretary of the Navy, Roosevelt, on a day when his superior Mr. Long had left him in temporary charge as Acting Secretary.[35] A few men only, in the inner circle of the war party, expected this extension of the war for the "liberation" of Cuba to the conquest of the Philippine Islands at the antipodes of the world. Albert Beveridge, a friend of Lodge and Roosevelt, in a speech at Boston on April 27, 1898, several weeks before any actual fighting had begun, gave almost the first public hints of this action.

> Cuba must fall into our hands, but that will be only when Spain is conquered. . . . In the Pacific is the true field of our earliest operations. There Spain has an island empire, the Philippine Archipelago. It is poorly defended. . . . In the Pacific the United States has a powerful squadron. The Philippines are logically our first target.[36]

Thus the armed force of the United States hurled her into the the race for imperial colonies in the tumultuous Orient.

An immediate problem now before the American politicians was the effect of such a war against Spain upon our relations with the other great powers. Here, too, swift and significant developments followed. From 1896 dates the beginning of a marked rapprochement with Britain, which was soon afterward to be cemented into a tacit alliance, a kind of "secret axis."

President Cleveland's recent Venezuela message had formed the climax of a long period of some thirty years of ill-feeling and strain between the United States and Britain. But its very explosion, with such unexpected force, had compelled Britain to overhaul her American policy in the light of an approaching fear of Germany and general war in Europe. The English proved conciliatory in recognizing the emphatic assertion of the Monroe Doctrine in its stronger form; the Venezuela boundary dispute was

[35] Mayo, *America of Yesterday*, p. 169.
[36] Bowers, *op. cit.*, pp. 69-70.

tactfully composed in a manner which accepted virtually all of the British boundary claims against Venezuela as just; and the two great nations closed the incident with a glow of good feeling induced by the framing of an arbitration pact now earnestly sought by Cleveland and Olney, which President McKinley eagerly signed in March, 1897. The difficulties of Britain in South Africa, the bellicose gestures of Emperor William II, further stimulated British courting of friendship with the United States. In 1898, while Germany and even France (having sizable investments in Spain) condemned the "bullying" tactics of the United States toward a weaker power, the British by broad hints gave their benedictions. From London, American Ambassador John Hay reported on April 5, 1898, a few days before the outbreak of war, that the commonest opinion left with him was: "I wish you would take Cuba at once. We wouldn't have stood it this long." Hay, of course, conveyed to Washington news of the "friendship and sympathy" shown in England as perhaps selfish in intent, but so "important and desirable in the present state of things. . . ." [37]

In high military circles in America, with some exceptions, fear of Britain seemed to depart. Mahan, in his program for increasing our sea-power, declared that he saw no need in the future to provide for renewed contests between America and Britain, whose interests, while they clashed at some minor points, now "coincided generally throughout the world." [38]

John Hay went even further. In a speech given after the opening of the war, on April 21, 1898, using the refrain "sharing of the white man's burden," he spoke of the thousand ties of origin, language, and kindred pursuits binding America and Great Britain: reasons enough for attaining a "good understanding." Finally he concluded, ". . . There is a sanction like that of religion which

[37] Thayer, *op. cit.*, Vol. II, p. 166.

[38] Where they appeared not to coincide, as at the time of the Venezuela boundary dispute, there were reasons enough for British moderation toward us. The unfortified border of Canada was a pawn for her good behavior. As Theodore Roosevelt remarked in January, 1896, at the time of the dispute, "We will settle the Caribbeans in Canada." (Puleston, *Mahan*, p. 131.)

binds us to a sort of partnership in the beneficent work of the world. Whether we will it or not, we are associated in that work by the very nature of things. . . . We are joint ministers of the same sacred mission of liberty and progress. . . ." The German ambassador at Washington, reading this speech, formed suspicions of a secret Anglo-American alliance.[39]

These omens, if omens they were, were plainer still in the speech of the young Albert Beveridge, who was soon to enter the Senate. Beveridge knew already of the expressions of good-will by leading English statesmen with regard to America's war in the Caribbean against Spain. But he knew also that Britain looked with favor at our penetration of the Pacific.[40]

The new American imperialism, according to Beveridge, plainly foreshadowed a partnership between the two nations. He continued:

> If it means Anglo-Saxon solidarity; if it means an English-American understanding upon the basis of a vision of the world's markets so that the results may be just . . . if it means such an English-speaking people's league of God for the permanent peace of this war-worn world, the stars in their courses will fight for us and countless centuries will applaud.[41]

From England in the powerful voice of the Liberal leader, Joseph Chamberlain, there came on May 13, 1898, as if in answer, the surprising speech prophesying a ripening accord between the two long-hostile sister nations: "What is our next duty? It is to establish and maintain bonds of permanent amity with our kinsmen across the Atlantic. . . . The union—the alliance if you please—the understanding between these two great nations is indeed a guarantee of the peace of the world."

[39] Dennett, *op. cit.*, p. 189.

[40] John Hay, after a conference with Lord Salisbury, reported to Washington that American retention of a "permanent foothold in the Philippines" brought no objections. England would be content if America should retain the Philippine Islands, asking only "an option in case of future sale," lest they fall into other, possibly German, hands. (Dennett, *op. cit.*, p. 191.)

[41] Bowers, *op. cit.*, p. 69.

Thus the entrance of the United States into that war which has been called our first war of commercial empire was accompanied by a positive, though tacit, extension of America's foreign connections, a departure from Washington's doctrine of isolation and "no entanglements." Thenceforth a tacit understanding, a shadowy "axis" or community of interests, appeared to be operating between Britain and the United States, and even between the United States and Britain's allies, Japan and France. There would be henceforth much well-informed talk of that vague "Atlantic System of States" which combined to hold the balance of world power against certain inland empires, notably Germany, and sometimes Russia. "McKinleyism," product of trusts and combinations at home, favored such a policy of combination, of an imperial world trust abroad. Many hands now worked to cement the Atlantic System, which was to bring such fateful consequences in the new century.

6

Meanwhile Theodore Roosevelt, who had so often and so vigorously inveighed against the comfortable classes in America for their want of patriotism, resigned from his civilian post and enlisted for active military duty, receiving the commission of Lieutenant-Colonel. With the aid of the more experienced Colonel Leonard Wood, he raised a volunteer cavalry regiment of "Rough Riders."

His motives were mixed and perhaps not even clear to himself, though as usual his intuitions were deep. Friends and family, who had sought to dissuade him, were firmly resisted. Suggestions that he pursued military glory for political purposes irritated him deeply. Secretary of the Navy Long, though he sometimes felt Roosevelt a perfect "bull in a china shop," urged him to remain at the helm of the Navy. Roosevelt refused; and Long a few years later wrote in his diary that, absurd as this action had appeared at the time, it had proved wonderfully right later. "His going into the army led straight to the Presidency." [42]

[42] Mayo, *op. cit.*, p. 162.

Roosevelt lived his dream of charging an enemy upon a horse at the head of a column of cowboys. He reveled in victory and gore—the "primitive" in him content even with the heavy battle casualties in his spirited but ill-trained regiment. Out of the disorder and comic opera that attended the Cuban skirmishes, the "political colonel" returned with a reputation for martial spirit and valor—enough for most men. In the field, by his colorful and pugnacious personality he attracted the attention of the press correspondents unerringly, as was his wont nowadays, and they made much of him. The legend of "Teddy" spread broadly. The charge of the Rough Riders on the little hills outside of Santiago was in effect a charge on the political heights that Roosevelt, in peacetime, had for many years been unable to scale.

The *mystique* of war which the swashbuckling Roosevelt expounded by voice and by example seized upon men of good society like a fever and had strangely varying effects. They entered the war with poor Spain as a high imperial lark. For example, the young multi-millionaire "radical" William Randolph Hearst, not content to fight the war with his "yellow" newspapers, equipped his own naval squadron, consisting of a large private yacht and several tugboats, with which he followed up the action of Sampson's conquering fleet at Santiago, and personally participated by capturing and rescuing several wretched, drowning sailors of the Spanish squadron.

Another of Roosevelt's contemporaries, his Harvard friend and clubmate Winthrop Chanler, also a son of old "Knickerbockers," had adventures still more curious which were a parody of those of the Rough Rider himself. Bored with social life at Newport and New York and Florence, Italy, and with his own pranks and escapades, the whimsical "Winty" Chanler inspired himself now with the martial fever of the hour and resolved to give battle even before the main armies met. He departed from Florida's coast one night in a filibustering tugboat, fitted out at his own expense, and landed somewhere on the uncharted beach of Cuba with the design of meeting and joining the besieged Insurgents. But "Winty" lost his way in the bush, was nearly bitten to death by mosquitoes, and was finally driven to his ship by Spanish guards, carrying with him a minor wound in the arm and feeling weary, starved, sick, and much the worse for wear.

Colonel Roosevelt, on the other hand, soon heard at the battlefield in Cuba, as he wrote to "Dear Cabot," that "The good people in New York . . . at present seem to be crazy over me." And Lodge replied at once: "I hear talk all the time about your being run for Governor or Congressman and at this moment you could have pretty much anything you wanted. . . ."[43]

But a few weeks after his "crowded hour" at Santiago (fully reported in the idolatrous newspapers), Roosevelt came bustling back to the States, landing at Montauk Point, Long Island, with the first returning troop transports. The war was clearly won; American armed forces had wrested possession of Cuba, Puerto Rico, even the distant Philippines from Spain. There was apparently no pressing need for Colonel Roosevelt's personal leadership in the field. Still in uniform, from his regimental tent he began promptly his march on Albany.

While his praises were sung and thousands cheered him as a new idol of the people, the agents of party organizations for the first time courted him. In Cuba he had received a letter from Benjamin B. Odell, lieutenant to boss Platt, informing him in effect that he would in all likelihood be awarded the Republican nomination for Governor—provided that he proceeded with tact.[44] The Republican party prospects had lately been injured by grievous public scandals arising from their corrupt and wasteful administration of the New York canal system; and a new popular hero, wearing the garland of victory in war, was exactly what was needed in this crisis.

The inner circle of the Republican party fixed upon Roosevelt as their candidate, despite many misgivings concerning his character. Chauncey Depew, the venerable president of the New York Central railroad, and one of the wisest old heads among Republican

[43] Lodge, *op. cit.*, Vol. I, p. 334 ff.

[44] Alexander, *Four Great New Yorkers*, p. 304.

elders, had won them over by his merry arguments. If Governor Frank Black were nominated, he said, there would be heckling on the subject of the canal frauds and Depew would be forced to state in public that the amount stolen "was only a million, and that would be fatal." But if Colonel Roosevelt were named, he could climb up on the stump and say with conviction:

> We have nominated for Governor a man who has demonstrated in public office and on the battlefield, that he is a fighter for the right, and is always victorious. If he is elected, you know and we all know from his demonstrated characteristics—courage and ability—that every thief will be caught and punished. . . . Then I will follow the Colonel leading his Rough Riders up San Juan Hill and ask the band to play the "Star Spangled Banner."[45]

The party leaders were convinced. They sent word to Roosevelt that they were ready to name him the regular Republican candidate for Governor if he would but call on Senator Tom Platt and give assurances that, once nominated and elected, he would not oppose or seek to injure the party organization or its chieftain.

In 1898 there was only one unpleasant, perhaps unimportant, incident that marred the Colonel's triumphal march on Albany. It is connected with Roosevelt's final parting from his Mugwump, his reformer, friends.

Though the Citizens' Union ticket had been defeated in the New York City mayoralty election the previous year, its showing had been so strong that plans were now laid for expanding the same movement into a state-wide Independent party. For the subsidiary offices of the state ticket, Independent candidates were to be named; but the most logical nominee for Governor would be the new hero of the day, Colonel Roosevelt. Had he not—save for certain regrettable lapses—long stumped with them for civil-service reform? And would not the endorsement of the intelligent voters (even though he was obviously to have also the "regular" Republican nomination) be in accord with his own innermost desires?

[45] Depew, *My Memories*, pp. 160-162.

The reformers too opened parleys with Roosevelt; and on September 1, 1898, a very earnest delegation appeared at the Montauk Point camp, among them the young littérateur John Jay Chapman, another amateur of politics, who knew Roosevelt socially and who has left us an intimate account of the proceedings. After a heated discussion of all the aspects of the case, the Colonel decided to accept the Independent nomination.[46] But no sooner had Platt and his stalwarts heard of the Independents' plan than they were thrown into alarm. For they had accepted Roosevelt as a political Lesser Evil, so that his bright shield might cover the regular machine men returning to state office under him, and not to have him encourage their enemies and detractors. A tug of war began. On September 10, 1898, Platt sent his lieutenant, the veteran Congressman Lemuel Quigg, to warn Roosevelt that he must absolutely disavow the "poisonous Mugwumps" and their "'good government' entanglements." A clear agreement was drawn up providing that Roosevelt was

> to acknowledge and respect his [Platt's] position at the head of the Republican organization . . . and you would consult with the Senator fully and freely . . . adopt no line of policy and agree to no important matter of nomination without previous consultation, and that you wanted him to agree to the same thing on his part.[47]

To the written memorandum of this conference Roosevelt at the time subscribed by letter, except for the reservation that he gave no promise to act "otherwise than in accord with my conscience." A week later he had a private interview with boss Platt, and was accepted into the fold. Then immediately after, on September 19, 1898, he wrote to his friend Chapman:

> Dear Jack,
> I do not see how I can accept the Independent nomination and keep good faith with the other men on my ticket.

There followed two weeks of explanations and recriminations, in which the Goo-Goos and, particularly, Chapman wrestled for

[46] Howe, *op. cit.*, p. 138. [47] Roosevelt-Barnes suit, pp. 2362-2363.

Roosevelt's soul. There was anguish on both sides; it was the parting of ways. Without Roosevelt the Independents' party and even the city reform clubs would vanish as going concerns. "I unloaded the philosophy of agitation upon Roosevelt," relates Chapman in his memorandum. "I pictured him as the broken-backed, half-good man . . . the trimmer who wouldn't break with his party, and so, morally speaking, it ended by breaking him." At times, during the long dispute, Roosevelt is said to have broken down and "cried like a baby." [48] Yet he held firm to his decision to renounce the Independent nomination, a decision which he made public in a letter to the newspapers on September 25, 1898. After this struggle with his reformer friends (and his own conscience) was over, Roosevelt always tended to speak of them most bitterly, even accusing them of "treachery." He claimed that he had not been given to understand that they intended to run candidates for the lower offices on his ticket in opposition to the rest of the Republican ticket. Yet this had been the very essence of their plan for building a new party throughout the state.

The significance of this incident, and of the minor public controversy that followed, was that Roosevelt dropped all connections with the reformers, but also gave up all chance of building a distinct and independent organization of his own, and so left himself henceforth entirely in the hands of the professionals.

Once more it was his "evil genius" Cabot Lodge who did most to persuade Roosevelt to abandon the Independents in a final break. They would lead but "to the defeat of the sound money men" and would undermine the results of the war, Cabot argued. John Hay, too, complimented Roosevelt upon his having shown himself in this painful affair both honest and practical, "a reformer by instinct and a wise politician; brave, bold, uncompromising, and yet not a wild ass of the desert." [49]

There was a brief scandal in the clubs, as reports of Roosevelt's faithlessness and his "surrender to Platt" were given by trust-

[48] Howe, *op. cit.*, pp. 140-143.

[49] Lodge, *op. cit.*, Vol. I, pp. 348-349; Roosevelt, *An Autobiography*, pp. 272-273.

worthy persons. But soon the obscure quarrel was forgotten. Roosevelt, wearing the sombrero of a Rough Rider, toured the state with an escort of cowboy warriors and a collection of flags for his rallies. There was talk of war and its rich fruitage, and not of reforming canal administrations. When embarrassing mention of the canal scandals was made, the bugles would blow and the drums roll. The citizens were exhorted not to help the Spaniards with their votes. "He really believes," remarked Roosevelt's embittered friend Chapman, that "he is the American flag." [50]

For all its brass music, the New York campaign was comparatively calm, as if the New Yorkers cared little for the war. However, the large corporations gave liberal donations to the party chest, Mr. J. P. Morgan coughing up $10,000; and the party workers labored willingly at the canvass. Colonel Roosevelt prevailed over his Democratic opponent by the close margin of 18,000 votes—yet without him the Old Guard might have lost this important election through its own follies.

A strong current of reaction against the war and its aftermath of prolonged, bloody conflict with the Filipinos now ran through the country. The typical Mugwumps, with whom Roosevelt had parted company, Schurz, Godkin, and Moorfield Storey, addressed the country more vigorously than ever as Anti-Imperialists. William Graham Sumner's eloquent protests that our great nation, in the name of patriotism, had "knocked to pieces a poor old bankrupt state" were widely noticed. Soon Bryan embraced the cause of Anti-Imperialism as furnishing the burning issue of the day. Thus Roosevelt's "spread-eagle" campaign in New York was of the greatest moment to the national administration. He brought happy omens that the "splendid little war" had been, after all, effective as a diversion, that the majority of the people would not repudiate a regime which carried the laurels of military victory, however dubious they might be.

At the outset of his term as Governor of New York, Roosevelt exuded confidence and good cheer. He told himself that he was

[50] Howe, *op. cit.*, p. 470.

going "to achieve results, not merely issue manifestoes of virtue." To his intimate friends, such as Winthrop Chanler, he confided that in spite of the Goo-Goos he expected to make "a pretty decent governor." And the charming Winty hastened to reply that no one doubted this, or believed Roosevelt doubted it. Otherwise "the imagination fairly boggles at the panic I should have suffered." Chanler pledged that he would give aid to the new Governor "by shooting Jack Chapman and his co-kickers with a putty blower." [51]

Theodore Roosevelt's term as Governor was neither brilliant nor interesting, like that of Tilden's reform administration a generation earlier, or Charles E. Hughes's or Alfred Smith's afterward. He made, actually, little more than "a pretty decent governor." He reigned by virtue of a compromise agreement with boss Platt, a compromise that was observed with tolerable good faith by both men, but was awkward and satisfied neither one. In those days the powers of the Governor of New York were peculiarly circumscribed, both as an executive and as an initiator of legislation. His office was apparently held "in trust" for the ruling party organization; while, as Elihu Root admitted, the wily Mr. Platt "simply ruled the State; for nigh upon twenty years he ruled." The capital was not at Albany, but at the corner of the sofa in the Fifth Avenue Hotel, where the county leaders met with Platt and said "Amen!" to his rulings.[52]

Platt, with a quietness and efficiency that made him famous under the soubriquet of the Easy Boss, managed a kind of central clearing house for political privilege, receiving fees regularly from the large corporations in his province and delivering services to them faithfully. This system of political-economic relationships, functionally similar to those in the other important states, was so firmly knit, so highly perfected by 1898, that even the popular hero Colonel Roosevelt, under the circumstances by which he tacitly accepted or recognized it, could do little.

[51] *T. R. Papers,* W. Chanler to T. R., Mar. 10, 1899.
[52] Root, *Addresses,* p. 202.

There is no doubt that he strongly desired to dismiss dishonest, corrupt officials from the public service and actually proceeded to do so, but in each case he had to consult, as agreed, the Easy Boss in order to replace them with reputedly more honest men selected from the organization's approved list. He would have liked to formulate some large policy with regard to the taxation and supervision of corporations and public-utility monopolies chartered by the state—a subject growing fashionable at the time, as we shall see—yet here too his hand was stayed.

Before he took office, Roosevelt relates, Platt asked him in a moment of pleasant humor what committee appointments he wished to suggest for the Legislature. Roosevelt had replied that he had no suggestions, and that in any case the Speaker had not yet been chosen. "Oh," responded Platt, "he has not yet been chosen, but of course whoever we choose as Speaker will agree beforehand to make the appointments we wish." [53]

It would be incorrect to say that Colonel Roosevelt as Governor of New York was merely the puppet of the boss. This was not the view entertained of him privately in professional political circles. The chronicle of Roosevelt's political growth is one alternately of compromise or "trimming," and of rebellious, bold-handed assertions of his independence, his integrity of character. Alternately, he accepts the system, makes his bargain with the boss, and then revolts. (We have seen his backward and forward movements while serving as Police Commissioner; and it is still the same.) Meanwhile his contradictory behavior illuminates all the more strongly the political conditions of the time because he is so atypical, so refreshingly different, so much more enterprising, than the common-garden variety of politician in his time.

In this connection we must remark Senator Tom Platt's careful efforts to pin down the young politician, as far as possible, by written agreements limiting his sphere of action. Such care evidently was unnecessary with those who preceded and followed him in office. A McKinley, in Ohio, did not have to be given sermons by

[53] Roosevelt, *An Autobiography*, p. 284.

Mark Hanna calculated to strengthen his respect for substantial moneyed interests in his state, nor weaned away from reputedly "unsound" or "heretical" notions. Roosevelt on the other hand came to the weekly Sunday breakfasts in New York with Senator Platt, those private conferences which were *de rigueur*, with obvious distaste. He apparently feared to be left alone with the oily, crafty old man; sometimes he brought his sister, Mrs. Anna Roosevelt Cowles, with him.

Attractive and jovial as was the picture that Governor Roosevelt made before the public (the mythical Rough Rider in politics, with his mask of furious energy, of "pure act" as Henry Adams described it), there was in him a more troubled, inward self known to only a few intimate friends, such as Cabot Lodge and Brooks Adams. It was that of an upper-class intellectual of uncertain convictions and limited knowledge, now facing the deeper questions of his time, in more responsible office, while endeavoring to push himself toward the further goal of his overweening ambitions.

The paradox of his character, which has so long troubled historians, derived from his being at the same time the playboy in politics, the picturesque Rough Rider who caught the eye of the crowds, all encircled by followers and flatterers, and the troubled intellectual, the "literary fellow" of aristocratic background who glimpsed something of the dangers and needs of his time, who was sensitive to the moods of the people—yet, at heart unsympathetic to them—who felt all these things and yet suffered from his own incapacity to rationalize them. Thus we may explain the recurrent lapses from announced high principles to gross compromise, the striking contradictions between word and deed, disparities far more prominent in a Theodore Roosevelt than in less honest and less sensitive political characters. We may understand the better also why, throughout the career of this "strong man," there seem to be hands guiding, propelling, manipulating him at every turn, the hands of men who were far more certain of their purpose than he.

The synthesis of political principles and maxims which were fittingly to be known as "Rooseveltian" took more definite form in his mind during the interlude at the Governor's mansion in Albany. In serious vein, he wrote now to his British friend, Cecil Spring Rice: "We have tremendous problems in the way of relations of labour to capital to solve." [54]

In his first annual message to the State Legislature, he found it politic to introduce some conciliatory sentences about the need for bettering the conditions of working men. But as soon as a serious strike broke forth in Buffalo, a short time later, he dispatched state militia to preserve order and property on the spot. Again, in a strike of construction workers at the Croton Dam project, he could not restrain himself from intervening with the armed forces at his disposal, who helped to defeat the strike. Labor, when it showed itself as an organized power, always made him react with instinctive violence. Union men knew this and remembered him for it all his life.

But at the same time the Colonel persisted in his critical attitude toward those whom he amusingly named in private conversation "the criminal rich." In 1899 the tremendous post-war "boom" was on; the bull market roared unceasingly in the stocks of companies being currently absorbed by the giant trusts created under Morgan's leadership. The Democratic leader Bryan now made the problem of the trusts, like that of "imperialism," one of his principal issues. He toured Ohio to oppose personally the re-election of Mr. Hanna to the Senate in 1899, holding that the voters must choose there "between plutocracy and democracy." [55] These would also be the terms of the national campaign in 1900, as anyone could see. Governor Roosevelt, who had so often ridiculed Mr. Bryan, now faced the problem of the multiplying and expanding trusts, everywhere laid to his own party's declared policy of tolerance. He told Cabot Lodge in April, 1899, that despite the booming prosperity seen on every hand, he noted a mood of "sullen discontent" and growing anger among the working classes and small tradespeople of his state—disturbing symptoms to the profes-

[54] Gwynn, *The Letters and Friendships of Cecil Spring Rice,* Vol. I, p. 293.
[55] Croly, *op. cit.,* p. 248.

sional student of the public pulse, who would soon adopt the very terms of Mr. Bryan in order to deal with them.

> I have been in a great quandary over trusts. I do not know what attitude to take. I do not intend to play the demagogue. On the other hand, I do intend, so far as in me lies, to see that the rich man is held to the same accountability as the poor man; . . . this is not always easy.

For many years Roosevelt and his friends had been wont to raise the slogans of nationalism and patriotism in opposition to sectional and class divisions. But now at Albany, facing a period of peace, he entertained doubts that the catalyzing force of militant patriotism would always be enough. Searching for Live Issues, he groped for new tactics and emblems, those which composed gradually the vague program called "The Square Deal." Brooks Adams, paying a week-end visit to Albany in the summer of 1899, held serious discourse with the Governor of the twin dangers of the materialistic trade-union and eight-hour-day movement among the lower classes, and of the possible "enslavement" of the nation by its trust magnates. Their minds played with the possibility of Roosevelt's "heading some great outburst of the emotional classes which should at least temporarily crush the Economic Man." [56]

Despite the hostages that he had given to conservative Republicanism, he was most eager at the outset of his term to figure as a vigorous reformer. He waited a few months, cast about for an issue, and soon found one in the shape of the Ford Franchise Tax Bill, long entombed in the committee rooms of the Legislature. This measure proposed a more adequate though quite moderate scheme of taxation to be placed upon public-service corporations of the state in ratio to the value of the franchises which they had obtained. Roosevelt's special emergency message late in April, 1899, calling for passage of the Ford Bill out of its turn, created a sudden excitement in financial and party circles, and brought the Republican elders hurrying to Albany to admonish him.

In the serious altercation with Platt which arose over the fran-

[56] *T. R. Papers,* T. R. to Hay, Jun. 17, 1899.

chise tax bill the differences between the ideas of the young and the old leader are well revealed. Platt urged the Governor to do nothing. He reminded the Governor warningly:

When the subject of your nomination was under consideration there was one matter that gave me real anxiety. . . . I had heard from a good many sources that you were a little loose on the relations of capital and labor, on trusts and combinations, and, indeed, on those numerous questions which have recently arisen in politics affecting . . . the right of a man to run his own business in his own way, with due respect of course, to the Ten Commandments and the Penal Code. Or, to get at it even more clearly, I understood . . . that you entertained various altruistic ideas, all very well in their way, but which before they could safely be put into law needed very profound consideration.

Platt concluded with an expression of fear lest "the notions of populism, as laid down in Kansas and Nebraska," would soon be exemplified by the leadership of the Republican party in the State of New York.

In answer, the Governor now set forth *virtually his whole profession of faith, that which he adhered to all his life.* He pointed out that "on the one hand" during the recent strike at Buffalo, he had "unhesitatingly acted . . . to put down mobs, without regard to the fact that the professed leaders of labor furiously denounced me for so doing. . . ." But "on the other hand," neither would he tolerate wrongs committed in the name of property, as by the public-utility corporations. He objected strongly to "the tendency to force everybody into one of two camps, and to throw out entirely men like myself, who are as strongly opposed to Populism in every stage as the greatest representatives of corporate wealth. . . ." On this score Roosevelt desired not to be misunderstood in any sense. He insisted emphatically that

these representatives of enormous corporate wealth have themselves been responsible for a portion of the conditions against which Bryanism is in ignorant revolt. I do not believe that it is wise or safe for us as a party to take refuge in mere negation and to say that there are no evils to be corrected. It seems to me that our attitude should be one of correcting the evils and thereby showing that, whereas the Populists, Socialists, and others really do not correct the evils at all . . . we Republicans hold the just balance and set ourselves as resolutely against improper corporate influence on the one hand as against demagogy and mob rule on the other. . . . I think it is in the long run the only wise attitude. . . .[57]

Despite the ill humor of the leader and his henchmen in the Legislature, Roosevelt therefore persisted in pressing for enactment of the Ford Bill. He threatened to call a special session; skillfully he used interviews with the press to arouse popular opinion, and implied that a disagreeable internal party struggle might ensue in the event that his wishes were resisted. Reluctantly the party machine yielded, although the bill was passed only on condition that certain compromise clauses be inserted which were designed to render its constitutionality doubtful.

From such victories Roosevelt's popularity waxed. Platt would warn him solemnly, however, that his future was being ruined; that no large corporations would be willing to contribute to his campaign expenses; they would neither forget nor forgive, while the public with its fickle memory would forget him in a brief season or two. There are signs that Roosevelt bore these strictures in mind. Once having scored a point for himself, he would turn about and allow a few cards to the adversary who still controlled the party's purse.

One of Governor Roosevelt's most helpful acquaintances of this period was Elihu Root, the gray-headed corporation lawyer who either as a legal representative or a lobbyist for his clients had been active in behind-the-scenes politics ever since the days of Boss Tweed in the 1860's. When certain legal technicalities appeared to disbar Roosevelt from the gubernatorial nomination in 1898, owing to his having declared residence in Washington rather than New York, the resourceful Root had quickly found an ingenious way out of the difficulty, winning Roosevelt's everlasting gratitude. A legendary remark suggesting Elihu Root's resourceful-

[57] Roosevelt, *An Autobiography*, pp. 300-301.

ness, and variously attributed to W. C. Whitney, Thomas Fortune Ryan, and J. Pierpont Morgan, was: "I have had many lawyers who have told me what I cannot do; Mr. Root is the only lawyer who tells me how to do what I want to do." [58] It was to the Ulysses of the New York bar (recently appointed Secretary of War by McKinley) that Roosevelt turned repeatedly for advice, especially on the new trust question.

After wrestling for long hours in December, 1899, with his annual message to the State Legislature, regarding measures for supervising monopolistic, semi-public corporations, Roosevelt sent the draft of his message to Root, confessing that he felt himself beyond his depth, and appealing for aid.

Root reads it and tutors him as follows:

> . . . You say "some of the wealth has been acquired by means which are inconsistent with the highest rules of morality and which yet under our present laws cannot be interfered with." I think that is a dangerous suggestion. It is not a function of law to enforce the rules of morality. . . . There is altogether too general an impression that it is immoral to acquire wealth, and far too little appreciation of the fact that the vast preponderance of the *grand fortunes which now exist in this country have been amassed, not by injuring any living being, but as an incident to the conferring of great benefits on the community.*

The "trust problem," according to Root, boiled down to seeing that wealth-getting did not infringe upon any individual's legal rights. So long as the rights of individuals were protected by law sufficiently, it was unnecessary to enact any legislation that would confine or injure business.

Roosevelt replied humbly:

> I see entirely the danger . . . such as my phrase might carry. I think that for it I shall substitute some of the sentences you write in your letter. There are, however, certain fortunes which do seem to me to be unfortunate in their effects with the country. . . .

[58] Jessup, *Elihu Root,* Vol. I, p. 185.

In his message to the New York Legislature, Roosevelt, as he admitted to Root, "cribbed" unblushingly.[59]

The grand fortunes may have been amassed, as Root argued, without injury to any living being; yet Governor Roosevelt now learned from the state banking examiners that there had been scandalous goings-on in the affairs of a certain trust company, purchased lately by a group of eminent financiers including W. C. Whitney and Thomas Fortune Ryan. The Governor's informants wrote him:

> They got rid of the old officers, put in creatures of their own, and proceeded to borrow for their own speculative uses, a large portion of the deposits. The collateral they gave was speculative . . . unmarketable in large degree, almost valueless in many cases. . . . They deliberately violated the Banking Laws and the Penal Code.[60]

Through the bank, the directors got control of an insurance company and disposed of the credit and funds of the latter in ways useful to themselves which the reigning Superintendent of Insurance made no effort to oppose. Roosevelt heard that the latter, Lou Payn, former Congressman, lobbyist and henchman of boss Platt, was the trusted intermediary of the ring of big speculators.

> . . . Being a frugal man, out of his $7,000 a year salary he [Payn] had saved enough to enable him to borrow nearly half a million dollars from a Trust Company, the directors of which are also the directors of an insurance company under his supervision. As Insurance Superintendent, he last year rendered such disinterested aid to Mr. Whitney, when Mr. Whitney's Metropolitan Railway was in danger of being made to pay a tax to the State, etc., etc., that in a burst of similar disinterestedness Mr. Whitney lends him offhand a hundred thousand. . . .[61]

The worst of it was that the newspapers, notably the *World* (March 12 and 13, 1900) with the help of a disgruntled em-

[59] *Root Papers*, E. Root to T. R., Dec. 13, 1899; T. R. to Root, Dec. 15, 1899; Jan. 4, 1900. Cf. also Jessup, *op. cit.*, Vol. I, pp. 208-210. Italics added.

[60] *T. R. Papers*, C. Bacon to T. R., April 19, 1900; also G. R. Sheldon to T. R., Jan. 18, 1900.

[61] Lodge, *op. cit.*, T. R. to Lodge, Jan. 22, 1900, Vol. I, p. 438.

ployee, ventilated these scandals, and Elihu Root was seen to have been the corporation counsel who approved the objectionable transactions. Roosevelt in this case acted with discretion. The *World*, which under Pulitzer often subjected him to its raillery, charged that he shielded certain high political and financial figures, notably Elihu Root. But in any case, he resolved that Lou Payn, Senator Platt's handy man, must give way to a new Superintendent of Insurance.[62]

The ousting of Payn brought fierce outcries from the party's stalwarts. Platt grew bitter; prominent financial leaders made testimonials on behalf of Payn, who for some time defied the Governor's efforts to dismiss him. In the end he departed. But Platt, who was grievously offended by the affair, was partly conciliated in having one of his "boys," whose reputation was not yet sullied, appointed in Payn's place.

A few "altruistic" measures (as Tom Platt cynically called them) were passed during Governor Roosevelt's term, including a tenement-house law, improved civil service regulations, and a new game law. But he had done nothing to prosecute the perpetrators of the canal frauds of 1897-1898; and while he was at odds with the party machine, he was charged by Goo-Goos with having "bowed to Platt on many an appointment." [63]

To his detractors he now answered in terms that were very characteristic of his temperament: "the fool reformers" were as bad as corrupt machine politicians. He ridiculed men who championed their favorite causes only as "a kind of tribute to their own righteousness," and without regard to opportuneness or the need for realistic compromise. To temporize, he held, was often the mark of the highest statesmanship. Or, as he said some years later,

[62] Elihu Root, now Secretary of War, remained silent, though it is evident the affair nettled him. "It is most distressing," he wrote at this time to one of his business associates, "to have the State Government made the tool of a lot of blackmailing scoundrels. I should be glad to know just what part Governor Roosevelt played in it." (*Root Papers*, E. Root to W. S. Johnston, Feb. 19, 1900.)

[63] Pringle, *Roosevelt*, p. 214.

during his libel suit against William Barnes: "I say emphatically that you must have regard for opportunism in the choice of the time and method of making the attack. . . ." [64]

Meanwhile the position of Colonel Roosevelt in the politics of New York State and his party continued to be precarious. Cabot Lodge was now curiously pessimistic when they discussed the "troubled waters" of New York machine politics, in which so many ambitious careers had foundered.

In a certain measure Roosevelt had "hired" his sword, as Brooks Adams had cynically advised him to do, to the masters of political parties; he had made his peace with the machine, which all his instincts and his education taught him to dislike. Yet he felt that his actual prospects were dark; his "career" might soon be ended. He heard of plans afoot to eliminate him from the Governorship, to deny him re-election, which he merited. Boss Platt wanted him out of New York altogether, Roosevelt heard. The big insurance companies, the corporation magnates who represented for him the "criminal rich"—involved in recent scandals, and incensed by the dismissal of Payn—pressed the Senator to rid them of the Rough Rider. "All the high monied interests that make campaign contributions of large size," he confided to Lodge, "and feel that they should have favors in return are extremely anxious to get me out of the State." [65] And beyond Albany the possible advance of the Rough Rider, popular figure though he might be, was limited. The McKinley-Hanna regime with its military conquests and prosperity was to seek vindication before the voters in 1900; and Roosevelt, though inwardly discontented, must remain regular. He could not hope to climb to the Cabinet offices, the realm of national and foreign affairs which truly fascinated him, or the highest office of all, unless he avoided "making mistakes," as an older counselor, H. H. Kohlsaat of Chicago, intimate of McKinley and Hanna, now warned him. He must, in short, take his orders and go where he was told. Especially upon the

[64] Barnes vs. Roosevelt, 366 ff.

[65] *T. R. Papers,* G. H. Lyman to T. R., Dec. 28, 1899.

"trust question" must Roosevelt avoid outspokenness. "I am anxious to have you inherit the McKinley machinery—& following," wrote the Chicago newspaper publisher. "You can get that only by sticking close to the President." He added mysteriously: "A man is often put in a hole by his would-be-friends." [66]

How vastly different was the situation of one of Roosevelt's Western contemporaries, the former Congressman Robert M. La Follette of Wisconsin, also a Republican, who now battled his way to leadership of his state organization. La Follette had been cast out of the temple in 1891 for the high crime of insubordination. Then, after a period of retirement, La Follette had determined to enter the struggle for public office in opposition to the entire Wisconsin machine, a course that Roosevelt, Lodge, and company had so sagely avoided. Wisconsin's party machine was as corrupt and complete as anything in the older regions of the country; yet it was not so deeply entrenched in the rural world; there were fewer crowded city alleys where its roots might flourish rankly as in Boston or New York. Thus La Follette could "go to the people" in a more effectively democratic commonwealth, agitating, educating them tirelessly against the bribe-givers. With the aid of his wife and a few college friends at Madison, he patiently built up his "personal machine." He and Mrs. La Follette by hand addressed thousands of letters, distributed tens of thousands of circulars. Evenings he made long carriage rides, to see his farmers and village shopkeepers face to face. His strength grew steadily from year to year, and his enemies accused him of "working stealthily" by candlelight. This was literally true; because he had no newspapers supporting him, no wealthy patrons, and was forced to knock at the farmers' doors after working hours, and make his appeals man to man, without formality, and by the light of a lantern or a guttering candle.

Thus by 1898 the relentless independent La Follette succeeded in forcing his own political program of administrative, fiscal, and electoral reform upon the state Republican party, though the nom-

[66] *Ibid.*, H. H. Kohlsaat to T. R., Aug. 9, 14, 1899.

inating convention, still partially under the Sawyer-Spooner control, denied him the Governorship. The obstruction of this program thereafter, the failure to enact the party resolutions into law, aroused a wave of popular anger, which made inevitable La Follette's triumphant election in 1900, an event that caused reverberations throughout the country. La Follette had transformed the dominant party in a great Western state "from below," after a decade of grim, incessant warfare. As its undisputed leader he now took over, with his own incorruptible band of followers, the University of Wisconsin "experts," Van Hise, Ely, and Commons, and the agrarian organizers who were sons of the Populists. Henceforth he need "consult" no one, take orders from no one—save the people, who, as La Follette said, "have never failed us. . . ."

But in New York, Governor Roosevelt, courageous and well-intentioned though he might be, felt the ground give way under his feet. For his strength was not built solidly upon a mass following, but derived from a bargain with the old professional organization. Thus he felt himself more or less helpless as many hands combined now to thrust him toward a kind of outer political darkness in 1900.

He should seek re-election as Governor, his admirers urged; then, retiring in 1903, hold himself in readiness for Presidential lightning to strike him. In one year as Governor there was too little time to enact a distinguished legislative program, or to render other signal services; but in his second term there would be opportunity to do this. It was against such a probability, Roosevelt knew, that the machine made ready to remove him. "Hurrahs" greeted the Colonel nowadays when he went forth to speak to the people, but he told himself always that mere "Hurrahs" did not encompass election victories.

After the death of Vice-President Hobart in November, 1899—he had indicated earlier that he wished to retire—there arose a "spontaneous" demand for Governor Roosevelt as running mate to President McKinley in 1900. Several months earlier, Cabot Lodge had written to Theodore that the Vice-Presidency offered interesting possibilities. "I have thought it over a great deal and I am sure I am right," he concluded. Later he wrote that Roosevelt was "tempting Providence by staying in Albany," where he might come a cropper, and firmly advised him to consider the Vice-Presidency if it was offered. Then on December 29, 1899, he reported confidentially that Elihu Root had been offered the nomination and had refused it.[67]

Other admirers and informants now brought word to the Governor that plans were being laid to bar his re-election and thrust him upon the Vice-Presidential "shelf." If he resisted, the whole press would be turned against him; and if he fought for the gubernatorial nomination, unlimited funds would be expended in aid of the Democratic candidate that year.[68]

Gripped by indecision, Roosevelt wavered for many weeks. He knew that the ways of Platt were dark and double; and he had won in 1898 by a slender margin which could be perhaps easily reversed. Moreover, he had managed to offend the trade unions; the American Federation of Labor, he thought, now seethed with anger against him because he had ordered out the militia at the recent Croton strike.[69]

Meanwhile the humorous little conspiracy of Platt and his collaborator, boss Quay of Pennsylvania, proceeded apace, though Mark Hanna openly disapproved of it. An emissary of the Easy Boss came to Albany a few days before the convention opened and advised Roosevelt that his renomination for Governor was improbable, and that public sentiment, especially among the Far Western delegates with whom the war had been popular, would make it hard for him to reject the Vice-Presidential office.[70] Waveringly Roosevelt thrust away the fool's cap of the Vice-President in public, while privately admitting that he saw nothing else to do

[67] *T. R. Papers*, Lodge to T. R., Jul. 12, 1899; Dec. 7, 1899; Dec. 29, 1899.

[68] *Ibid.*, C. P. Bacon to T. R., Apr. 19, 1900; Redfield Proctor to T. R., Apr. 21, 1900; Frederick Holls to T. R., May 3, 1900.

[69] Cowles, *op. cit.*, pp. 232, 240, 244, letters of Feb. 2, 1900; Apr. 30, 1900.

[70] Pringle, *op. cit.*, p. 218.

and was not abandoning the idea of it irrevocably. Lodge, the staunch old friend and mentor, continued to urge his acceptance of the office, though in guarded language, arguing that it would bring Roosevelt close to the Administration: ". . . I did not want you to think that with my views I was encouraging you to get into a position where you would be forced to take the Vice-Presidency." [71]

After some misgivings, the Rough Rider attended the national convention of his party at Philadelphia, wearing his "Acceptance Hat," the old cowboy sombrero of 1898. The only enthusiasm shown at this machinelike ceremony came with the "stampede" to nominate him for the Vice-Presidency. Mark Hanna's opposition to Roosevelt had ceased at the last moment, after telephone communication with President McKinley. "Don't you know that there is only one life between the Presidency and the Vice-Presidency . . . ?" he had exclaimed when another's name had been proposed, one even less offensive to him than the "wild man" of the Republican party.[72]

Although Roosevelt enjoyed the demonstrations made in his honor at the convention, he left it in a mood of deep depression. The Vice-Presidency seemed the tomb of all his hopes. He would pass four years in a futile and farcical role, presiding in routine fashion over the Senate debates which had never interested him, at an age when he might well have shone in more active parts.

His friend Cabot Lodge seemed curiously contented with the outcome. Much might be said of his strange behavior in this affair. Henry Adams, who had known both men for a whole generation, commented privately at the time that Cabot had resolved to "cut the throat" of his friend.[73]

Another intimate friend of both men, Winthrop Chanler, on hearing of the Vice-Presidential nomination, wrote to Roosevelt:

> Well, well, well! Long ago, when you first got the nomination for Governor, the astute Cabot told me that he wanted you to be Vice-

[71] *T. R. Papers,* Lodge to T. R., Apr. 19, 1900.

[72] Beer, *Hanna,* p. 310.

[73] Adams, *Letters,* Vol. II, p. 268.

President and enumerated all the advantages therein for you and the country. The Wily One has won the day, in spite of your titanic struggles to disappoint him. It is the first time that you have been beat, old man. Let the thought that it took the delegates from every State of the Union to do so, console you. I am glad because your being on the ticket makes a Republican victory almost a certainty. . . .[74]

Under marching orders, Roosevelt was designated to lead the nationwide stumping for his party, while the President, according to tradition, remained passive. The Vice-Presidential candidate was a "hybrid duckling" whom the Republican party had hatched, and, as Mark Sullivan has said, "the Republican party was Mark Hanna." [75] The humorous conspiracy to dispose of the adventurous amateur in politics and of his uncomfortable "heresies" was heartily enjoyed by boss Platt, Quay, and Boies Penrose, who had a hand in it, as well as by those great financiers who evidently approved of the scheme.

The long-cherished aspirations of the political adventurer and soldier Roosevelt, just as he attained a national popularity, seemed to have ended in farce. The Vice-Presidency was traditionally a "blind alley," a political grave. Yet McKinley and Hanna, heartily disliking the idea of having Roosevelt so near them, had ceased their opposition only at the last hour. In a sense, was not all the busy scheming to "shelve" Roosevelt a tribute to the force he now represented in their little world of practical politics? Unorthodox as were his methods, he had thrust himself into the field. Then by the romantic adventure in the Cuban battlefield he had won crowd popularity, had become for the first time a power as a vote-getter. The crowds in the Western cities had cheered him "like a Presidential candidate" when he attended veterans' gatherings and made a speaking tour in 1899. "Teddy," the emphatic stump speaker, all pent-up passion, with his bared teeth and clenched fists, was now a familiar figure to the millions, a force to be reckoned with. Moreover, it was an evil omen that the Western politi-

[74] *T. R. Papers,* W. Chanler to T. R., Jul. 10, 1900.
[75] Sullivan, *Our Times,* Vol. II, p. 380.

cians who disliked the McKinley administration's financial conservatism and the domineering of Mark Hanna, turned to the "unsafe" Roosevelt and joined with Platt and Quay to force him upon the Republican ticket, as a means of expressing their secret discontent. On the floor of the convention at Philadelphia in June, 1900, the little conspiracy had turned into a general ovation for the younger politician.

At any rate, one year and three months later—after the sweeping victory over Bryan—on September 6, 1901, the point of Senator Platt's clever joke was suddenly lost when the assassin Czolgosz discharged his revolver into the body of President McKinley. In high financial circles where solid contentment and confidence had been flourishing, panic raged; and Mr. Morgan himself was heard to swear mighty oaths. Eight days later the gentle William McKinley lay dead, and "that damned cowboy," as Mark Hanna called him, who had come hurrying down from his vacation retreat in the Adirondacks, was being sworn into office as President.

IV. TOWARD NATIONAL POLITICAL LEADERSHIP

THE MANAGERS of the ruling party had laid their plans with utmost care for 1900 and after. In the campaign for the re-election of McKinley, Mark Hanna, again the national chairman of the Republican party, sought both vindication by the voters and a crushing defeat of the old opposition party, now deeply committed to a partnership with Bryan's Western "radicals." Chairman Hanna, before an Ohio gathering in April, 1900, pointed with pride to the good fortune that had come in foreign war and in home business. His party, he promised, would continue to devote itself mainly to "the material interests" of the country. The opponents urged various reforms or experiments with the money system and the regulation of trusts, and demanded the liberation of the Philippines. In answer, Mark Hanna, often colorful and blunt in speech, coined a slogan from the terminology of poker players, a slogan that was to be a famous synonym for orthodox Republicanism: "I say, '*Stand pat!*'"[1]

The silver-tongued Bryan, chosen again as the Democratic standard bearer, inaugurated a nation-wide debate that season upon the issues of "imperialism" and the trusts, which he linked together in a very intelligent manner. Driven by a "greedy commercialism," he argued, our native monopolists, after exploiting the laborer and farmer at will, and crushing out small enterprisers, caused the country to depart from its democratic traditions in subjugating foreign people by force. For the Filipinos, under Agui-

[1] Croly, *Hanna*, pp. 303-304, 417.

naldo, were now engaged in tremendous guerilla war against American armed rule.

But the "boy orator" of Nebraska (no longer a youth) cast a less potent spell over the citizens than in 1896. His favorite financial cure-all, the free coinage of silver, began to seem old-fashioned in an era of roaring prosperity and good prices. Coming to New York during his tour, he had made an open alliance with Tammany Hall, saying: "Great is Tammany! and its prophet is Croker." It was a move that made the reformers and Anti-Imperialists unhappy, though it reflected well the divided character of the Democratic party, an amalgam of the "solid South," the Western agrarians, and the Eastern city machines.

Moreover, the new, glamorous war hero Colonel Roosevelt was a counter-attraction to Bryan during his own nation-wide stumping tour. ". . . The war had had the interesting and powerful psychological effect of diverting the mind of the American from his own woes, his currency troubles, his hard times," Ray Stannard Baker commented at this period. The citizens thought now "of glory and patriotism and expansion. . . ."[2] To these new interests the swashbuckling Roosevelt directed his appeals with a vehemence of speech and gestures that made him a favorite Republican orator. On all other questions Roosevelt spoke in a conservative key, warning his hearers against the insincere demagogism of the adversary, and deploring indiscriminate attacks upon large business interests.

It was Elihu Root, the Secretary of War, however, who sounded the strongest notes on behalf of the Hamiltonian party, which he did in a speech at McKinley's native Canton, Ohio, October 24, 1900. How pleasing this speech was to the greatest patrons of the Republican party is shown by the fact that Mr. J. P. Morgan thought it the finest oration of its kind he had ever heard or read, and obtained a manuscript of it to keep with his collection of the manuscripts of Rousseau and Keats, and the Shakespeare folios.[3]

[2] R. S. Baker, in the *Cosmopolitan Magazine*, May, 1900.

[3] Jessup, *Root*, Vol. II, p. 234.

The material results of "wise and successful government," Root said, were visible on every hand. Never in the history of the world was there a body of people "so well fed, well clothed and well housed." (That very summer, however, a desperate strike of 140,000 anthracite coal miners in Pennsylvania had been settled only through the urgent intervention of Mark Hanna.) Yes, continued Mr. Root, the country flourished, because "wise government" while not interfering with business and labor "gives to capital that confidence in security for its investment which draws it from the hiding places of distrust." As for Mr. Bryan and his followers, they had "learned nothing and abandoned nothing." They sought now, as in 1896, "to excite animosities and foment discord among the people; to deceive by the false promises of the demagogue; and to profit themselves by creating a warfare of class against class." Mr. Bryan would destroy the trusts? But most of the so-called trusts were great and strong "because they sell cheaper . . . are more efficient. This is not monopoly but competition." Bryan attacked those great industrial enterprises which employed labor and increased the wealth of the country; he had even proposed Federal licensing of large corporations engaged in interstate commerce. "Shades of Thomas Jefferson! What doctrines to be preached in thy name." Here was not "democracy" but domestic "Imperialism" with a vengeance. Absolute control over every business interest in the country would be established at Washington; the effect of politics and favoritism would bring an appalling destruction of values and liberties. Such a proposal was as grotesque as it was absurd.

Bryan had also charged that the existence of a large army, and the growing practice of using it in labor disputes, showed that "it was intended to suppress by force that discontent that ought to be cured by legislation!" But Root in his peroration cried that this was a defamation. "The American soldier is not a danger to liberty and law but their defender. . . . I challenge the just judgment of the people as between him and those men who, for their own selfish purpose, are aspersing and maligning him, while in distant lands he is braving hardship and disease and wounds and death in defence of our country's flag." [4]

The waving of the flag brought cheers that drowned out the cries of the Anti-Imperialists.

The Republican victory of 1900 was more sweeping, more decisive, than in 1896 and brought that which Chairman Hanna had craved: "a clear mandate to govern the country in the interests of business expansion." [5] Greater credit than ever now adhered to the President Maker who, as if with some future design, now for the first time endeavored to speak from the public rostrum and show himself more humorous, more tolerant, more prepossessing than in earlier years.

Years of undisputed rule were easily foreseen for the party of business men; and the large projects which had waited upon the November elections were pushed forward confidently. In New York, on the day of McKinley's second inauguration, the newspapers announced the approaching formation of Mr. Morgan's United States Steel Corporation, the world's first "billion-dollar-trust." At the same time reports were circulated of the combination of two rival transcontinental railroads, the Great Northern and the Northern Pacific, under the leadership of J. P. Morgan and James J. Hill. While in the Senate, Hanna, now a convinced Imperialist, pushed energetically his favorite measure, the Shipping Subsidy Bill, by whose provisions the friendly government would extend direct money subsidies to an expanding merchant marine competing with that of other imperial powers for the world's export trade.

The boom continued, and its foundation, as Hanna said in the summer of 1901, was "confidence—confidence in the future."

Then, on September 6, 1901, the shock of tragedy suddenly shattered all the smoothly working arrangements and plans. Mark Hanna, watching over the deathbed of the President, was seen to break down and weep like a child. Not only was his affection for

[4] Root, *Military and Colonial Policy*, pp. 27-64.

[5] Croly, *Hanna*, p. 341.

McKinley old and strong—though their agreement had become less perfect in the last days—but the patient labor of many years, and big deals planned for the future, seemed undone as the man's life ebbed away.

William McKinley may have been "nothing more than a very supple and highly paid agent of . . . capitalism," as Henry Adams remarked at the time.[6] Yet our government system was cumbersome at best; and McKinley's "suppleness" had made the divided authorities of the government function more effectively in the interests of business expansion than in nearly forty years. This successful functioning was grounded upon a structure of relations and understandings with the national party boss, Hanna, with the veteran leaders of Congress, and with the representatives of great financial and industrial concerns, that was inherently delicate and confidential. To entrust the command of this system to a youthful Theodore Roosevelt seemed grotesque.

It was not that Roosevelt was a Single Taxer or a Socialist in disguise; his background was in fact irreproachably conservative. But this political soldier, this playboy of reform politics, had never worked seriously at any trade; he had never had important business men as his clients nor acquired the respect for money that McKinley instinctively showed. To Hanna he appeared always "impulsive," frivolous, and "unsound"—for who could overlook his remarks upon the "criminal rich" or the "timid," "greedy" commercial interests? His restless ambitions would be urging him always to "do something," to "save" the country, when men like Hanna and Platt knew that there was no danger of a revolution, and all that was needed was to "stand pat." Finally to fix the contrast between the meddlesome young Roosevelt and the veteran, professional politician McKinley, one need but recall the awkward experience of the New York machine, which was a matter of common knowledge in the inner circles of the party. Those letters of agreement defining the sphere of the Governor and the boss, the reservations of Roosevelt regarding affairs affecting his "con-

[6] Adams, *Letters,* Vol. II, p. 356.

science"—such things were, of course, wholly unnecessary with a McKinley. Little wonder that a "bear market" raged in Wall Street.

With but a single thought the strong men in the ruling party hastened to encircle the "accidental" President with their counsel and their warnings. At Buffalo, whither Roosevelt had hurried instantly upon news of McKinley's fatal relapse, most of the Cabinet members were assembled. On behalf of the Cabinet, Elihu Root asked him to take the oath of office; and Root has related that Roosevelt whispered a question to him as to whether he should make any statement.

> Root told him he thought . . . the country was much disturbed and needed some assurance that would create confidence. He thought Roosevelt should declare his intention to continue unbroken the policy of President McKinley for the peace, prosperity and honor of the country. Roosevelt repeated the words just as Root suggested them to him, and Judge Hazel administered the oath. Root intended that Roosevelt's statement should constitute a binding obligation.[7]

The power of Mark Hanna, Roosevelt recalled in later years, was "such as no other man in our history has had." He was aware of this power, hedging in his own office, as McKinley's unofficial prime minister and national boss called upon him in Buffalo on that same morning. And to Hanna the same assurances given to the Cabinet were repeated. That evening Hanna returned by appointment, and the two men, who had never liked each other, held frank, intimate conversation. Without any beating about the bush, and without unmanly bowings to the new rising sun, Hanna assured Roosevelt that he would do all in his power to make his administration a success—subject to Roosevelt's following the McKinley policies. Hanna made it clear, however, that he was not committing himself to favor Roosevelt's nomination at the next election, but must leave that to the future to decide. Roosevelt thanked him and told him that he understood his position.

[7] Jessup, *op. cit.*, Vol. I, p. 238.

2

Theodore Roosevelt at forty-three aroused the interest of the country as the youngest President in our history, and one of the most attractive and sympathetic figures who had reached that office in recent decades. He assumed his burdens and dignities cheerfully on the whole, despite the tragic circumstances under which they had been gained. His energetic and informal methods of working, the ease with which he received and dismissed hundreds of visitors every day, his lively sallies, his original turns of speech, all occupied the press and the popular mind. "Every day or two," a correspondent reported, "he rattles the dry bones of precedent and causes sedate Senators and heads of departments to look over their spectacles in consternation." [8] From the outside, Roosevelt's many-sided career now appeared dazzling, meteoric; his personal force, irresistible.

In reality, Roosevelt knew that he was, so to speak, a *captive* President. As at Albany, so at Washington a nearly omnipotent boss, with power to make or ruin him, stood close by. Deferentially Roosevelt invited the boss to hold conferences with him at an early date at Washington; and from Cleveland came Hanna's reply, hinting plainly that the President must wait until he arrived to advise him "on many important matters to be considered from a political standpoint. . . ." Meanwhile, Hanna urged, " 'Go slow.' You will be besieged from all sides. . . . *Hear* them all patiently but *reserve* your decision—unless in cases which may require immediate attention. Then if my advice is of importance, Cortelyou [Private Secretary to the President] can reach me over the 'long distance.' "

Roosevelt answered that he would do exactly as advised. He would "go slow." [9]

Indeed from all sides, even by his relatives, he was besieged with the warnings to be cautious, to be "close-mouthed" and con-

[8] Sullivan, *op. cit.*, Vol. II, p. 394.

[9] *T. R. Papers,* Hanna to T. R., Oct. 12, 1901; T. R. to Hanna, Oct. 12, 1901.

servative. In truth, he understood the situation; and the urgency of these warnings seemed scarcely necessary. To his friend and biographer, Joseph B. Bishop, he confided his intention of avoiding disputes, of seeking to work with the managers of his party, rather than spend his term in strife with them as Grover Cleveland had done.

Moreover, he had felt in honor bound to retain McKinley's Cabinet, even his Private Secretary, Cortelyou, at his side. It was a conservative Cabinet at best; and two of its leading members were old friends and patrons, given to treating him with amused tolerance rather than respect. To the right of him sat Secretary of State John Hay; to the left, Secretary of War Elihu Root. The connections of these men ran straight to the highest circles of Wall Street. Possibly Hay was "one wheel of the old machine of Hanna and Pierpont Morgan, and Root the other," as the old gossip, Henry Adams, surmised.[10]

Another thread which led to the House of Morgan was the appointment by Roosevelt of Robert Bacon, one of the bank's partners, as Assistant Secretary of State—Bacon had been an admired classmate at Harvard. The frequent visits of George W. Perkins, whom Roosevelt had met at Albany, and who was generally charged with handling lobbying and political relations for J. P. Morgan and Company, also pointed to the continued political ascendancy of the great banking house. Perkins wrote frequently from Number 23 Wall Street to the young President whom he warmly liked, giving information of large financial projects in a manner that might commend them to Presidential tolerance. In urgent cases Mr. Perkins would sometimes call the White House on the long-distance telephone.

With regard to legislative matters, as in the preparation of his first message to Congress, Roosevelt went directly to Senator Aldrich's "Philosopher's Club" for advice and approval. "I shall want to see you before I write my message," he told the ancient Senator Allison of Iowa, "because there are two or three points

[10] Adams, *Letters,* Vol. II, p. 383; letter of Apr. 6, 1902.

upon which I do not desire to touch, until after consultation with you."[11] Mark Hanna, John Hay, Elihu Root, Aldrich, Allison, O. E. Platt, Robert Bacon, and George W. Perkins—all were consulted in the production of Roosevelt's first, eagerly awaited message to Congress.

Yet, notwithstanding these eminent advisers, Theodore Roosevelt as a young Republican had a contribution of his own to make. He clung tenaciously to those principles he had begun to advocate as Governor. In a confidential letter to his brother-in-law, Douglas Robinson, a New York stock broker who had besought him not to "upset the confidence . . . of the business world," he wrote in very characteristic terms that he intended to propound an attitude of even-handed "righteousness" toward the trusts.

> I intend to be most conservative, but in the interests of the corporations themselves and above all in the interests of the country, I intend to pursue cautiously, but steadily, the course to which I have been publicly committed . . . and which I am certain is the right course.[12]

For two years, as we have noted, the great movement toward concentrating industries into single trusts had been absorbing the attention of the country. Then, in the spring of 1901, came the launching of the colossal steel trust, followed by the fierce financial struggle for control of the Northern Pacific Railroad, which terminated in the pooling of the opposing Morgan and Harriman interests in the Northern Securities Company, a $400,000,000 holding company. McKinley himself had noticed, at the time of the Northern Pacific "corner" and panic, the virulence of the trust issue, and according to his official biographer, Olcott, during his second term "reached a firm determination to deal seriously with the evils inseparable from the rapid multiplication of the so-called trusts."[13] Roosevelt had learned that President McKinley had been turning over in his mind what to do in this matter. One often-advocated method of approach would have been to mod-

[11] Stephenson, *Aldrich*, p. 174.

[12] Oct. 14, 1901; Bishop, *op. cit.*, Vol. I, p. 159.

[13] Olcott, *McKinley*, Vol. II, pp. 299-300.

erate the protective tariff, which was "the mother of trusts." Despite his lifelong championing of protection, McKinley's final public speech at Buffalo proposed a series of reciprocity treaties with various countries for the mutual reduction of tariffs.

Roosevelt in preparing his first message had recourse to this identical solution: reciprocity. But when he broached this point to Senator Nelson Aldrich on October 28, 1901, he was advised to drop the whole business. This the President humbly agreed to do, saying: "All I shall do about the [reciprocity] treaties will be to say I call the attention of the Senate to them." Aldrich was also promised "a last looking over" of the message.[14]

To Hanna, intimately connected with the great oil and steel trades, Roosevelt also turned for advice on the trust question. Hanna wrote:

> I have been thinking (hard) about that portion of your message regarding "Trusts." It seems to me that there are some suggestions which may furnish ammunition to the enemy in a political contest—the question of "overcapitalization" which seemed to have created a doubt in your own mind strikes me as a delicate one.

The mention of "overcapitalization" Hanna advised him to drop entirely, assuring him also that organized labor was in general not opposed to combinations of capital. "They are not worried about the 'Trust' question. . . . Therefore may I suggest that you do not give it so much prominence in your message." Roosevelt had proposed some form of enforced publicity and investigation of books; but Hanna remarked, "The inquisition feature is most objectionable. . . . Pardon my suggestions—which have come from careful consideration. I see 'dynamite' in it."[15]

Roosevelt thereupon dropped his reflections upon the "overcapitalization" of the trusts.

True to character, Roosevelt in his first message to Congress did sound, at times, a critical note toward the huge monopolies whose apparition now frightened the average citizen. And this

[14] Stephenson, *op. cit.*, p. 180.

[15] *T. R. Papers,* Hanna to T. R., Nov. 10, 1901.

was the distinguishing feature of a very ambitious, long, involved paper, which touched a hundred different topics. He pointed frankly to the evil concerning which others had been silent. He also retained the statement that "knowledge of the facts—publicity" should be secured as a means of keeping the trusts a force for good and curbing their "occasional" tendencies to evil. When some of the corporations in their "eagerness to reach great industrial achievements" went too far, the government, he suggested, might inform itself and, while not "prohibiting" or "confining," should in some manner "supervise and regulate."

But modern business was delicate and could easily be thrown out of adjustment, he admitted. "Prosperity can never be created by law alone. . . ." It was not true, he argued, that "the rich were growing richer and the poor poorer." The country continued in an amazingly healthy and flourishing condition, thanks to Republican rule, and nothing must be done to disturb this needlessly.

Such is the gist of an essentially middle-road document that brought welcome relief to the anxious watchers in the counting-houses. It was a performance that ran constantly from "one hand" to the "other hand," as the informal political philosopher, Mr. Dooley, soon noted. Yet to dismiss it as purely opportunist would be to miss its nuances and to differentiate a Theodore Roosevelt in no way from his predecessor McKinley. Though still very moderate, the expression of a spirit critical toward the canons of the respectable can already be observed here. There are also, in references to the new imperial policies, accents of an intense nationalism. But here Roosevelt differs from the older leaders of the Hamiltonian party, who ignored the popular demand for the safeguarding of democratic, equalitarian rights under new forms of attack; he differs from them in seeking to give "a democratic meaning and purpose to the Hamiltonian tradition and method."[16]

Theodore Roosevelt, arriving suddenly in the office of President with its enormous powers under the Constitution, found that

[16] Croly, *The Promise of American Life*, pp. 168-169.

he actually held not much real power. Control of the party organization and of parliamentary activities seemed pretty thoroughly vested in Hanna, Aldrich, and a few of their associates. These men with their managerial or pivotal controls, buttressed by vast resources of money, could easily have moved to discredit and crush the unwelcome successor of McKinley, though it would have been a costly business, as in the case of Andrew Johnson. But Roosevelt acted warily, and, at the outset, respected the existing arrangements. He respected the huge, crude strength of Hanna, and the silent, confident force of the more polished Aldrich. How much he deferred to these men and their lieutenants is shown by the disposition of Federal patronage in his first administration—an inescapable sign, since the machinery of their "indirect" rulership rested as always upon the loaves and fishes of office.

To the famous corned-beef-hash breakfasts which Hanna served at the Hotel Arlington in Washington, Roosevelt came frequently for "consultations," just as he had formerly come to Platt's Sunday breakfasts in New York. A stupendous amount of patronage, in the shape of petty appointments, continued to be cleared through Hanna in 1902 and 1903, as is shown by the voluminous private correspondence between the two men. "I see by the papers," runs a characteristic message from Hanna, "that you are thinking of appointing Mr. ——— as ———. Please go slow about this. Will see you tomorrow." [17] Thus the army of Republican "workers," holding post-office, revenue, and lighthouse jobs throughout the country, continued to be provisioned by the national party boss.

In a similar manner Senator Matthew Stanley Quay of Pennsylvania, almost as powerful a boss as Hanna, was freely provided with minor offices. Concerning this old knave, who had been close to the gates of the penitentiary, Roosevelt once remarked, shrugging his shoulders, that it was not his fault if the people of Pennsylvania had elected the man as United States Senator. Also in the Western states, Roosevelt reinforced party orthodoxy against in-

[17] *T. R. Papers*, Hanna to T. R., Dec. 5, 1902.

surgence, by furnishing Henry C. Payne, his Postmaster General—rather than Governor La Follette—with Federal patronage in Wisconsin. Payne, who "represented" public-utility and railroad interests, was a "Standpatter."

In quiet fashion, Roosevelt passed out the desired loaves and fishes to these men who dominated what would later be known as our "invisible government." More publicly, however, he would point with pride to his selection of meritorious and distinguished young administrators to office, wherever possible, for in his heart the Mugwump, the civil-service reformer, still lived. Regarding the administration of the new colonies, where war and danger lurked, he decreed publicly that "no appointments . . . will be dictated or controlled by political considerations."[18]

But Theodore Roosevelt was never made to be a yielding, a complaisant character. Though he found his sphere sharply limited, he could not refrain from pressing instinctively, everywhere, to win more power; and this unremitting process was to end by changing the very traditions surrounding the office of the President.

At Albany he had learned how to carry out "horse trades" even with the wily Tom Platt, winning consent to reformist legislation, and credit for ousting crooked office-holders, in return for concessions to the boss's requirements in other directions. So in Washington, in a series of conferences with the wise old men of the party, the younger politician played a shrewd, determined game for the sake of concessions opening the road for his own ambitions.

A very plausible and appealing theory has been worked out by the late Professor Nathaniel W. Stephenson (based on a study of the Aldrich private papers) that Roosevelt at the outset of his term worked out a truce or "gentleman's agreement" with Hanna and Aldrich, which though circumscribing his field of operations gave him a free hand in certain areas. On August 23, 1902, there was a private gathering of the elder Senators, including Mark Hanna, at Oyster Bay, for an all-day conference. Again, on Sep-

[18] Bishop, *op. cit.*, Vol. I, p. 155.

tember 16, 1902, Roosevelt sailed across Long Island Sound to Narragansett, near Newport, where Aldrich's great castle stood, and conferred all day with the gentleman from Rhode Island and his colleagues in the Senate.

The upshot was that the President agreed to leave undisturbed the protective tariff system and the monetary system, those monumental achievements of the Republican party. However, as reports ran, he was "to have his head on all things outside of economics and finance." For instance, Roosevelt might have thought of "Bryanizing" a little. There was now a powerful popular movement for the Eight-Hour Day earnestly pushed by the trade unions and many liberal sympathizers throughout the country. Did Roosevelt agree with Hanna, Aldrich, Cannon, and company to avoid this subject? The idea of the Eight-Hour Day for labor was to spread widely, but without the blessing of the White House, where the counsels of Aldrich, Spooner, Allison, O. H. Platt (of Connecticut), and Mark Hanna were to prevail.[19]

Concerning the whole vague "trust question," which engrossed public opinion, the Republican elders, save for Senator Hanna, showed a certain resignation amounting almost to indifference. Much doubt existed that the government could actually curb the monopolistic corporations under existing laws and court rulings. Moreover, the legal character of the trusts was now being rapidly transformed by clever lawyers into new guises permitted by the New Jersey and Delaware charters. When Roosevelt, soon afterward, opened a government suit against one of the notorious new "holding companies," none of the Aldrich group objected.

Shortly after the second of these conferences, in September, 1902, Roosevelt departed upon a Western tour, and stopping at Logansport, Indiana, made an important "policy" speech touching questions of tariff and finance. Though there was said to be much discontent in the Middle West regarding the tariff and the trusts, he urged the need for continuity in our government revenue laws. To make abrupt changes was dangerous. "What we really need is

[19] Stephenson, *op. cit.*, p. 196; p. 243; Appendix, p. 453.

to treat the tariff as a business proposition," he declared, "and not from the standpoint of a political party." The nation could adjust its business to a given tariff schedule. But changes should be managed by experts, working "primarily from the standpoint of the business interests."

The philosophers of the Senate, both Allison and Spooner, at once wrote Roosevelt that his were brave words, "sound and wise . . . will do much to clear the atmosphere." They concluded: "Have done immeasurable good." And he replied (to Allison): "I thought I had substantially the idea that we agreed upon at the time you were in Oyster Bay." [20]

Roosevelt in short was not to disturb the economic legislation which favored industrial capitalism, nor the financial policy, the gold standard, favored by the Eastern bankers. In truth he was never highly interested in these matters, confessing that economic questions were beyond his grasp. But, in compensation, he could pursue freely a "spirited" foreign policy, and he could engage to his heart's content in vigorous but essentially "moral" crusades against the trusts, those "heejeous monsthers," as Mr. Dooley styled them.

3

As at Albany, so at Washington, Roosevelt studied the popular mood carefully and searched for Live Issues, the ideological raw material of the genuine politician. Nor were they far to seek.

For two years an agitated discussion of the coming of the great trusts was whipped up in the popular press; though it did not reach the intensity of the period between 1904 and 1912, discussion of the trust question was the paramount subject of the Rooseveltian Era. In the Middle West the problem of the high cost of living aroused discontent among an important minority that had always been allied with the Republican party. The high cost of living was widely attributed there to the appearance of the monopolies in steel, nails, barbed wire, shoes, wool, tobacco, all

[20] *T. R. Papers*, T. R. to W. Allison, Sept. 27, 1902.

the consumer goods which the farmer must purchase. In the usually safe State of Iowa, the rise of Albert Cummins as a dominant political leader, toward 1901, was a symptom; Cummins, though a Republican, preached tariff reduction as a measure with which to combat the trusts. In Wisconsin, where the radical La Follette now ruled, a strong anti-railroad movement flourished. And in Minnesota the merging of the two competing trunk lines, the Great Northern and Northern Pacific, had led to an attempt at a suit by Governor Van Sant against the parent holding company, the Northern Securities.

Rumblings of protest could be heard by sensitive ears throughout the Mississippi Valley, and especially in the "Granger" states, which so often threatened to quit the orbit of the Republican party. This movement, it was plain to see, Bryan would attempt again to take advantage of. In the winter of 1902, Bryan's followers in Congress, such as Albert S. Burleson of Texas, prepared to open fire upon the new President because of his initial "mildness" toward the big corporations.[21] But though breaches showed themselves here and there in the historic alliance between the Eastern capitalists and the Middle-Western farmers, it is doubtful that Hanna or Aldrich would have moved. They would have continued to "stand pat," while the breach widened.

Roosevelt, however, held different views; and was as confident of the correctness of his judgment as upon the eve of the Spanish-American War. He agreed with Bryan that the trust question was the Live Issue of the day. But in attempting vigorous legal action against the trusts, he alarmed the wise old men of the party far less than if he had struck at the protective tariff.

Not long before this, the railroad bankers, after the violent "Northern Pacific panic" of May, 1901, had composed their quarrel and decided to fling together, by a simple exchange of stock, the assets of three giant trunk lines. This alarmed even men of conservative opinion. A few more such moves on the chessboard of finance capitalism and, as Professor W. Z. Ripley com-

[21] *Bryan Papers*, W. J. Bryan to A. C. Burleson, Mar. 11, 1902.

mented at the time, the industries of the nation might be contained within one great holding company, controlled from one banking office, such as that at the corner of Broad and Wall Street in New York. The Northern Securities Company was widely held to be a menacing "Trojan Horse." James J. Hill, who was to be its titular head, admitted afterward that there had been talk of having him manage all of the railroads west of the Mississippi, covering two-thirds of the area of the United States, by means of one great holding company. Even Mark Hanna thought that Hill and Morgan might have gone too far, and McKinley himself would have acted against them in time.[22]

Shortly after his entrance into office, early in February, he asked his Attorney General, Philander C. Knox, who was formerly the attorney of Andrew Carnegie, for an opinion as to the legality of the new railroad holding company, the Northern Securities, whose creation had caused such an outcry. Knox advised that it was a violation of the Sherman Anti-Trust Act of 1890. Whereupon, in absolute confidence, Roosevelt ordered Mr. Knox to prosecute and bring the case to court.

News of the sudden, secretly prepared government action came to financial circles on February 18, 1902, with the effect of the proverbial bombshell. Mr. J. Pierpont Morgan, receiving the news while at dinner, appeared to lose his appetite, and expressed strong resentment at not having been told of the action in advance. Neither Elihu Root nor John Hay had known anything of it.[23]

Three days after the announcement of the government's suit to dissolve the Northern Securities Company, Mr. Morgan, "chaperoned" by Senators Mark Hanna and Chauncey Depew, arrived at the White House to pay a social call upon the new President. Theodore Roosevelt had met Mr. Morgan before and knew him slightly. But the encounter was dramatic.

The one man taciturn, huge, old, craggy and ugly of counte-

[22] Pyle, *James J. Hill*, Vol. II, p. 185; Beer, *op. cit.*, p. 246.

[23] "Root was much upset by it." (Adams, *Letters*, Vol. II, p. 374; Feb. 23, 1902.)

nance, was now almost a legendary figure in newspaper prose and caricature, legendary enough to terrify little children. Actually he was not the wealthiest of financiers, but the aggressive leader, heart and soul of the movement of combination in industry and finance, omnipotent in his control of affiliated banks and trust companies, seemingly invincible in his gigantic promotions. The movement he led, moreover, was held to be a part of progress and "natural evolution," hence inevitable. Creating ever new masses of debts and securities, huge new areas of capital investment, Morgan accelerated a tremendous credit inflation which wrought for a time a "boundless prosperity." He now stood at the very zenith of his strange, lonely career, as one of the sovereigns of the modern world.

The comparatively youthful, ebullient Roosevelt, on the other hand, was a kind of political adventurer to Mr. Morgan. He had never been in trade, though he sprang from the more comfortable or upper middle class. He had been a writer of books, a sportsman, a soldier, a government official. He occupied, in fact, a middle ground, and had said with conviction in his First Annual Message to Congress: "We are neither for the rich man as such nor the poor man as such; we are for the upright man, rich or poor." He had a thoroughly middle-class fear of labor in its militant moods, and had shown that he would not hesitate to use force against it. But on the other hand he shared a growing resentment and fear also of the mighty industrial overlords, including the one before him, who had accumulated a degree of power that seemed to brook all efforts of government to restrain them. He would soon say: "Of all forms of tyranny, the least attractive and the most vulgar is the tyranny of mere wealth, the tyranny of a plutocracy." The accent here upon vulgarity is not of the proletarian rebel, but of the aristocrat who, aware of the diminished power of his class, nevertheless professes to scorn mere "money-grubbers."

Linked with the aristocratic impulse another impulse could be noted, typical of a large *bureaucratic* class, the men in political or military service in Europe as well as America at this time, who stood outside of commercial life, but often felt bitterly that their devotion and exertions were unjustly overlooked. Roosevelt shared their "moral" conviction that ambitions might be nobly satisfied, not merely by the acquisition of wealth but by a patriotic career in arms, in service, or in directing grand imperial plans for the glory of country and people.[24] In short, no two men could have offered greater contrast than the youthful statesman and the old banker who confronted each other.

At this time there were few men who cared to face the gaze of this fierce old man. Railroad presidents and great bankers habitually avoided debate with "Jupiter" Morgan over his commands. Now Morgan evidently measured the politician and pondered over the possible difficulties he presented, for this politician was unlike others, whom he usually despised. Roosevelt, who had faced death in the Bad Lands of the Dakotas and in Cuba, stood on the precarious ground he had chosen. He was not to be dealt with by a direct approach. Morgan's impulse to violence, expressed in a letter he wrote the President from his hotel that night—a letter never delivered—was in some manner checked by his counselors. The first collision between these two men was less than deadly.

It was probably at a later, less public conference, that day (February 21, 1902) or the day after, that Morgan's complaints at not having been informed in time were heard.[25] It was then that Morgan made his famous, blunt proposal: "If we have done anything wrong, send your man [meaning the Attorney General] to my man [naming his lawyer] and they can fix it up." The President, however, held this to be impossible; while the Attorney

[24] Cf. C. A. Beard and A. Vagts, *The New Republic,* June 28, 1939, for a discussion of this bureaucratic outlook on life. Mahan in a letter wrote: ". . . The mere *opportunist,* the mere dollars and cents view, the mere appeal to comfort and well being as distinct from righteousness and foresight, in a word, mere selfishness and regard for present ease are being dropped rapidly behind and nobler, if somewhat crude and vainglorious, feelings are taking possession of the people. For after all, if the love of mere glory is selfish, it is not quite as low as the love of mere comfort." (Puleston, *Mahan,* p. 200.)

[25] Pringle, *op. cit.,* p. 256.

General, perhaps simulating the Rooseveltian pugnacity, added that they intended not to "fix it," but to "stop it."

"Are you going to attack my other interests, the Steel Trust and the others?" Morgan asked. To learn of this was the real object of his call.

"Certainly not," replied Roosevelt, "unless we find out that . . . they have done something that we regard as wrong."

After the banker was gone, Roosevelt pointed out to Knox how well "the Wall Street point of view" had been illuminated at this meeting. Mr. Morgan, he reflected, "could not help regarding me as a big rival operator, who either intended to ruin all his interests or else could be induced to come to an agreement to ruin none." [26]

Though it amused the President, there was not a little allegorical truth and keen insight in this notion of Mr. Morgan's. The political man could rise to the force of "a big rival operator," instead of remaining merely a "supple, paid agent" of the capitalist. That the political government might stand "above" the great capitalists, and act as impartial broker between the other great pressure groups, was another question that would wait long for its answer.

Meanwhile the actual outcome of the suit against the Northern Securities Company waited two years, until March, 1904, in the hands of the Supreme Court, which then issued a dissolution order favorable to the government's contention. The disposition of the company's assets, controlled by the court, inflicted no serious punishment upon the monopolists. Jim Hill, who angrily called Theodore Roosevelt "a political adventurer" and a poseur, vowed in 1902 that the purposes of the railway magnates would be met "in another way." Two certificates of stock, printed in different colors, would be issued instead of one, and that, as Hill remarked derisively, "would constitute the main difference." [27]

[26] Bishop, *op. cit.*, Vol. I, pp. 184-185.

[27] Pyle, *J. J. Hill*, Vol. II, p. 187.

The press and public opinion heartily approved of Roosevelt's suit against Northern Securities—though conservative organs denounced the action. Joseph Pulitzer, the owner of the independent, Democratic *World*, though personally hostile to Roosevelt, supported him at this time, on the ground that his actions appeased the masses of people. "The greatest breeder of discontent and socialism," wrote Pulitzer to his editor Frank Cobb, "is the . . . popular belief that the law is one thing for the rich and another for the poor." [28]

It was with the purpose of contending against such dangerous counsels of despair as Pulitzer alluded to, that Roosevelt, in the late summer of 1902, took the stump in a speaking tour of New England and the Middle West. In explaining and defending his action, which had roused up a spirited controversy, he argued that the trust question was essentially a *moral* question, and that he endeavored but to deal with it righteously. It was inevitable, with his half-aristocratic, half-bureaucratic outlook (detached from the economic motives of both the House of Morgan and the American Federation of Labor), that he should seek a synthesis emphasizing "the superiority of the moral to the material."

"Material prosperity without the moral lift toward righteousness," left to its own devices, he said, would bring but unhappiness and degradation to our country.[29]

He prophesied dangers to come from the jealousy of the classes.

> Not only do the wicked flourish, when the times are such that most men flourish, but what is worse, the spirit of envy and jealousy and hatred springs up in the breasts of those who, though they may be doing fairly well themselves, yet see others who are no more deserving, doing far better.[30]

Finally, Roosevelt argued, as one who but opposed the "misuse of property," who would prevent "wrongdoing" lest greater wrongdoing follow:

[28] Seitz, *Pulitzer*, p. 320.

[29] Speech at Bangor, Sept. 13, 1902.

[30] Speech at Providence, Aug. 23, 1902.

I am far from being against property when I ask that the question of the trusts be taken up. I am acting in the most conservative sense in property's interest. . . . Because *when you can make it evident that all men, big and small alike, have to obey the law, you are putting the safeguard of law around all men.*[31]

Roosevelt's words were timely; they came at a moment when the bright noon of McKinleyan prosperity sensibly declined; though business activity remained high, the distinctly higher cost of living began now to offset the gains of the four boom years after 1898. Roosevelt's mounting popular strength, however, maintained a unified support for his party among its old followers in the Congressional elections of 1902. His popular strength waxed even greater as a result of the part he played in the great coal miners' strike of that autumn. Here too he came to grips with the most powerful capitalists of the age; and here too his chosen tactics and maxims were vividly illustrated in action.

4

By 1898 the anthracite coal fields of eastern Pennsylvania were completely dominated by the combination of five coal-carrying railroads, either controlled or financed by the Vanderbilt family and Morgan. Centralization and well-maintained prices brought handsome profits to the coal operators and the railways, but the distressed position of the miners reflected the remarkable unevenness of our prosperity. The average earnings of a miner were increased, but the higher costs of the boom years after 1897 brought a sharp decline in "real" wages, leaving him not much better off than in 1880. Thus a union movement, corresponding in force to the monopoly movement at the top, and spurred by desperation, swept the coal fields in 1897.

Under the inspired leadership of the young, self-educated miner John Mitchell, the United Mine Workers organized the anthracite field and conducted the successful strike of 1900, bring-

[31] Speech at Boston, Sept. 6, 1902; italics mine.

ing a 10 per cent increase of wages, which was forced—during a Presidential campaign—by secret pressure of frightened Republican party leaders. In 1902 the miners struck again, this time with the object especially of winning union recognition as well as wage improvement. But the large mine operators, which meant the coal railroads typified by President George F. Baer of the Reading, were adamant; this time they would brook no secret political pressure and were resolved to administer—as Henry Frick used to say—a memorable lesson to the union.

On May 12, 1902, some 140,000 miners ceased work and remained idle throughout the spring and summer. Mark Hanna's National Civic Federation, organized lately to conciliate labor and capital, and numbering distinguished industrialists in its membership, sought in vain to intervene. Appeals were directed to President Roosevelt to press arbitration upon both parties, but no easy solution offered itself to him. An incident of mid-July, when a friend of the miners inveigled out of President Baer, and made public, the famous "divine right" letter—to the effect that "the Christian men to whom God in His infinite wisdom has given the control of the property interests of this country," would alone care for the interests of the laboring men—both hardened the miners and rallied public opinion to their cause.

Ten thousand militia patrolled the Pennsylvania coal field by September, but the mines were shut down, and their owners called for more troops, and Federal troops, as a means of protecting the strikebreakers whom they tried to bring in. Yet the union men behaved with admirable discipline and committed no violence. Meanwhile coal grew scarce and dear, rising from $5 a ton to over $30. September brought the first hints of autumn cool, especially to New England, whose high Republican leaders trembled for the consequences of the strike.

Lodge, in great anxiety, wrote Roosevelt in September that the price of coal was something one could not "argue with." The schoolhouses were closing. "Political disaster" loomed ahead. He ended: "We have powerful friends in business. . . . Can nothing be done—*not in public,* of course, I know that is out of the question, but by pressing the operators?" [32]

The coal barons remained obdurate. But behind the coal barons there stood, as everyone knew, one omnipotent being whose command they would doubtless heed more readily than that of the King in Heaven, whom Mr. Baer professed to worship. When interviewed at the end of August, the great man declared, however, that he knew nothing of the strike; he would not interfere.[33]

Meanwhile, "little flames of violence began to flicker out here and there, where cars carrying coal were seized and looted as they trundled past the dwellings of people who had no fires." [34] Inconspicuous news reports such as that of "prominent citizens of Arcola, Ill., including officials, lawyers, ministers," seizing a coal train and looting the coal, figured in the newspapers. "The coal strike of 1902 revealed how quickly a people's reverence for law becomes exhausted, when the pinch comes." [35]

Though the mood of alarm spread, and heart-rending petitions reached the President from miners and consumers, he remained embarrassed for a time. He had no legal authority to take action, he recognized; he had behaved independently toward the "big monied men," and doubted whether he could ask them for favors or exert secret pressure upon them; lastly, the coal operators were the more obstinate, because they had yielded to their employees owing to political interference in 1900.

Nevertheless he consulted Elihu Root, and turned to Mark Hanna for aid. The latter proceeded directly to New York on September 29, and saw in secret both Mr. Morgan and John Mitchell, President of the United Mine Workers. The terms of a settlement appeared within reach. But Mr. Baer, on behalf of the mine owners, when called upon in Philadelphia, absolutely refused to agree to a settlement save one brought about by starv-

[32] Lodge, *Correspondence,* Vol. I, p. 528.
[33] Corey, *House of Morgan,* p. 213.
[34] Wister, *Roosevelt,* p. 195.
[35] L. J. Ghent, *Mass and Class,* p. 127.

ing out his employees.[36] Finally, at the urgent suggestion of Governor Murray Crane of Massachusetts, Roosevelt summoned representatives of both sides to a conference at Washington on October 3, 1902.

Roosevelt appealed to the adversaries in the name of patriotism. Mr. George F. Baer, however, supported by his colleagues, burst into round abuse of the President, both for not having sent Federal troops and for having failed to prosecute the miners' union under the Sherman Anti-Trust Act, as Cleveland had done in the railway strike of 1894. Baer referred to the mild and personable Mitchell as a "criminal." The more courteous head of the miners' union, however, expressed willingness to submit the case to an impartial commission appointed by the President, a proposal which the latter considered eminently fair.

The conference ended in a storm, but Roosevelt now used the newspapers with his habitual skill, to make the public understand the cause of the deadlock; and popular anger at the coal barons mounted swiftly.

He wrote to Hanna of his disappointment over the failure of the October 3 conference, not only "because of the great misery ensuing for the mass of our people," but because the obstinacy of the coal operators would serve to "double the burden on us who stand between them and socialistic action." (Always, among the Rooseveltians there was talk of saving the country from socialism.) He concluded with the warning words: "I must now think very seriously what the next move shall be. A coal famine in the winter is an ugly thing." [37]

The situation was actually full of explosive possibilities. Cabot Lodge, beside himself with anxiety, wrote on October 11, 1902, that "The Socialistic feeling is growing apace, and the demand that the government take the mines—one of the greatest disasters that could befall us." [38] Yet the days passed, and Morgan, whose word many felt could end the deadlocked strike, waited silently, as with iron nerves.

[36] Croly, *Hanna*, p. 398.

[37] *Ibid.*, pp. 399-400.

[38] Lodge, *Correspondence*, Vol. I, p. 539.

Roosevelt, however, armed with immense authority and power, showed a resourcefulness hitherto unsuspected of him. With a purposeful indiscretion he began to utter thoughts out loud concerning the possibility of calling out the army. He informed his Cabinet that he should not even ask their advice, but would "act just as if we were in a state of war"—that is, with emergency powers. He might take over the coal mines, and the army would "dispossess the operators and run the mines as a receiver. . . ."[39] Plans for such action were actually drawn up with General Schofield, the army chief; and with Senator Quay it was also arranged that at a given signal the Governor of Pennsylvania was to ask for Federal troops to halt disorders.

Elihu Root, the old Wall Street attorney in the Cabinet, was worried enough to volunteer his aid to the President. He relates, in a memorandum of the affair:

> . . . Roosevelt contemplated sending troops to take possession of the mines. I do not know how far he intended to go. Theodore was a bit of a bluffer occasionally, and at the same time he had the nerve to go on—to take a chance . . . and trust the country would back him up.[40]

On October 9, 1902, Root wrote to Morgan, outlining a plan for a commission of arbitration "appointed by the President or by you," and asking for an early appointment. Two days later he arrived in New York and clambered aboard *The Corsair*, Morgan's very appropriately named yacht which rode at anchor in the bay. His impressions of Theodore's "impulsiveness" and "nerve," traits not hitherto or lately encountered in our political leaders, must have been effectively conveyed to Morgan. With the latter's approval, Root wrote an agreement, which he brought back to Washington.

The coal operators were advised by Morgan to accept a commission of arbitration, whose membership excluded any representative of the miners' union, being composed of several representatives of the mine owners, a philanthropic minister (designated

[39] Roosevelt, *An Autobiography*, p. 475.

[40] Jessup, *op. cit.*, Vol. I, p. 275.

by name), and a university professor versed in sociology. Upon this basis, with only minor changes, the strike conference proceeded to a settlement on October 15, 1902.

There was a last-minute hitch over the composition of the arbitration commission. President John Mitchell, on behalf of the mine workers, insisted that unless a labor man were included the pretense of arbitration was absurd, and his men would not abide by the decision. Frantic long-distance telephoning took place in the early morning hours of October 15 between the White House and the Morgan office, where Mr. Baer sat, as obdurate as ever, declaring that only a "sociologist" and no laboring man would be acceptable among the arbitrators. Suddenly it dawned upon Roosevelt that the mine operators would rather endure civil war and revolution than have anyone described *as a laboring man* upon the board of arbitration. But if he were called something else—"an eminent sociologist"—they would relent. Roosevelt recalls that he was overwhelmed with a sense of mingled relief and amusement when he realized that while the operators would "submit to anarchy rather than have Tweedledum, yet if I would call it Tweedledee they would accept with rapture. . . ." And he adds with scorn: "It gave me an illuminating glimpse into one corner of the mighty brains of those 'captains of industry.' " He thereupon gave the hononary degree of Eminent Sociologist to one E. E. Clark, grand chief of the Order of Railway Conductors, and the commission was complete.

At the other end of the telephone in New York, Robert Bacon and George W. Perkins, the Morgan partners, "eagerly ratified" this face-saving formula, and after some trouble forced the mine owners' spokesman, Baer, to accept it.[41]

The verdict of the arbitration committee was a compromise, which the miners afterward felt heavily favored their employers. Only two of the miners' demands had been partially met: the eight-hour demand was compromised at nine hours; the call for a wage increase of 20 per cent was answered with 10 per cent. The

[41] *T. R. Papers,* Roosevelt to H. C. Lodge, Oct. 17, 1902.

other demands were ignored by the arbitration board. Most important of all, union recognition, the real basis of the strike, the real lever of future collective bargaining, was rejected. Thus the road was left open for renewal of the struggle. The miners were none too happy with the outcome of their drawn combat; several times the vote of their delegates had been necessary to stiffen John Mitchell's attitude and prevent him from yielding to a settlement that would have been a complete victory for the operators. Whatever was won, was won not because of Roosevelt's "sympathy" but because of the determined and disciplined spirit of the mine workers.

However, they had gone promptly back to work, as the arbitration commission began its deliberations; coal moved again, and the whole country heaved a sigh of relief and applauded the President. The lion's share of the victory went to him for having forced a settlement of some kind, with bold hands. He could claim that he had defended the legitimate rights of labor, yet had been just to both sides.

Even the extremely conservative New York *Tribune* applauded the "generous and patriotic act of the President" in setting the mines in operation again, filling the empty coal bins as late autumn approached, and extricating the country from a menacing disaster. Was it "a sweeping victory for the miners" or "a bomb in labor circles"? None knew at the time. And the *Tribune* observed sagely that the "public," at any rate, was the gainer.[42] Moreover, the results of the November elections a few weeks later, strongly favoring the Republican party, attested the astonishing, growing popularity of the new leadership.

[42] The New York *Tribune*, Mar. 22, 1903.

V. TOWARD LEADERSHIP: "ROOSEVELTIANA"

THE LUSTY Roosevelt almost from the very outset, as we have seen, gave every sign of profiting from, fostering, and extending the renascence of political life that came to America in the first decade of the twentieth century. By his capacity and will, by his example, he was to carry on a notable revival of positive political leadership that was the historic feature of an enlightened, critical era. In a sense, he himself was carried along by a powerful current; but he was a vigorous oarsman, who enjoyed the race and steered boldly through the dangerous rapids as long as he could.

"I did not usurp power," he wrote in afterthought, "but I did greatly broaden the use of executive power." To the English historian, George O. Trevelyan, with whom he held a long, friendly, and rich correspondence, he said also:

> I have a definite philosophy about the presidency. I think it should be a very powerful office, and I think the President should be a very strong man who uses without hesitation every power that the position yields; because of this very fact, I believe he should be sharply watched by the people, held to a strict accountability to them, and that he should not keep the office too long.

The contrasts offered by this concept of executive leadership and power as against the usages of the immediate, pre-Rooseveltian past, are important. Political action ceases to be merely *negative*, must cease to act only to preserve the gains and privileges won by the ruling groups after the Civil War—the essential counting-house politics of the "Standpatters." It emerges from the closed office of the powerful desk politician and functions more largely than before in the open forum of public opinion. It operates less with Presidents and Senators and Governors acting as the puppets of more powerful managers behind the scenes. Instead, a more direct responsiveness to the popular will, to the sentiment of the masses, is sought. These changes were, to be sure, "relatively" rather than "absolutely" true. Moreover, the Rooseveltian pattern of leadership and power could not have been achieved if the historical and social currents of the age had not so strongly favored the spirit of change.

The evidences of political revival were to be seen on all sides and in many forms. The very atmosphere of the capital was altered. Around the attractive, many-sided personality of the President, a band of loyal followers and lieutenants gathered who were of a type not seen so frequently here in many moons. For while Roosevelt made the concessions of a *Realpolitiker* to the leaders of machines, he also threw open, more largely than before, a career to talent in the national government. In response to his many calls for educated men, for college men to enter public life, young enthusiasts inspired by a new ideal of public service and reform came to his banner. They occupied chiefly minor offices, since the high Cabinet posts were held by the men who had surrounded McKinley. They stirred things up in the dusty old government bureaus. In the Interior Department, an ancient stronghold of the corrupt, where the program of land and forest conservation began to be pushed earnestly toward 1902, the younger, newer men performed feats of patriotic devotion sometimes at the risk of life and health, sometimes at the cost of serious collisions with the men of the old administrative corps and their allies outside.

Here was one of the best sides of the Roosevelt administration, typified by the activities of Gifford Pinchot, the forester, who was himself a young man of education and fortune, actually appointed to his minor office by McKinley in 1897, but given full play and high authority under Roosevelt. James R. Garfield, son of the President who had been killed by a disappointed office-seeker, was another of the devoted young men of education and good family who attached themselves to Roosevelt. He was, naturally, an ardent civil-service reformer. Appointed at first head of the new Bureau of Corporations, established by a law of 1903, he was soon promoted to the office of Secretary of the Interior. At Capitol Hill, Albert Beveridge, brilliant and literary young Senator from Indiana, often described at the time as "engaging, vital, charming"—terms that could easily be used to characterize many of the Rooseveltians—became a devoted, admiring lieutenant of the President, often entrusted with the introduction and expounding of his characteristic legislative measures.

The circle of younger men who surrounded, advised, and took orders from Roosevelt came to be known as the "Tennis Cabinet," being thus differentiated from the Cabinet officers, who were too old and conservative to play at strenuous games in the President's leisure hours. Of the "Tennis Cabinet" and of the corps of younger men who were appointed to fill many offices under this administration, James Bryce, then serving as Ambassador at Washington, said that he had "never in any country seen a more eager, high-minded and efficient set of public servants, men more useful to their country than the men then doing the work of the American Government. . . ."[1] Some of them, now grown old, recall with tears of emotion the stirring days of their service under the beloved "T. R."[2]

"For that once in our history, we had an American salon," wrote a friend of Roosevelt's, nostalgically.[3] Theodore Roosevelt

[1] Rhodes, *op. cit.*, p. 398.

[2] "T. R. told us that we of the 'Tennis Cabinet' were much closer to him than his official cabinet. So he wrote and said to Jim Garfield and myself. . . ." (Hon. Gifford Pinchot to author, Dec. 8, 1938.) The "brain trust" of President Franklin Roosevelt developed directly out of the "Tennis Cabinet" of a generation ago.

[3] Wister, *op. cit.*, p. 125.

had long cherished a more cultured ideal of social life than his predecessors in politics.

To the Rooseveltian circle of men of society who were influential in politics and men of politics who were at home in good society, there was now added the prestige and authority of the White House center. The musty old mansion of tragic memories and ugly furniture was vigorously redecorated by the new President and his wife, at the start of their reign, so that it shone in all its parts. Brilliant seasons of fine dinners and spirited conversations, unlike anything since the days of Jefferson and Dolly Madison, succeeded each other until the social leadership of Washington seemed to rival that of New York and Newport.

Formality, pomposity and dullness, which had ruled at the state occasions of an uncouth Cleveland or a colorless McKinley, now departed. And save for those professional occasions when bosses and financial magnates must be invited, the *dramatis personae* also were changed. Roosevelt said:

> I am simply unable to make myself take the attitude of respect toward the very wealthy men which such an enormous multitude of people evidently really feel. I am delighted to show any courtesy to Pierpont Morgan or Andrew Carnegie or James J. Hill, but as for regarding any one of them, as for instance, I regard Professor Bury, or Peary, the Arctic explorer, or Rhodes, the historian—why, I could not force myself to do it, even if I wanted to, which I don't.

Theodore Roosevelt's many-sided cultural interests were well reflected by the presence in the Roosevelt salon of politicians who were also men of letters and historians, such as John Hay, Henry Cabot Lodge, and Beveridge; or the jurist, Oliver Wendell Holmes, whom he elevated to the Supreme Court bench; the French diplomat, who was a distinguished literary critic, Jules Jusserand; the artists LaFarge, John Sargent and Saint-Gaudens. Then, to mingle with these, he introduced the representatives of pioneering, exploring, and soldierly activities, of "the heroic virtues." He believed that "a high artistic and literary development is compatible with notable leadership in arms and statecraft." [4] Cowboys and former desperadoes and big-game hunters and pugilists might make their bow at the White House. But these invitations were issued with an eye to good fun and publicity; and they should not divert us from the significant point that Roosevelt in his social life exemplified a consistently aristocratic concept of culture and the good life; that he could "wear tails when the occasion called and be at home in them," [5] that he sought to gather about him an assembly of the "élite" whose aspirations were turned beyond the crude objectives of the Gilded Age.

None recognized better than himself, Roosevelt wrote in 1904 to a distinguished European poet, that ". . . we of the West, we of the eager, restless, wealth-seeking nation," after having reached "a certain, not very high level of material well-being," must turn to "the things that really count," the things of the spirit. "Factories and railways are good up to a certain point, but courage and endurance . . . love of home and country . . . love of beauty in man's work and in nature, love and emulation of daring and lofty endeavor, the homely work-a-day virtues and the heroic virtues—these are better still, and if they are lacking, no piled-up riches, no roaring, clanging industrialism, no feverish many-sided activities shall avail either the individual or the nation." [6]

These strictures upon wealth-getting and material comfort, these reflections upon arms and glory and culture, that come and go in Roosevelt's mind during his crowded years of power, all seem more or less consciously part of his now crystallized outlook on life. They give point to his relations with organized labor, his skirmishes with powerful financiers, his shifting tactics toward professional politicians, his bold foreign enterprises, and his constant pursuit of an ever-extending power.[7]

[4] Speech of Apr. 23, 1910, at the Sorbonne.

[5] Wister, *op. cit.*, p. 125.

[6] *T. R. Papers*, to Frédéric Mistral, Dec. 15, 1904.

[7] I have remarked that Theodore Roosevelt's values were in part "bureaucratic," in part "aristocratic." When in 1910 he made his remarkable European tour, as the guest of monarchs and nobles, he wrote to Trevelyan of his own surprise at the sympathy he had been shown by members of the Austrian Em-

2

The problem of power Roosevelt attacked with an intuitive and yet thoroughgoing art, by which future statesmen were to guide themselves more or less well. He saw that the throne of the President was, in effect, a most perilous seat, surrounded by predatory party bosses who might, at will, cut him off from the "big battalions" of party workers; by the managers of Congress who jealously circumscribed his legislative influence; by the lobbyists and lawyers of the great corporations, who furnished the "sinews of war" for party campaigns.

Methodically he courted the popularity of the crowd; this in itself was something of a departure, since no President in forty years had been personally popular with the masses, with the possible exception of General Grant. The second step was the effort to gain control himself of the party machinery and keep it in his own hands. The third step, following naturally, was that of raising war chests, duplicating the work of men like Mark Hanna.

From the White House, through extremely frequent press interviews as well as many speech-making forays, Roosevelt recommended himself to the "plain people" in many ways. For the first time the gentlemen of the press were given a permanent room in the White House. They responded by picturing the new incumbent as a human being, democratically informal and approachable to hundreds of people who visited him every day. He was shown dictating innumerable messages to Congress and to the nation, as

peror's court at Vienna. These feudal personages were impressed because, while he had been president of a republic, he (in his own words) "at the same time had done the kind of thing in war and sport which it would have gratified their ambitions to do . . . ; and then to my intense amusement, I found that they were in cordial sympathy with me because I had attacked the big financial interests, and because I frankly looked down on mere moneyed men, the people of enormous wealth who had nothing but their wealth behind them, and whose power was simply the power of the 'money touch.' " The Austrian nobles felt that Roosevelt had shown himself "aristocratic" in putting the vulgar men of "mere money bags" in their place. (T. R. to G. O. Trevelyan, Oct. 1, 1911, *T. R. Papers.*)

he strode up and down the White House rooms. He was heard shouting with bluff honesty to one whispering Senator: "We have no secrets here!" And to another, that his colleague who had just left the room was a crook. He appeared pre-eminent as a father and husband, a horseman, a wood-chopper, and above all as a hunter. On vacations he hunted the grizzly bear in full view of the national press. Thus he appeared as fearless before physical danger as he was unflinching in his pursuit of even-handed justice. In cartoon or popular song, the dynamic "T. R." appealed as effectively to the mass psychology of the huge middle class as modern dictators have done with the radio broadcast and pageantry. Truly he was the Great White Chief of all the American tribe.

The program that he began to call "my policies" or the "Square Deal" aimed to bring about a synthesis or combination of groups and classes, while preventing them from combining against him. He actually never made a frontal attack upon the whole system of privilege and secret control underlying the political government. Meanwhile his simultaneous onslaughts upon both "anarchists," or "unruly labor leaders," and the "criminal rich" appealed to the great middle class, as if bringing relief to the vague sense of insecurity that often haunted it.

It was Roosevelt's lifelong belief, based, as he told James Ford Rhodes, on his studies of history, that the downfall of the Grecian, Roman, and Italian republics was caused by the fact that when the rich got the power they exploited the poor, and when the poor got the power they plundered the rich. He was to stand midway between the two and prevent excess.[8]

In expounding a middle-road, middle-class program and seeking to make this effective, it was inevitable that Roosevelt should lean strongly upon the moral notes. Lacking the conviction of urgent economic necessity that drove on a Morgan in his trust-building career, feeling nothing of the inevitable class conflict that seemed to inspire a "Big Bill" Haywood, the Red labor leader of the West, he preached with an evangelical fervor the puritan pre-

[8] Rhodes, *op. cit.*, p. 395.

cepts he had long ago learned of duty, morality, honor, and "righteousness."

His more conservative and cynical Cabinet members noticed this trait, and sometimes after an especially fervent sermon twitted him freely. John Hay observed in his diary: "Knox says that the question of what is to become of Roosevelt after 1908 is easily answered. He should be made a bishop." Roosevelt himself said of his public utterances that "he knew there was not much in them except a certain sincerity and kind of commonplace morality which put him *en rapport* with the people. . . ."[9]

The paramount problem in America, Roosevelt felt, was to bring about a kind of "moral awakening," just as other mass leaders, in nations with different historical traditions, devoted themselves by a parallel effort to bring about a military "awakening." He too denied the economic man. Out of his preoccupation with the moral man came the characteristic Rooseveltian demand that the monopolistic corporation should turn itself into the "good" or "reasonable" trust. Because of the same preoccupations, he could ignore for a long time the movement for the eight-hour day and for the elimination of child labor.

The struggle for national unity against both "the turbulent or extreme labor people" and the "malefactors of great wealth" was presented as no affair of pale compromise, but was dramatized with all Roosevelt's natural vehemence of expression. Roosevelt stood as a man committed to righteousness, but he also stood forth as one of those who would be ever ready to "maintain right by force," to whom force was "one of the talents committed to nations by God. . . ." These were the words of his friend, Admiral Mahan.[10]

Roosevelt's readiness for violence of various kinds was seen late in 1903, when a bloodless revolt burst forth mysteriously in Panama, against the government of Colombia. Yankee men-of-war were on hand and the right of way for the Panama Canal overnight passed into the hands of the United States. "I took

[9] Hay, *Diaries*, Vol. V, Jun. 5, 1904; Jun. 21, 1904.

[10] "The Moral Aspects of War," *North American Review*, Oct., 1899.

the Isthmus . . ." Roosevelt would say, indiscreetly, some years later. His propensity to violence was supported by supreme conviction of his own rightness. It was a combination, a "way of getting things done" that impressed the crowds, and showed itself in domestic political battle as well as in the use of our armed forces overseas.

In January, 1903, an act establishing a Bureau of Corporations to engage in fact-finding in the field of the trusts was vigorously urged upon Congress by Roosevelt, but met with resistance from certain politicians who acted at the order of the Standard Oil executive, John D. Archbold. In a dramatic press conference, the President attacked those who blocked his bill. Then after exacting the oath of the reporters that they would keep secret the source of their information, he confided to them, for publication, that "Rockefeller" by telegrams to Congress opposed the Bureau of Corporations law. This proved later to be only approximately true. But in using Rockefeller's name, Roosevelt "demonstrated again his sound grasp of public psychology. . . . Rockefeller personified the evil of the trusts."[11] "Mr. Rockefeller, who had nothing directly to do with the case, declared himself shocked at the President's false revelations."[12]

A few weeks later he dramatized also his chronic clashes with organized labor. On May 18, 1903, a certain William A. Miller, employee in the Government Printing Office, was dismissed by his superior on the ground, as he claimed, that he had been expelled from his labor union. Roosevelt had the case investigated and ordered Miller's reinstatement. He had no objection to unions, he said, but no union rules could be permitted "to override the laws of the United States, which it is my sworn duty to enforce." The men of the American Federation of Labor met and passed resolutions of censure of the President's "open shop" principles. To Samuel Gompers, President of the A. F. of L., who came to protest in person, Roosevelt said, brandishing his fist: he must

[11] Pringle, *op. cit.*, p. 342.
[12] L. W. Busbey, *Uncle Joe Cannon*, p. 216.

govern his actions "by the laws of the land . . . without regard to creed, color, birthplace or social condition. . . ." He would no more recognize the fact that a man "does or does not belong to a union" than he would recognize before the law that he was a Catholic, a Protestant, or a Jew.[13] The trade-union men protested anew in hostile resolutions. But Roosevelt declared publicly that he would adhere to his "open shop" principles, come what may. He thought that "the labor unions and the trust magnates may perhaps unite against me," yet he would win through.[14]

A similar collision occurred May 10, 1905. Roosevelt, speaking in Chicago at a time when a large-scale, spirited strike of the teamsters' union was in progress, was met with a petition of the strikers' committee urging him not to permit Federal interference in their dispute. He replied with the broadest hints that at the first need, he would move with Federal forces for "the preservation of law and order, the suppression of violence by mobs or individuals."

Later that evening, speaking before a business men's club, he repeated these hints, saying that if organizations of laborers as well as capitalists were guilty of wrongdoing, they would be held to strict accountability. "The greatest and most dangerous rock in the course of any republic," he said, "is the rock of class hatred." Addressing directly the Mayor of Chicago, who was among those present, he pledged that the armed forces of the nation would stand behind the city and the state if ever the need arose.[15]

To Cabot Lodge, who complimented him fulsomely after reading a report of the affair in the press, Roosevelt replied that he had "used language so simple" to the strikers "that they could not misunderstand it. . . . So if the rioting in Chicago gets beyond the control of the State and the City, they know well that the regulars will come." [16]

Such incidents went far to pacify the middle class and large

[13] Bishop, *op. cit.*, Vol. I, p. 251.

[14] *Ibid.*

[15] Roosevelt, *Addresses*, Vol. IV, pp. 367-374, 374-376.

[16] Lodge, *Correspondence*, Vol. II, p. 121.

groups among the capitalists made uneasy by Roosevelt's unconventional proceedings under other heads. On the eve of the election of 1904, conservative Republican leaders such as Senator O. H. Platt of Connecticut were able to assure anxious capitalists and large manufacturers that Roosevelt was "sound"; the danger of the enactment of a national eight-hour law, inspired by the Roosevelt administration, was negligible. On November 1, 1904, Secretary of the Navy Metcalf wrote to Senator O. H. Platt: "No manufacturer need fear that the Department has sided, or is siding, with either those who advocate or those who oppose the measure."[17]

Toward the farmers as a class the Roosevelt administration moved with extreme care to avoid offense and disarm the periodic insurgence of the West. Certain favors were granted them, even by Aldrich's group in the Senate, as in the case of the Cuban Reciprocity Bill of 1903, which was adjusted in a manner satisfactory to beet-sugar growers. Anti-railroad agitation was partially appeased by the Elkins Act of 1903, which forbade the granting of rebates to shippers; though this, written by the railroads' friends in the Senate, was soon seen to give but slight relief from the burden of heavy freight charges.

In March, 1903, Governor Albert Cummins, the popular, plain-spoken Iowa lawyer, arrived at the White House to urge that Roosevelt advocate the repeal of certain tariff duties "as a means of opposing the trusts." A large faction among the farmers was now reported as eager either for tariff reduction or stern legislation to control trusts and railroads and the burdensome charges they seemed to impose. But here Roosevelt proceeded most cautiously. With a view to gathering popular strength in the West, he made ready for a long speaking tour through the farm belt. Yet before departing, early in April, he submitted his prepared speeches on the tariff and the trusts to Aldrich for advice and

[17] Stephenson, *op. cit.*, appendix, p. 460.

approval. "I want to be sure to get what I say on these two subjects along lines upon which all of us can agree." [18]

To Cabot Lodge he reported that the "free trade" agitation in the West troubled his mind. He was not certain of what he could get the party to do in this direction. The year before a Presidential contest would be "a most unwise one in which to enter upon a general upsetting of the tariff. . . ." The tariff, in any case, was "a mere matter of expediency," he thought. In other words, not a moral question.[19]

Roosevelt continued both to fear the temper of the Western agrarians and to lament the possible necessity for appeasing them by tariff reductions. Even a year later John Hay found him still "full of doubt and perplexity" as to tariff revision. Hay noted in his diary:

> He is getting very cross with his "fool friends" who urge him to "defy Congress and the people will rally to his support." He said he had sometimes succeeded in fighting the machine, but that was because he himself had chosen the occasion and calculated the chances.[20]

On his "swing" through the West in 1903, Roosevelt therefore confined himself to a castigation of "wicked" trusts and labor extremists. He showed himself to the farmers from the rear platform of his special train as one who, though an Easterner, had lived among them in the West for years, and knew their life, their world. Though wanting the organ voice of a Bryan, Roosevelt touched new heights nowadays as a dynamic speaker, preaching his middle-road sermons with a passion that sometimes seemed to strangle the words in his throat.

This long colorful tour of April and May, 1903, proceeded as far as the Pacific Northwest, and was interrupted by a famous bear-hunt in Colorado, and other picturesque, improvised episodes which Roosevelt now habitually indulged in. The people were intrigued with the Rough Rider and thronged about his train

[18] Roosevelt to Aldrich, Mar. 16, 1903; Stephenson, *op. cit.*, p. 219.
[19] Lodge, *Correspondence*, Apr. 22, 1903, Vol. II, p. 6.
[20] Hay, *Diaries*, Vol. V, Dec. 11, 1904.

everywhere to salute him, to his high satisfaction. Yet, momently, doubts assailed him and made him tremble for the future.

The "Hurrahs" were pleasant enough, he told a companion. The people were cheering the President of the United States. But the people forgot quickly; while the corporations and the great party bosses forgot nothing and forgave nothing. What if he should never even be *elected* to the office he now held? "*They* don't want it . . . Hanna and that crowd. . . . They've finished me. . . . I have no machine, no faction, no money. All this [waving his hand to indicate the crowd they had just left] has no significance. You see I cannot hope to be renominated without the support of my own State." The resistance to his nomination, in New York as elsewhere, Roosevelt ascribed to the hidden thrusts of Mark Hanna.[21] Thus it was no accident that, a short time later, on reaching the Pacific Coast, Roosevelt determined suddenly to bring into the open the secret struggle with the national party boss.

3

For two years the astute Mark Hanna had been watching Roosevelt's course, perhaps with inward misgivings, yet making no sign of overt opposition. The two men observed their bargain with each other, though at arm's length. Hanna had been "consulted" frequently; and he had helped the President in settling the coal miners' strike. But when various Republican state conventions at the end of 1902 passed complimentary resolutions recommending Mr. Roosevelt's nomination as the party's candidate for President at the next election, Hanna remained silent. In his very own province of Ohio, where a State Republican convention was to gather in early June, 1903, a plan was on foot to bring up a resolution favoring Roosevelt for 1904. It was directed by the faction led by Senator Joseph B. Foraker, Hanna's old rival, as a means of embarrassing Hanna. The latter, in a newspaper interview, was now forced to oppose the resolution for Roosevelt as be-

[21] McCaleb, *Roosevelt*, pp. 198-200.

ing premature, and unjust to other possible candidates, among whom he declared he was not numbered. Controversy flared up in Ohio, and Hanna telegraphed to Roosevelt at Seattle, on May 25, 1903, in apologetic terms, stating that he had nothing to do with raising the issue of the Roosevelt endorsement. "When you know all the facts," he ended, "I am sure you will approve my course."[22]

Roosevelt, who was busy raising up Western popular support for his aspirations, chose this moment to precipitate a public controversy with Hanna. He replied by telegraph, the same day, and made his dispatch public through the Associated Press.

> Your telegram received. I have not asked any man for his support. I have had nothing whatever to do with raising this issue. Inasmuch as it has been raised, of course, those who favor my administration and my nomination will favor endorsing both, and those who do not will oppose.

Roosevelt now openly announced his own candidacy and forced Hanna into a position where he must oppose him in the open or endorse him. In making public his reply he trickily suppressed the fact that it was a reply to a telegram from Hanna, couched in diplomatic and peaceable terms. To his Western audience, which had little sympathy with the Eastern rulers of the Republican party, he appeared to have hurled defiance at Mark Hanna.[23] To Lodge, Roosevelt indicated the little deception he practiced.

At Spokane, the next day, he delivered the hottest speech of the tour; jutting out his jaw and smiting one fist upon the other, he promised the equivalent of "a knockdown and drag-out fight with Hanna and the whole Wall Street crowd. . . ."

Facing the predicament of open party discord, outmaneuvered both by his Ohio rival Foraker and by Roosevelt, Mark Hanna beat a hasty retreat, wiring Roosevelt the next day that he would not oppose endorsement of him by the Ohio party convention.

The initial victory over Hanna, gained by a sudden thrust, and

[22] Croly, *Hanna*, p. 425.

[23] Lodge, *Correspondence*, Vol. II, pp. 18-20.

recorded in the national press, was an important step in breaking down Hanna's dominance of the party organization. Under the circumstances, also, it presented Roosevelt in a most appealing light to the Western citizens as the open adversary of the boss who represented the great "privileged interests." Thus his trip was concluded with triumphal ovations in the cities of the West.

Within little more than a year of taking his unexpected office the new President had shown his mettle as a political strategist with a flair for the attack. Thereafter his efforts to gain a real ascendancy over the party organization were pushed home steadily by discreet wielding of the patronage power. When, late in 1901, he discovered that fifteen officials of the Post Office Department, some of them reputable Republican leaders in their localities, were guilty of corrupt practice, he had them quietly removed. However, the replacements were made with an eye to creating a body of his own supporters.

The naming of the old spoilsman James S. Clarkson, whom Roosevelt had strongly denounced in his Civil Service Commission days under President Harrison, as surveyor for the port of New York, suggested an accommodation of his conscience with earlier ideals. From his post in New York the old spoilsman was reported to be occupied chiefly in "lining up" Southern Republican delegates for the approaching national convention. The dubious appointment (which was later reversed) of a certain W. M. Byrne as United States Attorney for Delaware, also caused some soul-searching among Roosevelt's admirers. The approval of a bill which increased Civil War veterans' pensions by some $5,000,000 per year—though existing pensions had been fairly generous—like the invitation to Dr. Booker T. Washington to the White House for luncheon, so pleasing to colored Republicans, was an instance of rather transparent domestic diplomacy. Thus he built steadily his own faction, his "machine."

While maintaining faithfully his "gentleman's agreement" with Aldrich and Cannon regarding economic legislation, he contended with Hanna in matters of party organization. In the affair of the

Ohio endorsement for his candidacy, he had shown increasing favor to Foraker, Hanna's enemy, who was further armed in the way of Federal appointments. The Roosevelt Papers show also that enormous patronage was dispensed to Senator Quay of Pennsylvania, perhaps even more frequently than to Hanna in earlier days. With Lodge, the dominant New England boss, and his colleague Governor Murray Crane, close business relations were constantly maintained, while in New York, where the aged Tom Platt was finally ousted by his ambitious lieutenants, Roosevelt cemented a practical alliance with the successor boss, Benjamin Odell. By all these dreary expedients Roosevelt gradually thrust himself into the real, rather than the titular, leadership of his party.

"Theodore, do not think anything about a second term," Mark Hanna had said to Roosevelt authoritatively after the death of McKinley. But in 1904, Hanna was sixty-six and in declining health.

Outwardly there was a reconciliation between the two men. Roosevelt paid Hanna the compliment of calling him generous and straightforward. "No one but a really big man—a man above all petty considerations—could have treated me as you have done during the year and a half since President McKinley's death."[24] However, Roosevelt showed determination to take care of his interests himself, in his own way.

In his later years, Hanna was treated more leniently by the national press, which had long pilloried him as an ogre covered with dollar marks. His spirit too had mellowed. By May, 1903, he could say to the Ohio Republican convention: "I believe in organized labor and I believe in organized capital—as an auxiliary." He too criticized capital for its selfish tendency to the "appropriation of the larger share," and in Chautauqua addresses frequently advocated the practice of the Golden Rule.[25]

Whether Hanna himself actually intended to run for President is one of the "problems" for scholars in our recent history. He denied repeatedly and publicly such intentions. He denied them to

[24] *T. R. Papers,* T. R. to Hanna, May 29, 1903.

[25] Croly, *Hanna,* pp. 407-409.

Roosevelt, sometimes in the form of jests. Yet he did not entirely close the door. The financiers of New York and Chicago leaned upon him still. Quietly they pushed preparations to launch his candidacy. They kept him informed of the general suspicion and uneasiness about the Rough Rider in Union League Club circles. Though Hanna too had moments in 1903 and 1904 when he was black with fury at Roosevelt, he bided his time, for his own reasons.

In conservative clubs and counting-houses brilliant intrigues may have been laid to nominate a less "impulsive," less unpredictable candidate for the Republicans in 1904. But Mark Hanna knew that this was now impossible, save at the cost of deadly party strife; even more, at the cost of business confidence. His theory of the public interest, nevertheless, held that the election of Roosevelt by a great popular majority was not desirable. He remained aloof and inscrutable because "he wanted to make the President feel and respect his power." [26]

Reports of constant intrigues by political "sappers and miners" in January, 1904, left the atmosphere of the White House nervously irritable. At a none too secret meeting in the Waldorf-Astoria Hotel, ten railroad presidents offered large subscriptions to the Republican chest "in case Mr. Hanna is the candidate." Their message to him was: "Stop making presidents and become one yourself." [27] News of Hanna's victorious campaign for re-election to the Senate in November, 1903, in spite of the furious onslaughts of Tom L. Johnson, was alarming also; once more he had held Ohio, and named his own Governor and Legislature. But not long after, on his return to Washington in January, 1904, he fell desperately ill.

A fierce unrepentant old man, in an agony of pain, lay dying. He looked back at his own past, so typical of his age: the large wealth he had begotten, the tremendous power he had suddenly seized and wielded so boldly, the far-flung, national, political battles in which he had triumphed. All this power was crumbling

[26] Croly, *Hanna*, p. 443.
[27] *The Nation*, Jan. 21, 1904.

away; while the young leader, medium of the strange new times, magnanimously called to inquire after him and left his card. The gesture touched the inscrutable old magnate's heart, and he responded with a last word of gratitude scrawled in his own hand.

On February 15, 1904, the threat of Mark Hanna's veto power in Republican party affairs passed away. Matt Quay of Pennsylvania had also died, alone and unwept, as the old sinner had wished to die. Boss Tom Platt of New York was retired and in his dotage; in Iowa, Allison was soon to make way for his more progressive colleague Senator Jonathan Dolliver and Albert Cummins; in Wisconsin, Spooner, another famous Republican veteran, passed out of the picture and was replaced by La Follette. Truly the old order was changing in 1904 as Theodore Roosevelt reached forward confidently to grasp the helm of the mighty party organization, President and party boss in one.

4

But who would find money, now that the great Receiver-General of the Republicans was dead?

To make a Rough Riders' legion of office-holders, Grand Army veterans and county or precinct leaders counted for much. But what was needed in order to operate the party Steam Roller in 1904 was money, money above all, and more money. Six months before the party convention Roosevelt, tacking sharply, set forth on his hunt for campaign funds, which he continued through the greater part of 1904 with his superabundant energy.

In February, 1903, Roosevelt promoted his Private Secretary, George B. Cortelyou (who had performed the same confidential function under McKinley), to the office of Secretary of the new Department of Commerce. Cortelyou was the close-mouthed type of political liaison agent; much like President Cleveland's Secretary, Daniel Lamont, he knew his way among the narrow lanes of downtown New York, where the national offices of railroads, insurance companies, and industrial concerns congregated so thickly. To Cortelyou was assigned the problem of raising a war fund.

To strengthen Cortelyou's hand, it was also the President's task to conciliate, as much as possible, the great financial magnates who traditionally supported the Republican party with their donations. Roosevelt's message to Congress in December, 1903, was extremely moderate in tone; it dwelt upon the splendid era of prosperity being enjoyed; it pointed with pride to the "sane and conservative" lines along which legislation was being enacted under his administration; and it gave notice that the malcontents of labor would be held as strictly to account as predatory wealth. On other delicate questions such as tariff and currency, the President was fairly vague. Thus the *Wall Street Journal*, on December 8, 1903, could exclaim that Mr. Roosevelt's policy "neither in intention or fact, is directed against wealth. We admire the courage of the President."

The President had submitted that message, before its completion, to Mr. James Stillman, head of the great National City Bank and a leader of the Rockefeller group, for criticisms and suggestions. At the same season he had made friendly overtures to Henry C. Frick, then a director of the United States Steel Corporation, as well as to J. P. Morgan himself, whom he invited for a consultation at the White House.[28] Yet those great silent men, Stillman, Morgan, and Frick, appeared at first allergic to Rooseveltian charm. The President was filled with anxiety, which he poured out to his close friends, Elihu Root, Hay, Taft, and Lodge. "The criminal rich and the fool rich will do all they can to beat me." The "gentlefolk," he told Owen Wister also, the people he met at the homes of friends or at his clubs, or had known at Harvard, were most bitter in their opposition to him.

From Boston, however, Lodge sent the cheering report that he found friendliness rather than hostility for his friend expressed in State Street, and "even in Wall Street there is a large body of men

[28] *T. R. Papers*, T. R. to J. Stillman, Aug. 29, 1903; T. R. to H. C. Frick, Jun. 9, 1903.

who are with you. . . ." Lodge would continue to do "missionary work" among the Boston bankers, and the President, he hoped, would aid him by continuing as before to show himself firm toward labor-unionists as in the Printing Office case.[29]

The view of Lodge is accurate. High financial quarters were always divided in their attitude toward T. R. rather than consistently hostile. Those who lost money in the market, owing to governmental action against the railroad "merger," were ready to blame him for their losses. Moreover his values, at once bureaucratic, military, and aristocratic, were different from those of most of the giants of Wall Street, who by dint of their "enlightened selfishness" daily contributed to the upbuilding of the nation. Yet there were not a few among the leading capitalists of the nation who felt that Roosevelt as President was much preferable to a Mark Hanna from the point of view of their own real interests; they bore his sermonizing cheerfully, for the sake of the greater real security he brought; they served, if need be, as "whipping boys" for the sake of his superb political acumen and uncanny control of the voting population. Such sophistication, a little rare in America, was long known to the older European capitalist societies, where men of money privately subsidized Radical or Social-Democratic statesmen, while submitting to being pilloried by them in public.

Among those who accepted Roosevelt's assertions that he acted in the long run "conservatively in property's interest," were George W. Perkins, partner of Morgan and Company, director of the U. S. Steel Corporation; and Joseph Medill McCormick, heir to part of the International Harvester Company fortune. Perkins, a most enthusiastic devotee of the Rough Rider, shared Elihu Root's conviction that by his picturesque methods he took the wind out of the sails of Bryan and other radicals, yet left Congress and the nation's purse-strings in safe hands. The vivacious Root would say: "Roosevelt's bark was always worse than his bite." It was Secretary Root, the old corporation lawyer, whom Roosevelt sent to New York to do missionary work among the men of the Union League Club, his old clients and clubmates.

[29] Lodge, *Correspondence*, Vol. II, pp. 19, 24, 57; Wister, *op. cit.*, p. 188.

Here, in a speech of February 3, 1904, replying to those who held that Roosevelt was "unsafe," Root said:

> But I say to you that he has been *the greatest conservative force for the protection of property and our institutions.* . . . There is a *better way* to protect property, to *protect capital,* to protect enterprise, than by buying legislatures. There is a better way to deal with labor, and to keep it from rising into the tumult of the unregulated and resistless mob than by starving it or by corrupting its leaders. . . . That way is, that capital shall be fair . . . fair to the consumer, fair to the laborer, fair to the investor; that it shall concede that the laws shall be executed. . . . Never forget that the men who labor cast the votes, set up and pull down governments, and that our government is possible, the continued opportunity for enterprise, for the enjoyment of wealth, for individual liberty, is possible, only so long as the men who labor with their hands believe in American liberty and American laws.[30]

Elihu Root, one of the most intelligent conservatives of his epoch, in these sentences expressed as happily as his chief could have wished the Rooseveltian ideology of "the better way . . . to protect capital." The President testified to this by his many profuse expressions of gratitude to Root. Thus by a form of educational or "missionary" work, the great patrons of the Republican party were induced to come forward and make their donations to the campaign chest.

How powerful was Roosevelt's hold upon the party organization in 1904 was shown by the fact that his handy man, George B. Cortelyou, who had held only a minor post up to recently, was named national chairman of the party, in place of the late Mark Hanna. At the convention in June, Roosevelt's nomination took place without let or hindrance. Even the usual feigned excitement among the delegates was lacking. "The cheering was mechanical," William Allen White observed. The ceremony of nominating Theodore Roosevelt formally was carried off by a New York politician, former Governor Frank S. Black (who privately detested the candidate), with "an electric fountain of rhetorical icicles."

[30] Root, *Miscellaneous Addresses,* p. 222; italics mine.

The galleries cheered heartily, at all events, and the politicians on the floor of the arena at Chicago, feeling that they had to do something, "for twenty long minutes . . . turned loose and cheered like mummers." [31]

Then, as if to demonstrate how much the two major parties actually functioned as a unit, the Democrats at their convention in St. Louis set Mr. Bryan in eclipse, and chose the rather colorless conservative, Judge Alton B. Parker of New York, as their leader. August Belmont and Thomas Fortune Ryan, who were believed to be in full control of the party of opposition (chastened by two successive defeats under radical leadership), thus offered a conservative counter-attraction to the more "impulsive" Roosevelt.

Few held doubts concerning the outcome, for the Rough Rider was at the zenith of his popularity.

Nevertheless, Roosevelt remained highly uneasy through much of the 1904 Presidential campaign. The applause of the public and the press he had been schooled to believe was but ephemeral; victories in elections depended upon the efficient working of the canvassing machine, upon the generosity of rich party patrons. The Secretary of War, William Howard Taft, who had been appointed to his office recently, when Root returned to the practice of law, had the impression that Roosevelt was unduly frightened and that certain interests were even using the critical moments of the campaign as occasions in which to wring promises from him. October came, and the President suffered, as John Hay drily remarked, "what we used to call in Ohio an October Scare." Dissensions among the Republicans of New York troubled his soul.[32]

To make matters worse, on October 1, 1904, Mr. Joseph Pulitzer's New York *World* (Democratic) enlivened the campaign by printing on its first page vigorous charges that Mr. Cortelyou, who as a Cabinet Secretary dealt with the corporations, in the post of national chairman drew golden streams of money from them for his campaign fund. How much were the beef trust, the coal trust, the tobacco trust, the oil trust, the railroads, the banks, the

[31] White, *Masks in a Pageant*, p. 313.

[32] Pringle, *Taft*, Vol. I, p. 261; Hay, *Diaries*, Vol. V, Oct. 8, 1904.

insurance companies contributing? What promises, the *World* asked editorially, were being given in return?

Thus it appeared that while the Square Deal President, through his public statements and his stump orators, directed appeals primarily to the masses of "plain people," whom he was to deliver from their wealthy oppressors, in private he made also the most impassioned demands for pecuniary support on the magnates who headed great trusts in railroads or in heavy industry.

Roosevelt also appeared "surprisingly and needlessly alarmed" to George Harvey, who was often the lobbyist for Ryan, Frick, and other great capitalists.[33] He was obsessed with the fear that by sheer trickery and pressure of money his opponents would outdo him, and that donations received for his campaign fund by Cortelyou were inadequate. Taking matters into his own hands, to a great extent, in October he undertook the most strenuous quest for additional funds, to be devoted to the last-hour canvasses in all doubtful areas.

What followed makes a very sad and perplexing chapter in the career of one of the most independent of Presidents: a chapter whose incidents have never yet been fully explained.

As the summer campaign drew to its close, widespread rumors were circulated that chairman Cortelyou was promising freely, to those he approached for donations, a more conservative turn in the Roosevelt administration. Taking note of these rumors, mentioned here and there in the press, the President on August 11, 1904, had written to the party chairman in the following terms:

> I should hate to be beaten in this contest; but I should not merely hate, I should not be able to bear being beaten under circumstances which implied ignominy. To give any color for misrepresentation to the effect that we were now weakening . . . would be ruinous.

And Cortelyou, who was running things in his own way, responded somewhat testily:

[33] Harvey, *Frick*, p. 298.

If I did not know you as well as I do I should resent your sending me such a communication. . . . I am conducting this campaign for your re-election on as high a plane as you have conducted the affairs of your great office.[34]

Yet the rumors continued busily as ever; and soon the ubiquitous little journalist and political philosopher Lincoln Steffens (now at the very height of his fame and influence) presented himself one day in September at the White House to make a proposal filled with splendid common sense. He suggested that the President, instead of offering in effect his immense popularity for sale to the great financiers, should ask "the common people who didn't want anything out of the government except general laws and an administration of justice and fair play" to contribute small sums to his campaign fund. Steffens offered to lay down between $1.00 and $5.00, and promised that a million other "little people" like himself would follow suit. The real point was that Roosevelt by such an appeal "would make the millions feel that it was their Government . . . and that you and your administration were beholden to the many, not to the few."[35]

There is no sign that Roosevelt did more than laugh at the notions of his witty friend with the Vandyke beard. The situation was far too serious. To him it seemed that the Republican party organization was in danger throughout the nation. A political party cost money; much money would be needed for watchers and captains to shepherd the tens and hundreds to the polls, especially in the "doubtful" State of New York where the Tammany men offered real dangers. Yet the money was not coming in as it should.

In the first days of October, Roosevelt, overcome by a kind of hysteria, telephoned from the White House to the National Republican headquarters in New York, and asked for chairman Cortelyou or Cornelius Bliss, the treasurer. They were out, and he spoke with Senator Nathan B. Scott, a member of the executive committee. "What is the trouble? . . ." the President asked.

[34] Bishop, *op. cit.*, Vol. I, pp. 324-325.

[35] Steffens, *Letters*, Steffens to T. R., Sept. 21, 1904, Vol. I, pp. 170-171.

"If the election was now, I fear we would be defeated," responded Senator Scott gloomily. The President was expected to win in the country, but his own state, New York, was counted as lost, and Mr. Bliss had no additional funds to give the state committee, which needed some $200,000 more.

"I will send for Mr. Harriman," Roosevelt then said.[36]

Roosevelt now did a fairly unprecedented thing. He made direct appeals for assistance to Edward H. Harriman, then the leading "angel" of the New York Republicans, and to Henry C. Frick, the steel baron, each numbered among the country's ten richest men.

John Hay records in his diary for October 8, 1904: "I lunched at the White House. Frick and Twombly [Hamilton McK. Twombly of the Vanderbilt family and interests] were there." [37] It may have been on the day before that Frick arrived, for he relates that he left New York with a party, in a private train, arriving in Washington as dusk fell, and came after dark to the White House, "entering by the door opposite the Treasury building." According to Frick's account, the occasion was pleasant, though the President appeared highly exercised over the scarcity of funds for the New York State canvass. The men of money promised that they would do their bit. Frick, according to an account by Oswald G. Villard, had the indelible impression that something in the nature of a pledge or promise was given in return. "He got down on his knees before us. We bought the ——— and then he did not stay bought!" [38] It is fairly doubtful, however, that T. R. with his now considerable training at political negotiation gave anything like a precise pledge.

Two days later, October 10, 1904, Roosevelt, who had occasionally kept in touch with Edward H. Harriman, wrote him also that "in view of the trouble over the State ticket in New York," he would like him to come to the White House within a few days for luncheon or dinner. Whereupon Harriman replied promptly, ac-

36 *Senate Committee on Privileges and Elections*, 1912, testimony, pp. 685-687.
37 Hay, *Diaries*, Vol. V, Oct. 8, 1904.
38 Villard, *Fighting Years*, p. 181.

cepting the invitation, stating at the same time that he was busy "correcting the trouble here," and promising that by the time of their interview "conditions will be very much improved." [39]

But if the railroad baron, reputedly worth a hundred millions, gave such assurances, why need a compromising dinner or luncheon be held? And Roosevelt, with a quick change of heart, on October 14, 1904, hastened to write (apparently without justification) that he had heard "in a roundabout way" of Mr. Harriman's embarrassment at visiting the President in the closing weeks of the campaign.

Now, my dear sir, you and I are practical men. . . . If you think there is any danger of your visit causing me trouble, or if you think there is nothing special I should be informed about, or no matter in which I could give aid, of course, give up the visit for the time being, and then, a few weeks hence, before I write my message [to Congress] I shall get you to come down to discuss certain governmental matters not connected with the campaign.

With great regard,

Sincerely yours,

Theodore Roosevelt.[40]

Mr. Harriman, however, a stubborn sort, evidently decided that helping to make a President was an expensive affair, and was resolved to look this one over in person. After a long-distance telephone conversation with the White House he too came on to Washington, on October 20, 1904. Again the occasion was friendly. Harriman was now politically prominent in New York because, as he testified some time later, he "owned" Governor Odell. His financial ties were with the Rockefeller dynasty, and often clashed with the interests of the House of Morgan. He appeared eager at this time to have Senator Chauncey Depew, who wore the "Morgan collar," kicked upstairs to the office of Ambassador to France, and replaced as Senator by ex-Governor Frank S. Black, who

[39] Kennan, *Harriman*, Vol. I, p. 183.

[40] *Ibid.*, Vol. I, p. 184.

would wear the "Harriman collar." Large affairs were on foot connected with control of the investment funds of great trust and insurance companies, as the Hughes investigation would show a year later, and a fierce financial struggle was actually being waged in secret for control of these institutions. Harriman left convinced that the President had pledged co-operation in the Senatorial business, as a way of clearing up New York's internal political strife. An understanding or "gentleman's agreement," positively denied afterward by Roosevelt, was attested by numerous witnesses at the hearings of the Senate's Committee on Privileges and Elections, in 1912.

Careful study of the testimony before the Senate Committee in 1912 made by witnesses hostile to Roosevelt shows that, in making a "deal" for Harriman's financial assistance in the campaign, the President hedged his promises with a superior cunning. Governor Benjamin B. Odell testified that his friend Mr. Harriman on his return from Washington gave him an account of the interview with Roosevelt. In regard to the kicking upstairs of Senator Chauncey Depew, which Harriman seemed to require in order to rearrange the New York political organization to his ends, "the President had said to him [Harriman] that *if it were necessary he would do as requested.*"[41] Roosevelt in his famous letter of October 8, 1906, written two years after the event, apparently "for the record," differed on this point, claiming that he told Harriman, "I did not believe it would be possible for me to appoint Mr. Depew Ambassador to France." Harriman, Odell, and company were thus consigned to the "Ananias Club" of immortal liars.

In any case, $250,000 was promptly raised by Harriman ($50,000 of this was his own money) and turned over, in good time, during the last days of October, to the Republican treasury.[42]

By October 24, 1904, John Hay could comment drily that Mr. Roosevelt's man, Cortelyou, "has all the money he needs—about

[41] *Senate Committee on Privileges and Elections*, testimony of Governor Odell, pp. 112-113; italics mine.

[42] *Ibid.*, hearings, pp. 112-113, 611-612, 693.

one half what Hanna had."[43] Roosevelt's obligations to the Malefactors of Great Wealth were ostensibly only half as large as those of President McKinley. But his public professions on this point, contrasted with his secret stern chase for funds, show both moral confusion and a fairly Machiavellian worldliness.

Near the end of the campaign he learned that some officials of the Standard Oil Company, with which he had broken lances publicly, had made a very large donation to Mr. Cortelyou's chest, and he wrote virtuously in a letter that became public October 26, 1904:

> I have just been informed that the Standard Oil people have contributed $100,000 to our campaign fund. This may be entirely untrue. But if true I must ask you to direct that the money be returned to them forthwith.

But Roosevelt appreciated how dire the need of money was for the legitimate and necessary expenses of a great national campaign, and proceeded to defend his real actions in the following terms. "It was entirely legitimate to accept contributions no matter how large . . . from individuals and corporations, on the terms on which I happen to know that you have accepted them," that is, that no improper obligations of any kind were involved. The donors, even the big corporations, understood that only a "square deal" for them could be expected. Of course these corporations, having a "tremendous stake in the welfare of this country," were but reasonable and proper in seeking the continuance of the Republican party by legitimate contributions. The Standard Oil, however, owing to its past record, lay in a special category.[44]

However, Mr. Cortelyou did nothing about the matter, and only in 1908 did Mr. Roosevelt learn that the money had never been returned.[45]

[43] Hay, *Diaries,* Vol. V, p. 320.

[44] Bishop, *op. cit.,* Vol. I, pp. 329-330.

[45] In effect, Cortelyou, though young at his work compared with Mark Hanna, had not done badly. From evidence brought out before the Armstrong Committee of the New York Legislature (Hughes' investigation of the insurance companies), the Clapp Committee in 1912, and the Barnes-Roosevelt suit for libel

While he was dictating the above letter—according to a reminiscence of Taft, divulged in a mood of anger—Secretary of State Knox came into the room and said to him: " 'Why, Mr. President, the money has been spent. They cannot pay it back—they haven't got it.' 'Well,' said the President, 'the letter will look well on the record, anyhow,' and so he let it go."[46]

Wall Street is a huge whispering gallery, and secrets spread rapidly there. On October 22, 1904, Daniel S. Lamont, the old Democratic wire-puller of Cleveland's administration, now a New York bank president, told the Democratic candidate, Judge Parker, of a secret conference at which Edward Harriman, James Stillman, Henry C. Frick, and George W. Perkins had decided that Roosevelt's election was a matter of necessity. They were convinced, as the New York *Sun* had said, that "the impulsive candidate of the party of conservatism" was preferable to the "conservative, temporizing candidate" of the party regarded as "permanently impulsive."[47]

A week before the election, on October 31, 1904, Parker issued his sensational public charge that Roosevelt had "extorted" money from or "blackmailed" the monopolistic corporations with promises of political immunity. The reports of Cortelyou's collections, as given in newspaper rumors, were cited as evidence. Five days later,

in 1915, a representative list may be compiled of the principal donations, as follows:

J. P. Morgan & Company	$150,000
N. Y. Life, Equitable, and Mutual insurance companies (combined)	148,000
George J. Gould (railroads)	100,000
H. H. Rogers and John D. Archbold (oil)	125,000
H. C. Frick (steel)	100,000
C. S. Mellen (railroads)	50,000
James H. Hyde (insurance)	25,000
James Speyer (banking)	25,000
James Stillman (banking)	10,000
Cuba Mail Steamship Company	10,000
William Nelson Cromwell	5,000
General Electric Company	3,000

[46] Pringle, *Taft*, Vol. II, p. 830; W. H. Taft to Helen H. Taft, Aug. 22, 1912.
[47] *Clapp Committee*, Vol. I, pp. 899-900; New York *Sun*, Aug. 11, 1904.

the President issued a thunderous denial in his most indignant phrases, which echoed throughout the land. That corporate donations had been accepted he did not contradict, but held this legitimate, as it had always hitherto been. Judge Parker's accusations were "monstrous" and by their falsity brought infamy upon himself. The vague, ungrounded assertion that there had been "blackmail" was atrociously false. ". . . If elected I shall go into the Presidency unhampered by any pledge, promise or understanding of any kind, save my promise, made openly to the American people, that so far as in my power lies I shall see to it that every man has a square deal, no less and no more." [48]

The election returns of November 8, 1904, overwhelmed, stunned even Theodore Roosevelt, as he said. He had won the largest majority and the largest vote in the electoral college that any candidate for President had ever received.

5

I have likened Theodore Roosevelt to an oarsman steering boldly past dangerous rocks and rapids. The current he rode was of course that of public opinion. In 1904 it ran more swiftly, stronger than ever in the direction of popular reform.

The political revival noted in the administration, with its more critical, sensitive, historically conscious leaders, came undoubtedly in response to the increasing pressure of a more enlightened public opinion. Toward 1904, after seven years of plenty, the financial boom stimulated by the policies of the Standpatters approached its end. Disturbed by uneven economic pressures, reflected by a rising cost of living which outstripped a rising wage level, and a period of more stringent business conditions—financial commentators often spoke of the period as one of "profitless prosperity"—the spirit of criticism, even of disillusionment, was intensified, and strongly favored the trust-busting activities of the Rooseveltian years.

[48] The New York *World*, Nov. 5, 1904.

To the American middle class, even more than to the working class, the new industrial trust became the great bugaboo. Almost everywhere men spoke of the coming end of business competition, perhaps of individual freedom itself, and of the approaching enslavement of the free American citizen. American society was developing into a hierarchy of classes, with the industrial barons at the top, wrote W. J. Ghent at this time in his prophetic work, *Our Benevolent Feudalism*. "The era of competition," he said, "whether free or unfree, is dead, and the means of its resurrection are unknown to political science."

This haunting question had already been raised repeatedly since the 1890's in our popular press, typified by Pulitzer's *World* and Hearst's New York *Journal*, though in hasty, transient form, mingled with sensational, invidious accounts of the debauches of the rich. But in the autumn of 1902, S. S. McClure, the clever publisher of low-priced popular magazines, while on the scent of "startling facts" with which to dazzle his readers, began to publish in *McClure's* Lincoln Steffens' series of articles on *The Shame of the Cities*, and Ida Tarbell's studies in *The History of the Standard Oil Company*. Here were authoritative reports that had been years in preparing, and now provided for a great mass audience a darker, more realistic picture of what our republic had come to be in the fullness of age.

Miss Tarbell, whose oil-digging father had once been "liquidated" by the Rockefeller clan in Pennsylvania, wrote with admirable restraint and clarity a history of the rise of a band of business dynasts who, so to speak, seized the country by the throat. The struggles, the intrigues of the oil barons, constantly defying the law upon shrewd legal advice wherever it restrained them, made history no less picturesque and conspiratorial than that of the Italian princes in the days of Machiavelli. In 1903 and 1904 the whole country talked of the Standard Oil "Octopus," of the mysterious John D. Rockefeller, who had long held himself deliberately in the shade, and whose possible wealth was only now dimly conjectured.

Meanwhile the vivacious Lincoln Steffens, then editor of *Mc-*

Clure's, had set off upon a great tour of the country on the trail of corrupt political rings that festered in our great cities. His series of "exposures," beginning in October (before Miss Tarbell's series) and continuing month by month, were carefully documented and lucidly, even brilliantly, written. They told almost for the first time a coherent but fearsome story of the alliance between professional political machines and business groups. Steffens' *The Shame of the Cities* had an enormous public success. Soon the leading publishers, such as Hearst and Collier, began to devote low-priced weekly and monthly magazines to a literature of informal social criticism, the literature of "exposure," to which T. R. one day would apply the striking name of "muckraking."

Steffens brought to his work a happy combination of qualities, human sympathy and "scientific curiosity." He did not wish to hunt down evil men; it was the process of evil itself that absorbed him. Political corruption, he would say in afterthought, "is a process. It is not a temporary evil, not an accidental wickedness, not a passing symptom of the youth of a people. It is a natural process by which a democracy is made gradually over into a plutocracy." [49]

Without drawing the conclusions at which he arrived long afterward, Steffens' inquiries nevertheless revealed an organic unity working throughout the field of local government. Everywhere, in St. Louis as in Philadelphia or Pittsburgh, there was the tribal chieftain who ruled over the local party organization, a William Flinn in Pittsburgh, a Butler in St. Louis. And behind the Flinns and the Butlers stood the dominant patron of the machine: a rich brewer in St. Louis, or a certain powerful, very secretive banker in Pittsburgh.

But if there were "villains," there were the heroes of Good Government, too. Like an American Diogenes, Steffens searched for honest men, and found and celebrated Tom L. Johnson, the Single Tax mayor of Cleveland. He pictured Johnson as a converted "robber baron" (converted by a reading of Henry George) who had once been a public-utility magnate, a lobbyist, a buyer of

[49] Steffens, *Autobiography*, p. 413.

franchises and privilege. Then he described how Johnson brought his wealth, his shrewd knowledge of men and the world, his original turn of thought, his picturesque circus tactics, to fighting the universal enemy: Privilege. ". . . Privilege causes the evil in the world, not wickedness; and not men," he would say. Once the temptations of Privilege were removed from the purview of business men—so that they no longer contested with each other for political advantage—then Democracy (which appeared to be a synonym for Christianity) became possible again. All would play fair together under just arbiters of the laws. Steffens himself shared fervently the belief of Johnson's disciples, such as Brand Whitlock and Frederic C. Howe, that fundamental municipal reform would teach men to do "the clean, decent thing." [50]

The city reformers felt that they worked at the "grass roots" of the industrial society. Many of them like Johnson and Folk of St. Louis were led to wage the holy war of the Single Taxers against "unearned increment" in ground rent. A score of embattled local reformers from Philadelphia to San Francisco staked everything upon activating the passive majority of honest citizens against the rings that defrauded them, and winning a more "direct democracy" by the expedient of the primary and the referendum. The movement of municipal reform, which Mark Hanna contended with in Ohio after 1897, spread more and more broadly during the 1900's, and assumed moral and religious overtones. Brand Whitlock, the radical young mayor of Toledo, declared at this time that he fought chiefly against "the cant and hypocrisy and iniquity of our system." Theodore Roosevelt, in his sermons upon righteousness, reflected the moods of the reformers of his age, who, as a Cleveland minister said, were but "trying to make Christianity possible."

Was democracy a failure? Steffens asked every month in his magazine articles that reached close to a million readers. "Will the people rule? . . . Is democracy possible?"

[50] Whitlock, *Letters,* Vol. I, pp. 171-172.

The public mind, more chastened and self-critical than in the booming, swashbuckling days of '98, now fixed upon these questions. It was haunted nowadays by a picture of the giant corporation extending its tentacles to crush out the small proprietor, the farmer, the laborer. This nightmare picture was soon brought home in all its horrifying details by a series of scandals in high financial quarters, resulting from battles and competitions among the money lords, that came to the surface toward 1904. The scandals of governmental and business misconduct were to bring certain celebrated inquisitions: those of the insurance companies by a New York legislative committee, with Charles Evans Hughes as its examining attorney; those of the powerful New Haven Railroad, led to trial before public opinion by the "people's attorney," Louis D. Brandeis. Thus, every day the evidence of legislative investigations and courts, summed up in the daily press, would be unfolding a monumental tale of financial and political skulduggery, broadly supporting the charges made already by the "muckraking" journalists. The public mind, filled with misgivings and mistrust, observed with a kind of terror the encroachments of the industrial trusts, and listened to incredible rumors of an all-powerful "Money Trust." This mood of dread and insecurity, especially in the middle class, underlay the trust-busting activities of the Rooseveltian era.

Senator Albert Beveridge, the ardent advocate of Hamiltonian ideals, early in 1902 prepared an important address to be given before a state convention in Indiana in which he defended both the new imperialism and the new order of trusts. The trusts, he said, were led by public-spirited men who reduced the costs of production by large-scale management, and who were too intelligent to penalize the public through needlessly higher charges. Scarcely had the speech been put in type when the beef trust (which Charles Edward Russell in Chicago was already investigating) greedily raised the price of meat. Beveridge was indignant, and wrote to George W. Perkins, his fellow-Hoosier, and one of his original backers:

. . . The beef trust in unjustly and arbitrarily raising prices is causing . . . indignation throughout the country. It gives demagogues an unjust opportunity to answer my arguments. Cannot you bring these foolish persons to terms? I am aware that you have your hands full, but it seems to me that . . . you can do nothing better than to see these people and give them a little sense.[51]

But Perkins, though a member of the House of Morgan now, and a lyrical advocate of the trusts, could do nothing; and his friend Beveridge found the incident deeply instructive. Soon the former panegyrist of big business determined to make a sharp turn to the left. "It was good form to be a liberal," as Frederic C. Howe recalls of those years. "Conservative lawyers, bankers, and men of affairs lent their names to radical movements. . . . The younger generation was to achieve the things that had been denied my own." And Beveridge, like so many other politicians, felt himself caught by the new currents. He planned in 1904 a Child Labor Bill, for which he would fight in the Senate. In May, 1903, Dr. Harvey W. Wiley, chief chemist of the Department of Agriculture, made public his "poison squad" experiments upon many publicly sold foods. And Beveridge soon after prepared to enter the struggle for a pure-foods law, to the dismay of the Chicago beef barons whom he had formerly defended. For Beveridge, in his change of heart, had discovered that after all ours was "a government of the people," and that it should not be pre-empted or controlled by the possessors of wealth. He too now believed that political democracy must endeavor to impose an even-handed justice, fair play, between the opposing economic groups.

Capital is all right in its place. It has a mission, and a mighty and beneficent mission it is. I do not object to capital. I defend it—only let it attend to its own business. And public life and special legislation for its own benefit are not its business.[52]

[51] Bowers, *Beveridge*, pp. 177-178; Apr. 8, 1902.

[52] Beveridge, "The Rich Man in Politics," *Saturday Evening Post*, Jun. 16, 1906.

Meanwhile the deep unrest that he had been noticing among the people pointed to the road that the future statesmen must travel.

I have been carefully studying the present unrest and interviewing numbers of people about it. I am coming to the conclusion that it is not a passing whim, but a great natural movement such as occurs in this country, as our early history shows, once about every forty years. It is not like the Granger episode or the Debs episode. The former . . . affected only the farmers; the latter only the workingmen. The present unrest, however, is quite as vigorous among the intellectuals, college men, university people, etc., as it is among the common people.[53]

The great currents of public opinion Roosevelt studied closely all his life. His hold upon the voters actually resided in the freedom with which he, unlike the Standpatters of the Hanna and Aldrich type, appeared to respond to public opinion. His propounding of the Square Deal in 1904, his air of independence, the unmistakable promise of bold-handed reform, all made for his unprecedented strength among the voters, a strength which he himself grossly underestimated.

The election returns of November 8, 1904, with their character of a political Tidal Wave had stunned even Roosevelt, as he admitted. It was now plain that he had overreached himself in pursuing secretly the masters of corporations for donations to his campaign chest; he had given hostages to the rich, reactionary Republicans, while stirring the emotions of the masses even better than he knew. This paradox provided deep perplexities for the future.

The plain people were jubilant at the outcome of the election of 1904. But so were certain of the masters of capital who felt that credit was owing to them for a share in the victory. Henry C. Frick of the U. S. Steel Corporation telegraphed the President on election night:

The endorsement of yourself and your policies by your fellow citizens is magnificent and truly deserved. Cordial congratulations!

[53] Bowers, *Beveridge*, pp. 223-224.

VI. PRINCIPALLY WORLD-WANDERING

THE OLD Senators who still ruled Congress seemed surprisingly unhappy over the sweeping Republican party triumph of 1904.

"What is to be done now with our victory is a pretty serious question," wrote the canny Orville Platt of Connecticut to Aldrich.[1] It was a question that Theodore Roosevelt, too, asked himself continually.

Originally a political "accident," he had won more real power than any of the dreary Republican worthies who had preceded him in his office since Lincoln. He was not only the chief magistrate, but the unchallenged leader of his party organization, seated in the driving seat of the Steam Roller. The opportunity for positive leadership lay open for him, with the Presidential power less restricted by indirect controls than ever before, as a similar opportunity fell one day to a later Roosevelt after re-election in 1936.

Moreover he could say, in this great hour, that his re-election, which vindicated his principles, was owing

> not to the politicians primarily, although I have done my best to get on with them; not to the financiers, although I have staunchly upheld the rights of property; but above all to Abraham Lincoln's "plain people"; to the folk who worked hard on farm, in shop, or on the railroads, or who owned little stores, little businesses which they managed themselves. I would literally, not figuratively, rather cut off my right hand than

[1] Stephenson, *op. cit.*, p. 250.

forfeit by any improper act of mine the trust and regard of these people.[2]

No one could utter braver sentiments than T. R., nor with firmer conviction, at a given moment. His second inauguration, celebrated by a crowd of 500,000 persons who streamed into the capital, witnessed his liberation from pledges to the dead man he had succeeded. "I am glad to be President in my own right," he said to John Hay.[3]

There is evidence that he weighed the trend of the recent elections, and the popular emotions that accompanied it, in serious spirit. One perhaps important symptom was the sharp rise of the tiny Socialist party, led by Eugene Debs, from 100,000 votes in 1900 to 400,000 votes in 1904. Roosevelt duly noted this when he remarked privately in February, 1905, that the growth of the Socialist party was "far more ominous than any Populist or similar movement in the past."[4] William Jennings Bryan, who also watched the popular pulse most carefully, told friends that he now feared the coming of socialism. The new party's rapid growth might lead soon to the capture of one of the older parties, as the Populists had managed to do in 1896. It was proof also "that the Democratic party has been too conservative to satisfy the reform element of the country."[5]

In serious vein, Roosevelt also pondered over the labor problem, though only a minority of American workers were Socialists, while the great majority pinned their hopes upon the economic action of the federated craft unions led by Samuel Gompers. In a long letter, written two days after the election to his Attorney General, Philander C. Knox (retiring now to enter the Senate), Roosevelt explored the possibilities of a Square Deal to labor. Hitherto, with Knox's aid, he had grappled chiefly with the great problems of the day that were connected with organized capital. To Knox, the

[2] Bishop, *op. cit.*, T. R. to Wister, Nov. 19, 1904, Vol. I, p. 345.

[3] Hay, *Diaries*, Vol. V, Nov. 8, 1904.

[4] Pringle, *Roosevelt*, p. 368.

[5] E. E. Robinson, *American Political Parties*, p. 289.

conservative attorney for Carnegie, Roosevelt gave credit handsomely for having given shape to policies which were only "half-formulated" in his own mind. But once in the Senate, there would be occasion for Knox to give as deep thought to the problem of labor as he had given to that of capital.

> More and more the labor movement of this country will become a factor of vital importance. . . . If the attitude of the New York *Sun* toward labor, as toward the trusts, becomes the attitude of the Republican party, we shall some day go down before a radical and extreme democracy with a crash which would be disastrous to the nation. We must not only do justice *but we must show the wage-worker that we are doing justice*. We must make it evident that while there is not any weakness in our attitude, while we unflinchingly demand good conduct from them, yet we are equally resolute in the effort to secure them all just and proper consideration.

Here we see in this confidential, artless letter how Roosevelt still never falters in his desire to play the Great Mediator. His hope of upholding the democratic doctrine of "equality before the law" in the conflicts of capital and labor corresponded significantly with the English and European political reform movements of this time, which conceived of social legislation as concessions to be made in time, as a form of "ransom" paid in order to safeguard society and its prosperity. The concessions might be costly; yet, as a Joseph Chamberlain intimated, their costs could be paid out of future profits, and would be outweighed by the gains in security from tragic upheavals.

Roosevelt argued:

> It would be a dreadful calamity if we saw this country divided into two parties, one containing the bulk of the property owners and conservative people, the other the bulk of the wage-workers and less prosperous people, generally; each party insisting upon, demanding much that was wrong, and each party sullen and angered by real and fancied grievances.

And what was the answer, what were the measures which, taken in time, would prevent such a fearful outcome? Roosevelt like the corporation lawyers Knox and Root wished to preserve the existing balance of property relations. Further than this he had no definite measures in mind, no time-table, no program. He seemed to offer only a standard, a kind of "moral" imperative, which his conservative colleagues often accepted, but as often wavered from, as it suited their material interests: ". . . Here in this republic, it is peculiarly incumbent upon the man with whom things have prospered to be in a certain sense the keeper of his brother with whom life has gone hard." For "the surest way to provoke an explosion of wrong and injustice is to be short-sighted, narrow-minded, greedy and ignorant. . . ."[6]

Yet vague as was the plan, and wavering the leader, it is true, as Herbert Croly later reflected, that Roosevelt groped in sound directions. His "new Nationalism" or "new Hamiltonianism," while strongly centralizing the government authority, made this augmented authority appear to be more responsive to the popular will; it served not as a bulwark against the rising tide of democracy, but as an effective instrument of the common national welfare. Even in compromise and failure, Rooseveltian leadership gave signs of what could be done; pointed to the "promise of American life."

"In internal affairs, I cannot say that I entered the Presidency with any deliberately planned and far-reaching scheme of social betterment," Roosevelt recollected in writing his autobiography. The more was the pity. What is remarkable at this stage is that, with a record-breaking victory to his credit, and holding an unchallenged position of leadership, Roosevelt confined himself so severely in his actual domestic policies.

While he wondered what to do with his victory, strong influence was brought to bear upon him to see to it that any reform or trust control activities should work, as he put it, "without paralyzing the energies of the business community."[7] From the West came two spokesmen of progressive measures, Governors Cummins

[6] *T. R. Papers*, T. R. to P. C. Knox, Nov. 10, 1904.

[7] *T. R. Papers*, T. R. to Sir George Trevelyan, Mar. 9, 1905.

and La Follette, with whom he held a long conference. La Follette advocated strong measures to control railroads and fix the rates they charged; Cummins urged a reduction of the tariff rates that would help, as he thought, to curb the trusts and lower the cost of living. Cummins, on leaving, expressed himself as satisfied with the interview, and counted upon Roosevelt's adherence to tariff reform. He recalled in later years that the President had shown him a passage in his forthcoming Message to Congress indicating as much.[8]

However, something very powerful moved Roosevelt at this juncture, and at almost the last hour before making public his message he veered and changed his mind. Senator Aldrich came to see him; Senator O. H. Platt likewise; and Speaker "Joe" Cannon also came to his desk. To Roosevelt's proposal to do something about tariff reform in the early future, Aldrich coolly answered: "Possibly." Senator Platt may well have reminded the President of the wisdom of holding to the "gentleman's agreement" of 1902 to avoid forbidden subjects. Cannon was even more forthright, according to his own later account. A struggle over the tariff would probably end in failure, and would moreover prevent enactment of the railroad bill Roosevelt had set his heart upon. By telegram, the sentences in the Message of December, 1904, referring to tariff reform, already given out to the press, were "killed."[9]

The Message to Congress of December, 1904, which was to announce a Roosevelt who had "come into his own," and which had been awaited with burning curiosity, proved to be a most moderate document. In a spirit of humanity it recommended laws fostering workmen's compensation and restricting child labor. It was silent upon the tariff issue. Its proposals for the extension of government control over the railroads were the most important ones. Responding to bitter criticisms of existing freight rates, Roosevelt urged

[8] Stephenson, *op. cit.*, p. 235, citing memorandum of A. B. Cummins.

[9] *Ibid.*, p. 462, memorandum of L. W. Busbey; cf. also L. W. Busbey, *Cannon*, pp. 208-209.

that Congress must accord a genuine power to the Interstate Commerce Commission—when complaints were brought—"to decide, subject to judicial review, what shall be a reasonable rate. . . ."

The terms of the Message were conciliatory. Great corporations, the President said, were "necessary," and for their "great and singular mental powers" the masters of corporations were entitled to large rewards. However, they must give due regard to the public interest.

Instant relief was felt now by the anxious railroad lobbyists and "railroad Senators" in Washington. Soon it became plain that, although an administration railroad bill was to be introduced in Congress, nothing would be done during the "Lame Duck" session, and that Roosevelt would not care to call a special session of the new, more liberal Congress, which would normally convene at the end of 1905. It was evident also that Roosevelt had as yet won no agreement of definite support for his bill from Aldrich and Cannon, who controlled Congress still with an unshaken grip. These men waited, and worked to gain time.

It was less well known that the great railroad master Edward H. Harriman, accompanied by his lawyer, quietly visited Washington several times in the winter of 1904-1905, and also in December, 1905, at the time of the new session of Congress. It is evident that in keeping with the friendly alliance between Harriman and Roosevelt, during the late campaign, Harriman was being "consulted" by those who advised the President in framing the proposed law. Yet Harriman disapproved of everything in the way of railroad legislation. He was not an easy man to please, and strain arose between the two aggressive men, more than a year before their public quarrel, almost immediately after the election to which Harriman had given such signal help.

The difficult course of Roosevelt's negotiations with both the railroad magnates and the Standpat leaders in Congress is reflected in certain letters to his Boswell, Joseph B. Bishop, and to Lodge. After a snarl of debate, the railroad reform bill, which had passed the House, died in the committee rooms of the Senate. It was evident that Roosevelt did not press the issue strongly and was easily resigned to waiting for another year, when perhaps the force of public opinion would come to his aid more strongly.

> My chief fear is lest the big financiers who, outside of their own narrowly limited profession, are as foolish as they are selfish, will force the moderates to join with the radicals in radical action, under penalty of not obtaining any at all. *I much prefer moderate action:* but the ultraconservatives may make it necessary to accept what is radical.[10]

In a similar vein he wrote to his old political mentor Lodge, saying that the railroads were opposing his reform bill vigorously and hoped to beat it. ". . . I think they are very short-sighted not to understand that *to beat it means to increase the danger of the movement for government ownership of railroads.*"[11]

These are scarcely the tones of one who, by a tremendous personal victory, had made himself the master of his party. Roosevelt's ventures in legislative leadership (actually very few) show instead that he accepted strict limitations of his power in this field; that he dreaded the wearisome, perplexing task of driving a definite program of legislation through Congress; that he feared the machinelike control of the Senate and the autocratic rule of Speaker Cannon, in the House, would be immune to direct attacks. This machinelike control, especially in the lower House, remained unchallenged by both Roosevelt and Taft, until the insurrection led by Congressman Norris of Nebraska in 1910 suddenly overthrew it.

It was true that the President sought to rally public opinion to his side by making certain fighting speeches, such as that at Philadelphia, January 30, 1905. Here, waving his Big Stick a little, he declared that our free people would not tolerate longer the vast power of corporate wealth, unless "the still higher power" of controlling this wealth in the interests of the whole people were lodged "somewhere in the Government." He asked for "justice" in the way of submitting the railroads to more rigorous supervision by the Interstate Commerce Commission, and gave warning

[10] Bishop, *op. cit.*, Vol. I, p. 428, Mar. 23, 1905; italics mine.
[11] *T. R. Papers,* T. R. to Lodge, May 24, 1905; italics mine.

once more that, without such measures, our republic might founder like republics of olden times amid the destructive contests of the Haves and the Have-Nots, the Poor and Rich.

Yet it was all too plain that his mind was distracted by the pernickety controversies that arose over the terms and details of a new empowering act for the Interstate Commerce Commission. Complex economic or financial problems always ended by boring him, for his mind, as his friends knew, was wanting in the spirit of orderly logic necessary to a law-making program. His heart, his emotions, were turned elsewhere in 1905—during this time of painful domestic controversy, financial scandal, and popular unrest—to more distant fields, abroad, where a role of glory, infinitely simpler and more attractive to his nature, beckoned him.

2

"The crowded year supreme" of Roosevelt's official life was unquestionably 1905, according to his authorized biographer. This was the year of the Portsmouth peace conference, bringing to an end the sanguinary Russo-Japanese war. It was the year also when the Morocco crisis brought western Europe to the verge of general war, a crisis in which the President exerted himself to play an important, perhaps a decisive, part in helping to stave off the debacle. Appearing now in the role of a brilliant principal in international *Machtpolitik*, lord of armies and navies, imperial ruler of colonies spreading from the Caribbean to the China Sea, and of their fifteen millions of natives, the Square Deal President inspired Henry Adams to call him "Tsar Rooseveltoff."

For by 1905 the United States formed no longer the "great republic of the West," living its busy life remote from the quarrels and intrigues of Europe's dynastic families; it was a "world power" in a world that had grown perceptibly smaller and whose navies had grown larger and swifter. Operating as the head of a world power was a business that fascinated the "small boy" whom Sir Cecil Spring Rice saw always in this President. As lord of the Army and Navy, and master of the country's foreign relations, his power in this sphere was well-nigh absolute and could even be exercised secretly, up to the point where treaties must be ratified by the Senate. Moreover, in the world outside our borders, the law of force, the law of the jungle, still ruled after all; and the Rough Rider, who preached that one must "speak softly and carry a Big Stick," was well fitted by his aggressive temperament to live in it. For his imperial contemporaries themselves, the Emperors William and Nicholas, or a Chamberlain and a Delcassé often exhibited a temperament no more mature than his. Even their intellectual spokesmen, who preached the ethics of racial superiority (The White Man's Burden) and the "struggle for life," in defending the imperial interests of the day, reflected a philosophy that was at once *"chaste, brutale, héroique et enfantine."* [12]

In the Far East, the interests of the United States as a "world power" now for the first time virtually collided with a whole constellation of the Great Powers. Inevitably the new American foreign policy had marked its enemies and sought to align itself with friends. The American penetration of the Pacific, the seizure of the Philippine Islands, was tolerated and encouraged, as we have seen, by the suddenly benevolent British Empire. More than one British financier-diplomat, like Lord Beresford, expressed the hope that the United States would work in more intimate relations with England in the Far East henceforth, and forestall the swift partition of China, especially by Russia and Germany.

"McKinleyism," with its trust in combinations abroad as well as at home, was responsive to British approaches. In John Hay's Open Door notes of 1899 and 1900 the policy of combination was clearly fostered. The great powers were circularized by the American Secretary of State for an agreement to guarantee to each other's citizens equality of commercial rights in the treaty ports already occupied. Their replies, in truth, were various and hedged with qualifications. But Hay, rather audaciously, declared the Open Door doctrine to be in operation. The declaration of the Open

[12] According to the historian Halévy, cited by Vagts, *Deutschland und die Vereinigte Staaten*, Vol. II, p. 1209.

Door policy gave to American activity in the Far East a humanitarian and righteous appearance, by appearing to protect China's integrity, and thus softened the blows of anti-imperialists at home. In the second place it pleased the American oil, textile, steel, and banking interests who were now entering the Chinese market more vigorously. The "growing necessity for protecting the new markets which American manufacturers and exporters had secured in the Orient, against the counteracting influence of other Powers . . . threatening the partial exclusion of American products," was met by Secretary Hay's skillful Open Door notes. The agreements he gained represented "a *coup d'état* for American foreign trade," according to one spokesman of financial interests.[13] Finally the Open Door agreements were seen to be helpful for the present to British interests in China, serving to stabilize things at a balance favorable to her, and were initiated by Hay, it is believed, as a discreet *quid pro quo* for British retirement from the Caribbean.[14]

John Hay, when he was named Secretary of State, was set down in secret German reports as a confirmed Anglophile. When attacked publicly on this ground by American politicians, he "writhed under the charge but did nothing except to deny it."[15] But even Richard Olney, who had written such ringing, war-like messages to John Bull in 1895, in his old age repented, and in 1900 declared publicly that America "must expand," that of necessity we must have a "friend" and that England alone could help or harm us.[16] Henry Adams, commenting on Olney's change of heart, remarked: "We drift inevitably back to the British. Economical and social interests are too strong. Our administration, whether Olney or Hay run it, must be British; Bayard or Frelinghuysen, or Fish or Seward—it is all the same."[17] Nor was it different when Theodore Roosevelt throned in the White House.

John Hay "believed in the British Empire." In England, "his

[13] *Bankers Magazine*, editorial, Jan., 1902.

[14] Dennett, *op. cit.*, pp. 291, 295-296.

[15] *Ibid.*, p. 388.

[16] R. Olney, "Growth of Our Foreign Policy," *Atlantic Monthly*, Mar., 1900.

[17] Adams, *Letters*, Vol. II, p. 270.

friends were always among the ruling classes: Curzon, Chamberlain, Balfour, Harcourt, the bankers, the landed gentry. . . ." It was a cardinal principle of his statecraft—as he declared one day, January 2, 1900, to the German Ambassador—that the "continued existence of the British Empire, even though somewhat humbled," would be of greater advantage to the world than its downfall.[18]

During the Spanish-American War, on May 7, 1898, Spring Rice, reflecting the benevolent British demeanor, had written Hay: "Therefore, as I say again, let us try while we can to secure what we can for God's language."[19] Hay answered that this was precisely in line with his own ideas. It was definitely in line with Roosevelt's ideas also. But Roosevelt was naturally a far more skillful political artist in furthering "friendship" with England, while standing for an unyielding "Americanism" before the home voters.

The British-American sharing of the White Man's Burden evolved rapidly in Rooseveltian days. While American armies, ranging from 60,000 to 100,000 men, formidable even for those days, were deeply engaged in "civilizing" the Filipinos, expansion operations in the Caribbean area were carried forward simultaneously. The late war and Pacific expansion had made the completion of a canal across the Isthmus of Panama a military as well as a commercial imperative. When, early in 1902, the bankrupt Panama Canal Company, launched by the ill-starred de Lesseps, expressed its willingness to sell its uncompleted property and rights to the United States for $40,000,000, Roosevelt moved rapidly to accept the bargain. With the authority of Congress, the earlier project, by which the American government was to build a canal across Nicaragua, was abandoned for that of Panama. The digging of this canal would complete a mighty link in the imperial chain spreading from the Atlantic seaboard to the China coast; and Roosevelt was extremely eager to have the great canal, planned more than fifty years ago, built by the end of his second

[18] Dennis, *American Diplomacy, 1896-1906*, p. 125.
[19] Gwynn, *op. cit.*, Vol. I, pp. 247-248.

term. But first the old Clayton-Bulwer Treaty of 1850, by which Britain and America were to share in the building of such a canal and hold it unfortified, must be altered, in accordance with the new demands of "Americanism" in the Caribbean.

Long-standing disputes between America and Britain had a way of being cleared up with miraculous speed, in these days when Germany's rising industrial and naval power was so keenly feared in Downing Street. The second Hay-Pauncefote Treaty, ratified in February, 1902, yielded to virtually all the American demands that the new canal was to be policed by American forces, and entirely built and owned by the American government. Following up the completion of this agreement (chiefly prepared under McKinley), Roosevelt undertook by aggressive diplomacy to settle the old Alaska boundary dispute between Canada and the United States. Once more the British seemed ready to yield in changing the line in southern Alaska in accordance with American claims; and evidently perceiving this, Roosevelt did not neglect to hasten them on by drawing out the Big Stick in 1903, flourishing it toward Canada, and speaking out loud about the possible mobilization of American troops at the frontier. The final judgment of the Arbitration Commission, which terminated the affair, represented a cheap foreign triumph for Roosevelt, since the chief of the British delegation, Lord Alverstone, appeared to have been instructed in advance to yield to all the American claims.

Roosevelt's combative manner successfully concealed his real or secret acceptance of the "inevitable" Anglo-American partnership. His innate tendencies were almost as anti-German as John Hay's; and like many high officers in the American navy he singled out the rising German power as "the enemy," while England was held to be the friend of the future. While Britain yielded up control of the Caribbean despite her West Indian possessions, and recognized the new status at Panama, the Germans might not abide by the Monroe Doctrine unless they were encouraged to do so by show of force. The talk of German expansion in South America, even of a possible German naval war against the United States, reached the President. Possibly he knew of Admiral Dewey's strange pre-

Rice (now familiarly "Springy"), though he was unfortunately stationed at St. Petersburg, equally intimate communications and warnings inspired directly by Downing Street, or sometimes discreetly by Edward VII himself, constantly poured into the White House. Roosevelt flung himself, with a forwardness and zest that no other American chief magistrate had shown, into the "game" of world politics, as if it were an end or a joy in itself, fascinated by its dark and double intrigues, its high and intangible privileges, or dangerous shiftings of chance, that made it all so much more fun than framing and passing a tariff bill.

Shifting his attention from the Caribbean to the Far East, which had been John Hay's special province up to the time of his long illness, in the latter part of 1904, Roosevelt took a strong hand in Pacific affairs. There the final phases of the world-wide contest for colonies and markets were being enacted with breathless speed. The dominant course of world power politics, ever since the end of the nineteenth century, was fixed by England's desperate efforts to gather a coalition of allies against the day when Germany would attempt to destroy her Empire. Germany, the *arriviste* state of Europe, had experienced belatedly an amazing increase of industrial output—her steel-producing capacity increased, between 1881 and 1911, from a figure that was 48 per cent of England's to one that was 220 per cent. In turn, Germany, growing swiftly in population, commerce, and naval force (which the vainglorious William II did nothing to conceal), was possessed with justifiable fear of "encirclement" by her rivals. By 1904 this dominant polar antagonism, around which other rivalries were aligned, and which could be studied in Africa or Polynesia, expressed itself in concealed form in war between Russia and Japan.

Less than two years after the declaration of the Open Door doctrine for China, the "co-operative" policy was a dead letter. England, which had given but lip-service to the Open Door agreements, signed her first Anglo-Japanese Treaty of Alliance early in 1902. Japan now turned to British support and abandoned efforts to conciliate Russia, with whom she clashed constantly in

North China and Manchuria, and war between the two nations was now possible. England could remain unconcerned, since her growing interests in South China and the Yangtze Valley and her immense Indian possessions were rendered all the safer from possible Russian pressure. Meanwhile the German Emperor, pursuing his own designs, pressed his cousin Nicholas to fall upon Japan, seize Korea with its warm-water ports, and make sure of Manchuria as well. The German purpose, it has been judged, was to "mire" Russia in far-off Manchuria, so as to relieve Germany's eastern frontier in Europe from the danger of Russia's vast armies. Beyond this, there were obscure negotiations on foot, pointing to an eventual sharing of North China loot between Russia and Germany, in return for a promise of German support for Russian acquisition of Manchuria—in violation of the Open Door agreements. The vast but obscure schemes of the German rulers also envisaged binding Russia to their projected *Drang nach Osten*, the Berlin-Baghdad drive, though eventually Russian diplomacy saw no good for itself in this adventure. Meanwhile the German rulers, without cost to themselves, riding upon the backs of the Russians, plainly hoped to snatch increased territory in Shantung, north of China's Great Wall, to add to their fortified base at Kiau-Chau, and thus make it more defensible. The expected war began on February 8, 1904, with England, the secret ally of Japan, remaining passive, yet by the threat of her navy giving France (Russia's ally and financial backer), as well as Germany, reason for neutrality.

Britain intended to remain strong in the Orient, not by doctrines but by an alliance with the Japanese regarding mutual aid and "spheres of influence." Japan was a rising power. The weakening of Russia would make her more manageable after the war, and lead to her eventual attachment to the British system of alliances. English officials who watched over the future of India and the Near East were delighted at Russia's embroilment in Manchuria. Meanwhile in April, 1904, during the early stages of the war, the English concluded a second, important treaty, the Entente Cordiale with France, settling all matters of the control of Egypt and Morocco between them. The Kaiser's confused, poorly sustained diplomacy had been outdone at every step by the wily British maneuvers; when the British alliance with Russia was signed three years later—despite William's manly wooing of "Nicky" at Björköe—the encirclement of the too aggressive, heavily armed Germany was a reality.

4

Into this web of international pressures, intrigues, secret treaties, and fomented conflicts, the restless Roosevelt now trod. The American interests lay for the moment in safeguarding our possessions in the Philippines, lately pacified by Governor-General William H. Taft; but the paramount object was to maintain the Open Door for foreign trade in China, whatever the fortunes of the Russo-Japanese War. Hitherto American policy in the Far East, as McKinley and Hay had conceived it, had been identical. But the diplomatic struggle for free and impartial trade rights, among the concessions and spheres of influence of the various powers, was to be a long, losing fight. When Roosevelt sought to uphold the balance of power and made peace moves, ostensibly "for the sake of humanity," Britain moved not to persuade the Japanese.

As soon as hostilities started, the Kaiser appealed to the President, his American "admirer," through Ambassador Sternburg, to urge the belligerents to observe the neutrality of China "outside the sphere of military operations." This excluded, of course, Manchuria and North China, which the Kaiser evidently hoped would fall partly to the larger adversary, Russia, and partly to himself. Roosevelt agreed to circularize the powers with a note to this general effect, after altering the declaration in an important sense, to urge the observance of neutrality *in the whole of China's "administrative entity."* Thus it was from Washington rather than from Berlin that the circular note, boldly reasserting the Open Door policy, was issued on February 10, 1904.[28] The Kaiser thus acted

[28] Dennett, *op. cit.*, pp. 407-408.

as if piously supporting the Open Door doctrine together with his admirer, Roosevelt. This stratagem had little effect on the powers lined up for this war, who responded but indifferently. The Kaiser in this affair behaved with much duplicity toward his American friend, by secretly assuring Russia that he would recognize her conquest of Manchuria. The British government treated the Roosevelt declaration with suspicion, as if words about the territorial integrity of China mattered little against the realities of war and invasion, and of genuine British interests and combinations elsewhere in the world.[29] Russia, suspecting an American neutrality that was actually benevolent toward Japan, paid no heed to Roosevelt's enunciations from Washington upon Chinese territorial integrity. Roosevelt could not understand the Kaiser's underlying motives, but in collaborating with him to a limited extent he at times aroused the suspicions and fears of the British, who hinted that he was being led around by the nose, and insisted that the Kaiser plotted a great coalition against them.

The Rough Rider, in these moments, leaves us with the impression of one moving innocently between the lines of two enemy camps, filled with hidden gunpowder, while assuring the two implacable enemies that there is really nothing to quarrel about. He plainly did not grasp the character of the treacherous ground mined with secret alliances over which he walked, and trusted by informal diplomatic approaches to foster reconciliation, and to win German and British support for his own Pacific balance of power. More than once he assured Spring Rice, and the British Ambassador at Washington, Durand, that reports of the Kaiser's scheming against Britain were misguided. Meanwhile British coolness to his own pursuit of peace and balance in the Far East deeply disappointed him. In the opinion of most students of this period in world politics, Roosevelt failed completely to perceive the deep animosities between the two strongest European powers, as he ignored the real character of their commitments. In the end, more or less wittingly, "inevitably" he drifted into one of the two camps and thus rendered the other all the more desperate.

[29] Griswold, *Far Eastern Policy*, pp. 98-99, 102.

Meanwhile the war had gone hard for Russia, and her dubious friend, the Kaiser, also found no further gains to be derived from it. In January, 1905, before the battle of Mukden, and again in April the American President pressed his good offices for a mediated peace upon the Russian Czar and the Japanese government without effect. For many months, in voluminous diplomatic correspondence and informal approaches through his personal lines of communication, von Sternburg, Spring Rice, and Ambassador Jusserand, he strove to force the two warring nations into a conference, while at the same time he labored to bring England, France, and Germany to the support of his efforts. He believed, as he relates in his autobiography, "that a further continuance of the struggle would be a very bad thing for Japan, and even worse for Russia." At first Roosevelt had been almost as warm a friend of Japan's as England, fearing the Russians more strongly, and expressing in private a willingness to come to the aid of the Japanese, in force if need be. But the sweeping character of the Japanese victories ended by alarming him. At this rate all Asia, and the Philippines included, would be at the mercy of the new conquerors, and unexpected dangers were suggested. Meanwhile, though the usually ferocious Kaiser appeared favorable to Roosevelt's peacemaking, the English were silent, and held off, clearly refusing to second his efforts. Roosevelt, standing between the two alignments, could make nothing of the mutual suspicions and terrors felt on each side, even after the sensational visit of the Kaiser to Tangier in Morocco, March 31, 1905, which suddenly shifted the real theater of world struggle to northern Africa and the Mediterranean Sea. Roosevelt's ignorance was partly due to the lack of an active espionage organization at that time.

In his far-flung interventions and his world wanderings the American leader was like a willing soldier who does not see the whole of the battle front, nor the general configuration of the struggle. He did not know, for instance, until very late, that the English were silent because they were preparing to renew their secret alliance of 1902 with Japan in much stronger form, protecting their main Asiatic possessions more definitely than before—

this at a time, March-April, 1905, when the Japanese waited anxiously for the second Russian fleet steaming around the world to meet them.

But it was time for the war to end. The drain upon Japanese human and material resources was heavy; while the Russians accumulated a tremendous debt to French bankers and investors. Roosevelt, then, did not "stop" the Russo-Japanese war, as we now know. The closing of the purse strings at French and Anglo-American financial sources—for American bankers such as Kuhn, Loeb and Company also gave liberal aid to the Japanese—served as much as the sweeping naval victory of Togo, on May 27, 1905, to halt the war.

In April the French government had already hinted that Russia was ready to make terms. The Japanese, of their own accord, desired that the American President (rather than France) should act as mediator; and the first formal overtures for peace were made by them to Washington, May 31, 1905, immediately after their great naval victory. A week later, pressed by William II, the lethargic ruler of all the Russias indicated to the waiting American ambassador at St. Petersburg that if Mr. Roosevelt desired to act "on his own initiative" in treating with Japan, Russia would agree to a peace conference. The formal invitations to the belligerents then went forward; and Roosevelt busied himself with the essential preliminary work for the conference, which was set for August 10, 1905, at Portsmouth, New Hampshire.

It was to be an affair of novelty and pageantry, the arbitration of a great and terrible war between mighty empires, by the American President. World interest centered upon Oyster Bay, where the President received the envoys with simple ceremony upon the Presidential yacht; then shifted to the little New England city of Portsmouth. A visitor found Roosevelt weary but happy; he had been working tirelessly to carry through the affair, and feared obstacles and treachery at every turn.[30]

At the conference, the Japanese pretended to be firm in their

[30] Bishop, *op. cit.*, Vol. I, p 405.

demand for a huge money indemnity, as well as the various territories and spheres of influence they had marked out for themselves or conquered. The Russians, on the other hand, proved to be as hard to bargain with as ever, especially where money was concerned. Roosevelt, though he had favored Japan earlier as the ostensibly weaker adversary, was now keenly aware of the "yellow peril" to the Philippines, and unwilling to see Russia driven out of the Pacific. Therefore his main efforts were directed on the one hand to inducing the Japanese emissaries to give up the notion of indemnities—Russia was bankrupt, and it would have been necessary to capture Moscow to wring money from her. On the other hand, he strove to persuade the Russian government to yield as far as possible to Japan's territorial demands, for the fortress of Port Arthur, a protectorate in Korea, and cession of the southern half of Sakhalin Island. In the end nearly all of the Japanese real, minimum demands were accorded—after long and close negotiation, Russia contenting herself with the boon of having escaped an indemnity. In a sense, Roosevelt's intervention worked well for Japan, who he knew could not continue the war effectively.

Japan was left as virtually the dominant sea power in the Pacific, restrained after 1905 only by her economic exhaustion and her alliance with Britain. Probably her government had not actually counted upon wresting money from Russia; yet the failure to do this was attributed to President Roosevelt's interference. Mob rioting broke out in Tokyo, and Roosevelt—instead of the British government, to whom the peace was extremely important—became the scapegoat, "drawing the resentment of the Japanese people onto his own unpracticed shoulders." [31]

The war had been ended not a whit sooner than the British desired it to end, after their new secret treaty with Japan was initialed. But they wished it ended, within limits, for soon they would also have important treaty business on foot with the wretched Russians. Therefore the happiest solution for them diplomatically was for neutral America rather than themselves

[31] Griswold, *op. cit.*, pp. 121-122.

to stay the hands of their military allies from further conquest.[32]

Moreover Roosevelt, who congratulated himself upon having re-established a balance of power in the Pacific, had actually confirmed a status favoring the Anglo-Japanese domination, while German aspirations in China were thoroughly checked, her concessions in Shantung becoming untenable. The Russian Bear, most of all, had had his claws clipped in the Orient, and threatened less forcibly the British domain in India as well as China. Thereafter, rumors in the chancelleries of Europe told of how the English terrified the Czar with pictures of another Japanese attack upon his possessions (an attack which in 1905 had led to a bloody internal revolution), and which the English alone could restrain. Thus Russia soon became more eager to join the Anglo-French Entente in the West.

Universal applause for the peace-making President accompanied the signing of the historic Portsmouth Peace Treaty on September 5, 1905. Roosevelt in his toast to the Russian and Japanese emissaries at the opening of the conference had said that he prayed for a "just and lasting peace" not only for the two powers here represented, but for "all civilized mankind." [33] It was with this end in view, ostensibly, that he participated and intruded himself so vigorously into the affairs of the whole world. In studying the pattern of bold Rooseveltian interventions in the incessant struggles of the world's imperial rivals, we must ask ourselves constantly how much the real interests of the American republic were aided, and how much this international activism in Washington

[32] Roosevelt was scarcely neutral in the negotiations. For on July 29, 1905, preceding the peace conference, Secretary of War Taft on a tour of inspection to the Philippines was instructed to call at Tokyo as the President's special plenipotentiary. He bore a "memorandum," in effect a secret treaty, by which the United States was to recognize Japan's acquisition of Korea, while Japan agreed not to attack our Pacific possessions, the Philippines, etc. Yet the status of Korea, as a part of China's "integrity," was to be settled at the approaching Portsmouth conference. The Taft-Katsura "memorandum," and the later Root-Takahira "gentleman's agreement," remained in force, putting the United States in an informal alliance with Japan and Britain in the Far East.

[33] The New York *Tribune*, Aug. 6, 1905.

actually changed the order of things or furthered the humane end of world peace.

No sooner were measures taken to quench the flames in one part of the world, than they roared up in another place. Even while the Russo-Japanese War drew to its close, and Roosevelt's mediating efforts were bearing fruit, the world crisis over Morocco, with its menace of a general war of all the great powers in Europe, burst forth in the early spring of 1905. The mercurial President's attention now swung to the focal point in the Mediterranean, where once more he would endeavor to play his characteristic, leading part.

Once having begun, he must continue. After the Portsmouth Conference, Roosevelt said:

> In foreign affairs, we must make up our minds that, whether we wish it or not, we are a great people and must play a great part in the world. It is not open to us to choose whether we will play that great part or not. We have to play it. All we can decide is whether we shall play it well or ill.[34]

5

On March 31, 1905, the anxious motives of the German Emperor in seeking new friends, even as far afield as North America, became painfully clear. On that day he had disembarked at Tangier, Morocco, from a German cruiser, and, addressing the Sultan of Morocco in a deliberately "aggressive" speech (while trembling nervously at his own audacity), declared his hope and wish that Morocco would remain independent and free to the trade of all nations. The inwardly tormented, outwardly bellicose William II acted in accordance with the deliberate plan of his Foreign Minister, von Bülow, who convinced him that the hour had come to smoke out the secret terms of the Anglo-French Entente of 1904, relative to the partition of northern Africa, by an open challenge in that area and a demand for the Open Door. The German government in the discussions that followed William II's

[34] *Presidential Speeches,* Richmond, Va., Oct. 18, 1905, Vol. IV, p. 461.

visitation demanded that the status of neutral rights in Morocco be clarified, and that a conference to determine this question as well as that of "neutralization" of the Moroccan government be held. This the French, who were on the ground, refused; the English supported them, and secret mobilization began. Thus, as we have seen, the stage setting of the world-wide imperialist drama was shifted from the frozen prairies of Manchuria to the tropical, palm-fringed shores of Morocco.

William II and von Bülow, whose courting of Roosevelt had both titillated and mystified the man, now called upon him earnestly to defend with them the sacred and enlightened principle of the Open Door, the "co-operative" policy, in northern Africa as well as in China. The United States was asked to join Germany in requesting the other interested powers to agree to an international conference regarding the future status of Morocco, a conference in which the United States was to participate as an equal member, by virtue of previous though somewhat obsolete conventions with former Sultans. The Germans revealed the utmost anxiety to escape from the isolation which threatened them in the hostile world arena.[35]

The Emperor urged upon the President the gravity of the situation, telling him in memoranda transmitted through Sternburg that the Moroccan question was not an isolated one, but might lead either to war or to a new grouping of the world powers. "If England is successful in causing the refusal of France to join in a conference to settle the Morocco question, Germany will have to choose between war with France or between an understanding with France with regard to Morocco. . . . Everything he [William II] thinks depends on the attitude *you* may

[35] A. Vagts, *op. cit.*, Vol. II, pp. 1835-1843.

Dr. Vagts, after long study of German archives touching this period, attributes the idea of calling for American participation to the purpose of showing "peaceful" intentions on the part of Germany. Should war have come—and only the resignation of the French minister, Delcassé, averted it—then American participation in the preliminary discussions would have been a gauge of Germany's good faith in seeking peaceful solutions.

consider fit to take toward a conference of the treaty powers to settle the Morocco question."[36]

Thus "everything depended upon" Theodore Roosevelt, the Emperor of Germany assured him! General war, for which secret preparations were under way—or peace. The Kaiser through his Ambassador communicated charges of the plotting of England and France to gain an absolute ascendancy over Germany, and urged the President not to permit such an outcome, which would vitally affect the balance of power in the East, perhaps to the ultimate injury of American interests there. America must therefore help to bring about the conference over Morocco. Yet at this very time William himself returned to the wooing of Czar Nicholas, to whom he proposed a military alliance against England at a conference on board his yacht July 24, 1905.

Faced with the possibility of working for the balance of power in the Western World, to the advantage of Germany, Roosevelt turned less than impulsive, and hesitated prudently. With a very moderate enthusiasm, while admitting that the United States took only slight interest in Morocco, he made diplomatic overtures to both the French and the British governments for holding an international conference. In London, Lord Lansdowne appeared cool to any suggestion of a conference, and determined to fight in behalf of France if Germany attacked. Roosevelt, still unaware of the shaping of secret military alliances in Europe, and the secret agreements between France, England, Italy, and Spain to divide Morocco and Tripoli, decided at length to press for the international conference that might lessen the European tension, and also further peace in the Far East.

He approached the French, then, in serious vein. To Jules Jusserand, with whom Roosevelt was also upon very intimate, informal terms, he remarked that it might be advisable to make "concessions . . . that one can honorably make to avoid a conflict. . . . You must grant some satisfaction to the immeasurable

[36] Bishop, *op. cit.*, T. R. to Whitlaw Reid, Apr. 28, 1906, Vol. I, p. 471.

vanity of William. And it would be wise to help him save his face, if by doing so one could avoid war."[37]

Roosevelt then offered to employ his "initiative" in bringing about the conference, in a spirit friendly to France. Although United States interest in Morocco was slight, vigorous support would be lent France, if such a conference were held, in order to see to it that "unjust attacks by Germany upon French interests" would not succeed.[38]

In short, although the President in the Far Eastern war had favored Japan against Russia, in the Western crisis he favored France against Germany, saying, "France was right," and promising that he would not serve as a "decoy duck" for the Kaiser. Most important of all, he told the French ambassador in advance just what he would say to the German ambassador in regard to a conference whose conditions and limits were to be fixed by the French and the English![39] Moreover, the United States would not "accept the invitation to the conference unless France was willing." Upon these safe terms, France agreed on June 23, 1905, to let the President intervene for the maintenance of peace.

Roosevelt might flatter the Kaiser and remain his "admirer," desirous of going "hand in hand" with him; but in a pinch, to the intense disappointment of the German Foreign Office, he drifted toward the French, and more or less knowingly, the Anglo-French orbit.

He did continue to reason, like Admirals Mahan and Dewey, that while England could be forced to act as our friend, Germany, if she disposed of her European rivals, was to be feared as an ultimate enemy. Was not the configuration of the "Atlantic System" that John Hay saw accepted also by Roosevelt, in spite of his outward obeisances to William II? By this concept, America was

[37] *Documents Diplomatiques Français,* 2" Série, Tome VII, Paris, 1937. Jusserand to M. Rouvier, Jun. 18, 1905.

[38] Bishop, *op. cit.,* Vol. I, p. 478.

[39] *Documents Diplomatiques,* 2" Série, Tome VII. Jusserand to Rouvier, Jun. 25, 1905.

bound to be vitally affected by a shift in the western European balance. As Henry Adams stated it: "We have got to support France against Germany, and fortify an Atlantic system beyond attack; for if Germany breaks down England or France, she becomes the center of a military world, and we are lost." These were prophetic words, stating a formula which, right or wrong, was to be followed by American statesmen of either party in all the great crises of the twentieth century.[40]

Recently published documents, issued by the French government in 1937, reveal more strongly than ever how decidedly Roosevelt swung to the support of France in the Moroccan crisis.

On June 6, 1905, secret negotiations between France and Germany had led to the resignation of the bellicose Premier Delcassé, as partial appeasement for Germany. Yet nothing further was yielded in Morocco. The conference was to be one whose program, by the terms of the Anglo-French Entente, was fixed inalterably in advance. For the Kaiser to accept such a limited conference, under such narrow conditions, meant to take the appearance of things in place of the substance of them. He was to satisfy himself with the resignation of the hated Delcassé and the mere acceptance of a conference by his adversaries, while silently a great diplomatic triumph was scored for the Anglo-French Entente, which both excluded Germany from northern Africa and fashioned an iron ring of "encirclement" around her.[41]

At a time when tension between Germany and France made direct negotiation difficult, Roosevelt played the important part of pressing the Kaiser (through Sternburg) to swallow the bitter pill as really good candy. The French Diplomatic Documents, now reaching to 1906, show that in framing these letters to the head of the German government, the President showed them to Ambassador Jusserand in advance of delivery. "The letter to Baron von Sternburg . . . the President let me modify . . . while he dictated, and adopted without hesitation divers suggestions which

[40] Adams, *Letters*, Paris, Aug. 27, 1905, Vol. II, p. 461.

[41] Vagts, *op. cit.*, Vol. II, pp. 1858, 1860-1864.

I permitted myself to make."[42] In these messages Roosevelt warned Germany of the consequences of war.

> Without mentioning the certain loss of your colonies and your fleet which England will bring about, suppose that you triumph over France, the addition to your State of a new French Province would only increase the number of your enemies within your frontiers: it would be like a poison to you.[43]

Jusserand remarks in his secret reports to Paris that Mr. Roosevelt favored the cause of France more and more in public statements at this time. Roosevelt and Jusserand agreed also concerning the formula for the conference: there was to be officially "no program" and no discussion of points where either power was "engaged by honor, by previous engagements"—in short, a huge loophole permitting the program to be fixed in advance. Jusserand remarks:

> In all this the President has certainly sought as best he could and with the sincerest friendship, the most practical means in his judgment for avoiding the calamity of war. He has in any case despite the advances and solicitation of William II, refused to do or say anything that might range him on the side of the Germans in this quarrel. On the contrary, it is our cause that he has wished to defend, while observing, nevertheless, all the forms rendered necessary by the character of the German sovereign, and without which his words would have no effect.

Jusserand even paid tribute to Roosevelt's political courage in ignoring a numerous German voting population in America.[44] "Germany was to have her conference; France, Morocco." To Germany a momentary, illusory prestige from the affair; to France, empire over rich territories she had seized, and to Britain security for the imperial "life-line" running via Egypt and the Suez Canal to the Orient. Such is the consensus of German historians.[45]

[42] *Documents Diplomatiques,* IIe série, tome VII, pp. 126, 134, 157. Jusserand to Rouvier, Jun. 23, 24, 26, 1905.

[43] *Ibid.,* p. 157.

[44] *Ibid.,* pp. 180-181.

[45] Vagts, *op. cit.,* Vol. II, 1864.

Roosevelt declared that he feared a war that was to be a calamity for all of civilization, "what would literally be a world-conflagration." Hence he busied himself in sending to the Kaiser pleas couched in the most fulsome terms of flattery, that he preserve the peace of the world and earn the gratitude of untold generations, by accepting the empty conference offered him. The willingness of France to confer, he pretended, was a magnificent "triumph" for the Kaiser's diplomacy. Let him not cloud his high and honorable fame by raising difficulties over mere "minor details." [46] These minor details, as Roosevelt himself soon admitted privately, gave the "kernel of the nut" to France, and but the shell to Germany.

Henry Cabot Lodge, the chairman of the Senate Foreign Relations Committee, declared that the "local dispute in Morocco is a matter of indifference to us, but it is of very great importance to give France all the help we can." [47] Both Lodge and Roosevelt now expressed fear of the "young, aggressive military power, Germany." In designating Henry White to head the American delegation, Roosevelt wrote him:

> I want to keep on good terms with Germany and if possible to prevent a rupture between Germany and France. But my sympathies have at bottom been with France and I suppose will continue so. Still I shall try to hold an even keel.[48]

Elihu Root, now Secretary of State after Hay's death in July, 1905, instructed White that the American delegation must be careful to avoid injuring the Anglo-French Entente, "or be made a means of breaking that up. . . ." White was to "help France get what she ought to have," but also to make it as difficult as possible for anyone to pick a quarrel.[49]

At the Algeciras Conference, sitting from mid-January to April, 1906, the American delegation labored to throw the moral influ-

[46] Bishop, *op. cit.*, Vol. I, pp. 481, 484-488.

[47] Lodge, *Correspondence*, Aug. 14, 1905, Vol. II, p. 172.

[48] *T. R. Papers*, Aug. 23, 1905.

[49] Nov. 28, 1905; Nevins, *White*, p. 267.

ence and diplomatic weight of the United States into the balance for peace—though on conditions unfavorable to Germany. According to the amusing account of Harold Nicolson, whose father Sir Arthur, hero of *The Portrait of a Diplomatist,* was the British representative at the conference, the Americans worked with the British and French delegations almost better than they knew to force German surrender on all important points.

At one stage of the affair, March 21, 1906, the Kaiser balked at accepting the Franco-British formula for predominantly French police and military rule of the Moroccan ports (a disguised, or "creeping," annexation). Roosevelt once again put pressure upon the Germans, threatening before Sternburg to publish the entire correspondence with the Kaiser (some of it of very embarrassing nature) if a break-up of the conference were forced by German resistance. On the other hand, if the Emperor would yield, Mr. Roosevelt would issue public statements crediting him for the success of the conference and preservation of peace, and would also undertake to receive at the White House a delegation of German war veterans with special honors, as an occasion for public manifestation of United States friendship for Germany and her monarch. Roosevelt contended that the Emperor had promised to accept a solution which he, Roosevelt, held to be "fair." Reports of increasing anti-German feeling in America, again, helped the Emperor to yield on this point. The public encomia for the Emperor by the President and the public reception of German veterans at the White House were then duly demanded and given.[50]

A year after the Algeciras Conference, the British were able to complete their military alliance with Russia. Thus "encirclement" was complete, and the Central Powers lived thenceforth in an atmosphere of military nightmare up to August, 1914. Years of active Rooseveltian intervention in world power politics, as the head of a world power, changed in no way the developing alignment of the great powers that brought nearer the catastrophe of the first imperialist world war. In the Pacific, the Taft-Katsura "memorandum" preserved a friendly alliance between the United

[50] Bishop, *op. cit.*, Vol. I, pp. 500-502.

States and Japan and paralleled and supported the Anglo-Japanese alliance. In the European area, the Square Deal President, despite his fleeting wishes for friendly relations with the German Emperor, ended by supporting firmly the French, and therefore the English, "line" in the Morocco crisis, thus bringing the United States solidly into the Anglo-French axis. For the first time in our history, America was directly involved in the family quarrels of the great European Powers. From the conquest of the Caribbean, the Panama Canal venture, the penetration of the Pacific and China, to the American-European policy indicated at Algeciras in 1906—when our "frontier" first approached the Rhine River—there was a procession of fateful steps leading to an ever deeper involvement of American policy in the power politics of two hemispheres.

VII. THE POLITICS OF REFORM

WHILE Theodore Roosevelt, figuratively speaking, wandered over the world, an imperial monarch with silk hat and Big Stick, the political weather along the home front in America grew unsettled and stormy. Nor was he, who kept always such a sharp eye to the weather, unaware of the unfavorable signs of popular unrest. Returning from his rather glamorous forays among emperors and their plenipotentiaries, he might recall that large tasks of domestic reform and lawmaking, more prosaic and arduous than foreign conquests or diplomatic enterprises, were still left undone. This was largely owing to the obstinacy of the conservative and "greedy" rich, he would recall, and of their Standpat representatives in politics.

> I don't at all like the social conditions at the present [he wrote to Secretary Taft]. The dull purblind folly of the very rich men, their greed and arrogance, and the way in which they have unduly prospered by the help of the ablest lawyers . . . these facts and the corruption of business and politics have tended to produce a very unhealthy condition of excitement and irritation in the popular mind, which shows itself in part in the enormous increase in the socialistic propaganda.
>
> Nothing effective, because nothing at once honest and intellectual is being done to combat the great amount of evil which, mixed with a little good, a little truth, is contained in these outpourings. . . . Some of these socialists, some of them [are] lurid sentimentalists; but they are all building up a revolutionary feeling, which will probably take the form of a political campaign. Then we may have to do too late, or almost too late, what had to be done in the silver campaign [of 1896] when in one summer we had to convince a good many people that what they had been laboriously taught several years ago was untrue. . . .[1]

[1] *T. R. Papers*, T. R. to Taft, Mar. 15, 1906.

Here as in his letter to Knox of the year before Roosevelt expresses candidly his fear of the coming of deep class divisions into our politics, with the struggle of the Have-Nots against the Haves imperiling the existing order of things. Once more, it is his conviction, constantly expressed, that he could manage the masses of the people if the "arrogant rich" did not obstruct his program of moderate concessions. At the moment the fate of the long-postponed railroad reform bill urged by the administration hung in the balance in the Senate. As before, the coterie of elder statesmen, headed by Nelson Aldrich of Rhode Island, persisted in opposition tenaciously and skillfully. Would they delay, obstruct, until it was too late?

Albert Beveridge, who, sensing the tide of opinion, fought nowadays in Congress as a champion of social justice, wrote to Roosevelt that it was too late for the slogan of "Let well enough alone!" He concluded:

> The truth about it is that nearly all the older politicians are like a bunch of belated travellers who have come to catch a train and stand on the platform waiting for it, when as a matter of fact the train has passed on a long while ago.[2]

The mind of the great middle class continued to be obsessed by the fear of the trusts. Miss Tarbell's *History of the Standard Oil Company* appeared in 1904 in book form and was read by an army of readers. Thus a work of contemporary history contributed to the long series of public prosecutions undertaken against the chieftains of Standard Oil, now to be climaxed by the action of the Department of Justice under Roosevelt.

In February, 1905, *Everybody's Magazine*, following the course of *McClure's*, began publication of a series of articles by Charles Edward Russell which were a study of the methods of the Chicago meat-packing companies—"The Greatest Trust in the World." Each month that year half a million readers learned with horror that the methods of the great beef trust did not halt at poisoning its customers. The feeling of nausea aroused by

[2] Aug. 2, 1906; Bowers, *op. cit.*, p. 238.

the scandals concerning the Chicago packers was enhanced the following year when Upton Sinclair's *The Jungle* appeared. A Federal investigation followed these disclosures, and a stormy demand for a national pure-food law was heard in the land. But even while alarm and anger at the infamies of the trusts penetrated to the pit of the American stomach, Thomas W. Lawson, in his studies of "Frenzied Finance," which appeared in *Everybody's*, disabused not only the "lambs" of Wall and State Streets but the thrifty who entrusted their money in savings accounts and insurance policies to great and respectable institutions.

In December, 1904, Lawson, a spectacular market-plunger, who had fallen on lean days and turned "informer" against his erstwhile confederates, announced somewhat casually that he was going to "cause a life insurance blaze" that would be long remembered. Earlier he had told how rulers of the Standard Oil ("The System"), by controlling a great bank, such as the National City Bank of New York, were able to manipulate the money and security markets at will. Lawson described how the manipulation of the recently formed Amalgamated Copper Company stock had brought to investors a loss of one hundred millions of dollars. Bank deposits belonging to the public, he contended, were diverted to assure control by "insiders" of the $153,000,000 copper trust. But now, he charged, the assets of the four largest insurance companies, totaling three billions of dollars, formed a reservoir of speculative capital for masters of the stock market. The huge New York Life Insurance Company, he said, lay under the control of the Standard Oil; and the policyholders' life savings were at the mercy of the Standard Oil crowd in speculative and piratical adventures.[3]

The public sensation caused by Lawson's general charges against the formerly sacrosanct insurance companies—and met by them only with evasive denials or embarrassed silence—led the publisher of the powerful New York *World* to enter the case. Soon specific exposures followed Lawson's allusions; President John

[3] Filler, *Crusaders for American Liberalism*, pp. 190-193.

McCall of the New York Life Insurance Company resigned, for reasons that remained obscure; in the equally large Equitable Life Assurance Society, dissension burst forth among the executives at the same time. After September, 1905, the investigations of a New York legislative committee into insurance company affairs engrossed the public. Its legal counsel, who examined a long line of political, social, and financial celebrities, was Charles Evans Hughes, described then as "young, thin, pallid, insistent, with merciless, cold gray eyes and a mouth suggesting a steel trap." [4]

The pitiless Mr. Hughes drew a detailed picture of corruption in high places. For many years the great insurance companies, subject to state laws, had exerted themselves to influence state and national governments by regular secret distributions of money to politicians under the head of "legal expenses" or "supply department." George W. Perkins, Morgan's partner and vice-president of the Equitable, usually handled the lobbying and corruption funds. But more important than the tales of the "House of Mirth," set up in Albany for the entertainment of local statesmen, was the picture of interlocking controls by which insurance funds were kept on deposit with chosen banks or trust companies, which were, in turn, subsidiaries of the insurance companies. A second important use of insurance reserves was to invest them in new securities financed by bankers who were also directors of the insurance companies. Thus members of the firm of J. P. Morgan and Company, or Kuhn, Loeb and Company, sitting as directors of the New York Life, or Equitable, would approve readily of the purchase of securities originated and sold by themselves as investment bankers.

The contest of the Morgan and the Rockefeller-Harriman groups for control of the Equitable Life Assurance Society, inheritance of the frivolous young James H. Hyde, now became comprehensible to intelligent Americans. For the prize at stake was nothing less than control of billions in institutional reserves.

[4] The New York *World*, Oct. 11, 1905.

Thus little by little the real contours of the new system of monopoly capitalism, which conquered ever larger areas of American life, became known to thoughtful Americans through the writings of critical journalists and the cross examinations of great lawyers, such as Hughes and Brandeis, who prosecuted the "robber barons" before the bar of public opinion. Among the comfortable but democratic middle classes, uneasiness over the progress of the monopolists grew until it became the central political problem of the age.

Among the working classes, discontent and opposition took stronger form after 1900. An active minority, perhaps a fourth of organized labor, followed Eugene Debs, the inspiring leader of the 1894 general railway strike, in building a new party devoted to the principles of Marxian socialism. Debs delivered in 1904 six to ten speeches every day and carried the message of socialism into every state and territory with such burning zeal that he became a national figure. Yet the majority of the trade-unionists continued to hold by Samuel Gompers' "pure and simple" trade unionism. This meant the solid building of the federated trade unions as a national system, the unending fight for more favorable hours and wages, and for immediate, rather than ultimate, political advantages.

Though the main body of trade-unionists avoided the party of socialism and voted Republican or Democratic, to "reward friends and punish enemies," the mood even of conservative labor grew exasperated in 1906. For many years, ever since 1898, Gompers and P. J. McGuire of the A. F. of L. had lobbied patiently before Congress in an effort to win an amendment to the Sherman Anti-Trust Act that would eliminate its application to labor combinations. In 1906, labor circles reeled under the blow of the famous Danbury Hatters' decision of the Supreme Court, imposing punitive money damages against all the members of a union that had engaged in a strike and boycott.

Gompers now toiled in earnest to exert the force of labor in elections. The American Federation of Labor sent speakers into various districts to oppose the election of Congressmen who had shown a strong anti-labor spirit.[5]

In the Rocky Mountain region, where mining was one of the principal industries, a more militant labor movement had grown up since the late '90's in the shape of the Western Federation of Miners. Here in this rude world but recently carved out by pioneers the industrial conflict often took the form of pitched gun battles between strikers and civil or military authorities. In February, 1906, former Governor Steunenberg of Idaho (who had once called for Federal troops to put down a strike) was assassinated. The alleged confession of a suspect implicated the heads of the Western Federation of Miners—Haywood, Moyer, and Pettibone—as supposed accomplices; and because these men resided at the time in Colorado, an Idaho sheriff took the bold step of kidnapping all three of them and bringing them to face justice in Idaho, scene of the assassination.[6]

The trial of Haywood, Moyer, and Pettibone became a *cause célèbre* of 1906. Throughout the country funds were raised, petitions circulated, and even the American Federation of Labor made the case its own. The writ of injunction in labor cases was bad enough; but now the kidnapping of labor leaders, shorn of those civil rights that all criminals had to defend themselves in an extradition process, aroused immense indignation. To their defense came the colorful Chicago lawyer and radical philosopher, Clarence Darrow, who had defended Debs in 1894; the prosecuting attorney in the long-drawn-out trial was William E. Borah of Idaho. "Big Bill" Haywood and his colleagues were finally acquitted, on the ground of insufficient evidence; but out of the passions roused by this struggle came greater strength for the new Industrial Workers of the World, fathered by Haywood, Eugene Debs, and Daniel De Leon. The I.W.W., planned as an industrial union and dedicated to the "class struggle," proposed to continue the fight by violent as well as peaceful means, "until the workers of the world organize as a class, take possession of the earth and

[5] Gompers, *Seventy Years*, Vol. II, pp. 239-240.

[6] Sullivan, *op. cit.*, Vol. III, pp. 481 ff.

the machinery of production, and abolish the wage system."[7]

To a Theodore Roosevelt, sensitive to the public pulse and also respectful toward violence, the rise of militant "syndicalist" leaders like Haywood, the sudden growth of the Socialist party under Debs, the coming of intellectuals like Darrow to their camp, were signs of a falling political barometer forecasting social storms. Against such eventualities, of which he had so often given gloomy warnings, he must prepare to act, to throw all his powerful influence and force into the balance.

2

But while the labor movement now directed a constant pressure on the political government to yield anti-injunction laws, trust-act amendments, and the eight-hour day, the farm regions too showed signs of a growing disaffection which endangered the ruling party's historic alliance between business and agriculture. Rural discontent was of course chronic, since the protective tariff had long favored manufacturing as against farming. Its recurrence between 1901 and 1904, after several years of good farm prices, followed by a period of sharply rising living costs, was scarcely surprising. The Roosevelt victory in the 1904 elections had brought to Congress a group of agrarian leaders who called themselves Progressive Republicans and voiced the traditional demands of the farm belt. Of these leaders the most prominent was Robert M. La Follette, twice Governor of Wisconsin, and now elected to the United States Senate.

The press of the whole country watched the march of Wisconsin's "Little Giant" upon Washington with mixed curiosity and fear. He had delayed his departure for the East, in the autumn of 1905, and had gone to Chicago with his advisers to complete the last details of the new railroad tax law for Wisconsin, born of many years of struggle. En route to Washington, where he arrived in mid-January of 1906, he was much inter-

[7] Brissenden, *The I.W.W.*, Appendix II, citing preamble to constitution of 1908.

viewed and gave out vigorous public statements on the issues of the day.

The Senator, who was born in a log cabin in Primrose, Wisconsin, child of desperately poor settlers, was a man of wholly different stamp from those who ruled the councils of the brilliant Roosevelt administration. There was grimness and anger in him; he had taken his stand long ago as the champion of the "little American"; thus the contest for office had been made longer and harder, but he arrived at last in the national capital with his hands singularly free. Nor did he need to give thought to the diplomacy of machines and bosses. It was this thoroughgoing, unswerving independence that made political observers rate La Follette, in a day when more than one picturesque crowd leader held the stage—such as Bryan, Pitchfork Ben Tillman, or Tom Johnson—as by all odds the most "dangerous" of the radicals.

La Follette was a Mid-Western Solon. The "Wisconsin Idea" which he championed was a product of the intensely democratic Middle West farmers, who had in earlier times demanded principally liberty from the state. Now the sons of the frontiersmen had turned with the later Populists to erect governmental safeguards to preserve their liberties from abuse by the corporate monopolies of modern times. In pursuing this general plan for Wisconsin, La Follette "consulted" not railroad lawyers nor lumber barons, but professors at the University of Wisconsin, such as Ely, Commons, and Van Hise. A special office for a statistical research director to aid the State Legislature was created, and this contributed largely to the effective writing of laws. Soon, in contrast with the wavering course of a Theodore Roosevelt whether at Albany or at Washington, La Follette had succeeded in pushing through a large body of new statutes, bringing sweeping reforms of child labor and working conditions for women, corporation practice, taxation of railroads and public utilities, primary elections, labor disputes, workmen's compensation. For other states, Wisconsin became a sort of experimental social laboratory where new legislation was carefully tested and perfected in the light of knowledge gained from similar experience in all parts of the world. By developing and applying, for example, the device of the administrative commission of "experts" to regulate and judge of technical questions, which the popular mandate could not accurately decide, La Follette made a very high contribution to our political knowledge. These were the methods pursued later with notable success by men like Alfred Smith (in his liberal heyday) and other followers. What would the Little Giant do? Would he rend asunder the Republican party, as Bryan had rent the Democratic party ten years before? Would he capture its national leadership? Would he continue in his triumphal progress, overriding all opposition single-handed until he reached the Presidency itself?

The Old Guard in the Senate were prepared to waste few courtesies on La Follette. With a touch of wry humor they appointed him to the Committee to Investigate the Condition of the Potomac River Front, a committee which had never yet held a meeting, as La Follette relates, nor had a bill referred to it. Their precautions were justified. From the date of La Follette's arrival, there began the first strong movement of "insurgence" in Congress since the Free Silver uprisings of the early 1890's.

From the start, La Follette declared himself a devoted supporter of President Roosevelt's policies. Debate was proceeding, carried over from the previous session, upon the long-deferred railroad reform bill; and despite the unwritten law that new Senators must make themselves scarce for at least their first year, La Follette, in protest at the bowdlerizing of the administration bill, began on April 19, 1906, his famous first three-day set speech, an open call to revolt against the Aldrich dictatorship. This speech was held, as the correspondent of the Sioux City (Iowa) *Journal* reported, to be "a deliberate insult to the Senate," as well as a defiance of party discipline. In retaliation the Senators showed the new member extreme discourtesy, and one by one they left the chamber, until only three remained to watch him, one of them the aged Allison of Iowa. Walking up and down, "shaking his pompadour in a fine frenzy," and pointing his finger at old Allison, La Follette made his famous prophecy of doom:

Mr. President, I pause in my remarks to say this. I cannot be wholly indifferent to the fact that Senators by their absence at this time indicate their want of interest in what I have to say upon this subject. The public is interested. Unless this important subject is rightly settled, seats now temporarily vacant may be permanently vacated by those who have the right to occupy them at this time.[8]

Several years later, La Follette reverted to his prediction of 1906, pointing out that twenty-four Senators who had refused to lend him their ears, a huge proportion of those who stood for the next election, were now retired to private life.

Theodore Roosevelt's sharp veerings, his lapses into reform, so to speak, can be understood only in relation to the growing pressure brought upon him by the radicals. Left to his own devices, he tended to wait, to hesitate, to temporize, like so many other professed reformers who were ready to believe that the mere occupation of office by themselves meant the winning of the battle. But the arrival of a La Follette, fresh from his provincial successes, to a leading place in national politics was a portent and a reminder.

Now Bryan, the "peerless leader" of the opposition party after 1904, began to urge radical policies for the Democrats. His influential weekly newspaper, *The Commoner*, kept up a constant fire of criticism upon Mr. Roosevelt, pointing out week after week the compromising features of his tactics. According to the indefatigable adversary, Roosevelt was dangerously "Hamiltonian" and believed that "the well-born were born to rule"—a very accurate judgment of the President's convictions. Great opportunities lay before the powerful President, said Bryan, but his own instincts led him to protect the "plutocracy," whatever he might say in his set speeches year after year. Bryan challenged him on a series of issues. What was President Roosevelt doing (1) to advance the Eight-Hour Day, even to the extent of enforcing it in the District of Columbia on government contracts? (2) What was he doing to bring about a constitutional amendment permitting "more democ-

[8] *The Commoner*, May 25, 1906; La Follette, *Autobiography*, p. 414.

racy" through the Direct Election of Senators? (3) What of more vigorous prosecution of monopolies? Why were horse-thieves who broke the law given criminal punishment, while trust magnates who broke the law went unpunished? (4) Why was nothing done about the infamous court injunction used in labor disputes? (5) Why was there still no strict regulation of the railroads, after all these years? Why did President Roosevelt still oppose giving to the Interstate Commerce Commission the real power to initiate and fix railroad rates? What truth was there after all in the legend of the "iron man in the White House"? Bryan's organ asked.[9]

Thus after years of good fortune and comparatively smooth sailing Theodore Roosevelt faced an increasingly troubled and critical public opinion at home after 1904. Though he stood at the zenith of his power and glory, thanks chiefly to foreign exploits, his hesitations were noticed, his compromises were measured by would-be rivals for popular leadership.

The danger of party cleavage was always perfectly real to him. In the northwestern tier of states, hitherto staunchly Republican, he felt the constant clamor for downward revision of the tariff and increased trust prosecution. The clamor for more effective railroad regulation, led by La Follette and others, threatened to become a veritable "prairie fire." Yet for nearly two years, up to 1906, the clique of Aldrich and Cannon that still ruled Congress had warily forestalled legislative action.

The essence of Roosevelt's diplomacy, as Professor C. E. Merriam has pointed out, lay in pursuing tactics of combination, and in avoiding the "permanent consolidation of any one group against him. . . ." His "on the one hand" and "on the other hand" policy enabled him to hold the middle class, and alternately to attract and repel the labor group and the business group. "Broadly speaking . . . he was always detaching part of a group, commercial, labor or otherwise, and preventing solid opposition against him."[10] It was in very fear of a rupture within his party and of a

[9] *The Commoner*, Nov. 18, 1904; Dec. 9, 1904; Apr. 13, Apr. 20, 1906.

[10] Merriam, *Four American Party Leaders*, p. 34.

combination of militant sectional and class movements, including Bryan, La Follette, and even Debs, that the Square Deal President now turned resolutely to the unpleasant business of writing large reforms into the statutes. For more than four years he had preached the Ten Commandments, yet no signal legislative achievements were credited to his name.

3

In the late summer and autumn of 1905, at the very climax of his foreign diplomatic adventures, the President in a series of speeches indicated that he was turning to renew his delayed "drive" for domestic reform. On August 11, 1905, at Chautauqua, New York, he spoke of the beef packers as violators of the trust laws, and hinted that their very efforts to evade or resist the law would soon bring sterner laws for their supervision. A few weeks later, in another public address, he promised that he would again seek the passage of an act reinforcing the supervision of the railroads by the Interstate Commerce Commission. He declared that he was opposed to the government ownership of anything that might "be left in private hands," but it would be impossible to go on without "controlling" the railroads. Recently, some public scandal had been caused by the report that a great railway, the Santa Fe, had continued granting rebates to certain large shippers such as the Standard Oil in spite of the Elkins Act of 1903, which expressly forbade such practices. Roosevelt now urged that the I.C.C. must have the power to examine the books of the railroads. He hoped to see all the necessary power granted to the government, but, he qualified, "I would far rather see some of it granted . . . than see a pretence of granting all in some shape that really amounts to nothing."[11]

Roosevelt's speeches that summer and autumn bespoke preparations for an approaching conflict. He talked less often nowadays of the capitalists who "in making fortunes for themselves have

[11] Roosevelt, *Speeches,* Vol. IV, pp. 450-476.

done good to all of us." The recent literature of exposure, sensational articles on the beef trust, the Hughes investigation of the insurance companies, had hardened public opinion and permitted stronger measures of attack. In December, 1905, Attorney General W. H. Moody ordered trust prosecutions by the Federal authorities in many fields. The huge Standard Oil and American Tobacco companies were already under investigation; in addition eight indictments were found by Federal grand juries in December against the Armour, Swift, Cudahy, and Morris packing companies of Chicago, and against certain railroads, notably the Chicago and Alton, accused of granting special rebates on freight charges to the stockyard companies.[12]

Thus the tumultuous Rooseveltian battle for domestic reform was under way as the new "progressive" Congress arrived to hear the President's annual message of December 9, 1905, demanding a varied program of legislation, including a pure-food law, a new enabling act for further measures of forest and soil conservation, a law requiring publicity for party election expenses, and, most important of all, a law that would compel the railroads to grant "just and reasonable" rates. Once more, however, nothing was said about tariff revision.

It was the reading of Upton Sinclair's novel *The Jungle*, early in 1906, that led this literary President to take up the fight for a pure-food law. Finley Peter Dunne ("Mr. Dooley") firmly believed that Mr. Roosevelt was moved to his very bowels by the famous passage in Sinclair's work which describes, with a Zolaësque realism, how a careless workman falls into a vat and is turned into sausage.

> "Annyhow, Tiddy was toying with a light breakfast an' idly turnin' over th' pages iv th' new book with both hands. Suddenly he rose from th' table, an' cryin': 'I'm pizened,' began throwin' sausages out iv th' window. Th' ninth wan shtruck Sinitor Biv'ridge on th' head an' made him a blond. . . ."

[12] The New York *Times*, Dec. 14, 15, 16, 1905.

While controversy raged over the truth of Sinclair's tragic and powerful novel of the stockyards inferno, the President dispatched special agents to the scene, and soon had from them a sober report that was if anything more revolting still. A Pure Foods Bill, often advocated by the enthusiastic Dr. Harvey W. Wiley, chief chemist of the Department of Agriculture, was now rapidly pushed through Congress. A companion measure, the Meat Inspection Bill, covering specifically control of the great meat-packing plants, was written by Albert Beveridge, with Roosevelt's strong approval, and introduced in Congress as a "rider" for an appropriation bill.

But the packers and the cattlemen rallied and descended upon Washington with one of the most tenacious lobbies ever seen there. Once more the struggle for "constitutional liberty" (for packing houses) raged in Congress. In the lower House, the teeth of the Beveridge bill were drawn one by one; and only torrential speeches in the Senate and new exposures (through publication of the government's report) were enough to save part of the bill. Beveridge suspected that the President yielded too easily to the opposition, and the two men clashed angrily. In truth, the law was so rewritten that inspection of meats was to be at government expense, rather than that of the accused packers. Amid the popular hue and cry, with Beveridge appealing to the Senate not to "surrender to the next biggest monopoly in the United States, after the Standard Oil," even Aldrich yielded his assent, and a creditable measure was passed at length—a minor victory for the Rooseveltians.[13]

Much closer to the heart of the Rooseveltian politics lay the movement for the conservation of America's natural resources. In the "great barbecue" that followed Lincoln's Homestead Act of 1862, the distribution of the national domain in the West had proceeded in an incredibly rapid and wasteful fashion. The approaching impoverishment of our forests and of our soil—then a nearly incredible notion—was first heard of in the 1890's. Professor Frederick J. Turner, in his famous historical essay, *The Significance of*

[13] Bowers, *op. cit.*, p. 230.

the Frontier in American History, now pointed to the end of the great frontier movements that had been recurring, in wave after wave, since the sixteenth century.

Thanks to a small group of public-spirited citizens an act of 1891 passed by Congress provided for the withdrawal from sale of certain public lands suitable for forest reserves. Thus a far-reaching principle was established that turned away from unbridled individualism and fixed responsibility for the country's natural resources, in some measure, upon the national government. Roosevelt while Governor of New York was one of those who began to support projects for setting up state forest reserves. But in 1902 the movement was given further impetus when a law devised by Senator Newlands of Nevada, providing for the reclamation and conservation of water-power resources, was placed on the statutes.[14]

The heart and soul of the conservation movement was Gifford Pinchot, Theodore Roosevelt's friend and a member of the "Tennis Cabinet." This handsome, wealthy young man had made forestry his life work, having spent years studying the forest reserves of France, Germany, and Switzerland. Returning to America, where he served as head of the government's Forest Service after 1897, Pinchot began to preach conservation everywhere, not merely for the sake of forests, but as a program for a "new patriotism . . . of national service." It meant not merely growing big trees and digging irrigation ditches, but the husbanding of vast resources for the welfare of the people as a whole. It set up the ideal of national husbandry in an age that seemed to be up in arms against land-grabbers or exploiters of political privilege profiting by the unearned increment of land speculation. With a collective

[14] In the years 1862 to 1926, under the Homestead Act and amendments, the government issued 1,391,128 patents for approximately 226,159,053 acres of land, which passed to private ownership. In addition 137,000,000 acres were granted to railroads or to states for railroad building. Of the private lands "commuted" or granted title after six months, by payments of $1.25 to $2.50 per acre, a huge share was taken by large corporations through their agents. A land-office agent estimated for the government that inspection showed that of "commuted" homesteads not one in a hundred was ever occupied as a home. (Hibbard, *History of Public Land Policy*, pp. 387, 389.)

plan that looked toward the future, it opposed the waste and confusion of individual and local land usage. The cause of national conservation, in short, was peculiarly appealing to the Rooseveltians. Roosevelt and his friends, who recoiled at the notion of socializing the railroads, could take up the fight for conservation as a cause embracing all their convictions of "moral righteousness" in government. Planned conservation, as the ardent, mystical Pinchot contended, would not merely save our public resources from the control of the monopolists, but guarantee "an equal opportunity for every American citizen to get the fair share of the benefit" from these resources. It would both create and distribute wealth; it would carry democracy into new ground, making of our country a "Nation of Homes," a society of small landholders, "bringing the Kingdom of God on Earth." [15]

With the aid of Gifford Pinchot and Secretary of Interior Garfield, Roosevelt explored the provisions of the old Act of 1891; he found that he could withdraw large quantities of government lands from distribution, and after 1902 he aggressively pushed the withdrawal of forest reserves until he could claim that by 1909 he had increased their area from 43 to 194 million acres. Private corporations, railroads, utilities, and mining companies, which used government lands, were restricted or regulated under a plan of "stewardship" for the public. Soon public undertakings that equaled the vast cost of the Panama Canal were under way for the development of inland waterways, the irrigation of deserts, and the preservation of power sites.

The program of conservation was popular among the majority of the citizens, and La Follette, who sometimes spoke harshly of Theodore Roosevelt, called it the most constructive and permanent achievement of his period in office. Yet the removal of large lands from private use did not go unopposed. Claim hunters and their political allies, especially in Western states having rich mineral or timber land, were aggrieved and began to resist Roosevelt's measures actively. Nevertheless, thanks to the enthusiasm he engen-

[15] Pinchot, *The Fight for Conservation*, pp. 26, 115.

dered for conservation, an important act was passed in June, 1906, enlarging the Forest Service and extending its authority.

In the following year the Roosevelt administration pressed its fight for conservation to new victories. A stubborn group of opposition Congressmen who desired to curb the President's occasionally high-handed actions in this field managed, with the help of skillful lobbyists, to have Congress pass a bill prohibiting further withdrawals of public lands in the six northwestern states, unless authorized by Congress. To veto this bill—presented as a "rider" to a routine Department of Agriculture appropriation bill—would have been awkward. Therefore Roosevelt had Garfield and Pinchot map out every acre of the public domain that had a bush on it and could serve for potential timberland. These lands, sixteen million acres in all, he removed from the reach of land-grabbers, by an eleventh-hour executive decree, in accordance with the law of 1891. Then, this done, he humorously signed the new bill which revoked his power to take such action. The opponents of the Forest Service, he recalled afterward, "turned handsprings in their wrath; and dire were their threats. . . ."[16]

4

By strenuous fighting for conservation, for pure-food and meat-inspection laws, and by frequent indictments of trusts, Roosevelt appeared to wage the struggle for reform with increasing vigor. His main objective, however, was still the passage of stronger laws regulating the railroads. To the press he stated frankly that the hour was late, that the people must have relief from the burdensome rates of the railroads. Yet in this contest he feared the outcome. The railroads, he felt, were "crazy" in their hostility. In the winter of 1906, while the railroad bill was being debated, Mr. Harriman and his lawyer, Sidney Webster, came several times to Washington and expressed the strongest objection, not only to the railroad bill but to investigations of the Harriman lines being made

[16] Roosevelt, *An Autobiography*, pp. 404-405.

by the Interstate Commerce Commission. It was plain that Harriman, who had raised $250,000 for the campaign of 1904, was becoming alienated, although in endeavoring to learn what he desired the President could get nothing but "general allegations or sweeping accusations" from him.[17]

In a public address on October 19, 1905, Roosevelt had already hinted that he would willingly accept *only a part* of the power he sought in order to regulate the railroads; it was a hint of compromise. His Message to Congress of December 9, 1905, whose main feature was the appeal for railroad control, also reiterated his prudent position of the year before: "My proposal is not to give the Interstate Commerce Commission power to initiate or originate rates generally, but to regulate a rate already fixed or originated by the roads, upon complaint and after investigation." The new rates to be established were to be, of course, "subject to review by the courts." Full publicity for the accounts of the railroad was another condition he favored.

The remarkable thing was that twenty years after the Interstate Commerce Act had become law, the Commission it established had almost no power to interfere with the activities of railroads. One of the members had even resigned lately, making public protests at the impotence of this regulatory body. Even its limited power had been stripped away—chiefly on the Constitutional ground of "due process"—by the remorseless reasoning of the Supreme Court, the court which Senator Aldrich was said to trust in as he trusted in Providence. The Commission could not of its own authority fix rates for the railroads, for such action might result in "confiscation." On the other hand, if a fair valuation of the railroad properties could once be established, as La Follette urged, then "reasonable" rates permitting fair profits might be fixed. But the very mention of government appraisal of the railroad properties and fixing of their rates aroused terror of a red Socialist revolution in Senatorial breasts.

In January the act enlarging the powers of the Interstate Com-

[17] *T. R. Papers,* T. R. to Sidney Webster, Jan. 31, 1907.

merce Commission, in line with the President's moderate views, was introduced in Congress by Representative Hepburn of Iowa. After brief debate, the bill was quickly passed by the Lower House —Speaker Cannon evidently offering no resistance—and committed to the charge of a committee of the Senate for consideration. Here, the leader of the "Railway Senators," the multi-millionaire Elkins of West Virginia, was chairman; beside him stood Nelson Aldrich, the "dictator," with divers faithful Republican followers. Tillman, on behalf of the Democratic minority in the Senate's Committee on Interstate Commerce, it was expected, would be able to accomplish nothing, and the bill would either be strangled by amendments or altogether killed.

The Old Guard was willing to grant power to the government commission, ostensibly to fix rates, upon complaints brought before it; provided, first, that complaint could be made difficult, costly, and infrequent. That is, a grain shipper with a grievance would be obliged to retain a lawyer and send him to Washington to defend his petition. In the second place, rate cases were to be reviewed after considerable delays, and judged before Federal courts, involving further costly legal process and (probably) very conservative judgment. This was what was meant by allowing for "broad court review" of railroad rate cases. Now the trouble with Hepburn's bill, as sent from the Lower House, was that it provided for no special intervention by the Federal courts, save those normally offered under the Constitution. Aldrich therefore prepared to amend the Hepburn Bill; it was rumored also that rather humorous, dilatory tactics were planned in the shape of a long series of "joke" amendments. Suddenly, to the astonishment of the Senate leader, one of the "regular" Republican members, Jonathan Dolliver of Iowa, rebelled, and with two other Republicans joined the Democratic minority to report the bill favorably.

Dolliver, the genial, studious giant with a pleasing gift for Lincolnesque oratory, long a popular and useful ornament in the conservative organization, had for several years, since 1903, shown signs of wishing to break from the leash. Like Governor Cummins of Iowa, who was soon to enter the Senate in place of the ancient

Allison, Dolliver was sensitive to the strong current of discontent running again through the Granger states. Allison, who had reared him as his protégé since the '80's, and raised him to the party's Inner Circle, had often stayed Dolliver's hand when he thought to revolt, saying: "Don't do it now. Wait until I'm gone. I know it is wrong. . . . I have only a little while left, and I haven't got the strength to break away. But wait until I am gone. . . ." [18] Yet Dolliver now took a leading hand in the railroad bill, and prepared to issue a report in defiance of the Standpat dicta, saying nothing of "broad court review" and leaving the disposition of railway rate cases as the Lower House had voted it.

On the 15th of February, 1906, Aldrich had an interview with the President—possibly a stormy one—of which neither divulged anything to the public. Aldrich fought for delay, and even turned for aid to certain friends on the Democratic side of the Senate. Meanwhile Dolliver worked in close collaboration with Roosevelt to advance the new bill.

When the Senate's Committee on Interstate Commerce reported out the bill, it was seen that the Republican majority had split its vote. The Eastern faction, among them Aldrich, Foraker, Elkins, and Kean, opposed the Hepburn Bill; the Western Republicans, Dolliver and Clapp, joined with the Democratic minority under Tillman to bring about favorable recommendation. This development, undoubtedly forced by the crafty Aldrich, gave him the occasion for his astonishing maneuver by which "Pitchfork Ben" Tillman, the Southern radical Democrat, was designated to report the bill out of committee without the official indorsement of the Republican party. Thus if the bill came to grief or created evil consequences it would not be a Republican affair. Moreover Dolliver, who had hoped to sponsor the bill, was out-flanked, while the President would be placed in an awkward position. For not long ago Mr. Roosevelt had had a resounding personal quarrel with the irascible Southerner Tillman and had barred him from the White House.

[18] La Follette, *Autobiography*, pp. 432-433.

Yet Tillman accepted his mission in good faith. As in the stirring campaign of '96, beside Bryan and Altgeld, he girded himself for a general onslaught upon entrenched corporate wealth and privilege, eager to garner what credit he could for the Democratic party. The President, meanwhile, after enjoying Aldrich's strange pleasantry, made conciliatory statements to the press, declaring that he "did not care a rap" for personal difference, and, in the interests of railroad reform, would co-operate unstintedly with the Democratic leader, "Pitchfork Ben."

For sixty days, during the months of March and April, the Senate chamber rang with a great "Constitutional debate" over railroad control. One by one the conservative Republican orators arose and attacked a measure which ostensibly had the support of their own administration. Foraker of Ohio, the grey-haired hero of the Civil War, condemned the Hepburn Bill as "Democratic" in its inspiration. This old politician, not yet known as the "hireling" of the Standard Oil Company that he was, was heard with respect when he pleaded passionately for liberty to railroad owners. The policy of centralized control that was embodied in the Hepburn Bill, he argued, would "feed on itself . . . and spread like a conflagration until in some form or other it comprehended and applied to every other kind of business, for such were the teachings and plans of Socialism." [19]

Senator Philander Knox of Pennsylvania, formerly Attorney General in Roosevelt's Cabinet, pointed out that the bill placed some ten billions of railroad property under the arbitrary control of government agencies, "beyond the protecting clauses of the Constitution." He urged the inclusion of an amendment providing for "broad judicial review" of all railroad rate cases (which would be, in effect, an invitation to endless court suits). Otherwise, sacred rights, "painfully won from the tyrannies of the past, rights adhering to the rich as well as to the poor, would be forfeited. . . . The courts," cried Knox, in a ringing peroration, "are the guardians of our rights and liberties." [20] Thus the theme of

[19] *Congressional Record*, May 18, 1906.

the opposition was the danger of a tyranny of the poor over the rich!

While Aldrich and his Senatorial lawyers fought to defeat the Hepburn Bill by ingenious constitutional arguments, or sniped at it with a series of amendments, a crowd of Democratic and Republican "Granger" Senators, led by Tillman and Dolliver, defended the bill in torrents of words. They fought for "narrow court review," limiting the injunctive power of the Federal courts to suspend the government's action in railroad-shipper disputes; else, they contended, the floodgates of litigation would be opened. The issue was, simply put: should the Interstate Commerce Commission be given veritable power over the railways, or illusory powers that would be haltered in the courts?

The President for a time pursued the fight with uncommon force and resourcefulness, though Aldrich held the votes of forty Senators in his hand. As Mark Sullivan has recalled it, Roosevelt arranged with his admirers among the newspaper correspondents that a series of vigorous articles on the railroads and on Senators sympathetic to them should appear during the debate over the railroad control bill. In January, 1906, there appeared in the *World's Work* a powerful attack upon Senators Aldrich, Hale, Spooner, Elkins, Penrose, Foraker, Depew, and Kean, as "representatives of corporate business everywhere. . . ." In *McClure's Magazine* for March, 1906, Ray Stannard Baker published a careful, documented study of the evil tendencies of the railroads and their abuse of political privilege.[21] Rumors were circulated in the press, evidently inspired, that the President even hoped to send a few railroad presidents to jail, believing that it would have a wholesome effect on the situation.

News of sensational charges against the Standard Oil and the American Sugar Refining companies, developing from current investigations, was hinted at, as if held over the heads of the opposition. Also, in a series of public addresses during the early spring

[20] *Ibid.*, Mar. 28, 1906.
[21] Sullivan, *op. cit.*, Vol. III, p. 241.

of 1906, Roosevelt made what then seemed radical proposals—proposals for an inheritance tax that would gradually level wealth, and for Federal laws regulating insurance companies within the District of Columbia. These were the days when Roosevelt thundered most heavily against the "malefactors of great wealth." Yet, whatever the popular effect of these broadsides, votes were still lacking in the Senate to encompass the passage of the Hepburn Bill, which he had made the spearhead of his program of economic reform.

In the early stages of the Senate deadlock, Roosevelt made great efforts to gather together a Senate majority. Through an intermediary he communicated privately with Senator Tillman, the Democratic floor leader, and made an "arrangement" for collaboration between the Democrats and himself. Tillman reported that he could count upon the aid of from twenty-six to twenty-eight of the Democratic contingent of thirty-three Senators. In addition, Dolliver promised the support of between twenty and twenty-two Western Republicans, making a majority of from forty-six to fifty votes out of ninety. The delicate negotiations for a coalition with the Democrats—a rather bold undertaking for a Republican President—were completed at a conference on April 14, 1906, in Attorney General Moody's office, both Tillman and Dolliver being present. Roosevelt, as Tillman declared, promised to "stand by" the coalition and contribute executive pressure in support of the bill, whose terms, providing for "narrow court review," were agreed upon.[22]

Roosevelt's public struggles with Aldrich often partook of the character of mock warfare. He respected and bowed before Aldrich's power. "My experience . . . has made me feel respect and regard for Aldrich," he told Taft in 1903, "as one of that group of Senators, including Allison, Hanna, Spooner, Platt of Connecticut, Lodge, and one or two others, who . . . are the

[22] Tillman's account, *Congressional Record,* May 12, 1906; Stephenson, *op. cit.,* pp. 307-308.

most powerful factors in Congress." Though he disagreed with them radically on many questions they were "the leaders, and their great intelligence and power, and their desire . . . to do what is best for the government, makes them not only essential to work with but desirable to work with." [23]

To work instead with the Democrats, in order to pass a bill which Aldrich opposed, meant not only a break in the party harmony, but final departure from the President's tacit "gentleman's agreement" with the Standpatters. It was a decision before which Theodore Roosevelt hesitated deeply. Fortunately, conciliators were there to devise a compromise between the "narrow" and "broad" court review positions, difficult as that seemed. And then the magic of Aldrich accomplished the rest: subjection of the dynamic President, in his first large battle to lead Congress.

Aldrich's magic consisted at this time simply in his subterranean connection with friendly "Railway Senators" among the Democrats. The veteran Joseph Bailey of Texas, a florid, old-fashioned orator, with large black hat, sedate black suit, and string necktie, was at that time the real leader of the Democrats in the Senate. Though he publicly appeared to be sponsoring the "narrow" review clauses of the Hepburn Bill, as well as other popular measures urged by the Democracy, public scandal not long afterward stamped him as a partner in certain dubious oil enterprises that eventually came under the control of the Rockefeller clan. Legend also has pointed to him as the secret lieutenant of Aldrich on the Democratic side, who brought about, when needed, the sudden switch of two or three vitally necessary Democratic votes to the conservative side. For example, one of the amendments that Bailey proposed, an "anti-injunction" clause, had the air of being so radical that the Supreme Court would certainly nullify the whole railroad act.[24]

Tillman himself, according to his memorandum of the proceedings, "suspected the Texan [Bailey] . . . of holding secret con-

[23] *T. R. Papers*, Roosevelt to Taft, Mar. 13, 1903.

[24] S. H. Acheson, *Joe Bailey, The Last Democrat*, p. 201.

ferences with Aldrich," and, as he reported to Roosevelt, kept a close watch on his colleague, lest he "sell out." [25]

Just when victory over the Standpatters seemed assured—though with the dangerous help of a coalition of Democrats and Western Republicans of the La Follette type—the game passed from the President's hands. For at the Democratic caucus, on April 18, 1906, when noses were counted, to everyone's surprise it was found that several recruits were missing. This was all that Aldrich needed.

For Roosevelt the deadlock had been wearying, and the adventure of working with the Democrats, who would seek credit for railroad reform, politically hazardous. He pressed the distraught Tillman to produce the missing Democratic votes; but though Tillman pleaded for time, they were not found in the last two weeks of April. After having held the threat of a coalition with the Democrats over Aldrich's head, Roosevelt was now ready to abandon the comedy of intrigue, and to "trade" or compromise. He wished, as both Lincoln Steffens and La Follette complained, simply to "get something through"; he would content himself in the end with "half a loaf," when half a loaf was worse than none.

On May 4 Nelson Aldrich called at the White House. Reports of this secret interview held that the "dictator" of the Senate was suave and gracious in victory. Roosevelt, judging from his letter to Lodge, acknowledged his defeat in "sporting" fashion, and vowed that Aldrich, who represented only "ten per cent of the people," would be vanquished the next time. Meanwhile an election was approaching, and they must think of the fortunes of their party.[26]

A compromise amendment, made ready by the practiced Senator Allison, was now quickly produced. It had the language of strong railroad reform, but it offered the legal realities of *broadest court review* and restraint in favor of the railroads, in the shape of occult clauses permitting "interlocutory injunctions" and other court in-

[25] Roosevelt to Allison, the New York *Tribune*, May 16, 1906.

[26] Lodge, *Correspondence*, Vol. II, p. 370.

terventions which would limit government control. On the morning of May 4, 1906, it was understood in Washington that the harassed President had yielded suddenly and given his approval to the "Allison amendment," abandoning the Tillman-Dolliver reform coalition. When the Republican compromise terms were made known a week later, they were universally described as a "gold brick."

The vociferous Tillman and his fellow Democrats were outraged by the bad faith, and even "betrayal," they had suffered at the hands of the President. Roosevelt, they cried, had ended by yielding to Aldrich. He was "so constituted," as Senator Rayner of Maryland remarked, "that he cannot look at a trap without fooling with the spring." [27] The Hepburn Act emerged, however, as a simon-pure Republican party measure, supported by the Old Guard. The embittered Tillman then disburdened himself of a remarkable "confession" on May 12, 1906, before the Senate, relating how the President had sought him out and agreed to use his services as leader of the opposition party, then cast him aside in order to effect a compromise with his own party leaders. Roosevelt issued angry denials from the White House; charges and counter-charges filled the air with confusion as the memorable session of Congress drew to its close in June.

Roosevelt had been on the verge of forcing through Congress a measure that would have substantially increased the power of the Interstate Commerce Commission over railroad rates. It would have meant a bitter conflict within his own party, the possibility of overthrowing the old leaders and creating a new political alignment upon progressive and conservative beliefs. Instead he had recoiled, accepted a half-measure that brought no relief from the abuses that agitated a large part of the public. In defending himself, he argued that the bill he signed was the "same thing" that he had asked for; yet few believed him.[28]

[27] The New York *World,* May 12, 1906.

[28] The Hepburn Act extended the authority of the Interstate Commerce Commission over pipe lines, express companies, sleeping-car companies, and railway terminals; it was given the power not to fix rates, but to nullify rates found

As if to conceal his embarrassment, on May 4, 1906, the day when his compromise with Aldrich was announced, Roosevelt delivered his fiercest broadside against the industrial trusts in a message to Congress which laid bare the secret practices of the Standard Oil and sugar-refining trusts and the coal-carrying combination. He promised that his Attorney General would institute prosecutions against all these wrongdoers at an early date.[29] But one of the newspaper men present continued to question the President concerning the Hepburn Act amendments, and his explanations appeared labored. Finally, the reporter who had admired him exclaimed bluntly: "But Mr. President, what we want to know is why you surrendered." To this Roosevelt made no direct reply.[30]

5

By the summer of 1906, Theodore Roosevelt's crusade against the monopolistic trusts seemed to have reached its climax. He was now the very head and front of the anti-monopolistic movement that gripped the plain people of America, and made repeated vows that he would continue the fight until the industrial trusts, which had been as "subjects without a sovereign," were liable to Federal jurisdiction.

In March, 1904, the Supreme Court's decision in the Northern Securities case, reversing its previous opinions of 1895, had dissolved a great railway holding company, and cleared the path for further vigorous prosecution of the trusts. To the President, who sought to serve as an "honest broker" between the rival interests of the republic, this was a notable vindication of the course he had chosen. His aides, James R. Garfield, Herbert Knox Smith, Attorney General W. H. Moody, and later Charles Joseph Bonaparte,

unreasonable, on complaints of shippers. "Far from satisfying agrarian demands, the Hepburn Act only stimulated the progressive surge which was soon to induce a political earthquake. . . ." (C. A. and M. R. Beard, *The Rise of American Civilization*, Vol. II, p. 568.)

[29] The New York *World*, May 5, 1912.

[30] Stephenson, *op. cit.*, pp. 314-315, citing memorandum of Richard Hooker.

who succeeded Moody in 1906, worked at his order with a large force to gather information and evidence concerning the monopolized industries. The facts, when they were assembled, astonished Roosevelt himself, though he had occasionally glimpsed at close hand something of high financial chicanery when he served as Governor of New York.

Apparently the snowballing movement toward the consolidation of business had gone on pell-mell, with little regard for honor or truth, or the principles of the Decalogue which Roosevelt so earnestly preached. By 1904 (when a temporary halt in the trust movement followed the Northern Securities decision), there were some 318 greater or lesser industrial trusts, which consolidated 5,300 separate manufacturing plants and were capitalized at over seven billions of dollars, five-sixths of them organized since 1898, and nearly half of them under the favoring New Jersey corporation law which tolerated holding companies. The greatest of all holding companies, the United States Steel Corporation, under a New Jersey charter, controlled 170 subsidiary concerns.

In the case of the other great holding company, the Standard Oil Company of New Jersey, both a "holding" and an operating company, Roosevelt aides brought reports of extraordinary malpractice: there was evidence of over 1,900 violations of the Elkins (rebate) Act of 1903. The Standard Oil had continued, as before, the beneficiary of secret freight rates which gave it a crushing advantage over its competitors; sometimes it paid as little as one-fourth the shipping charges exacted by railroads of "outsiders"; often it forced the railroads to add a surtax increasing the freight costs of its competitors in the oil trade, who, by 1904, were virtually extinct. The sugar trust was found guilty of systematic cheating in payments of customs duties by the use of short-weight scales, in addition to its other unlawful acts in restraint of trade; the American Tobacco Company was little better; while the misdeeds of the combination controlling the Chicago packing industry ran the gamut from poisoning its customers to secret rebates and price extortion.

Roosevelt, learning all this, boiled with honest indignation, which was now shared by all except the great financiers themselves and the Marxian socialists, who believed that the trusts prepared the way for the future society of collective, socialized industry. In a series of fierce verbal onslaughts he promised "without fear or favor" to prosecute the wealthy malefactors, whom he now branded publicly, side by side with Red revolutionists, as "undesirable citizens." In effect, his record by 1909 was impressive when compared with that of his predecessors; forty-six suits for violation of the Anti-trust or Interstate Commerce Act were begun, and over half of these cases were relatively successful in bringing indictments and fines. The most famous of these suits were against the Standard Oil Company of New Jersey and the American Tobacco Company.

What was the real object of the crusade against the trusts? Charles Joseph Bonaparte, who was Attorney General from 1906 to 1909, in a speech in October, 1906, said that it was to restore "fair play" in American business. This wealthy civil-service reformer and distinguished lawyer, who had been a contemporary of Roosevelt's at Harvard, by an amusing metaphor likened the conflicts in the business world to those of pigs in a huge pig pen. The fatter the pigs became, the more money for their owners, and the better for the American people, provided there was a fair field and no favor. But, he added:

> Our big, strong, greedy, over-prosperous trusts . . . crowd their smaller and weaker fellows from the feeding-trough, so that they don't get their fair share of our national prosperity. The problem is how to fence off the great beasts so as to give the little ones a show.

Thus President Roosevelt and the Republican party, he declared, were simply trying "to keep each trust in its pen." [31]

The contradictions of such a policy, which sought "fair play and no favors," which differentiated between the "bad trusts" and the "good trusts" (which presumably did not crowd hard against the other pigs), are characteristic of Rooseveltian policy. A quite mod-

[31] Bishop, *Bonaparte*, pp. 128-130.

erate, limited objective was pursued, in contrast with the violence of language used.

"Trust busting" continued in an atmosphere of loud and intemperate controversy, which the press followed with sensational news stories. Week by week, in 1906 and 1907, large corporations fell under indictment, while conservative spokesmen, university presidents, professors of economics, and financiers complained that the Reign of Terror was "tearing down" things and undermining public confidence. It was true that a subsidiary of the Standard Oil of New Jersey on August 13, 1907, was condemned by Federal Judge K. M. Landis to pay a fine of $29,000,000; the American Tobacco Company, organized by the late W. C. Whitney and Thomas Fortune Ryan, was also forced soon after to dissolve into several of its constituent parts. Some of the tobacco company's property was even seized forcibly by Federal officers.

TOBACCO TRUST GOODS SEIZED BY GOVERNMENT

CUSTOMS COLLECTOR TAKES POSSESSION OF 8,750,000 CIGARETTES IN TRANSIT UNDER SHERMAN ACT—DRASTIC SECTION OF LAW USED FOR FIRST TIME.[32]

Thus ran newspaper headlines in 1907. Yet the amount of goods involved, worth $7,252.50, was a mere bagatelle for a concern worth a hundred million dollars. The assessment against the Standard Oil was subject to appeal before the Supreme Court, and after litigation for four more years was canceled, and nothing was lost. Finally, the companies that suffered from dissolution decrees, reappearing eventually as separate entities, worked together as a "community of interests," and maintained secret price agreements as harmoniously as ever.

None of the wealthy evildoers was ever put in jail. After from thirty to forty years of "trust busting," beginning with Theodore Roosevelt, the whole effort to prevent monopoly and restraint of trade was judged by a contemporary historian to have failed ut-

[32] The New York *World*, Oct. 22, 1907.

terly.[33] Mr. Louis D. Brandeis, who in his earlier career as a lawyer fought some rousing legal battles with monopolistic corporations and was often in touch with Roosevelt's Department of Justice, felt that this President was "not objective in his thinking" upon the trust question. Brandeis also had visions of setting American business free. Roosevelt, in self-explanation, declared that he worked for "the moral regeneration of business"; he directed simply a "movement for honesty." After a time, when the going became more difficult, when business conditions were unsettled or depressed, he halted his efforts; as if enough honesty had been generated to last for some little while.

Meanwhile, certain episodes of the trust-busting crusade lent drama to the epoch. The Standard Oil clan, on the whole, remained sullenly silent under assaults upon their moral character. But this was not true of Edward Harriman, the railroad master, whose vast combinations were often financed by the more speculative members of the Standard Oil family.

Harriman was filled with a deep sense of grievance. Theodore Roosevelt, he believed, was under a certain "moral obligation" to him; yet his efforts in personal conferences during two years had won him no favor. In the autumn of 1906 rumors were heard that the government would move to separate his two transcontinental lines, the Union Pacific and the Southern Pacific, and heavy selling in the stock market undoubtedly placed Harriman under some financial strain.

The government attacks upon his property, he felt convinced, were acts of the basest ingratitude for his earlier services; also they seemed to be acts of vengeance, following his stern refusal in the summer of 1906 to donate any money to the Republicans' election chest, when a request was carried to him by an emissary of Roosevelt's. In the second place, he believed that they were inspired by his powerful rivals in the financial world. According to the memorandum of one of Harriman's attorneys, Maxwell Evarts, who attempted to intercede in the quarrel, Roosevelt burst

33 Faulkner, *American Economic History*, p. 542.

out on one occasion: "Well, you don't know what Morgan and some of these other people say about Harriman." [34]

Evidently the Morgan partners, who came far more frequently to the White House than was generally realized, carried dark tales about the great financial rival, Harriman, to the trust-buster. And there was not a little to be said about the "reorganization" of the Union Pacific, or the notorious looting of the small bankrupted Chicago & Alton by the Harriman band in 1904. Harriman could never be dissuaded from the belief, expressed in his official biography, that Theodore Roosevelt played favorites in his trust-busting games, a practice that might yield immense profits to Harriman's adversaries.

At this moment of strain, an employee stole several of Harriman's letters and sold them first to Mr. Hearst, and then to Mr. Pulitzer's New York *World,* which on April 2, 1907, published one letter addressed to Sidney Webster, corporation counsel. In this Harriman, writing in December, 1905, spoke of his disillusionment with his political friend Roosevelt, of the promises that had been made to him, the sums of money Harriman had raised in return for these promises, and the subsequent bad faith shown. He had helped Roosevelt "at his own request," and had merely been used to "further his own [Roosevelt's] interests." Harriman vowed that he had been gulled and would never trust politicians again.

In retort, the President handed to the press a letter of his own of a somewhat earlier date, October 8, 1906, to Vice-President James Sherman. (Often he had letters ready—and not fortuitously—in these emergencies.) Here, replying to reports concerning Harriman's dark mutterings against himself, the President presented his own relations with this man as having involved no promises, no obligations, and no requests whatsoever for money donations. (!) It was one of T. R.'s famous "letters for the record." [35] But it closed with the startling words that labeled Harri-

[34] Kennan, *Harriman,* Vol. II, p. 224.
[35] The New York *World,* Apr. 2, Apr. 3, 1907.

man "as undesirable a citizen as Debs, or Moyer or Haywood. The wealthy corruptionist, and the demagogue who excites . . . class against class, and appeals to the basest passions of the human soul, are fundamentally alike and are equally enemies of the Republic." Strong words, that deeply wounded the mighty Harriman, pilloried with socialists and syndicalists, raising a memorable storm that enlivened the trust-busting battles.

The clash with Harriman, the powerful legal onslaughts upon the Standard Oil family of corporations, are extremely noteworthy because at this very time the relations between the White House and J. P. Morgan and Company, by contrast, were so uncommonly sweet. After the Northern Securities affair in 1902, there was almost no trouble with the House of Morgan, and the great banker evidently avoided challenging the great politico in his own province. Instead, Morgan's underlings, Perkins and Gary, more prepossessing, more ingratiating than the bluff old man, plied the President with flattery. Elbert Gary, the president of the United States Steel Corporation, wrote to Theodore Roosevelt frequently saying that he shared his views upon "righteousness," that Roosevelt's investigation of the steel trust had "done good rather than harm," that Gary himself had benefited by following Roosevelt's example and heeding his appeals.[36] Accounts of the steel trust's "profit-sharing" system, applied to a few well-paid workers, were sent to the White House, while nothing was said of the twelve-hour day and the number of spies employed to eliminate union organizers. Thus the biggest of all trusts went unmolested. The gigantic International Harvester Company, organized by Morgan and George W. Perkins, also was granted immunity as a "good" trust. Nor were serious difficulties provided for the Morgan-Vanderbilt coal-carrying railroads, or for the fabulous New Haven railroad monopoly, which by 1906 had swallowed up almost all the surface and marine transportation in the six New England states.

[36] *T. R. Papers,* Roosevelt to Paul Morton, Jan. 24, 1907.

Possibly Roosevelt felt that by attacking one sector at a time, and also avoiding a general frontal advance—by directing his fire now upon one flank and now another—he made victory more certain. In any case, at the time of the government attacks upon the Rockefellers and upon the Harriman lines in the winter of 1907, there was a good deal of uneasiness in financial circles and railway stocks fell sharply in Wall Street. Rumors that the Interstate Commerce Commission planned a series of large "raids" against other railroads brought cries of protest and finally, on March 11, 1907, a visit by a delegation of New York magnates, headed by Mr. Morgan himself. To them Roosevelt said that

> . . . No raid was contemplated by the Commission; that nothing would be done in a spirit of resentment, or that would have a tendency to add to, or even continue, the existence of the prevailing public mistrust.[37]

A little later Charles S. Mellen, president of the New Haven, who so proudly wore the "Morgan collar," dashed into the White House to inquire of Roosevelt himself if, under the provisions of the Sherman law, his road would be allowed to keep its Long Island Sound steamers. Roosevelt assured him that "so far as I and my Administration are concerned, if you do not sell, you will have no trouble about those steamship lines." Yet the simultaneous ownership of both railways and competing steamships was a glaring instance of non-competition, of restraint of trade, of monopoly. Again, a few weeks later, Mellen returned to ask Roosevelt if the Interstate Commerce Commission would object to the New Haven's buying the Boston & Maine—a measure which Louis D. Brandeis contested on behalf of independent stockholders. The President said: "I would buy it, if I were you."[38]

In the spring of 1908, following the exposure of scandalous and fraudulent transactions by the management of the New Haven railroad, there were reports that a government suit would be launched. One day the news of this was released, but an hour later

[37] *Commercial and Financial Chronicle*, Mar. 16, 1907.

[38] Statement of C. S. Mellen in The New York *Times*, Nov. 11, 1915.

orders came by telephone from the White House to all press associations to kill the news. It was rumored that Morgan's man, Mellen, had again appealed successfully to the White House at the eleventh hour.[39]

These waverings cast a strange light on Theodore Roosevelt as an example of the "honest broker" in politics, a magistrate judging impartially between the rival pressure groups within the state. Gradually the energy of the trust-busting crusade diminished, despite strong talk by Roosevelt of "criminal prosecution of trust magnates." Attorney General Bonaparte cautioned him to go slow in 1907, a year of depression. "I have been on the lookout for several months for a good case, but the chance of getting conviction, and a sentence of imprisonment after the conviction, seems to me to be very poor," Bonaparte wrote in August, 1907.[40]

Despite "trust busting," the United States remained essentially what it had been, "the paradise of capitalists." The great corporations contributed almost nothing in taxes in return for the enormous police and judicial protection they enjoyed. There was no Federal income tax, nor inheritance tax; there was virtually no compensation for workmen killed while at labor; the labor of women and children was subject to almost no restrictions, and efforts to restrict it locally were halted by the Federal courts on Constitutional grounds. The very Sherman Anti-Trust Law itself was used to restrain labor organization. In the commodities and securities markets the most piratical adventures by the speculative leaders of the day were carried off, everywhere with impunity, to the loss of the investing public. Even in 1904 great monopolies, such as the Amalgamated Copper Company, were able to corner the world copper market and double the price of this metal. In that year also a general stock-market panic was traced to the hand of the Rockefeller group, operating through the huge National City Bank. Theodore Roosevelt had moved public opinion powerfully, to be sure, when he left office after seven years.

[39] Lief, *op. cit.*, pp. 146-147.

[40] Bishop, *Bonaparte*, pp. 139-140.

His effectiveness, however, was largely limited to the sphere of "morals."

He clung to his middle-ground position out of deep convictions, and lashed out to the right and the left of him. After using his invectives against the oil trust, he turned to denounce the labor leaders, Haywood, Moyer, and Pettibone, as "undesirable citizens." Thus, as Eugene Debs passionately protested, the chief magistrate publicly condemned men who were then still held innocent under the law, and for whose defense thousands of poorer citizens throughout the country raised funds from their modest earnings.

He veered repeatedly from condemnation of the "criminal rich" to admonitions also to those who, following his example, attacked the rich and the powerful with excessive zeal or, perhaps, with baser motives than his own. Reading the series of articles by David Graham Phillips entitled "The Treason of the Senate," he became very exercised, and on March 17, 1906, at the Gridiron Club dinner in Washington, he lashed out at those who wrote the literature of exposure with an immortal epithet: "Muckrakers." He had taken as his text the passage from Bunyan's *Pilgrim's Progress*, treating of the "man with the muckrake, the man who could look no way but downward with the muckrake in his hands . . . who continued to rake to himself the filth of the floor." The "Muckrake" speech, subsequently repeated at a public ceremony, April 14, 1906, perplexed and disheartened Roosevelt's liberal friends. While denouncing "bad" capitalists, he had also accused the "Muckrakers" of seeking "to make financial or political profit out of the destruction of character," of creating a "morbid and vicious public sentiment." The purpose of the speech, as Roosevelt admitted to his friend Lodge, was to strike at "agitators, at corrupt or sinister or foolish visionaries . . . at preachers of social unrest and discontent. . . ."[41] It balanced the record.

[41] Lodge, *Correspondence*, Vol. II, p. 247.

VIII. THE POLITICS OF DEPRESSION

THE POLITICAL government in the years before the first World War seemed to gather to itself more centralized power than anyone would have dreamed of in recent times. This power now seemed fixed securely in the hands of the man who was at once chief executive of the government and boss of his party. It was commonly remarked among students of political affairs in those days that the President now "overshadowed" all other authorities. Besides his military and police power, he had the right to investigate the management or examine the books of any corporation in the country; he could more or less control railroads valued at fifteen billions of dollars; he sought in addition the power to regulate life-insurance companies with billions of dollars in assets; and it was said that he bent his energies to have laws enacted licensing all corporations engaged in interstate commerce. He could enjoy "smashing" a financial titan like Edward H. Harriman. To a conservative dean of the Yale Law School, all this spelled "the menace of growing centralization."[1] To an intellectual like Herbert Croly, the Rooseveltian tendency meant the redemption of our politics, provided energy and unity of command in a government that had been hitherto divided in all its parts, and made for "the promise of American life." However, the weaknesses in this system, concealed behind its front of deceptive strength, were seldom grasped by those who exclaimed with the editor of the liberal New York *World*, "Where will it all end? Despotism? Caesarism . . . ?" Perhaps the great corporations,

[1] The New York *World*, Oct. 13, 1905.

under pressure, would be driven to the extremity of "launching a revolution" in order "to take possession of the national government." Yet such desperate measures were entirely needless.

"We still continue to enjoy a literally unprecedented prosperity," Theodore Roosevelt announced with pride in his Message to Congress of December 3, 1906. Fortune had thus far smiled upon his work.

That very winter and in the following spring symptoms of the declining phase of the business cycle were at hand. Financial stress was reported in European centers. Would such adverse developments disturb American industrial activities? Many "experts" thought not, holding that our fabulous supplies of gold, our immense bank reserves, our increasingly strong position as a creditor nation, would henceforth eliminate such panics and depressions as those of 1873 and 1893.[2]

Nevertheless money grew dear—that is, interest rates mounted—toward the end of 1906; grain and stock markets suffered sinking spells, and large railroads were hard pressed to obtain loans for their construction needs that spring of 1907.

By the early autumn of 1907, the credit strain was intense; a half dozen large New York banks were reported to be in difficulties, while thousands of depositors, who struggled to withdraw their savings, stood in long, funereal lines day and night. Farmers could obtain no loans to move their crops; factories were shutting down; hundreds of thousands of laborers were made idle and hungry. The deluge had come; and the "overshadowing," "Czar-like" President could only look on, bewildered.

In spite of moral exhortations of the Square Dealer and his followers, the raging financial panic of October, 1907, revealed many weak spots in our economic system. The immediate or external cause of trouble now appeared to be extravagant "financiering" rather than "overconstruction," as in the 1870's and 1890's. Taking advantage of a legal loophole in the revised New York

[2] Noyes, *American Finance*, p. 364.

State general trust-company law, numerous financiers had toward 1900 launched new trust companies, accepting demand deposits from the public and doing a general banking business. In addition the fashionable new trust companies were almost as free of control as the "investment trusts" and holding companies of a generation later, those of the 1920's; the size of cash reserves, unlike that of banks, was subject to their own discretion; they could buy and sell stocks; they could, as in the case of one trust company, use their own stock as collateral in order to buy other trust companies, until a "chain" of trust companies formed a pyramid that was based on the shaky foundations of very speculative shipping, oil, and copper securities, accumulated for the enrichment of the inner circle of directors. Should any of the stones at the base of the pyramid be dislodged, then the whole structure of overlying banks and trust companies would come falling down.

This was precisely what happened in the week of October 14, 1907, with the group of interlocking trust companies controlled by the shipbuilder C. W. Morse and his partner, the audacious copper baron, F. Augustus Heinze. The stock of the United Copper Company, an independent concern, crashed suddenly from $50 to $10 a share, and with it fell various oil and shipping stocks. At once several large trust companies and banks were in trouble, including the Knickerbocker Trust, the Trust Company of America, the Mercantile National, and others affiliated with the Heinze-Morse enterprises. More than a year before, mysterious warnings of exactly such developments had been given by Jacob Schiff, the head of Kuhn, Loeb and Company, who advocated the establishment of a central bank of reserve.[3]

Now it was discovered how much the Rough Rider, in his collisions with great financial leaders, had "undermined" confidence. In a speech at Chicago, October 22, 1907, which was widely noticed, Roosevelt's former friend and adviser, President Nicholas Murray Butler of Columbia University, exclaimed: *"Do not wreck the credit system."* Roosevelt's reforming activities, especially his

[3] The New York *Times,* Jan. 5, 1906.

recent threat to use the criminal law against monopolists, Butler said, would end by destroying the economic basis "upon which our prosperity and our happiness rests." To such appeals the President answered that he acted but to "turn on the light." In a speech at Nashville, he took notice of the charges that "the policies for which I stand" were responsible for the financial troubles of the moment, and replied that he doubted if this were true. Yet even were the charges true, "it will not alter in the slightest degree my determination that for the remaining sixteen months these policies shall be persevered in unswervingly." [4]

The onward sweep of the crisis would reveal whether the government and its law stood "above" the corporations and their magnates, as Roosevelt boasted. On the very day that Roosevelt spoke at Nashville, October 22, 1907, a large trust company in New York, the Knickerbocker, closed its doors.

In October, J. Pierpont Morgan, the "personal dictator" of the American financial world, had gone to Richmond, Virginia, to attend the General Convention of the Protestant Episcopal Church. As a prominent layman of this church he was busy with all the ceremony and beautiful psalm-singing of a clerical convention when news, more or less surprising, of the tragic bank panic reached him by telegraph on October 19, 1907.

To his friend Bishop William Laurence he confided that he was going back to New York on Saturday, the 19th. "They are in trouble in New York. They do not know what to do, and I don't know what to do, but I am going back."

The Bishop, who happened to return with him in his private car, remembered him as "in the best of spirits" without suggestion of care or anxiety and singing lustily away at breakfast.[5] Morgan sang while banks crashed; their white-faced officers had turned to him for aid. Was it pure religious faith that made him so cheery in these dark hours?

Since 1893 Morgan, by his personal force and will and by his

[4] The New York *World*, Oct. 23, 1907.
[5] Laurence, *Memories of a Happy Life*, pp. 251-252.

strategic relationships with the largest railroad, industrial, and banking concerns, had managed to assert his leadership. In October, 1907, all eyes turned to him as the dictator of the financial world. What passed then for a central banking system consisted of the great New York Clearing House banks, who could decide whether or not the checks of the other metropolitan banks should be accepted for exchange. The bulk of the Clearing House members, as the Pujo Committee investigation would soon show, consisted of institutions directed by Morgan, by his ally George F. Baker, head of the First National Bank, and by James Stillman, head of the huge Rockefeller-owned National City Bank.

As soon as Morgan arrived in New York on Sunday evening, October 20, the city's leading bankers gathered in his home. There, in the famous library with its rare examples of medieval art, its miniatures and Shakespeare folios, the men of money sat in night-long conference with the Morgan partners, Perkins, Davison, and Steele, who carefully thumbed through their assets and liabilities. There the decision upon the clearing of checks was made. Morgan himself sat in a small adjacent alcove, playing a game of solitaire and smoking his big black cigar. One by one the proposals and estimates would be brought to him on pieces of notepaper. Some he would comment upon in his brief, stolid way; some he would accept; others he would silently tear up. The presence of Stillman, of Baker, of Schiff beside him suggested the mobilization of most of the nation's liquid wealth under Morgan's leadership.

Early in the morning Morgan came, "in his coupe drawn by the familiar gray cob," to 23 Wall Street, the low corner building with large, Roman-arched windows. He passed "through a line of trust company presidents and financiers" reaching from the swinging door outside to the glass-enclosed private office inside. Among those who gathered in the musty old counting house were Edward Harriman, Thomas Fortune Ryan, Elbert H. Gary, Henry C. Frick, and August Belmont, former rivals and enemies who had now closed their ranks. The very head of the national government, frightened by events he could scarcely comprehend, now sent his Secretary of the Treasury, George B. Cortelyou, hurrying to the corner of Wall and Broad Streets with $35,000,000 of the Treasury's surplus funds to throw into the breach.

It was the master of banking who now appeared to hold power of life and death over the nation, a power reflected in the newspapers of the day:

> Above the tumult of hysteria and fear one voice sounded strong, clear and reassuring. . . . One face grim and determined shone through the clouds of doubt and foreboding.
>
> It was the voice and the face of J. Pierpont Morgan, called to the throne of finance again; made master of more millions than ever a human being controlled before; with the wealthiest of corporations as his vassals, with financiers of international repute as his aides, and the great U. S. Treasury as his almoner.

Across the street to the frenzied stock exchange word went forth: *"Mr. Morgan requests that you do not sell the market."* It was a threat. To the bankers and financiers who waited to learn of their fate, there was but one command: "You must put yourself unreservedly in the hands of Mr. Morgan." The only questions asked were: "What are you worth? What have you got? How have you been doing business?"[6]

Then the cash and gold marshaled by the banking consortium—the Rockefeller banks contributing nearly as much as the national Treasury—were deposited with those institutions which it had been decided to support. A large part of the government deposits, as Secretary Cortelyou admitted afterward to a Congressional committee, was handed over as call loans to hard-pressed stockbrokers.

The panic and depression were real enough; it had been long brewing. The form it took and the methods of defense used reflected the paramount importance of finance capital in the modern business system. Singular incidents that occurred during the tumult and confusion revealed at the same time how the dominant group of finance capitalists condemned and destroyed rival operators

[6] The New York *World*, Oct. 24, 1907.

whom they had silently marked out as their prey; how by a tacit agreement the Morgan and Rockefeller "crowds" moved swiftly to eliminate menacing opponents, to seize long-coveted prizes in the shape of valuable industrial property, and place these forever among the mass of their own possessions.

Thus it was common rumor in Wall Street that F. Augustus Heinze, the Montana copper baron, had long been a thorn in the side of the Rockefeller copper trust, known then as the "Amalgamated" and controlling the Anaconda mines. Heinze, the independent, owned newspapers and banks as well as oil companies. He paid more liberal wages to miners, signed agreements with the union, and yet in the copper market competed successfully in price with the "Amalgamated." Since 1904, H. H. Rogers, then active head of the Standard Oil combination, had tried to ruin or buy out Heinze. "Rogers . . . told Rockefeller what a dangerous man Heinze was, and they probably both agreed to fight him forever."[7] There was the strange fact that at the height of the panic on October 23, 1907, a New York newspaper published alarming reflections upon the management of a large bank, the Heinze-controlled Knickerbocker Trust Company; and at noon that day the bank closed its doors.[8] The blocks of securities held as collateral for Heinze and Morse were then taken up by new hands, at panic prices. Other banks were saved—except the Knickerbocker Trust—on condition that Heinze, Morse, and their allies resign as directors and officers.[9] Thereafter the independent producers who threatened the monopolies, whether in copper or in shipbuilding, disappeared from the scene.

Like the Rockefeller band, the Morgan group also imposed its terms of surrender. To those who appealed to him, Morgan is credited with having said: "Why should I get into this? I've done enough. I won't take all this on, unless—" and then a gesture signifying "unless I get what I want out of it."[10] Thus it was said

[7] C. W. Barron, *More They Told Barron*, p. 53.

[8] *Commercial and Financial Chronicle*, Oct. 27, 1907, p. 1060.

[9] Noyes, *op. cit.*, p. 371.

[10] Corey, *The House of Morgan*, p. 345.

that when the Trust Company of America, which suffered a tremendous run, losing $34,000,000 of deposits within a few days, was saved by Morgan's bringing up funds of the New Haven railroad, a valuable railway franchise lying in the vaults of this bank as collateral passed into the hands of Morgan's road.[11]

But there were even greater prizes that fell as wreckage of the financial storm to the masters of banking who gathered at Mr. Morgan's home.

On the week-end of November 2, 1907, Elbert H. Gary, president of the United States Steel Corporation, was seen by watching newspaper reporters to enter Morgan's brownstone mansion on Madison Avenue. Henry C. Frick and George W. Perkins, directors of the steel trust, were also reported to have joined him. What the conferees discussed in their nocturnal meetings, it soon appeared, must have been the tremendous bargain which had been temptingly offered in the shape of the Tennessee Coal and Iron Company. This large, independent property, located in a strategic part of the South and believed to possess enormous iron ore deposits, was valued lately at from $150 to $160 a share (of $100 par value), but controlling stock, it was learned, had been assigned to Moore & Schley, a large concern of stockbrokers who were now in serious straits. Mr. Gary earlier had been offered control of the company for $100,000,000, or at $150 a share, but insisted that the price was double what he was willing to have the United States Steel Corporation pay for it. Now, in the midst of the panic, his terms were met, and a bargain was struck by which the steel trust gave its own 4 per cent bonds, worth $40,000,000, for Tennessee Coal and Iron's stock, worth at the time 160, or actually $80,000,000.[12]

The only problem about this "deal" in the minds of the gentlemen congregated at Madison Avenue, New York, was the incalculable one: the President at Washington. Would the United

[11] Barron, *op. cit.*, p. 171.

[12] *Commercial and Financial Chronicle*, Oct. 27, Nov. 3, 1907.

States Steel Corporation, by adding the new property, be liable to prosecution under the Sherman Anti-Trust Act?

On Sunday night, November 4, Mr. Gary telephoned to the White House, spoke to the President's Private Secretary, William Loeb, and succeeded in making an appointment with the President for himself and Henry Frick the very morning following. Taking a special train at once, the two financiers roared through the night to Washington, arriving there early in the morning, and insisted upon calling the President from his breakfast—before the stock exchange opened in New York.[13]

Gary then told the President that a large concern, presumed by Roosevelt to be a "big trust company," would have to go into receivership unless a quantity of shares in Tennessee Coal and Iron were taken from its hands. Gary, in his most pious manner, intimated strongly that the steel trust had no keen desire to purchase the property in question, but would do so only as an altruistic measure. With the President's approval, they would even pay a price "somewhat in excess of its true value," in order to relieve the situation.

Their own company, they argued, controlled slightly more than 50 per cent of the nation's steel trade, and with the new property would still control less than 60 per cent. They insisted upon learning of the government's attitude before the market opened that day.

"I answered," Roosevelt noted after they had left, "that, while of course, I could not advise them to take the action proposed, I felt it no public duty of mine to interpose any objections." Later, in testifying before the Stanley Committee, he explained, "It was necessary for me to decide on the instant, before the Stock Exchange opened, for the situation in New York was such that any hour might be vital."[14] The name of the business concern which was scheduled for failure he had not been told, and he preferred not to ask for it.

[13] Tarbell, *Gary*, pp. 201-204.

[14] House of Representatives, *Investigation of United States Steel Corporation* ("Stanley Committee"), pp. 1371, 1375.

At five minutes before ten, Mr. George W. Perkins, waiting at a telephone in the office of Morgan and Company, heard the voice of Gary giving "the glad tidings" from Washington. Instantly word was flashed to the stock exchange and a buying demonstration swept the market upward.[15]

For the Morgan-dominated steel trust, which in its early years often threatened to go into receivership owing to its burden of "watered" stock, the purchase of Tennessee Coal and Iron with its vast reserves of ore proved to be a masterly stroke. Gary admitted a few years later that he would not sell the new property for ten times its cost.

2

The boast of Roosevelt was that the door of the White House would swing open as readily to the labor leader as to the financial magnate. Yet no labor leader was known to have left his door with something equivalent to the government's blessing for executing a plundering raid upon a billion dollars' worth of property. Only lately Mr. Gompers, appearing on behalf of the American Federation of Labor, had presented "Labor's Bill of Grievances," and had been dismissed with evasive replies.

If at times a glimmer of the truth dawned upon Roosevelt, he would admit his own abysmal ignorance of economic problems, which were, after all, the fundamental problems of his time. ". . . When it comes to finance, or compound differentials," he remarked once to Professor J. Lawrence Laughlin, "I am all up in the air."[16] "Judge" Elbert Gary, like all other Morgan men, felt that he owed much to this President, and at the end of his term the steel magnate wrote gratefully:

> Notwithstanding that I hear from some of my acquaintances . . . that the present agitation, investigations, prosecutions have a tendency to depress business and slacken prosperity, it is my opinion that sooner or later, probably sooner, the results will be beneficial. . . . I do not

[15] *Ibid.*, pp. 940-941, 1605-1606.
[16] Pringle, *Roosevelt*, p. 432.

hesitate to say that your influence as President of this great republic has been of benefit to me personally and I feel equally certain that it is beginning to have good effect on others who have been reluctant to see their faults.[17]

Under the stress of a great financial storm, which he knew not how to navigate, he turned more and more to the counsel of the men who commanded the big dreadnaughts of the money market. Sometimes he suspected dimly that perhaps the "malefactors of great wealth" were scheming "to bring about as much financial stress as possible" in order to effect a reversal of his declared policies, or to replace his type of government with a reactionary one. This thought occurs in a speech of August 29, 1907, shortly before the decline in financial markets assumed panic proportions.[18] He wrote to one prominent banker, Higginson, that in spite of the pleas that he make reassuring gestures toward the business interests, he could not drop his action against the railroads and monopolies, for such a course would be indefensible "the moment the . . . flurry in Wall Street is over." "I cannot grant an illegal immunity," he concluded, in almost apologetic tones.[19]

But the "flurry" became a long, fierce downpour; and Roosevelt's mood and spirit changed noticeably under stress. In 1907, generally, his attitude was defensive. Soon he was quietly granting indulgences and immunities on every side. The great magnates who came to him asked always for a "breathing spell"; they asked only that the Federal government "keep its hands off them." [20]

He had always worshiped naked power; and now he appeared to bow before the reality of overwhelming economic power. The funds of the Treasury were deposited, for the emergency, where the imperious Morgan directed. Prosecution against the New Haven railroad, as we have seen, was postponed. George W. Perkins, Morgan's lieutenant, who had designed the structure of the

[17] McCaleb, *Roosevelt*, p. 240.

[18] Roosevelt, *Speeches*, Vol. VI, p. 1351.

[19] *T. R. Papers*, T. R. to H. L. Higginson, Aug. 12, 1907.

[20] *Ibid.*, T. R. to H. L. Higginson.

International Harvester Company, a virtual monopoly in the manufacture of farm machines, came to him on August 22, 1907, when this company was known to be under investigation, and urged that it be spared. It was a "reasonable" corporation; it exercised no undue restraint of trade; it gave work to thousands of men, and incomes to thousands of small investors. And Roosevelt quietly dispatched a message to Bonaparte, his Attorney General: "Please do not file this suit until I hear from you." [21]

Herbert Knox Smith, the Commissioner of Corporations, who investigated the International Harvester Company for the President, now reported that it was not an "obvious" monopoly. Justice must therefore be done to a "good" trust whose only wish was to obey the law. Perkins had told Smith that his company, like the other Morgan combinations, was endeavoring to "uphold the policies of the administration and to adopt the methods of modern publicity. . . ." There were no "moral grounds for attack" on the International Harvester Company, Smith concluded; and if one were made on "purely technical" grounds, then Perkins and his associates threatened to fight. Smith concluded:

> While the administration has never hesitated to grapple with any financial interest, no matter how great, when it is believed that a substantial wrong is being committed, nevertheless it is a very practical question whether it is well to throw away now the great influence of the so-called Morgan interests, which up to this time have supported the advanced policy of the administration.[22]

Here in the intimate language of one of Theodore Roosevelt's "Tennis Cabinet" the cat is let out of the bag. We perceive that the Roosevelt administration up to this time (August, 1907) had enjoyed support from "the great influence of the so-called Morgan interests" and *as a practical matter feared to throw this support away*. The decision was made to spare the Harvester Company. This decision and the grounds for it, when examined in 1908 by a Senate Committee, Roosevelt always refused to explain. The

[21] *T. R. Papers*, T. R. to Bonaparte, Aug. 22, 1907.
[22] U. S. Senate, 62nd Congress, 2nd Session, *Senate Documents*, p. 694.

Committee tried to reach the records in the custody of Herbert Knox Smith and the Bureau of Corporations. But Roosevelt ordered Smith to deliver the papers to him, to be held until he stepped out of office. They could only be got, he said, by impeachment. ". . . If they were made public, no end of trouble would ensue." [23] The affair of the International Harvester, like that of the Tennessee Coal and Iron two months after, strongly reveals the narrow limits within which the power of the Honest Broker was exercised.

While Roosevelt stood forth as the fearless adversary of "plutocrats" like Morgan (whom he appeared to assail in public), in private an effective alliance was made—not with Morgan, but with his more prepossessing, more ingratiating lieutenants Gary and Perkins.

The Standard Oil men on the other hand, ever since Miss Tarbell's historical study had appeared, were obvious political targets and easy to pillory. Financial scandal also pursued Harriman. But the character of Morgan and Company for reputable dealing stood high, and few of the "Muckrakers" attacked this group—save for the large scale of their operations—until after the crash of the New Haven railroad. While the Rockefeller men remained silent under attacks, and came not to Washington to ask either for mercy or indulgences, the Morgan lieutenants (several of whose friends were in the Cabinet itself) came often to "consult" the President and appeared to defer to him and to court his approval earnestly by good works.

In November, 1907, rumors of the President's strange services to the leaders of Wall Street circulated actively, and certain of his admirers, such as William Allen White, wrote asking what truth there was in these reports. He replied stoutly: ". . . I shall not 'surrender' to the bankers, or to any one else, and there will be no 'secret, midnight conferences' with any big financiers, or any-one else." [24]

[23] McCaleb, *op. cit.*, p. 249.

[24] *T. R. Papers*, T. R. to T. E. Watson, Nov. 12, 1907; to W. A. White, Nov. 26, 1907.

3

"It is difficult for me to understand why there should be this belief in Wall Street that I am a wild-eyed revolutionist," Roosevelt wrote pathetically to Jacob Schiff. Some day, the men of wealth and substance would realize, he prophesied, that they had been utterly mistaken in their opposition to him, "even from the standpoint of their own interests; and that nothing better for them could be devised than the laws I have striven . . . to have enacted." [25]

As a consequence of the panic and depression of 1907, Roosevelt's attitude toward the great industrial combinations which he had thought to break up, or at least control with a firm hand, began to change noticeably. He began to fear that he might have gone a little too far. As he said to the English historian Trevelyan, he had seen his problem as that of instituting reforms without paralyzing business initiative. He still refused to admit that his "policies" had brought on panic; panic developed from business corruption, "trickery and dishonesty in high places. . . ." But on further reflection he began to believe that "very possibly the assaults and exposures which I made, and . . . which were . . . imitated in the several States, have brought on the panic a year or two sooner than would otherwise have been the case." [26]

To William Allen White he wrote that he felt his reign was ending "under a more or less dark cloud of obloquy," though through no fault of his own.[27]

Yet by sending out word that he would "do everything I can to the very verge of my power to restore confidence," he seemed for the moment to justify the reproaches which the magnates heaped upon him. He even went to the length of issuing certain public statements calculated to instill firmness and hope in the stock markets.

[25] *Ibid.*, T. R. to J. H. Schiff, Mar. 28, 1907.
[26] *Ibid.*, T. R. to Hamlin Garland, Nov. 23, 1907.
[27] *Ibid.*, T. R. to W. A. White, Nov. 26, 1907.

In 1908 the Supreme Court handed down a number of decisions which showed that its members looked not only at election returns but sometimes even at the barometer of the stock ticker. The cancellation of the $29,000,000 fine against the Standard Oil in July, 1908, suggested that moderation in trust busting was now desired. The way was also prepared for the famous "rule of reason," by which the mere size of a corporation was to be judged no offense in itself. Although the President resumed the suit against the Standard Oil at once, there was actually a partial truce in the war against the trusts for nearly three years after 1907; then, under another President, when circumstances warranted, the fate of the trusts would become a political football again.

Roosevelt's friend and patron, George W. Perkins, nowadays passed for a philosopher of big business. He spoke at Chamber of Commerce meetings and published pamphlets and articles urging that corporations should be permitted to grow as big as they wished; they should be subject to "regulation" instead of "repression" or "strangulation." A commission made up of men who were "master minds," who knew intimately the interests of business, should replace the mere politicians and sit in judgment of business problems.[28] Perkins' solution sounded much like that of the protectionist Republican manufacturers who insisted that the tariff should be revised only by its "friends." Yet by the beginning of 1908 Theodore Roosevelt's views had shifted until they resembled closely those Perkins constantly preached.

He now dwelt upon the *inadequacies* of the Sherman Anti-Trust Act and the Interstate Commerce Act. In a message to Congress he said:

> It is profoundly immoral to put or keep upon the statutes a law, nominally in the interests of public morality, that really puts a premium on public immorality, by undertaking to forbid honest men from doing what must be done under modern business conditions.

[28] G. W. Perkins, *Wanted, a Constructive National Policy*, Aug. 7, 1910 (pamphlet).

And again he declared:

It is a public evil to have on the statute books a law incapable of full enforcement; because both judges and juries realize that its full enforcement would destroy the business of the country.[29]

Senator La Follette thought these criticisms of the trust laws were a sort of "executive sanction to violate the law."

It is true that the President's behavior suggested that he was carrying out a retreat from reform. Actually this maneuver was concealed, as was so often done by "social-democratic" politicians in Europe, by turning more boldly radical than before in speech. For under the stress of business depression and unemployment and declining farm prices, the mood of the public was, if anything, more critical, more edged with discontent than in the more prosperous years before 1907. Thus Theodore Roosevelt, in a season of popular agitation, and with election approaching, publicly advocated a series of boldly progressive measures. He recommended that Congress pass a direct income tax and inheritance tax; that the government institute a program of workmen's compensation for its employees, partly as an example to be followed by private business. He proposed even that the abuse of the injunction in labor disputes should be curbed; and finally, adopting La Follette's ideas, he declared that the problem of railroad rates could be met only by granting the government power to make a valuation of railroad property and fix rates according to "a fair rate of return." [30]

All this sounded alarmingly radical, until one recalled that the much-compromised and -amended Hepburn Act, moderate as were its provisions, had barely won passage through Congress under its present iron control. Moreover, in these very proposals that sounded so drastic there were also passages, as Roosevelt himself pointed out, that advised important changes in the anti-trust

[29] McCaleb, *op. cit.*, p. 240.

[30] *Presidential Messages*, Message to Congress, Jan. 31, 1908, Vol. VII, pp. 1597 ff.

laws, "in order to make legal proper combinations." [31] Finally, by 1908 the President had lost all control over Congress; and in the Lame Duck session, following the election of November, a loud quarrel broke out between the White House and Capitol Hill. Ordinary appropriations desired by Roosevelt were delayed or refused passage; Roosevelt might still give lip service to progressive, reform proposals as he did in his final messages, yet Congress paid no attention to words that were uttered as if "for the record," and which he himself knew would be wholly ignored. Actually he had abandoned nearly all actions against the trusts and the railroads, writing to a friend in a chastened mood: "As a matter of fact I have let up in every case where I have had any possible excuse for so doing." [32]

To avoid ending his long service as President under a "dark cloud" was an important consideration with such a man as Theodore Roosevelt. It was a coincidence that during the autumn of 1907, while the gloom of depression fixed itself upon America, new strain appeared in the relations of America and Japan; and to these problems the President turned his attention with renewed zeal.

Strong anti-Japanese agitation had broken out in California, and a violent movement to eliminate all Japanese immigration was revived in stronger force than ever. The "memorandum" of an agreement between Taft and Katsura, in 1905, had failed to work. Against the discriminatory and punitive measures of California, the Japanese government protested firmly and with great dignity. Japanese subjects must be treated upon a footing of perfect equality with Europeans; upon this ground the Japanese never yielded. Thus Roosevelt, who strongly deplored the local persecution of the Japanese in California, despite fair and conciliating words, saw relations between the two countries drift from bad to worse. In America the demagogic newspapers of Hearst, both in San Fran-

[31] *T. R. Papers*, T. R. to H. L. Higginson, Feb. 19, 1908.
[32] McCaleb, *op. cit.*, p. 256.

cisco and New York, whipped up a storm of fear over the "Yellow Peril." Throughout the world there was much secret diplomatic gossip of an approaching conflict; and yet, as Roosevelt now recognized, the Philippine Islands were virtually indefensible for our navy—our "Achilles heel" in the Pacific.

Roosevelt said afterward of the Japanese: "I had . . . become uncomfortably conscious of a very, very slight undertone of veiled truculence in their communication . . . and I finally made up my mind that they thought I was afraid of them." He heard also that "the Japanese war party firmly believed that they could beat us" and that other foreign experts also thought so. It was time then for a "showdown." [33]

Suddenly it became known that tremendous preparations had been going on in American navy yards; and soon the news of Roosevelt's decision to send the American battle fleet on a voyage around the world competed in popular interest with accounts of the financial panic. The fleet was to proceed via Cape Horn and the Pacific Ocean, the tour to include a "friendly" visit to Japan, in response to an equally "friendly" invitation. Such a voyage by so large a fleet, requiring such great supplies and organizational labor, had never been attempted before; many doubted that it would succeed. Others strongly believed that the Japanese navy under the formidable Admiral Togo would attack and defeat our ships in the Pacific.

On December 16, 1907, amid enormous popular excitement, the great battle fleet, numbering sixteen battleships with attendant supply and auxiliary vessels and 12,000 officers and men, saluted the President of the United States on the yacht *Mayflower* and steamed out of Hampton Roads. It was to be gone for nearly fifteen months, practicing and maneuvering upon its way around the world, and advertising our navy as one of the most efficient sea forces and the second most powerful, after Great Britain's. Roosevelt recollected:

[33] Bishop, *Roosevelt,* Vol. II, p. 249.

In my own judgment the most important service that I rendered to peace was the voyage of the battle fleet around the world. I had become convinced that for many reasons it was essential that we should make it clearly understood . . . that the Pacific was as much our home waters as the Atlantic. . . . I determined on the move without consulting the Cabinet, precisely as I took Panama without consulting the Cabinet.[34]

Thus, in a troubled hour, without informing the representatives of the people—who sought for a time to withhold funds for the expedition—Roosevelt turned boldly to what was little less than a warlike gesture. He gave his personal orders to the officers of the fleet to keep the peace; but "they were to take exactly the same precautions against sudden attack of any kind as if we were at war with all the nations of the earth. . . ."

Japan might have regarded the move as a provocation, as many authorities predicted. But Roosevelt thought, as he told Tirpitz in 1910, that "we had gained three months" for preparation so that "if they did make war it would be proof positive that I had followed exactly the right course."[35] He noted with satisfaction that all trouble with the Japanese government and press "stopped like magic" as soon as they found that our fleet had actually sailed and was in good trim.

At first, apprehension had mingled with excitement over the possibility of a war. Then, as the great fleet sailed smoothly around the coast of South America, to San Francisco, Japan, the Philippines, and, via European waters, toward home, pride in the navy swept over the country. It was a moment of high triumph for Mahan's sea-power doctrine, since not a few German and British authorities had doubted if so large a fleet could be sailed round the world. The United States was now silently accepted as a great naval power in the Pacific. These mighty floating engines of war advertised a mobile fighting force that could throw its weight wherever it chose. The Japanese had chosen to show a peaceful demeanor, and received the fleet when it arrived with a three-day

[34] Roosevelt, *An Autobiography*, pp. 548-549.

[35] Bishop, *Roosevelt*, Vol. II, p. 250.

celebration of "amity," in October, 1908. Almost a year earlier, at the mere mention of the project, Japanese diplomats had taken the initiative to bring about the Root-Takahira "gentlemen's agreement" restricting Japanese immigration to the United States. Possibly the British ally, in ways as yet unrevealed, exercised a restraining influence. "A real identity of British and American interests in the Far East, based on the common immigration policy [of excluding the Japanese] of the United States and Great Britain's Pacific Dominions, was beginning to emerge." [36]

Roosevelt's campaign to win popular interest in appropriations for a big navy was also furthered. As an English commentator predicted in October, 1907, in the London *Spectator:*

> Next time Mr. Roosevelt or his representatives appeal to the country for new battleships they will do so to people whose minds have been influenced one way or the other. The naval programme will not have stood still. We are sure that . . . this is the aim which Mr. Roosevelt has in mind. He has a policy which projects itself far into the future.[37]

Once more, in the field of foreign and military action, Roosevelt, escaping from the vexing obstacles which beset his course at home, acted with the free hand of an autocrat.

On February 22, 1909—his term soon to expire—he stood again at Hampton Roads, addressing the returned fleet from the flagship, with tears in his voice. This was his hour of highest glory. He spoke of how he and all Americans had "thrilled with pride" as the hulls of the mighty warships lifted above the horizon. "You have steamed through all the great oceans; you have touched the coast of every continent. . . . We are proud of all the ships and all the men. . . ." [38]

4

As all things mortal must come to an end, so the brilliant Theodorian reign approached its term in 1908, and the President who

[36] Griswold, *op. cit.*, p. 128.
[37] Cited in Roosevelt, *An Autobiography*, p. 550.
[38] *Ibid.*, pp. 557-559.

had had the longest uninterrupted term since Ulysses Grant's busied himself with the problem of a succession.

By "playing a great part in the world," as befitted a "great people," Theodore Roosevelt maintained his remarkable popularity to the very end; his foreign forays had a way of following hard upon domestic troubles and reverses that might have dimmed his glory. It must be recalled that the dubious affair of the Tennessee Coal and Iron Company was little spoken of until very late in 1908; the act of submission to Morgan's men, as in the International Harvester case, was not definitely suspected until 1912. To the nation, especially to its large middle class, he remained the "trust buster" at home and the wielder of the Big Stick abroad. Moreover, his uncommon passion for publicity had made the attractive, independent, and forthright sides of his personality part of the everyday knowledge of millions of Americans, who for several years were both diverted and stimulated by him and who truly loved him. But besides holding the affection of the masses as no other recent politician save perhaps the "magnetic" James G. Blaine had held it, Roosevelt's mastery over the Republican party organization was complete.

Little doubt exists that a "third-term movement" of considerable force could easily have been engendered. Politicians in the lower ranks of his party would have welcomed his renomination. A hundred or more of the convention delegates were Federal officials appointed by Roosevelt, and the whole mass of Southern delegates, representing the Republican "rotten borough," would have been compliant enough. As late as May 29, 1908, Roosevelt said: "There has never been a moment when I could not have had the Republican nomination with practical unanimity by simply raising one finger." [39]

Yet, following his triumphant re-election in November, 1904, he had given an unequivocal pledge to the people that he would not be a candidate again for the office of President. The taboo of a third term had ruled Americans ever since Washington's time.

[39] *T. R. Papers*, T. R. to Rev. Lyman F. Abbott, May 29, 1908.

In recent memory, only Ulysses Grant had tested its force in a nominating convention; what the people as a whole felt upon the matter was still unknown. To this taboo Roosevelt himself bowed, saying in a letter to Sir George O. Trevelyan, ". . . The strong man may readily subvert free institutions if he and the people at large grow to accept his continued possession of a vast power as being necessary. . . ." Yet at the same time he expressed the poignant regret that, having acquired and demonstrated his large public power, he must nevertheless "at a fixed date of the calendar abandon certain struggles . . . of vital concern to the national welfare." Alas, he was but forty-nine years of age as he wrote these lines! [40]

Though he must practice a Roman self-denial, the possibility of effecting a succession that would foster *continuity* of Rooseveltian policy and influence obsessed him. For, like Andrew Jackson, he was in a position to name, to "make," the President who succeeded him.

Of his Cabinet members, Elihu Root, who had become Secretary of State after Hay's death in 1905, was the ablest and most distinguished personality, whose long services seemed to make him worthy of elevation. Despite their different careers and background, the two men were in tolerably close agreement in supporting moderate reforms that would work conservatively in property's interests. Elihu Root thought there was really no difference between his own principles and "what Theodore thinks he believes," even though Theodore undoubtedly had given him some bad moments.[41]

Roosevelt, who was deeply fond of Root, and once said that he would willingly "walk on his hands and knees . . . to see Root made President," thought for a long time of setting the old corporation lawyer in his office. There he would have served the people as their advocate as loyally and skillfully as he had formerly served Wall Street. Yet this scheme was eventually aban-

[40] *Ibid.*, T. R. to G. O. Trevelyan, June 19, 1908.
[41] Jessup, *op. cit.*, Vol. II, p. 182.

doned, for the West would only see Root in his professional corporate connections, and the heat of a campaign might illuminate these connections unpleasantly.[42]

New York's brilliant and independent reform Governor, Charles E. Hughes, was also of Presidential stuff, but was passed over quickly by the king-maker, who sought instead a man more amenable to his own influence. It was the Secretary of War, his good friend Taft, then apparently the most deferent and devoted member of his Cabinet, to whom he finally turned to hand the crown.

William Howard Taft, at fifty, had had one of the most distinguished and fortunate careers among the Rooseveltians. Originally he had been a protégé of McKinley; but it was under the Square Deal regime that he had figured prominently before the public, as Governor General of the Philippines, as Secretary of War, and lately as Roosevelt's active lieutenant. Taft's strong Ohio connections, his eagerness to accept minor public office, had aided his first steps in politics. He too had gone to a great Eastern university, Yale; he had been something of a local reformer in youth; and at the same time, while serving as a judge of an Ohio court during the industrial warfare of the 1880's, had shown a strong antilabor bias (much like Theodore Roosevelt's), which had commended him to both Presidents Harrison and McKinley. He came of a wealthy family, politically influential—his father, Alphonso Taft, had been an Ambassador and a member of Grant's Cabinet; he possessed education and administrative ability; he was handsome, immensely fat, and of an amiable, smiling disposition. He appealed, even as early as 1903, to conservative groups in the Republican party, who had singled him out as one of their own. ". . . The trust people and probably some of the machine politicians," he loyally warned Roosevelt at the time, were engineering a movement to have him, Taft, nominated in place of his chief.[43]

[42] Davis, *Released for Publication*, p. 54.

[43] Stephenson, *op. cit.*, p. 221, Taft to T. R., Apr. 27, 1903.

Actually Taft had an overwhelming inclination to jurisprudence. His heart's desire was to reach the bench of the Supreme Court. Yet brothers and wife, and all sorts of powerful influences, persuaded him to refuse the robe of the Justice, repeatedly offered him by Roosevelt, so that he might remain available for the Presidency in 1908. Nevertheless it was as a judge, reflecting over evidence, alone, independent, that he was happiest. For all his stout, cheerful, robust exterior, he did not make friends and confidants easily. In all his life, marked with a tolerable if not brilliant juridical and administrative success, he had scarcely ever run for an elective office or learned to be happy jostling about among the lower orders of politicians, giving and taking pleasantries, patronage, and political favors. What Roosevelt did not foresee was how difficult it was going to be for a man who had no talents for the arts of political intrigue—which he himself ate, drank, and breathed—to acquire them in short order.

In those days Taft posed as a militant Square Dealer. When the decision to give full administration support to Taft's candidacy was finally made, early in 1908, Taft indicated to everyone that he stood unswervingly for "Roosevelt policies." If defeated "because I am close to Roosevelt, then . . . I ought to be defeated on that account," he wrote to one of those who prepared his campaign. He declared that he enjoyed being in Roosevelt's Cabinet. "My strength is largely as his friend." [44] Thus it was Taft, more than anyone else, who promised *continuity*.

Indeed, he sometimes expressed even more clearly, more logically than his chief, the great underlying principles of Rooseveltian policy: defense of the existing social-economic system; defense, above all, of property rights against more radical movements or even a possible revolution of socialism.

> I agree heartily and earnestly in the policies which have come to be known as the Roosevelt policies [Taft wrote in a private letter of 1907]. These policies, stated succinctly, are that the guaranties of the Constitution shall be in favor of life, liberty and property and shall be

[44] Pringle, *Taft*, Vol. I, p. 329.

sacredly maintained; *that the guaranty with respect to the right of property would be undermined by a movement toward socialism*; that this movement has gained force by the use of accumulated wealth and power in illegal ways . . . to center financial control in a few hands. . . .[45]

And Roosevelt, he concluded, had finally roused the people to the necessity of enforcing the law against rich and poor alike; he had begun to curb those violators of the statutes who by their excesses would have precipitated a revolution not only against the rich but against all property-holders.

Roosevelt himself was convinced that there was little to choose between himself and Taft as "friends of conservatism and order" who would fight the evils and excesses of monopoly.

He would have felt more unhappy about leaving the Presidency, he wrote privately to Trevelyan in a letter of June 19, 1908, were it not that ". . . in Taft there was ready to hand a man whose theory of public and private duty is my own, and whose practice of this theory is what I hope my own is. . . ."

But between the spirit and the letter, between the theory and the practice of a doctrine, there is often a world of difference. Roosevelt had defended property, law, and order, while using the terms of the radical Bryan; thus he was enabled, as he boasted, to keep the adherence of the "one-suspender men"; the rural West remained hopefully attached to the Republican party.

In his letter to Trevelyan which reviewed the significant episodes of his two terms, Roosevelt related how, time and again, simple farmers from the hinterland appeared at the White House, all clean and sober for the occasion, and asked to see him, saying that they wanted only "to shake that honest hand." Roosevelt never failed to appear before them. These horny-handed old fellows touched his heart; to have won their enduring affection was one of his principal political achievements—something that a Taft would know little of.

In short, while Roosevelt collaborated in Congress with those

[45] Pringle, *Taft*, Vol. I, p. 339.

"broad-minded," "patriotic" statesmen, Aldrich, Cannon, and their group, he also conducted a great crusade for "righteousness" that both entertained and heartened the masses. Taft sometimes thought that his friend could literally run with the hares and hunt with the hounds. Could he himself, less imaginative, more methodical, with a mind that moved in straight lines, with limited knowledge of the dark, double ways of politicians and Congressmen, do as much, according to the same tactics?

In mid-January, 1908, Roosevelt indicated plainly that Taft was his political heir. Both were in agreement upon the continuity of policy, and even, in some measure, upon the continuance of most of the officials who made up the Roosevelt administration and gave it its spirit of devoted public service. Both men also agreed apparently that the new administration, if Taft were elected, would limit itself rather to "retrenchment," to the "consolidation of gains" made previously, while experimental legislation was to be avoided if possible. To this extent the Roosevelt policies were to be modified. In general, all circumstances of the transfer of power revealed how much Theodore Roosevelt desired to continue as a force in American politics, perhaps even as the Strong Man of the new government.

From the beginning of 1908, Roosevelt threw into motion all the machinery of publicity he commanded, as well as that of the party organization, in behalf of the Taft candidacy. The hunt for convention delegates was pushed rapidly; Private Secretary William Loeb and Assistant Postmaster General Frank Hitchcock, in preparation for the convention, helped canvass for Taft adherents under Roosevelt's orders.

In addition, Taft men were appointed to strategic Federal posts, which would give them occasion and leisure to aid in the party canvass. Within two months, by March 20, 1908, some 552 delegates out of a possible 980, a clear majority, were claimed for the "Crown Prince"—having been rounded up swiftly by methods of which Taft was not too closely informed. The bulk of expense for the pre-convention campaign was met by Charles P. Taft, the wealthy half-brother of the candidate. Henry Cabot Lodge was designated as "temporary chairman" to conduct the actual convention; and with his help plans to avoid a "stampede" for the Rough Rider were carefully completed. (The Taft family were highly suspicious on this point up to the final hour, according to certain witnesses.) The party platform was "dictated" by Theodore Roosevelt; the successful nominee's formal speech of acceptance was to be written under the eye of the incumbent President.[46] The party's Committee on Credentials, as under Mark Hanna's rule, could pass usually upon delegates approved by the party leader, in disputed cases, and reject opponents. Thus the various Favorite Son movements were easily checked by the Steam Roller machinery, now driven by Theodore Roosevelt. That summer the nomination of Taft was brought about smoothly before a routine convention whose cheers were given mainly for the retiring President.

The platform adopted by the Republican party was liberal in tone. It favored at last a moderate reform of the extremely high protective tariff in force ever since 1897. On this score Taft himself had been outspoken in his public statements. Certain radical demands, such as that of La Follette, for a plank urging the direct election of Senators and more complete government control of railroad rates, were resisted. A spirited effort made by the labor leader Samuel Gompers to win support for an anti-injunction plank was rebuffed. Taft, whom the Democrats would call "the father of the injunction," owing to his record as a Federal judge, said that he would never act to weaken the power of the courts to defend property. Moreover, the National Association of Manufacturers, which took an active part in the Republican convention this year, fiercely opposed the very mention of the labor issue. A compromise plank, wrought in the most cautious phrases, was actually worked out; and when Gompers indignantly objected to it, he was told to "go to Denver"—the site of the Democratic party convention.[47]

46 Stoddard, *As I Knew Them,* pp. 341-344.

47 Gompers, *Seventy Years,* Vol. II, p. 262.

5

Late in 1906, William Jennings Bryan, the orator of American protest, had returned from a most remarkable world tour, filled with new visions and hopes for new departures. Before an enthusiastic multitude that gathered in Madison Square Garden, New York, to welcome him and to hear him, he sounded ringing calls to battle.

> Plutocracy is abhorrent to a republic; it is more despotic than monarchy, more heartless than aristocracy, more selfish than bureaucracy. . . . It is already sapping the strength of the nation, vulgarizing social life and making a mockery of morals. The time is ripe for the overthrow of this giant wrong. In the name of the counting-rooms which it has defiled . . . in the name of the home which it has despoiled; in the name of religion which it has disgraced; in the name of the people whom it has oppressed, let us make our appeal to the awakened conscience of the nation.

Then seizing the bull by the horns, so to speak, with his eye upon the approaching national contest, he announced his decision to make the nationalization of the railroads the Burning Issue of the day: "I have . . . reached the conclusion that railroads partake so much of the nature of a monopoly that they must ultimately become public property . . . and be managed in the interests of the whole community." [48]

Bryan, who had seen his own proposals, adapted originally from the old Populist platforms, taken over by Roosevelt, now served notice that he intended to drive the opposition party forward again toward more radical and more popular policies. Though the Democratic party convention of 1908 was to be cautious, avoiding commitment to government ownership of the railroads, it turned once more to radical policies and leadership.

Bryan sensed the maneuvers of retreat planned by the ruling party. The choice of Taft as Republican standard-bearer, which

[48] Werner, *Bryan*, pp. 152-153.

was so promptly approved in Wall Street circles, gave Bryan the opportunity to seize Democratic party leadership from the hands of the Eastern and Southern conservatives who had met disastrous defeat in 1904. Thomas Fortune Ryan had financed the party in late years, and controlled it through his Tammany Hall and Virginia political friends; he was now pushed into the background. Long before the national convention opened at Denver, twenty-one states had pledged their delegates to the Nebraskan as the party's overwhelming choice for the nomination. Under Bryan's guidance the old party responded, ostensibly, to "the increasing signs of an awakening throughout the country." Its admirable platform contained a series of outspoken resolutions, urging downward revision of the tariff, prohibition of "interlocking directorates" among large corporations, a direct income tax, the direct election of Senators, the elimination of the injunction in labor disputes. The *leitmotif* of the platform was expressed by the phrase: *"Shall the people rule?"* [49]

Once more the "substantial men" ceased their active support of the Democratic party after Bryan's nomination. Woodrow Wilson, president of Princeton University, who had political ambitions, at this time wrote to a friend of his desire that "we could do something, at once dignified and effective, to knock Mr. Bryan once and for all into a cocked hat." Conservative Eastern elements typified by George Harvey, publisher of *Harper's Weekly*, and a confidential aide of T. F. Ryan, had publicly proposed the name of Dr. Wilson himself in place of Bryan; yet little attention was paid at the time to his maneuver. Instead, the mass of organized labor, led by Gompers of the A. F. of L., joined the Western farmers in giving enthusiastic support to Bryan's canvass.

Taft, supported by a unified, disciplined party organization—in contrast with the discordant Democrats—wore the mantle of Theodore Roosevelt that summer. In his speeches, he warned the country that Bryan and his followers were "irresponsible" by nature. Bryan would punish the rich. He was opposed to the accumulation

[49] Robinson, *op. cit.*, pp. 295-296.

of wealth under a strong government. But under the Republican administration, the Roosevelt policies would be continued in a practical spirit, and both the rich and the poor would be held equal before the law. Thus Taft seemed to embody those qualities of "calm thought and moderation and sober judgment" that prominent personages such as Nicholas Murray Butler had found wanting, after the panic of 1907, in the "intemperate" Roosevelt. Taft was "sound." Yet at the same time his public speeches held fair words promising continuance of the Rooseveltian reform activities. He summed up the last four years as "a great struggle between the national administration and certain powerful combinations in the financial world. . . ." He would continue the struggle, for, if the old abuses remained unchecked, if "the tyranny and oppression of an oligarchy of wealth cannot be avoided, *then socialism will triumph*, and the institution of private property will perish." [50] Taft also pledged himself to aid in bringing forth a "reasonable" revision of the protective tariff in force, especially in the schedules for those industrial products such as steel rails and raw materials which no longer needed protection.

Such was Taft's tone in public, especially during the campaigning in Western cities. It was remarked, not long afterward, that Taft had the air of leading a continued reform movement in the West, and at the same time of promising a "restoration" in the East. For, in private, Taft often sounded as if he held notions quite different from his friend Theodore's of how the country must be saved from socialism.

Though the new leader was not a strong or brilliant campaigner, he gained, thanks to the help of the President, the expected electoral victory over Bryan. He held the ground that Roosevelt had conquered, and even extended it in the electoral college returns. It was significant, however, that Bryan increased the Democratic vote by a million over that of 1904. The Socialist party, though it gained only moderately this year, aroused and educated the whole country by its spirited campaign conducted far and wide by

[50] Duffy, *Taft,* p. 204; italics mine.

Eugene Debs from his "Red Special" train. The extreme radical vote, however, was made fragmentary by the intrusion of William Randolph Hearst who, that year, contending with both party organizations, launched his "Independence" party as a venture of his own.

The divergence between the two friends, Taft and Roosevelt, in temperament, in tactics, in the immediate influences they each reflected, really showed themselves during the election campaign. In the month following the election, December, 1908, occurred the first of their differences that foreshadowed the lamentable and historic quarrel between the two statesmen.

Roosevelt knew that under Taft the program of saving the reluctant capitalists from their own excesses would be pursued in a far more prudent spirit. "You see, *you have often preached caution to me* . . ." was a characteristic phrase Roosevelt used in a letter he wrote to Taft a year before the election.[51] Yet in practical diplomacy the proverbially impetuous Theodore could administer many lessons to the habitually tactless Taft. Taft must not be seen playing golf, then a rich man's sport; he must stop at hotels, instead of the homes of rich Republicans; he must shake hands with the people, and allow himself to be handled as public property. These were practices which Taft had not followed of his own accord in ruling over millions of little brown brothers in the Philippines.

Roosevelt told Ray Stannard Baker in August, 1908, shortly after Taft's nomination, that his protégé was a "cool-headed lawyer," such as the country now needed. He concluded:

> Well, I'm through now. I've done my work. . . . People are going to discuss economic questions more and more: the tariff, currency, banks. They are hard questions, and I am not deeply interested in them; my problems are moral problems, and my teaching has been plain morality.[52]

[51] *T. R. Papers*, T. R. to Taft, Sept. 19, 1907; italics mine.

[52] R. S. Baker in *The American Magazine*, Sept., 1908.

In the same vein he told another journalist, in the last days of his administration, that the time had probably come to cease the "crusading" that he had felt himself forced to do to save the country from "intolerable conditions imperiling everything." Henceforth all attention would be given to "what you call the business problems of government," which had no appeal to Roosevelt. Taft, however, would know how to "round out and shape up the policies of the last four years." He had a legal mind. "He's a constructive fellow, I am not. . . . The ground is cleared for constructive work. . . ."[53]

Taft himself, in formally accepting the nomination, had tried to differentiate his purposes from his predecessor's:

> The chief function of the next administration in my judgment is distinct from and a progressive development of that which has been performed by President Roosevelt. *The chief function of the next administration is to complete and perfect the machinery by which these standards may be maintained*, by which the lawbreakers may be promptly restrained and punished, *but which shall operate with sufficient accuracy* and dispatch *to interfere with legitimate business as little as possible.*[54]

Here at any rate was a hint of Taft's natural, human prompting to be President in his own right. If he had not sought to be this, his whole solid, respectable, determined family would have pushed him to it. To write the speech of acceptance cited above, the candidate had made a journey to Oyster Bay and submitted his work to the approval of the overshadowing party chief. But then he had journeyed to his native Cincinnati and closeted himself in the bosom of his family, who persuaded him to accept certain changes and amendments.

The family, especially Charles P. Taft (the half-brother) and brothers Henry and Horace, were all strong characters. Not the least of these was his wife, whose dislike and suspicion of the Roosevelts was often noticed. Mrs. Taft, who had been triumphantly right in advising her husband not to enter the Supreme

[53] Stoddard, *op. cit.*, pp. 352-353.
[54] The New York *Times*, Jul. 29, 1908; italics mine.

Court, urged him to separate himself as much as possible from the "Roosevelt policies." She said: "Let the Corporations rest for a while." [55]

Charles P. Taft, for example, would never have passed for a good Rooseveltian. He was a successful corporation attorney, had seen a good deal of the inside of political life—once as Congressman for a single term from Ohio, but chiefly from behind the scenes. For many years he had contributed a generous annuity to fill out his distinguished younger brother's income from public service, and for the sake of his brother's elevation to the Presidency he had donated large sums, representing a small fortune. But the election being over, brother Charles also discovered political ambitions in himself; he announced that he would stand for the Senate in Ohio, after the retirement of Foraker. Presumably he hoped to go to the Senate, "as the Mark Hanna" of his brother's administration. But a public outcry at Charles Taft's schemings, at his attempt to pass over those Ohio party veterans who were next in succession for the Senate, caused the whole plan to be hastily abandoned.[56]

Another glimpse we have of this curious, rich brother, is on the occasion when he is closeted with Mr. J. P. Morgan at the latter's home, and he sends an urgent message to brother "Will," just then passing through New York, to join him promptly at Morgan's for a conference. However, the new President felt obliged to rebuke his brother, pointing out the impropriety of such a visit, and asking that Charles Taft and Morgan come instead to see him in Washington.[57]

Yet the President-elect in his first letter to Roosevelt after the election tactlessly attributed his success as much to his brother's money as to Roosevelt's political support: "You and my brother Charley made that possible which in all probability would not have occurred otherwise." [58]

However, a passage in another letter of this time from Taft to

[55] Pringle, *Taft*, Vol. I, pp. 329-330.
[56] Stoddard, *op. cit.*, p. 349.
[57] A. Butt, *Letters*, Vol. II, p. 443.
[58] Sullivan, *op. cit.*, Vol. IV, p. 315.

Colonel Roosevelt was phrased in the terms of that extreme deference which, I suspect, led Roosevelt to name Taft his Crown Prince:

> I can never forget that the power I now exercise was voluntarily transferred from you to me, and that I am under obligation to you to see that your judgment in selecting me as your successor and bringing about the succession shall be vindicated according to the standards which you and I . . . have always formulated.

This letter was made public by Roosevelt during the rupture of 1912.[59]

It is clear that the brother heartily disliked Roosevelt, and hoped that Will would not think too long of his obligations to the other man, or preside under his shadow. The influence of Charles P. Taft, like that of the first lady, "Nellie" Taft, was thrown squarely against the idea of "continuity." One perceives this source of discord at an early date in the new regime, according to the gossiping journal of Major Archie Butt, who was the personal military aide of both Presidents. Speaking of his brother to Archie Butt early in 1909, Taft said, laughing:

> What troubles Charlie is, he is afraid Roosevelt will get the credit of making me President and not himself. . . . I am always amused at Charlie's determined position that Roosevelt had nothing to do with my nomination and election. . . .[60]

More important still for Roosevelt's hope of continuity of policy was the retention of certain Cabinet officers and minor officials by the new administration. Taft, in a pleasant humor after his big victory, had voluntarily promised as much in the case of James Garfield, Secretary of the Interior, and certain others; and Roosevelt had conveyed the good news to those Cabinet members who wished to stay in the service. Then, belatedly, Taft realized that he might want to select new men, who would be beholden entirely

[59] The New York *Times*, Apr. 27, 1912.
[60] Butt, *Letters*, Vol. I, p. 104.

to him rather than to "T. R.," men who would be fitted for the different tasks he had in view. Therefore James R. Garfield, the head of the "Tennis Cabinet," and enthusiastic conservationist, was asked finally to give way, and was replaced by a lawyer and politician, who for a time had been his assistant: Richard *Achilles* Ballinger, former Mayor of Seattle. Taft was determined to dismiss Roosevelt's friend Garfield "because I *knew* him," he said later.[61] The selection of Ballinger, who soon proved to be a vigorous opponent of Rooseveltian policies and sought to reverse them, was a key case; he was to be the "Achilles heel" of the new administration.

In the awkward interim period, Taft wrote most apologetically to Roosevelt of his regret at changing the Cabinet personnel, "with a view to a somewhat different state of reforms, which you have instituted, and which I must carry on." But this scarcely relieved the strain, which had begun immediately after the election, when Roosevelt found that he already counted for very little in national affairs.[62]

The final exchange of letters between the outgoing and incoming executives consisted in mere amenities, labored and cold, despite Taft's attempts at epistolary endearments. At the very end Roosevelt spoke with irritation of his protégé, saying to Mark Sullivan: "*He's weak. . . .*" News that Taft, before assuming office, had made gestures of submission to the rulers of Congress, Senator Nelson Aldrich and Speaker Cannon, in order to further his legislative program, ran about Washington. Roosevelt had worked with these men, had advised Taft to do so; but he had

[61] Pringle, *Taft,* Vol. I, p. 386.

[62] Taft to Roosevelt, Feb. 1, 1909, McCaleb, *op. cit.*, p. 271; also Gifford Pinchot to author.

Political action is a continuous, eternally unfinished process. There existed unfinished business in the State Department, a "gentlemen's agreement" with Japan in which Taft as Secretary of War had had a hand; the Big Navy program was also an important part of Rooseveltian policy; the work in progress in the Department of the Interior and the Forest Service (which Gifford Pinchot continued to head) involved reclamation, setting up land reserves, eternal warfare against land-grabbers—all this depending greatly on the continuance of the personnel and *esprit de corps* created under Roosevelt.

been accustomed to holding them at arm's length, or even to appearing as their opponent in public. Taft, it was now said, was using utterly different tactics, calculated to bring about a kind of Restoration Period. At the Gridiron Club dinner, held in Washington early in April, 1909, at the very outset of the new regime, the players burlesqued a "Restoration." Aldrich and his colleagues in the Senate, as well as Joe Cannon, were shown as having the run of the White House, and were told by its incumbent: ". . . Fix up the tariff to suit yourself and the boys." It was an extraordinarily accurate forecast.[63]

Theodore Roosevelt could scarcely conceal his depression as his term of official rule drew to its end. Part of this was because he so thoroughly enjoyed the burdens of his great office. Part was undoubtedly due to disappointment in his hope of a large, continuing, indirect power, through transfer of the Presidency to his once deferent and humble lieutenant Taft. The evening before the inaugural ceremonies, March 3, 1909, the Tafts were, in accordance with custom, White House guests. In a letter four years later Taft still vividly recalled the dinner gathering that evening as "that funeral."[64]

The real end of the seven years' reign actually came at the large luncheon which Roosevelt tendered to the "Tennis Cabinet" on March 1, 1909. Here were present his favorite Cabinet members such as Garfield, and the intimate friends among the minor officials such as Gifford Pinchot, who would have laid down his life for him. Roosevelt toasted his "generals" for the last time, thanking them for their able, loyal service, and saying magnanimously that the credit which had come to him, as the chief, belonged truly to them. His words were simple, but they were very moving; and the thirty-odd guests who had long loved him, and who had never suffered from boredom in his service, could scarcely abide the thought of his exile. Many of them, conquered by emotion, broke down and wept unashamed.[65]

[63] Dunn, *Gridiron Nights*, pp. 216-217.

[64] Pringle, *Taft*, Vol. I, p. 393.

[65] Roosevelt, *Presidential Addresses*, Vol. VIII, pp. 2177-2179.

BOOK TWO

IX. AN ATTEMPTED "RESTORATION"

THE FOUR years of the Taft administration, designed to be a period of "calm" and "confidence," were filled with the turmoil of controversy. These were years of political drama, both sensational and inwardly significant. The "inwardness" of the political drama—like that of the preceding eighty years of American political history—can best be charted in terms of centripetal and centrifugal movements. The bureaucratic tradition and the needs of the deep-rooted party system work to pull things together; the economic and sectional forces in society work with outward-driving thrusts, to break up the partisan lines, to clash among themselves, then to coalesce into a new balance.

So, under the outwardly amiable Mr. Taft's reign, movements of tremendous energy, the stronger for having long been pent up, worked again, driving the liberal middle class, the farmers and organized labor in a crusade for "social justice"; and, gathering an unheard-of force, threatened to destroy the former equilibrium of the old party system.

For a long time the leaders who dominated the ruling party more firmly than ever, the so-called Old Guard—now that the Great Hunter devoted himself to pursuing lions and water buffaloes in Africa—ignored the signs of gathering stormy weather as much as the Chief Magistrate himself ignored them. They went forward with plans for their "Restoration"; they returned to high-handed methods of forcing the bonds of party discipline upon dissenters, or attaining the practical ends in view by tactics already too crude and old-fashioned for existing public opinion. By such measures they aroused and shocked great numbers of citizens who were nowadays more jealous of their rights, more discontented, more aware of the painful contrasts between the "promise of American life" (which a Theodore Roosevelt often seemed to hold out to them), between the "American dream," and the ugly realities of the time. Against such stresses and discontents, the strenuous, acrobatic "Teddy" had held the ruling party together and bedazzled the voters. Even a powerful (Democratic) opponent, Joseph Pulitzer, conceded that Roosevelt had worked wonderfully to overcome "discontent and socialism among the masses. . . ." If Roosevelt had committed a hundred times more mistakes, or had been a hundred times "more impulsive, changeable, unpresidential in dignity . . . inaccurate, loud and vociferating," Pulitzer thought, he must be given eternal credit for his service to the nation in turning "the great machinery of the government and the force and majesty of the law" toward prosecuting the "great offenders." [1]

The change from Roosevelt to Taft, as Elihu Root drily said, was like changing from one of the new automobiles to a horse-cab.

William Howard Taft, in equipment of education and training, was superior to most of the mediocre types selected for the Presidency by politicians. Yet it cannot be said that he was a man of real intelligence or large character; the considerable mass of his intimate letters and papers and the details of his private life, published lately, do not add to his stature. He appears Pickwickian rather than tragic. In his heart he had wished not to be President but to be a Supreme Court Justice. He had been pushed into the office in spite of himself, as he was to be pushed into other misadventures. Thus he approached his difficult role, in which so few Americans have distinguished themselves, with not a little fear and trembling. The sum of his errors or blunders would overcloud the sum of his creditable achievements while in office. For he was not a bold fellow, and lacked the imagination and flashing intui-

[1] Seitz, *op. cit.*, letter of Aug. 7, 1907, p. 320.

tions of strategy that his friend Theodore possessed. He was well-meaning and strove to please more than one faction in order to have harmony; yet he won few friends because of small, narrow traits of character easily exposed by the stress of public life, and contrasting strangely with his vast, loose, genial physical bulk. He shrank from strenuous political combat, longing for peace and order; yet opened himself to heavy attacks from various sides, and lived through a long nightmare of political war.

From the start of his administration Taft proceeded as if "the time for rhapsodies and glittering generalities" had passed—these were his own words. He proposed to continue on the road of "even-handed" justice to the poor or rich without fear or favor. But the Ship of State must be held to its course more steadily than before by the large, fat man at the helm. Government was to be conducted with more Constitutional purity, with more thorough legality than under the "impulsive," wayward, sometimes high-handed T. R. And who could best assist him in steering such a course? The people best fitted, he argued, to administer the government "without injury to the business interests" were "those lawyers who understand corporate wealth. . . ." The distinguished corporation lawyers whom he installed in his Cabinet, from Philander Knox, as Secretary of State, to George W. Wickersham, as Attorney General—he reasoned, a little too logically—by knowing corporate evils well would be best able to put the trusts in their place. They would gain a better hearing before Congress than the "more radical members" of his party. Taft expected to be criticized for the composition of his Cabinet. But even before assuming office he was reconciled to being "charged with reactionary tendencies." [2]

Taft little thought that he was already sowing dissension in his own administration. Under Roosevelt one of the intangible gains was the improvement that had been brought about in certain branches of the public service by the introduction of vigorous, educated, and genuinely patriotic young men. In the Departments of

[2] Pringle, *Taft*, Vol. I, p. 182, letter of Feb. 23, 1909.

the Interior and Agriculture—the former long malodorous for its grafters and claim thieves—Roosevelt's favorites, Garfield and Pinchot, had been leading a veritable crusade against waste, grabbing, and speculation in national lands. Their enthusiasm had spread to the young men in the ranks, lower officials and agents, some of whom, as in the Forest Service, endured willingly hardships and adventures in which life and limb were endangered for the great public cause. It is out of such devotion and *esprit de corps* that the administration of a good society is developed. And here, though perhaps guilty of oversights or at times of overzealousness, Roosevelt and his followers had made solid beginnings.

The appointment of Richard A. Ballinger, the lawyer-politician from Seattle, to replace Garfield as Secretary of the Interior, suggested the reversal by Mr. Taft of the conservation policies that had brought such credit to the preceding administration. Ballinger had for several years been Commissioner of Public Lands, working under Garfield; then had resigned early in 1908 to return to the practice of law and increase his earnings. His connections with Western politicians and land claimants who were interested in lands that the government had withdrawn was found afterward to have been close and friendly. What purpose lay behind the appointment of a Ballinger? To the Pickwickian Taft, the problem shaped itself as one of being more strictly legal or "Constitutional" in dealings with the public lands. He had the impression that Secretary Garfield had been overzealous, while he termed Gifford Pinchot a "fanatic." Ballinger would be more careful. Under him there would be a change of emphasis—but also dissension, from the very start, between his faction and the Pinchot faction of ardent conservationists.

For the legislative program being prepared under the new administration, a change of emphasis was also the rule. A revised tariff act and a new central banking and monetary act, demanded for years by great financial interests, were the most important measures planned. Immediately after his election Taft held a number of conferences with Senator Nelson Aldrich, the boss of the Senate, and Speaker "Joe" Cannon, the boss of the House of Representatives. These were the wise, strong leaders, with whom Roosevelt, it must be said, urged Taft to collaborate. But whereas Roosevelt would certainly have engaged in horse-trading with these Standpatters, reports soon indicated that the President-elect had yielded them a free hand in framing the new protective tariff. A special session of Congress was to be called for the tariff legislation; and the new act, Cannon predicted as early as November, 1908, would be drawn up largely in accordance with the wishes of the "intimate friends of the protective tariff"; that is, the protected manufacturers.

There were times when Taft felt deep misgivings about his "wicked partners"—as he sometimes called Cannon and Aldrich in private speech. The powerful Speaker, a cynical and profane old man, given (alas) to whiskey and poker, he found especially distasteful. There had been some talk of the new President's helping the Progressive wing of the Republican party to elect another Speaker who might impress the public as less cheerfully cynical than "Joe" Cannon. But as reports of Taft's secret conferences with Cannon and Aldrich spread, the Progressives knew that this was not to be; the President would give them no aid or comfort.

Before taking office, Taft wrote to his brother Horace that he had made an "investigation" to learn whether Speaker Cannon could be beaten, and found him "so strongly entrenched . . . that it was impossible. . . . I therefore gave up any hope of doing so or any effort to do so." [3] The search was not exhaustive, apparently; and the spirit shown here is like the courage of the Sabines rather than the Romans.

Two weeks after his inauguration, Taft wrote a long letter to Theodore Roosevelt bidding him *bon voyage*, and describing also, in somewhat gloomy terms, the series of compromises or "arrangements" made with the Standpatters which he clearly foresaw would bring down upon him the anger of the reform wing. But

[3] Duffy, *Taft*, p. 237.

the die had been cast; the party caucus, led by Cannon, had spoken and marked out the party "line." And Taft wrote:

> I have no doubt that when you return *you will find me very much under suspicion by our friends in the West.* I think I am already so because I was not disposed to countenance an insurrection of thirty men against 180 outside the caucus. . . . I knew that unless I sat steady in the boat, and did what I could to help Cannon and the great majority of the Republicans to stand solid, I should make a capital error in the beginning of my administration in alienating the good will of those without whom I can do nothing to carry through the legislation to which the party and I are pledged.

Taft is already "on the defensive." Cannon and Aldrich, he argues, had promised "to stand by the party platform and to follow my lead. They did so, I believe, for you, in the first Congress of your administration." Actually the initiative, the party leadership, which Roosevelt had held, passed to Aldrich, Cannon, and their associates in Congress. And Taft implies this when he expresses the fear that he may not be able to manage Congress as well as had his predecessor. He lacked, as he felt, Roosevelt's prestige and popular support as well as

> . . . the faculty for educating the public . . . through talks with correspondents, and *so I fear that a large part of the public will feel as if I had fallen away from your ideals;* but you know me better and will understand that *I am still working away on the same old plan* and hope to realize in some measure the results that we both hold valuable and worth striving for.

There are moments of pathos in this long letter when Taft appears to wrestle for the shrinking friendship of his great benefactor and friend. He explains his not having consulted Roosevelt more, on the ground that he had refrained from imposing upon the outgoing President's "well-earned quiet." (But when did Theodore Roosevelt ever ask for rest or quiet?) He insists that he is still following the lights of his patron, "the same old plan"—of exorcizing that Old Devil, socialism—but Roosevelt would not have done that with the open public assistance of the "wicked partners," Cannon and Aldrich. Finally the letter is the confession of a soldier weary before the battle has been joined, and seeing the future as through a glass darkly.[4]

The plans for a "Restoration" were, nevertheless, pushed forward rapidly. Opponents were brushed aside or chastised; the state of public opinion was ignored.

Nelson Aldrich, the real leader of the ruling party, thankful that the erratic, unstable Roosevelt was abroad, busied himself with vast, Hamiltonian plans for establishing a central bank of reserve—the embryonic Federal Reserve System—made possible by the recent passage of the Aldrich-Vreeland Act of May 30, 1908. He had traveled to the great financial centers of Europe, studying the foreign banking systems with Davison, of Morgan and Company, and George Reynolds, of the First National Bank of Chicago, by his side. Returning, he conferred with Paul M. Warburg, member of Kuhn, Loeb and Company, who had also labored long in the vineyard for a new banking act, but expressed fear that the political obstacles were too great to be overcome.

". . . You say that we cannot have a central bank, but I say we can," exclaimed Aldrich with his determined mien and piercing eyes.[5] It was with the same ruthless, determined spirit that he approached the task of enacting new tariff schedules under the law which was to bear his name. Aldrich had had the determining voice in the framing of financial and tax laws for thirty years. He saw no great obstacles before him now; least of all in the White House, whose incumbent now responded readily to his least call. Aldrich, though erect and proud as ever, was seventy; he was older than he realized. He had forgotten nothing and learned nothing.

2

Since 1906, William Jennings Bryan's farm paper, *The Commoner,* then widely read throughout the interior, had been speak-

[4] Duffy, *op. cit.*, letter of Mar. 21, 1909, pp. 226-227; italics mine.

[5] Stephenson, *op. cit.*, p. 340.

ing hopefully of a possible alliance between the independent or "Progressive" Republicans, as they now came to be called, and the Democratic opposition. Such an alliance would seize the balance of power from the conservative leaders. It was broached actively in the spring of 1907, when there was much talk of a union between La Follette and Bryan.[6] In the more recently founded farm paper, *La Follette's Weekly*, doctrines but little different from those of the Bryan Democrats were voiced, and nearly all the new Senators from the West, such as the brilliant William E. Borah of Idaho, seemed to take their tone and inspiration from the Little Giant of Wisconsin. They gave warning that the plain people, the farmers and the producers, were too largely ignored in Washington. They reiterated interminably the views to be read in *La Follette's Weekly* that

> The Middle West, that great agricultural Mecca [sic] between the Rockies and Alleghenies, between Canada and the Gulf, is the battleground upon which the American farmer, the American laborer, the American capitalist, must fight his political, his moral, his social battles. It is the crucible of God—the "melting pot"—where the best of all the races of the world have congregated and amalgamated to produce America's working citizens, who love their country and are not ashamed of honest labor. . . . It is the bread basket of the world. It is here the American farmer must fight for a "square deal." [7]

The clamor for "more direct democracy" often heard from the West, the demands for stronger control of the railroads and trusts, for the curbing of speculation in grains, for tariff reform (in the interest of the agriculturists), for direct primaries, direct election of Senators, reform of the rules of Congress, even popular control of the judiciary through the "recall of judges"—the cry for all that would equalize the political unbalance now rose stronger than ever, a crescendo of protest.

After 1906 the filibustering tactics of La Follette in the Senate

[6] *The Commoner*, May 24, 1907.

[7] *La Follette's Weekly*, Jul. 17, 1909.

meant something more than the behavior of a Lone Wolf in politics. If the imperious Aldrich had read *The Commoner* or *La Follette's Weekly* he would have seen that La Follette worked systematically to bring about a new grouping of the opposition, one that would burst through the old superstitious limits of the parties. A beginning of this was to be seen in the struggle over the abortive Hepburn Act in 1906. Theodore Roosevelt had flirted for a time with a Democratic-Insurgent-Republican combination, based upon economic—that is, anti-railroad—lines, but then abandoned it.

The same combination was headed in the summer of 1908 by La Follette in the contest over the Aldrich-Vreeland Act, which broadened the monetary basis of the national banks and provided for a Monetary Commission, headed by Aldrich, to draw up a plan for a central bank of reserve. Here again was the specter of that United States Bank which the common people, and especially the farming class, had fought since the days of Alexander Hamilton and Andrew Jackson. Once more, as La Follette argued, it was to be a central bank cast in a form desired by the great financiers and with all its vast centralized economic powers placed in their hands.

La Follette used sensational methods in an attempt to alarm the country; in a final effort to prevent passage of the monetary act he filibustered for three days. He ranged over all subjects interminably, harping especially upon his favorite reform measures. He treated his listeners to an unvarying flood of irony; he railed at the machinelike control of the Senate's Philistines by the "little handful of men" that dominated its important committees. He was literally Peter the Hermit "alone in the Senate," thoroughly hated by most of the members of its comfortable little club, yet building himself an ever greater following in the *Hinterland* beyond the Mississippi River. When La Follette weakened, members of the Democratic minority willingly took his place. It was while one of them, the blind Senator Gore of Oklahoma, paused in his flight of words—thinking his allies were present to take up the burden—that the clerk of the Senate, by previous arrangement, instantly called Aldrich's name, and the filibuster was broken. The Aldrich-Vreeland Act was then swiftly passed.[8]

La Follette's example of systematic defiance of the Congressional and party "hierarchy" was considered a most dangerous provocation by the Old Guard. Manifestation of a similar insurgent spirit in other Republicans now brought fearful parliamentary reprisals in the House of Representatives. The thirty "young insurgents" from the West (of whom Taft had spoken in his letter of farewell to Roosevelt) had joined with the Democrats in a fight to depose Speaker Cannon at the start of the special session in 1909. One by one, Cannon demoted the "insubordinates," such as George K. Norris of Nebraska and Victor Murdock of Kansas, from the committee chairmanships and privileges they had earned by years of service.

In the Senate, Jonathan Dolliver, the Iowa veteran, in addition to La Follette, was also marked for demotion. He had combined with the Democrats in 1906 in an effort to bring about a more drastic railroad act; he had been guilty of other sins of insubordination. The unforgiving Aldrich excluded Dolliver from membership in the powerful Finance Committee of the Senate, a committee to which he should have gone by seniority as well as personal distinction. Dolliver had hoped, by attaining the important committee post, to lead in the framing of a historic tariff-reform act which might bear his name, thus paving the way to higher things. The failure of appointment was a most bitter blow. La Follette had often appealed in vain to this lovable giant, whose heart was known to be on the progressive side, to join him in opposition, to stand "at the head of a movement here in the Senate and the country, for the public interests." Dolliver could now believe what his colleague La Follette said of the "tyranny" of the financial East over the West. For he learned that when appeals were made to Aldrich on Dolliver's behalf, Aldrich had said firmly and coldly

[8] *Congressional Record*, Vol. 42, Part 8, 60th Congress, 1st Session, May 29, 30, 1908.

that it would be impossible for them to work together in preparing a new tariff.[9]

Meeting Dolliver in the corridor of the Senate, one day after the committee appointments were announced, La Follette said to him:

"Jonathan, are you pretty nearly ready to have that conference with me?"

He answered: "Yes, I am coming over to see you."

"Well," I said, "come now."

And he went with me to my committee room. We spent several hours together.

From that day, Dolliver is said to have resolved that he was going to be "independent." He had saved his money and put it into a farm.

"I am going to judgment in the next twenty years," he said, "and I am going so that I can look my Maker in the face. . . . I can take my books, my wife and children, and, if I am dismissed from the service for following my convictions, I will go out to my farm and stay there until the call comes." [10]

3

The Payne-Aldrich Tariff Act of 1909 differed little from earlier Republican legislation in its field. Nor did it differ in the bitter debates, the rumors of corruption, the criminations and recriminations, it aroused. What chiefly distinguished the contest that began shortly after the special session of Congress opened was the fact that Democrats and Republicans as such were no longer clearly divided upon the line of protection. Even the Southern Congressmen now sought protection for Louisiana sugar or Alabama iron or tobacco. Opposition formed chiefly among the "Insurgent" Republican Congressmen hailing from the Granger states such as Wisconsin, Minnesota, Nebraska, Iowa, and Kansas. Nor did these men demand Free Trade—in a world of competing com-

[9] Stephenson, *op. cit.*, p. 345, citing memorandum of Senator Albert Cummins.

[10] La Follette, *op. cit.*, pp. 432-434.

mercial empires which erected Chinese walls of customs duties about themselves. On the contrary, a number of them sought increases of duties that would specifically aid agricultural and forest products such as hides and lumber. But mainly they fought against the Payne-Aldrich tariff as a means of fighting the tariff-favored trusts, which, a large minority of the Western Republicans believed, were responsible for the high cost of manufactured consumer goods. The tariff contest of 1909 was waged on economic rather than on partisan lines. It was accompanied by the strongest revolt within the Republican party since the Free Silver struggles of the 1890's.

The elaborate, technical business of writing a national revenue law was as usual little understood by most of the public, which looked on with mixed, confused sentiments. It was a situation made to order for Aldrich, who had been framing tariff laws for thirty years by his own system of compromise, horse-trading and "sudden thrusts." The only doubtful factor, this time, was that the Republican party platform in 1908 had declared itself for genuine and "unequivocal" revision of the tariff, and the President in various campaign addresses (though not in his inaugural) had been more outspoken still in urging necessary downward revisions of rates. The problem was therefore how to give the appearance of supporting the President's moderate demands, or how to sacrifice him a little while saving his face.

The bill introduced before the Lower House by Chairman Sereno Payne of the Ways and Means Committee on April 10, 1909—after some cursory hearings of "experts" and lobbyists—promised very slight reductions in the schedules, causing not a little disappointment. But soon it was improved by the addition of an amendment, providing for a direct income tax, a clause which it was now hoped the Supreme Court would not nullify as in 1895. But Aldrich's bill, presented in the Senate in the guise of a series of amendments and made ready with remarkable speed by April 12, 1909, administered a shock in that it embodied *increases* rather than the promised reductions. The Senate's "dictator" presented his bill with only a brief oral statement, asking immediate consideration of its 300 pages and hundreds of increases over the rates in the House bill.

Even before the bills were introduced, a large Wall Street investment house, Hayden, Stone and Company, had sent out a telegraphic market letter to its clients informing them that "we are reasonably sure . . . there cannot be any radical reduction." [11]

Ten days later, the attack of the dissident Republicans led by La Follette and Dolliver burst forth with a vehemence that none had awaited. Where was the downward revision promised to the people? they asked. Their first onslaught made a "profound impression" upon a public opinion already deeply agitated by great financial scandals and depression.[12]

But Aldrich asked coolly in return: "Where did we ever make the statement that we would revise the tariff *downward?*" Soon the Standpatters were to avow openly that all the talk of lowering the tariff rates was but a "concession, a sop thrown by those lacking in confidence to the voters." [13]

The "Payne Bill" had shown a desire to appease the consuming public, placing iron ore, hides, and wood pulp on the free list, and a forty per cent reduction in duties on shoes. It was when this bill with its amendments returned from the Senate's Finance Committee that, as in Lewis Carroll's tale, the Cheshire Cat gradually disappeared until only the grin was left. But Aldrich had promised President Taft that the tariff act would be in accord with his pledges, so that he would have no occasion to veto it. What would the President now do? the press asked.[14]

The new President was even more undecided than he appeared, as his letters now show. Taft wanted, Lodge said, only "a tariff that will strike the country favorably." [15] But his own view of what

[11] *Collier's Weekly*, Apr. 3, 1909.

[12] The New York *Times*, Apr. 23, 1909.

[13] *Congressional Record*, Jun. 8, 1909, p. 2950; Apr. 22, 1909, p. 1499.

[14] The New York *Tribune*, Apr. 13, 1909; *Literary Digest*, Apr. 17, Apr. 24, 1909.

[15] Lodge, *Correspondence*, Vol. II, p. 334.

this would be was not firmly asserted; he seemed unready to exert Presidential force to impose it, and inclined rather to let Congress (and its managers) lead the way. Thus he seemed to lean now to one side, now to the other. La Follette and Beveridge, who communicated with the President, felt sometimes that he encouraged them to "insurge" and raise the pressure from their side against the Standpatters. "Saw Taft—he is with us," Beveridge wrote his wife on one day.[16] But Aldrich proceeded confidently without fear of lightning bolts from the White House. Indeed the crafty old horse-trader was prepared to make certain seeming concessions to Taft, in items lowered from extremely high rates and no longer important to the great lay Republicans of big industry; free hides, a lower rate on lumber and upon leather gloves, and reduced tariffs for the Philippines were gifts which, in June, filled the President's heart with joy.[17] Yet in the case of the all-important wool and cotton schedules, which Aldrich insisted upon as representing his own requirements, Taft showed himself complaisant or indifferent. Thus Dolliver, with a flash of wit, was led to remark in the Senate one day that Mr. Taft was "an amiable man entirely surrounded by men who knew perfectly what they wanted."

But it was worse. Privately, to friends, to his brothers, to members of his Cabinet, to Elihu Root, Taft actually complained that Speaker Cannon was not playing square with him, that he mistrusted Aldrich's motives in keeping certain rates too high; that the attitude of the Standpatters was "most unfortunate." [18] These were his private thoughts, for at heart he felt himself something of a "low tariff man." But, in action, he invited Aldrich and his coterie to White House good-will dinners, fed them of his meat and good wine, and then bowed to their councils.

In the last week in May, as the tariff debate prolonged itself, Jonathan Dolliver heard that the President had turned against the Insurgents, saying that "he would not have anything to do with

[16] Bowers, *op. cit.*, Jun. 12, 1909, p. 349.

[17] Butt, *op. cit.*, Vol. I, p. 162.

[18] Jessup, *op. cit.*, Vol. II, p. 220; Pringle, *Taft*, Vol. I, pp. 429, 430.

such an irresponsible set of fellows." Beveridge on the floor of the Senate, May 25, 1909, cited passages from the President's speeches of 1908, promising moderate but definite reductions of the tariff rates, so that they would bear less heavily upon the masses of the people. He called upon the Republicans to support the President's original declarations and keep the party faith. The next day when Beveridge visited the White House, he found, as he said, "the coldest atmosphere I ever encountered in politics." [19]

Taft now came to think Beveridge, ardent supporter of Rooseveltian policies, an insufferable egotist and poseur, who bored him to death. He hated to meet the "fanatic" La Follette even at a public ceremony; and thought it equally a waste of time to see those "blatant demagogues," Dolliver and Cummins,[20] men who talked incessantly, wearyingly, shrilly, and endangered the future of the party itself.

Legends of the overweening vanity of the Insurgent leaders, La Follette, Beveridge, Dolliver, and Cummins, have been perpetuated by certain historians. ". . . Of the sum of the egos of all 96 Senators, the 10 Insurgents had more than half," according to Mark Sullivan. Yet in the tariff battle of 1909 this group of Senators, who had only hitherto fired occasional, sniping shots at the Old Guard, made a demonstration of organized minority resistance, of devoted teamwork, that was spectacular and rare in our parliamentary history.

From the rostrum of the Senate Chamber they educated the people. A "prairie fire" was growing in the West, as one keen observer related at the time. Men talked everywhere of the need for new leadership, and a "new national party." Such a development was "nearer than the Republican party of 1855." [21] It was the sense of this historic opportunity that fused the bloc of Insurgent Senators, including La Follette, Beveridge, Dolliver,

[19] Bowers, *op. cit.*, p. 343.

[20] Pringle, *Taft*, Vol. I, pp. 430-431.

[21] Mark Sullivan in *Collier's Weekly*, Dec. 11, 1909. In those days Mr. Sullivan was an ardent Progressive.

Cummins, Bristow of Kansas, Moses Clapp of Minnesota, Knute Nelson, and Norris Brown, into a determined, well-drilled team, whose members each mastered the parts they must play. Soon, as they knew, they were to be proscribed, "outlawed," and must depend solely on the voters of their own states for continuance in public life. They were convinced that they had nothing more to look for in the Aldrich-Cannon leadership and must either rebuild their party from within or form a new alignment.

"It is incumbent upon the reformer who seeks to establish a new order to come equipped with complete mastery of all the information upon which the established order is based," La Follette wrote not long afterward. La Follette brought to the group the Wisconsin tactics of mastering facts, of using exact knowledge as a weapon against the adversary. The work of organized opposition was thereupon divided among the Insurgent Senators: thus Dolliver prepared to speak on the cotton rates, La Follette on the wool and other textiles, Cummins on the metals, while Beveridge acted as floor leader. They engaged experts to furnish them with information in each field, and from the early days of May to the torrid ones of June, gathered together every night at La Follette's or Beveridge's apartment—with a case of beer to quench the large Mr. Clapp's thirst—and prepared their speeches and mapped out the strategy of debate in consultation.[22] Every evening they planned questions which they would ask of each other on the morrow, on the floor of the Senate, in order to bring out plainly all points to the most innocent listeners. That spring the American people, hearing of the concerted attacks, day by day, learned something of what tariff legislation meant.

Dolliver, for instance, whose speeches were probably the most interesting and wittiest of the period, delivered an all-day speech on the cotton-textile schedules, which he proved to be higher than the Dingley rates of 1897, tremendously favorable to Massachusetts mill owners, whose lobbyists had demanded the new rates. Aldrich, greatly put out of countenance, warned Dolliver that he

[22] La Follette, *op. cit.*, pp. 441, 442, 445.

was assaulting "the very citadel of protection." But Dolliver answered with the defiant challenge that henceforth he would take his orders from his constituency and not from Mr. Aldrich. He perorated:

> I want to see an end to the scandal that has accompanied the framing of every tariff bill. . . .
>
> So far as I am concerned I am through with it. I intend to fight it. I intend to fight without fear—I do not care what may be my political fate. I have had a burdensome and toilsome experience in public life now these twenty-five years. . . . I do not propose that the remaining years of my life, whether they be in public affairs or in private business, shall be given up to a dull consent to . . . all these conspiracies, which . . . use the lawmaking power of the United States to multiply their own profits and to fill the marketplace with witnesses of their avarice and of their greed.[23]

The Insurgents made serious charges of secret alterations of the tax rates, such as the reduction of the cigarette tax in committee at the demand of the tobacco trust. Beveridge told of how the same trick had been worked before; and how it was being worked now. And his accomplice La Follette would rise and ask him with malice: "Does the Senator think that remarkable legislation . . . was an oversight?" [24]

Aldrich grew angry, embarrassed, silent. At times he demanded discipline. The tariff would be passed, he hinted, as written by the majority; the majority were on his side. He threatened Beveridge and the others, styling them "free traders" and no Republicans. Yet day by day the testimony of Aldrich's "experts" seemed overweighed by the Insurgents' marshaling of facts. At last it was apparent that they actually meant to vote against the bill. Aldrich was astonished; he had thought they talked but for the record. In answer to his menaces, Cummins of Iowa replied: "There will come a time presently when the clamor of millions who want re-

[23] *Congressional Record,* May 3, May 5, 1909; Tarbell, *The Tariff,* p. 357.
[24] *Congressional Record,* May 14, 1909.

lief will sound like the roar of a thousand Niagaras from one ocean to another." [25]

Aldrich scorned to consider such warnings; he pressed on to votes. Danger existed, because the House version of the tariff bill included an amendment providing for an income tax of 2 per cent upon incomes of over $5,000, the Democrats joining with the Insurgents to support this clause. Aldrich, who fought the income tax for twenty years, was finally forced to the unpleasant expedient of accepting as a compromise measure the proposal of a corporation excise tax of 2 per cent, in return for which the Insurgent-Democratic combination abandoned the personal income tax. Then, as a separate measure, both Houses passed a resolution for a Federal income-tax amendment to the Constitution to be submitted to the states.

The Payne-Aldrich revenue bill, when it was finally passed, contained good mixed with evil. Its increases were moderate; there were provisions for sliding rates, and for a tariff commission to be appointed by the President. But the nation, deeply aroused by the long, sensational debate in Washington, remembered chiefly the ruthless tactics used in forcing passage. They saw that the protective tariff rates were made higher when it was pledged that they should be made less burdensome. The ten Insurgent Senators who, burning their bridges, voted opposition to the very end, were known thereafter as martyrs to Aldrich's "Star Chamber" proceedings. ". . . A promise to a people is sacred!" Beveridge had exclaimed, when the final roll call was taken.

While the President cheerfully signed the bill, the citizens were already protesting that they would be forced to pay more for their woolen clothing. Even conservative newspapers such as the New York *Sun* (on August 2, 1909) made gloomy predictions of an approaching civil war within the Republican party which would continue "until the leadership of one faction or the other is driven from power." At the other side of the country, the farm paper of La Follette drew its own conclusions, saying:

[25] *Literary Digest*, May 15, 1909.

The lesson has been a costly one to the people, but it has been well-learned. . . . The tariff-favored trusts won out. . . . But their victory will unquestionably be short-lived. Soon the people who must buy food and clothing and other necessaries of life will send other representatives to Washington.[26]

It was the evident truth that underlay such dire predictions as those above, the reports from field agents of a "prairie fire," that sent the indolent Mr. Taft upon a speaking tour of the Middle West late that summer. He had decided to "get out and see the people and jolly them." [27] From Minnesota the party wheelhorse, Representative Tawney, who had much to do with the recent tariff act, had called for help in a local election campaign. Taft planned to make his speech at Tawney's native town of Winona, in the heart of the radical agrarian region, a defense of the Payne-Aldrich bill. Unfortunately he delayed writing his speech until the last hours, when it was prepared with great haste.

Neither the Republican party nor himself, ran Taft's speech of September 17, 1909, had promised that tariff rates would all be revised downward. (This resembled unpleasantly Aldrich's equivocations.) Then, after a long, labored defense, he concluded: "I would say without hesitation that this is the best tariff bill that the Republican party has ever passed, and therefore the best tariff bill that has been passed at all. . . ." [28]

Only afterward, when he took account of the outburst of ridicule this speech evoked in the press, did Taft realize that he had made a political mistake. In this same speech he also made disparaging allusions to the Insurgent Senators, challenging them either to "stay in line and work for party solidarity," or leave the party openly, as their individual consciences dictated. The "Progressive" Senators accepted this as an attempt to "read out of the party" those who opposed the Payne-Aldrich bill.[29]

[26] *La Follette's Weekly*, Aug. 14, 1909.
[27] Pringle, *Taft*, Vol. I, p. 457.
[28] The New York *World*, Sept. 18, 1909.
[29] *La Follette's Weekly*, Sept. 25, 1909.

The Mid-Western countryside rang with the protests of the Insurgents, recorded in numerous newspaper interviews:

TAFT HAS SURROUNDED HIMSELF WITH CORPORATION ATTORNEYS

TAFT HAS MADE STUDIED EFFORT TO REPUDIATE THINGS PREDECESSOR STOOD FOR

The Insurgent leaders were now more determined than ever to overthrow the Old Guard and recapture the Republican party for Lincoln's plain people. It was nothing less than this that La Follette and his colleagues patiently planned: once a half dozen large Western states were seized, the rebuilding of the party from within could be completed rapidly, as in Wisconsin. That summer and fall the Insurgent leaders, returning to their constituents, told their tale of outrage and betrayal and won strong local approval. Some of them as in the case of Beveridge were soon to face re-election campaigns, and they arranged to stump for each other.

Jonathan Dolliver, ill and worn out from the long summer debates, nevertheless addressed a cheering letter to Beveridge in September. Formerly the very paragon of regularity and tolerance in Congress and party, Dolliver wrote as one who had come to see the light of revolution late in life.

If we had a direct line from the skies we could not have done a better job for ourselves than we did when we stood on our convictions against all comers including the Big Chief [Aldrich]. The penalty of doing right exists only in the imaginations of grafters and time-servers. If you never see the inside of the Senate Chamber again, the last three months of your labors will make your life notable and famous when biographies are written. . . .

We don't need money to fight them. *We will go in with the common weapons of justice and common sense and make a new era in national life. . . .*[30]

When the "man mountain" of Iowa, Dolliver, believed that the central party organization could be defeated with "the weapons

[30] Sept. 14, 1909; Bowers, *op. cit.*, p. 371; italics mine.

of justice and common sense," surely the times were out of joint. The plans for a "Restoration" had grievously miscarried. It was scarcely a year since the Rough Rider had gone abroad, and the party he had held unified was torn by internal strife. Soon a wave of scandal would engulf it.

As the party elections of 1910 approached, Elihu Root, now Senator for New York, had forebodings of disaster, and went about "like old Noah," warning his political associates "that this is no ordinary shower but a flood," and that they had "better hurry up and get into the Ark." Yet few of his friends believed him.[31]

[31] Jessup, *op. cit.*, Vol. II, p. 154.

X. THE BALLINGER CASE: AN AMERICAN AFFAIRE DREYFUS

THE CONSERVATION of America's immense natural resources for the benefit of the people made the chief glory of Theodore Roosevelt's years in power. Not only were great forests of magnificent timberland saved from destruction, but millions of acres of coal, of mineral land, and above all of water-power sites were held from pre-emption by claimants who would eventually have turned them over to the hands of monopolistic groups.

The soul of the conservation movement in the early years of the present century was undoubtedly Gifford Pinchot. His eyes, as Owen Wister recalled, seemed to look always "as if they gazed upon a Cause," and his face was "one of marked and particular beauty, in which enthusiasm and asceticism" were blended.[1] There were those who, like President Taft, could be ironical at the expense of this "fanatic," this "transcendentalist." But that his idealism was constructive and invaluable could scarcely be denied.

In their zeal the conservationists undoubtedly exceeded a Pickwickian interpretation of the law. Garfield as Secretary of the Interior and Pinchot as an under-officer of the Department of Agriculture used their authority to compel those who developed power sites or established electric power lines across government lands to charge only moderate rates for their services. These tactics were extremely irritating to the forerunners of the Electric Bond and

[1] Wister, *op. cit.*, p. 114.

Share Company and other utility monopolies.[2] When Taft became President, he immediately put a stop to this practice, upon legal grounds. In any case he thought Pinchot "a good deal of a radical and a good deal of a crank. . . ."[3] But Gifford Pinchot, though a minor government official, enjoyed the influence of a full Cabinet officer; he had been a favorite at Roosevelt's court, and to dismiss him would have meant an open repudiation of Rooseveltian principles.

However, Taft's naming of Richard A. Ballinger as Secretary of the Interior—despite his awareness that Pinchot and Ballinger worked with poor accord—was an indication that limits were to be marked out for the conservation movement. Henceforth everything would be done "within the law" and according to the "limited powers" granted by the Constitution, even though land-grabbers and public utilities benefited thereby.

No one offered greater contrast to Gifford Pinchot, surely, than Secretary Ballinger. His face and manner was that of a hard-headed "old school" lawyer and politician who had grown up with the West. Taft appointed him, probably, at the urging of Western party leaders, remarking at the time that the appointment "would satisfy the West coast."[4] In the Far West conservation policies were said to be less popular than elsewhere. The Western politicians demanded continued liberal distribution of public lands in their vicinity to "pioneers" who would settle and develop them. In reality the latter-day pioneers were often but claim agents leagued with the politicians, to whom the Department of the Interior had been a source of spoils for a century. Eventually the claims would turn up in the hands of some large syndicate that could furnish the capital or build the railroads necessary for the exploitation of the copper, coal, or timber lands.

Under the Roosevelt administration, for several years, Ballinger as General Land Commissioner had exhibited only restrained en-

[2] Stahl, *The Ballinger-Pinchot Controversy*, pp. 77-78.

[3] Pringle, *Taft*, Vol. I, p. 480.

[4] *Ibid.*, Vol. I, p. 478.

thusiasm for the current conservation policies. In one case, in 1907, he had shown himself ready to approve certain claims for coal lands in southern Alaska, known as the "Cunningham Claims," which special agents of the Interior Department had considered as being of fraudulent title. There were reports that most of these claims to Alaskan coal lands were being taken for the Guggenheims, who were then developing copper mines in Alaska, or were to wind up in the hands of a "Morgan-Guggenheim syndicate" eventually. One special agent of the Interior Department who had become suspicious of the Cunningham Claims opposed Ballinger's action so vigorously that Secretary Garfield was induced to delay approval of them until further government investigations were completed.

In March, 1908, Mr. Ballinger resigned from the service and resumed the private practice of law in Seattle. It happened oddly enough that among the private cases he defended was that of the self-same Cunningham group which still petitioned the government for title to some 5,280 acres of coal land. Later, Ballinger explained that he took this case largely as a friendly service, accepting only the small fee of $250, which barely paid his expenses for a trip East. The fact that while employed in the government service he had obtained information of possible value to his clients presented no ethical problems to his mind. The Cunningham affair, however, continued in suspension; and there matters rested until 1909, when by a most curious coincidence Ballinger, returning to the Interior Department as its chief, took it under consideration once more.

From the start Secretary Ballinger showed that he believed in a form of conservation that encouraged private exploitation of government lands in the Western states and territories. Within thirty days after taking office he, with Taft's approval, restored to entry a great part of the land that his predecessor, under Roosevelt, had withdrawn "illegally" in a sort of last-hour coup.

It is apparent from the Taft Papers that Gifford Pinchot came at once to Taft and protested vehemently at Ballinger's reopening of large water-power sites to entry. Pinchot contended that Taft by supporting Ballinger's orders was going back on the principles of the Roosevelt administration which he had vowed to continue. And Pinchot would not endure such a change silently, but, he hinted, would resign from the service he loved and defend the cause of conservation before the public.[5] There were three conferences in April, 1909; and though Taft did not enjoy the visitations of the "fanatic," he retreated, and ordered Ballinger, who acted under protest, to restore the water-power lands in question to the forest reserve.[6]

Under the surface a constant struggle was now waged between the two adversaries, Pinchot and Ballinger, and their respective cohorts; and Taft, aware of the dangerously growing dissension within his government, was alarmed and wearied by it. He wondered how to end it without running the political danger of banishing Pinchot, who had already threatened to resign. Large principles and even vast natural wealth were at stake; yet the President did not treat the matter in this light. Then, at the end of the summer, the internal struggle suddenly rose to a climax.

In August, 1909, Pinchot, through Forest Service officials, got wind of the contested Cunningham Claims and learned that Ballinger was endeavoring to have them validated, although more than one subordinate who had investigated the claims reported that they were fraudulent. Louis R. Glavis, the young chief of the Field Division of the Interior Department who had been in charge of this case, had come to the conclusion that certain of the Alaskan coal lands, including forest reserves under the jurisdiction of the Interior Department, were to be disposed of to claimants who evidently represented the Morgan-Guggenheim "Alaska Syndicate."

Glavis had been in the service about four years, and had the reputation of being a very able, intelligent, and faithful official. He was only twenty-five years old and it was not surprising if he

[5] Gifford Pinchot to author, Dec. 18, 1939.

[6] Stahl, *op. cit.*, pp. 85 ff.

took to heart the many moral exhortations of Theodore Roosevelt that one should fight to the uttermost for the welfare of the nation against the forces of money and greed. In 1907 he had already crossed swords with Ballinger, when the latter was his superior as General Land Commissioner, and by a direct appeal to Secretary Garfield he had prevented the disposal of the Cunningham Claims. But now Ballinger, in full command of the department, pressed Glavis to have the Cunningham affair concluded in short order, or have the claim approved. Glavis was distraught at this command, since his investigations required traveling over wild territories and seeking the depositions of persons who sometimes lived thousands of miles apart. He telegraphed to Washington, pleading for more time. On May 17, 1909, he went to Washington himself and saw Secretary Ballinger, submitting his partially completed report. Ballinger and his legal aides thereupon overruled Glavis's judgment on the fraudulency of the Cunningham Claims. But Glavis, who later exhibited a remarkable memory and mental capacity, felt that he knew the law and that a great deal was at stake. He relates:

> Without consulting with my superiors, I went to Attorney General Wickersham and stated the matter to him. I understand that he asked Mr. Ballinger to refer the matter to him. . . . Ten days later the Attorney General . . . upheld my contentions and saved the Alaska Coal cases.[7]

That is to say, Glavis was given further time for investigation. But soon the Interior Department superiors pressed him again to hasten the affair. It was now mid-July and Glavis, who had returned to the West, saw Ballinger, then visiting Seattle, and made a last, vain appeal for more time to prepare for a final hearing.

By now the whole affair was overshadowed by mutual suspicion and hostility. Glavis knew that his own position was precarious, that his cause was seen with little favor and would eventually be overruled. But more than his own career, the Alaska coal cases

[7] *Collier's Weekly*, Nov. 13, 1909.

involved "the future coal supply of the United States." The hidden interests who, thanks to their railway dominance in Alaska, would soon take over the coal fields, would in his opinion secure "a monopoly similar to that of the Pennsylvania coal fields today." [8] As a last resort, Glavis appealed for aid to a friend, A. C. Shaw, who was an assistant to Gifford Pinchot in the Forest Service. He saw Pinchot on August 5, 1909, at Spokane, and held a long talk with him, and Pinchot thought the story was serious enough to warrant sending the young official with a letter of introduction to President Taft himself.

The stout Chief Magistrate was vacationing at Beverly, Massachusetts, after the steaming days of the tariff warfare, when, on August 18, 1909, Glavis came to him with his complaints and charges, over the head of his superior officer. Glavis charged that entries for over 5,000 acres of valuable coal and timber land had been made for the indirect benefit of the Morgan-Guggenheim syndicate; like Gifford Pinchot, earlier, he accused Secretary Ballinger of being faithless to the conservation program inaugurated under Roosevelt and officially espoused by President Taft. Later, on September 5, 1909, Glavis returned and delivered into the hands of the President a large dossier, several hundred pages of technical reports, and testimony taken in the field.

It was plain that Taft was in no humor to enjoy the high-handed, even insubordinate performance of the minor official Glavis—though it was done in the name of public duty. Besides, Glavis came straight from Pinchot, who stood behind him, and who was believed to be responsible for recent press criticism of the administration's handling of conservation problems. Taft was busy preparing for his speaking tour in defense of the unpopular Payne-Aldrich tariff; he was busy and yet needed rest—and golf,

[8] L. R. Glavis to A. C. Shaw; testimony of Jan. 26, 1910; 61st Congress, *Investigation of Interior Department*, Vol. 34. Conflicting views have been expressed upon the value of the Alaska coal lands. Mineral resources are usually of uncertain value, until promotional capital, machinery and transportation are applied to exploiting them. At the time, 1909, there was much talk of railway building in southern Alaska by larger railroad interests.

which made him happy. During that week of September 6, 1909, the President was visited by Attorney General Wickersham and by Secretary Ballinger, who came with his legal counsel, Lawler. It is evident that the whole unpleasant matter, including the Glavis documents, was taken up with these men. Normally a ruling in the case should have come from the Attorney General. But Mr. Wickersham, as it transpired, was extremely busy with many more important affairs all that week; and so it came to pass that Mr. Ballinger, the accused, with the aid of Mr. Lawler, his counsel, judged the Glavis charges and presented his summary report to the President.

It was of course a judgment that completely exonerated himself and set down Glavis as a neurotic young man, filled with delusions of grandeur and obsessed by mere "shreds of suspicion." Taft now moved with unusual promptness, since the dangerous Pinchot was in the background of the case; he disposed of the whole business (as he hoped) with a vigorous public letter addressed to Secretary Ballinger, exonerating him and requesting him to dismiss the offensive Glavis. Afterward, he would claim that he spent several days and sat up until three o'clock one morning going over the evidence in the case.[9] In reality he asked Oscar Lawler, the attorney assigned to the Interior Department, to draft a report "as if he were President," exonerating Ballinger, which Lawler did. This was duly signed by Taft, with perhaps a few slight changes introduced by him.

The letter of September 13, 1909, to Secretary Ballinger, Mark Sullivan wrote at the time in *Collier's Weekly*, appeared as "a ponderous, sweeping letter of exculpation and endorsement intended . . . to refute all present charges against Ballinger and make future ones impossible." Taft told Ballinger that he had "examined the whole matter most carefully" and reached the conclusion that Mr. Glavis's case was without substantial evidence. For having attempted to file "a disingenuous statement unjustly

[9] Taft to Senator Knute Nelson, May 15, 1910, the New York *Times*, May 16, 1910.

impeaching the integrity of his superior officers," Taft authorized Mr. Ballinger to dismiss the said Glavis from the service, as the Secretary had intended.

The President, as he departed on his Western tour to quench Western prairie fires by this forceful public statement, doubtless intended to teach a lesson not only to Glavis but to Pinchot and his fellow agitators. Newspaper talk of Alaskan land-grabbing had started in the latter part of August, and La Follette already thundered accusations against Ballinger for helping the "water-power grab." The source of the public rumors lay within the government itself: the Forest Service, conducted by Pinchot.

2

But while Taft was falling into grievous blunders in his Minnesota speech, another prairie fire was kindled in the East by his letter to Ballinger. It was the heyday of social reformers, who spoke through many organs. One of the largest and most powerful of the muckraking magazines was *Collier's Weekly*, whose owner was a close friend of Gifford Pinchot, and whose editor was the able Norman Hapgood. In a vigorous, well-informed editorial, Hapgood attacked the Taft administration that week, arguing that the Roosevelt conservation policy was being abandoned, that frauds were being committed again in the oft-pillaged Interior Department, and that the well-meaning Mr. Taft was being led around by the nose. Taft's letter exonerating Ballinger, it was hinted, was not even written by the President; and the President perhaps knew nothing about it.[10]

To Pinchot the punishment of Glavis was a blow at himself and all his works. To defend conservation and "bring the Kingdom of God on earth," he must now help to right the wrong done to Glavis. To the Insurgent bloc of Congressmen the "Ballinger-Pinchot case" seemed a heaven-sent opportunity for renewing their drive against the administration; and they rushed into the

[10] *Collier's Weekly*, Sept. 25, 1909.

fray with a single accord. Soon the great muckraking magazines, which now flourished more widely than ever despite Roosevelt's prohibition, took up the issue; and month by month, in *Hampton's*, *McClure's*, or *Collier's*, attacks upon the Department of the Interior were published. One article pictured Mr. Ballinger as a frank and crude opponent of conservation; it cited his own words in an interview and accused him bluntly of acting in collusion with the Morgan and Guggenheim interests.[11] But the greatest sensation was caused by publication in *Collier's Weekly* on November 13, 1909, of the long, detailed, carefully prepared article by Louis Glavis himself, telling the story of his investigations and preferring charges against Secretary Ballinger. (Though Glavis had been offered $3,000 to tell his story, he had refused payment of any kind, wishing only to clear his name.) The article was prefixed by a sensational headline devised by the editors:

ARE THE GUGGENHEIMS IN CHARGE OF THE DEPARTMENT OF INTERIOR?

The storm now broke in its full force. Demands were made everywhere for a public investigation of the Interior Department by a Congressional committee. On the other hand, Payne Whitney, a scion of New York society, heard talk at the Union League Club of a million-dollar libel suit against *Collier's Weekly* and brought advance news of this to Editor Norman Hapgood and to Pinchot, who had engendered the whole controversy.[12]

One day in December, therefore, Louis D. Brandeis received an urgent telegram from Norman Hapgood, who knew him, asking him to come at once to the offices of the New York firm of Winthrop and Stimson. There Brandeis found a conclave of legal talent, including Henry L. Stimson and George Wharton Pepper, who was engaged by Gifford Pinchot. In addition, James R. Garfield, Norman Hapgood, and Louis R. Glavis were present, the last-named explaining the case to the lawyers. At this meeting

[11] J. L. Mathews in *Hampton's Magazine*, Jan. 1910.

[12] Hapgood, N., *The Changing Years*, pp. 185-186.

Brandeis was strongly impressed with Glavis's sincerity and sense of honor.[13] The Boston reformer and lawyer consented to enter the case. It was understood that a Congressional investigation impended; and plans were laid by the lawyers to represent Glavis and Pinchot at the forthcoming hearings, and thus defend also the owners of *Collier's Weekly*. It was the latter who had retained Brandeis as the strongest lawyer they could get.

Above all things, Taft had dreaded a contest with Gifford Pinchot. At the very time of his dismissal of Glavis and exculpation of Ballinger, on September 13, 1909, he had written: "My dear Gifford . . . I urge that you do not make Glavis's cause your own." The President begged him to take no hasty action.[14]

Yet the logic of events drove Pinchot and the other devoted followers of Theodore Roosevelt into the growing opposition movement against Taft and his Old Guard allies. But yesterday the achievements Pinchot had long dreamed of, in the field of land conservation, had seemed very near. But now it was plain that long-cherished plans and policies of conservation were to be compromised, if not abandoned. This was the meaning of Glavis's dismissal. Pinchot therefore entered the struggle with all his heart. On December 31, 1909, he wrote a long letter to Theodore Roosevelt, then still in Africa, giving his own account of the evil things that had happened since his hero had gone to hunt lions and kings.[15] He also turned to the Insurgents in Congress, who from the opening of the session in December had been fighting for a resolution for an inquiry into the Department of the Interior. To Senator Dolliver, who had led the Progressive opposition to the Payne-Aldrich tariff, Pinchot addressed a long letter on January 6, 1910, that was intended to be read publicly from the floor of the Senate. In this the fiery Chief Forester explained how he had come to mistrust the policy of the President's Cabinet

[13] Lief, *op. cit.*, p. 157.

[14] Pringle, *Taft*, Vol. I, p. 491.

[15] In the early spring of 1910, Pinchot made a journey to Italy, to meet Roosevelt and present "at his [Roosevelt's] request" his account of the controversy. (Gifford Pinchot to author.)

advisers; how he had permitted his two aides, Shaw and Oliver of the Forest Service—though it was clearly an improper and insubordinate step—to help Glavis prepare his case against Secretary Ballinger. Like Glavis, "the most vigorous defender of the people's interests," they had acted out of a high sense of duty, risking their official position rather than the public property. But they had taken this step only after appeals through official channels to the President had failed. The President, Pinchot contended, suffered under "a mistaken impression of the facts."[16] The real question, he said, was "between government by men for human welfare and government by money for profit, between the men who stand for Roosevelt's policies and the men who stand against them."

This indignant letter, exploding like a bombshell in the Senate, gave notice that the break between the Roosevelt followers and the administration had come. It brought from the President the dismissal that Pinchot had courted.

Somewhat tardily, the President realized how the rebellion was growing; how the radical West was breaking away from his party and his attempts at leadership, and how the mantle of Roosevelt, which he had so proudly assumed in 1908, was being torn from him by the friends and political heirs of Roosevelt. He saw a "cabal" against him, rather than an inevitable combination of diverse groups and forces. Assailed on one side because of the unpopular tariff bill, the administration was now assailed on another side for its alleged betrayal of the conservation program. Quietly measures of defense were taken which would strengthen the government for its test.

Pinchot, after his deliberate act of insubordination, made a farewell speech on January 8, 1910, before the assembled officials and clerks of his bureau, to whom he had been as a romantic hero. It was a parting challenge, greeted with rousing and rebellious cheers:

[16] *Senate Documents*, Sixty-first Congress, Third Session, No. 719, pp. 1283-1285.

This fight must go on. It is larger than any man's personal presence or personal failure. . . . Stand by the work! Hold fast to the standard we have set together. Never allow yourself to forget that you are serving a much greater master than the . . . Administration.[17]

3

President Taft had been reconciled, from the beginning, to working with the veteran Speaker "Joe" Cannon, because it was "impossible" to dislodge him. However, the Insurgent bloc in the House had other ideas about Cannon. Led by the mild-mannered little George W. Norris of Nebraska, they had been plotting their stroke of state for nearly four years since March, 1906, and to this end had held frequent conversations with the Democrats, who shared with them a deepening sense of wrong. Not only were the Outs and Insurgents shorn of committee privileges, but with increasing arrogance during the "Restoration Period" Cannon had injured them politically by ignoring or postponing indefinitely consideration of bills introduced for the benefit of their districts and states.[18]

When the resolution for an inquiry into the Department of the Interior was introduced before the House in January, following Pinchot's letter to Dolliver, Cannon as usual was ready to appoint the House members of the joint committee from his own list of complaisant Standpatters. Possibly, as the Insurgents charged at the time, even the very terms and provisions of the resolution were to be written and the personnel of the committee packed as Ballinger directed. But by the ruse of waiting for an hour when the chairman of the Rules Committee had gone out to lunch, Representative Norris succeeded in having the House elect its own choice of members. The majority were "sound" Republicans; but the presence of an alert opposition minority, including one strong Insurgent from Kansas, E. H. Madison, and two able Democrats, made a passive "whitewashing" of the affair impossible.

[17] Stahl, *op. cit.*, p. 128.

[18] *The Commoner*, Mar. 9, 1906.

Cannon had long managed the House in the spirit of partisan chairmanship perfected by "Czar" Thomas B. Reed in 1890; his despotism depended upon control of the Ways and Means, Rules, and Judiciary Committees. To call up a bill, the legislator must needs go hat in hand to the Speaker's private chambers, negotiate with him, and seek his good will by promising services in return. Then, perhaps, he might be recognized on the floor at some stated time, weeks or months later. Otherwise measures never came to a vote; they died a silent death in the "morgue" of the Judiciary Committee, garroted by the trusted appointees of Speaker Cannon.[19] This despotism had grown less and less benevolent with passing time, and more and more cynical; until on March 16, 1910, ignoring the signs of growing rebellion, and wishing to punish the insurrectos anew, the old Speaker pushed his autocracy to new extremes. Now he sought to abolish the custom of "Calendar Wednesday," a day on which members had a little more than their usual prerogative to be called upon and to speak for their own measures.

On a roll call, so aroused were the less hardened members of his own party that the Speaker was beaten by a sizable vote. The patient Norris had made a study of the rules and precedents in which Cannon had skillfully entrenched himself and for a long time had held himself prepared for just such an emergency as the roll call produced. Suddenly Norris brought forth a resolution that he had carried in his pocket for many months, moving that the Committee on Rules be elected by the House instead of being appointed by the Speaker, as heretofore. There followed a tremendously long and excited debate, lasting for nearly thirty continuous hours and reported by the press in the terms of a great military battle. The control of the Rules Committee was the foundation of the Speaker's autocratic power; and Cannon by every possible resource, all through the day and the night, fought to retain it.

Against the cry of the Standpatters for party discipline, emotional appeals rang out, as that from the respectable Gardner of

[19] Mark Sullivan in *Collier's Weekly*, Mar. 13, 1909, Apr. 3, 1909.

Massachusetts, son-in-law of Henry Cabot Lodge, who demanded the end of "arbitrary rules" and restoration of the "principle of representative government." Norris exclaimed passionately:

I would rather go down to my political grave with a clear conscience than ride in the chariot of victory, a Congressional stool pigeon, the slave, the servant, and the vassal of . . . the owner of a *legislative menagerie.*

Efforts were made, as often before, to rally the sheeplike Tammany Democrats to the rescue of the beleaguered speaker, but Norris denounced them, crying: "Hold up your manacled, wounded, bleeding, shackled hands and let the country see your parliamentary slavery!"

The mood of disaffection among the regulars had gone too far. In the end the Western Republicans with the aid of the Democrats prevailed, and by successive votes forced Cannon to crushing defeat.

In his last extremity, Cannon reverted to the vernacular and exclaimed wearily, "Well, boys, I am a little shot up." Then, as if challenging fate, he himself moved to declare the chair of the Speaker vacant. At this dramatic turn, equal almost to an impeachment, even the Democratic floor leader, Champ Clark of Missouri, burst into tears. The Insurgents and Norris himself, however, shrank from this final step and sustained Cannon in the chair to the end of the session. But the appointive powers of the Speaker were thenceforth severely curtailed, and new, liberal rules were adopted. It was the most humiliating defeat ever suffered by a Speaker of Congress.[20]

Thus, within a year of Roosevelt's departure, an Insurgent-Democratic coalition ruled the House of Representatives. The majority party was divided, its parliamentary machine smashed. Meanwhile the broadening political struggle for "more democracy" that had suddenly liberalized the procedure of Congress it-

[20] Sullivan, *Our Times,* Vol. IV, pp. 380 ff.; *Collier's Weekly,* Mar. 26, Apr. 3, 1910; Neuberger, *Norris,* pp. 39 ff.

self swept on toward new triumphs. More than the political fortunes of Mr. Taft was involved. The schemes for legislation on currency and a central bank of reserve had been maturing quietly in Aldrich's committee chamber. The uprising in Congress and the electoral defeat assured by its demoralizing effect now doomed the plans upon which Aldrich had set so much store. The central bank plan was to wait for years, and was to be shaped by alien hands in a manner wholly different from the purpose of its original authors.

The Insurgent leaders and the opposition party now had a free hand to direct the attention of the country to the hearings of the "Ballinger-Pinchot case" before a committee of Congress. The turmoil in Congress in 1909 and 1910 had aroused the public to the highest pitch of excitement; and it now followed with rapt interest the extraordinary inquiry into a branch of the executive power which, under the masterly strokes of the "people's attorney," mounted to an utterly unforeseen climax in the month of May.

4

The Ballinger-Pinchot hearings began January 26, 1910, and continued, with some recesses, for nearly four months. In inquiring into the charges made against Mr. Ballinger and his conduct of the Interior Department, the Committee of Congress named Pinchot and Glavis among the important witnesses to be heard. After a time, out of the distinguished counsel available, Brandeis was chosen as the principal attorney for the conservationists. With his rare powers of concentration and analysis, he mastered in a comparatively short time the evidence and the law touching the case. Soon Brandeis in his firm, quiet, businesslike way dominated the proceedings; and the affair to all practical purposes became a struggle between Brandeis and the administration and all its defenders, whom he prosecuted day by day before the bar of public opinion.

Louis D. Brandeis, a native of Louisville, Kentucky, and descendant of German Jews, had settled in Boston, and there for more than a quarter of a century had developed an extremely successful legal practice. Often he had served as counsel for large corporations, railroads, and trusts. Then toward 1896 a growing fear of the evils which the trusts wrought possessed him. Thereafter he began to devote a regular part of his time to free service in behalf of various popular reforms, free-trade, and anti-monopoly movements. In court and Congressional hearings he appeared as the advocate of the public and the consumers, winning the unofficial title of "people's attorney."

Toward 1905, in fighting the monopolistic expansion of the Morgan-owned New Haven railroad, he opposed no less an adversary than J. P. Morgan and Company, with extraordinary success. Deeply informed of the methods of the big financiers, thorough in his mastery of facts, he stood forth as the most dangerous foeman who had appeared to challenge the "robber barons" of his time. A certain political-economic philosophy, which may here be simply defined as an applied latter-day Jeffersonism, now crystallized in his mind and was to be presented soon in a series of brilliant polemical pamphlets which shaped the progressive thought of this era. To Brandeis' view the problem of democratic distribution of land and resources was now of central importance, and drew him powerfully to the defense of Pinchot and Glavis.

Brandeis, then in his early fifties, was in the prime of life, and in the courtroom had the reputation of a formidable, hard-hitting antagonist. He was very tall and slender, carried himself with a slight stoop, and had a strongly marked face and deep-set piercing eyes that were not easy for an opposing witness to meet. His habitually gentle voice and manner could change with unexpected swiftness when he was ready to strike one of his terrible, paralyzing blows. Against his unhurried resourcefulness of mind, the administration defenders—the committee chairman Senator Knute Nelson and the committee majority, typified by such stalwarts as Senators Root and George Sutherland—found themselves at a sore disadvantage.

Glavis, in his straightforward, clear, extremely well-organized testimony of late January and February, gave a picture of an administration profoundly hostile to the conservation policies set forth by Roosevelt and supported by Congress previously. The points set forth in his *Collier's* article, regarding Ballinger's pressure upon him to approve the Cunningham Claims; Ballinger's professional relations—in the interim when he had resigned from the government service—with the Cunningham claimants; his connection with Cunningham's partner Charles J. Smith, Washington political boss; and charges that the claims were in all likelihood to pass, by option, to the Alaska Syndicate controlled by the Morgan and Guggenheim interests—all this was brought forth. No evidence of corruption or illegal conduct by Ballinger was indicated; only incompetence, dubious ethical behavior, and faithlessness to the declared conservation policies of the government.

Brandeis stressed both the human and the political aspects of the case. Glavis, who had been flung out in disgrace, was defended as a fearless and patriotic public servant; Pinchot too was made a symbol of public-spirited doctrines and constructive social visions which the administration had betrayed. To Brandeis, a Ballinger represented privilege, the power of the Morgans, while Glavis was the "little fellow," the independent in public service. Once more, as in the contest with the New Haven railroad monopoly, Brandeis found himself contending with the overshadowing bankers, here reaching out in secret for the natural wealth left to the public domain.

As in preceding "public" cases, Brandeis directed his main appeal to the force of public opinion. What good was there, he asked, in conservation, if it meant that our natural resources were to be preserved for the rich, while the great multitude of citizens were left "dependent upon certain large capitalists, dependent upon the very limited number of the rich"? [21]

Besides using the committee hearings as a sounding-board for the progressive principles that he and his clients embraced, Brandeis' object was to establish clearly the competence and honesty of Glavis, particularly, and the incompetence and faithlessness of the administration. (Thus the threatened libel suit against *Col-*

[21] Lief, *op. cit.*, pp. 174-175.

lier's Weekly would doubtless be discouraged.) Besides exposing the character of Ballinger and his aides, the lawyer tried to illuminate also the circumstances under which Glavis had been judged and dismissed. A request was made, therefore, to have the report, on the basis of which Taft and Attorney General Wickersham had recommended exonerating Ballinger and ejecting Glavis, submitted as evidence before the committee. After some delays Taft submitted Wickersham's report, a huge dossier containing nearly all related evidence and documents in the case, amounting to some 500,000 words. This bulky report, giving the grounds upon which Glavis had been dismissed in September, was evidently intended as a sixteen-inch gun that would silence all questions.

Examining the documents which included (a part of) Glavis's charges and the replies of Ballinger and three other Department of Interior officials who had been charged with improper conduct, Brandeis began to scent something wrong. It was like a detective story in which the criminal, after completing a "perfect crime," leaves exposed the simplest, the most obvious evidence of his wrongdoing. The vast "Wickersham report" was dated *September 11, 1909,* two days before Taft's letter to Ballinger dismissing Glavis, and less than a week after Glavis had brought (September 5, 1909) his accumulated, written evidence to Taft. It dawned upon Brandeis that the report had been deliberately *antedated.* This was a wholly unexpected development which startled the lawyer, filled him with indignation at the hypocrisy of the administration, and shook his very faith in the government.

The indignant lawyer one night took Norman Hapgood, the editor of *Collier's,* out for a walk and imparted his exciting discovery. Neither Taft nor Wickersham could possibly have made himself acquainted with the facts of the case between September 6, 1909, the day of Ballinger's visit to explain things to Taft at Beverly, and September 11, the date of the report. Glavis, Brandeis reasoned, had simply been dismissed at Ballinger's request, while Ballinger had probably prepared his own exoneration, to be rubber-stamped by Taft.

It was the date affixed to the Wickersham report that had

aroused his suspicions, and the great length of the report had confirmed them. It was filled with the discussion of technical points, and Brandeis himself had taken a full week merely to read it. How long should it have taken to prepare and write it? Some time in November, when attacks multiplied and when a Congressional inquiry was feared, Taft's men had decided to compose their elaborate report of the affair. Then *they had dated it prior* to the time of Glavis's punishment. (For up to now, there existed only the brief memorandum letter of September 13, which Taft had asked Ballinger's legal assistant to write for him.) They had done this "in order to make the public think that in supporting Ballinger, the Attorney General and the President, instead of a political white-wash, had given to the case an attention which at that time they actually had not given to it." [22] By a routine check-up Brandeis informed himself of the daily program of appointments and the movements of Taft and Wickersham in the week of September 6, 1909. Thus he was assured that there had been no time for either one to study the merits of the case at all. Finally, *certain points raised by Glavis, not yet included in the report he had handed Taft, but expressed only in the* Collier's Weekly *article of November 13, 1909, were answered in the "Wickersham report" dated September 11, 1909!*

There were now damning enough traces of the combined dishonesty and stupidity of the administration, but they were circumstantial. Brandeis desired to force from them the admission of their own turpitude. He began now to hint that something was missing in the documents furnished to the committee of Congress conducting the investigation. Day by day he asked patiently, insistently, for reports or memoranda that, he claimed, were being withheld; and each day he was refused.

Then one night in February a young man named Kerby, stenographer in the office of the Secretary of the Interior, and formerly private secretary to James R. Garfield, came to the Pinchot home in Washington with an astonishing piece of news. His conscience

[22] Hapgood, *Changing Years*, pp. 388-389.

had been troubling him, because he had read in the newspapers of a presumed missing memorandum in the Ballinger case; and he himself had in his possession the stenographic notes of the very memorandum, since it had been originally dictated to him. Brandeis was called in, and the confession was repeated, under pledge of secrecy, since the young man feared for his job. The opponents of the Taft administration now had all the knowledge they needed, although there was some uncertainty as to how the information could best be used. Brandeis showed scruples in refusing to call Kerby as a witness against his superiors.

Thereafter Brandeis redoubled his demands for all papers or memoranda that had passed from Ballinger and his aide, Oscar Lawler, to Attorney General Wickersham and the President. An assistant to Ballinger, Finney, who was examined, was asked point-blank:

Brandeis: Is it not a fact that this summary of the Attorney-General which purports to have been made September 11, 1909, bearing the date September 11, 1909, was, as a matter of fact, not completed for more than two months after that time?

Finney: I do not know when it was written, Mr. Brandeis.

The conspirators grew uneasy under the lawyer's pointed questioning. Ballinger, giving testimony, was at once defiant and nervous, and made a poor impression. Yet Brandeis was able, during the cross examination of Secretary Ballinger late in April, to trap the adversary in further false denials.

Brandeis: What did Lawler take with him when he went to Beverly the latter part of the week? [23]

Ballinger: A grip with some clothes in it. I do not know what else he took.

Was there not a memorandum? Was not Ballinger at this very moment withholding this memorandum? "Your question implies an insult! . . ." Ballinger exploded. On the witness stand, Ballinger took the line of denying everything, gave the lie to his

[23] Of Sept. 6-13, 1909.

foes, and called their charges "imaginative" or "maliciously false."[24]

At the committee hearings Brandeis now told the country confidently that President Taft was too busy to have written the letter of September 13, 1909, exculpating Ballinger, without outside help, and that the Wickersham report on which his letter was supposedly based had been antedated. In Congress the Insurgents rose and expressed concern at a government that concealed its actions and suppressed evidence thereof. At first the White House issued formal denials that any material evidence or papers were suppressed. It was left to Attorney General Wickersham to make the damaging admission that his long, bulky report to the President was not completed on the day it was dated, September 11, 1909, but some time afterward.

Finally,[25] on May 14, 1910, the confusion and uncertainty surrounding the whole affair were dispelled when Kerby, the stenographer—probably induced by the offer of a job from a large newspaper chain, that of E. W. Scripps, which desired the news—gave public testimony before the committee. He told how Assistant Attorney General Lawler, with Ballinger's aid, had written the letter exculpating Ballinger, which Taft had simply signed. The original memorandum for the letter had been burned; but Kerby had kept his stenographic notes and had them photographed.

The capital was in turmoil. It was felt, with not a little sense of shame, that the President and Attorney General Wickersham had acted hastily, without a real effort at inquiry, when Glavis

[24] The New York *Times*, Apr. 30, 1910.

[25] A long account of the Ballinger affair is given from the point of view of a defender of President Taft by Henry F. Pringle in *The Life and Times of William Howard Taft*, New York, 1939. It is based largely on the Taft Papers and information furnished by Mr. Wickersham. Yet Mr. Pringle, the authorized biographer, finds serious "errors" and "indiscretions" in the conduct of both the President and his Attorney General. My own account is based on a partial reading of the Hearings and Testimony before the Joint Committee of Congress Investigating the Department of the Interior, as well as published studies of the case, such as Miss Stahl's monograph; also upon conversations with Mr. Gifford Pinchot and Justice Louis D. Brandeis, retired. However, opinions and judgments offered here are my own.

came with his accusations. Ballinger and his aide had dictated Ballinger's own exoneration, and the whole affair was concealed and defended afterward, many assumed, either because real wrongdoing was at the bottom of it or because the Taft people were determined to undo the whole conservation program. In reality the members of the Taft administration had committed no unlawful deed; but out of timidity and a sense of the weakness of their position, in the face of expected attacks, had been led into a series of subterfuges—especially, the "antedating" of the long Wickersham report—as a means of bolstering their case.

In Presidential circles consternation reigned as the scandal of the Ballinger exoneration gripped the country. On one day the White House declared that the allegations of the stenographer, Kerby, were "absolutely without foundation." But on the next, May 15, 1910, President Taft in a letter to Chairman Nelson of the Joint Committee of Investigation admitted the truth of Kerby's testimony. He admitted that he had told Lawler to write the letter exculpating Ballinger and firing Glavis. He admitted also that the subsequent report of Attorney General Wickersham had been "antedated." But this, Taft now alleged, was because he had heard much "oral" testimony in the week of September 6, 1909, and he and Wickersham had decided to set back the date of the completed report as of the time of the oral evidence heard when they were considering Glavis's charges. The "explanations" which Taft and Wickersham presented were considered disingenuous, even by conservative newspapers, and did little to lessen the shock and disgust widely felt.[26] The country believed that Taft and Wickersham had engaged in rather clumsy-handed (even needless) dissimulations, and had been caught in the act by the unfeeling Mr. Brandeis.

Ballinger and his aides were not shown to be venal; they were only trying on legalistic grounds to "give away for nothing" certain resources, the lands which, according to the government's declared policy, were to be reserved for the benefit of the people.

[26] The New York *Times,* May 15, 18, 1910.

Ballinger and his aides, as the Brandeis brief summed it up, not only would have discredited Pinchot and Garfield, but would have sacrificed the honest Glavis, thus perpetuating

> in this country an act of injustice as great as that done Alfred Dreyfus in the Republic of France, and for very similar reasons. The reason here is that men in exalted station must be protected at all hazards, and if they cannot be protected by truth then suppression and lies must be resorted to.

With the sudden, absurd, unawaited outcome of the case, the ruinous libel suit against the magazine which had attacked the administration was dropped. The committee of Congress, made up chiefly of "regulars," which would normally have delayed its recommendations for a year or two, was pressed by its large Insurgent-Democratic minority to make a prompt report. The Standpat majority eventually gave its blessings to the Taft administration and to Ballinger. But the dissenters issued—at the height of an election campaign—a powerful minority report sharply criticizing the President and advising the censure and removal of Ballinger. Though Taft staunchly defended his Secretary of the Interior as the victim of a lying conspiracy, the latter resigned, pleading ill-health, some six months later. In any case the Cunningham and other claims which Glavis had styled as fraudulent were withdrawn by Walter Fisher, the admirable Secretary of the Interior who succeeded Ballinger.

The "Ballinger-Pinchot" case, coming upon the heels of the tariff controversy and the uprising against Speaker Cannon, was a culminating political disaster for the "Restoration" government. As the party that "betrayed conservation" the Republicans were slaughtered, electorally speaking, in the balloting of November, 1910. A strong Democratic majority occupied the Lower House, while enough Insurgents from a half dozen Western states that had broken away from party orthodoxy sat in the Senate to keep the Upper Chamber also hostile to the administration.

Theodore Roosevelt had returned in the late spring of 1910 to find the country aflame with political discontent and controversy.

The great sectional division of the 1890's which he had closed was opened again. The ex-President generally held himself at a distance from his successor in the White House. Though in the campaign of 1910 he endeavored to help his party and the President by some moderate stumping efforts, the results were disappointing. Beveridge, La Follette, and other Insurgents who made pilgrimages to Oyster Bay, left saying that Colonel Roosevelt, as he now preferred to be called, was "more progressive" than ever.[27]

For the ruling party, the prospects were exceedingly dark. Nelson Aldrich, the chief of the Standpatters, weary of it all, announced that he would not stand again for the Senate at the end of 1910. The opposition party, long out of power, saw large opportunities beckoning in 1912. Meanwhile, it was significant that shortly after the elections, in December, 1910, Senator La Follette with the aid of Louis D. Brandeis and others who had fought in the battle for conservation began to organize the dissident wing of the Republican party as the National Progressive Republican League.

[27] Bowers, *op. cit.*, pp. 312-313.

XI. "DOCTOR WILSON"

One fine afternoon in September, 1910, two large, handsome Irishmen proceeded to the charming town of Princeton, New Jersey, and knocked at the door of the president of the University. They observed the beauty of the trees that sheltered the old house; their eyes also took in the terraced garden below, now in its late summer glory, that the wife of the scholar had long tended. Ushered into the library of the master, they viewed with not a little feeling of awe the rows upon rows of books that lined the room to the ceiling.

One of the men was ex-Senator "Jim" Smith, for twenty years New Jersey's Democratic boss, and the other was his son-in-law and first lieutenant, "Jim" Nugent, the boss of Newark. Both were simple, rough-hewn men of politics; but they were men of feeling too, and while they waited shared together a sense of foreboding.

Smith finally said to his companion: "Can you imagine anyone being damn fool enough to give this up for the heartaches of politics?"[1]

The mission of the two political bosses was to confer with "Doctor" Woodrow Wilson, as they called him, upon his forthcoming campaign for the Governorship of New Jersey. A short distance in time beyond the November elections (whose favorable outcome was firmly counted upon) lay the work of preparation for the Democratic Presidential nomination, which was the real objective of the Doctor and his supporters. The man who a few minutes later stood before them was even stranger to them than the place

[1] Kerney, *Political Education of Woodrow Wilson*, p. 62.

and the bold, far-flung plans. He was well on in middle age, bespectacled, gray-haired, and with a cool gray eye. His medium-sized figure was spare and firm; his face bony, deep-lined, with its wide mouth and sharp jaw, no thing of beauty or sweetness. It was a face which to Smith and Nugent seemed a mask of grim-mouthed, inscrutable expression, compounded of the asceticism of the preacher and the super-salesmanship of the college president. A type, in short, wholly unfamiliar to politicians.

Such was Dr. Woodrow Wilson at fifty-three, after a long and apparently distinguished academic career, as he prepared to leave the seemingly peaceful sanctuary of Princeton to launch himself upon the sea of troubles that was American local and national politics. What was worse, he knew pathetically little at first hand of practical politics; he knew what he had read in books, in his fine library. He was a self-confessed amateur, an innocent; and the two shrewd, successful men of affairs, who had eaten and drunk of practical politics since their childhood in the grimy north Jersey towns, scarcely knew where to begin with him.

How Woodrow Wilson came to be "discovered" late in life, how the Presidential crown was offered him, and how he wrestled for it, is an absorbing tale, not without picturesque contrasts and rich in lessons. Born in Staunton, Virginia, the son of a Presbyterian minister, he was of Scotch-Irish stock. Although the Wilsons and the Woodrows had not lived long in the South (his mother, Jessie Woodrow, migrated with her parents as a child of nine from Scotland), they were as proud as most Southerners. The boy grew up during the painful epoch of Reconstruction, and was one of those educated, but poor, Southerners who moved northward in search of opportunity. Yet if he was poorer than his classmates at Princeton, the minister's son was a fellow of strong ambitions and almost pretentiously intellectual tastes. After preparing for the bar, he had found his beginnings at this profession in Atlanta, Georgia, fruitless, and turned away from it with distaste to teaching. Slowly he advanced himself as a fellow at Johns Hopkins, then as a professor of government and history at several Northern colleges, finally at Princeton.

As a scholar, in his chosen field of political science, he had shown a certain promise when in 1885, scarcely thirty, he published his *Congressional Government.* It was a treatise essentially upon the divided authorities of our system of political "checks and balances," a piece of special pleading for the British system of concerted parliamentary leadership. At the height of the Gilded Age, and its crude taste, the young Wilson's studies had led him to admire English literature and political thought; Edmund Burke and the late Walter Bagehot, fastidious Tory apologists, were his chosen mentors. It is important to note that as early as 1885 he had preached unified executive leadership, rather than "divided" and "limited" government, with its cumbersome competitions of the three branches of the service, executive, judiciary, and legislative. In the 1880's and 1890's, Wilson believed, effective "leadership" would have overcome much of the turbulent party strife that weakened our government system; it would have placed emphasis upon programs and policies and removed it from patronage and spoils.

It was in this spirit that Wilson wrote voluminously on law, history, and politics in various magazines and learned journals; in the *North American Review,* the *Atlantic Monthly.* Indeed, he hoped for a long time to win distinction as a writer on public affairs, to have a career in literature. But when he searched his soul, as in those vivid early letters to his fiancée, he showed an honest awareness of his own limitations as a writer; his work was of secondary order. He felt himself temperamentally indisposed to the methodical labor of the secluded scholar, and realized in moments of self-knowledge that his real aspirations were for a role in public and administrative life.

Confined for long years to the study and the classroom, Wilson was a man who longed for a life of action, of struggle, and this to be passed before the eyes of the world. It was really because of his gifts as a lecturer that he rose steadily through the academic ranks. As a graceful phrase-maker and orator at university clubs and dinners of business men who donated funds to universities, he grew more eminent still. In those days he echoed habitually, in a manner pleasing to his listeners, the conventional sentiments they entertained upon public and educational questions.

With the retirement of Princeton's president in 1902, the professor of political science was chosen in his place, reaching a safe and honorable berth at middle age, as one of America's eminent men. But Dr. Wilson was to be denied a life of peace. Within two years he was embroiled in a kind of long drawn-out "village feud" at Princeton, over the administration and expansion of the graduate school. The factions of Graduate Dean West and Wilson fought unremittingly in a seven years' war; and their ill will assumed new forms when Wilson in a sudden, liberal move attempted to eliminate the expensive and fashionable eating clubs long favored by the students' fraternities. Those who had opposed Wilson's efforts to control the graduate school now opposed also his effort to "democratize" Princeton undergraduate social life. The trustees were divided into hostile factions; the university's rich patrons began to cut their endowments—a fatal blow. For years Wilson was the center of an internal storm of university politics, which it became increasingly difficult to hide from the public. In the end, the opposition became overwhelming; though Wilson was a tenacious fighter, the moneyed men among the trustees whom he had always courted, that is, a majority of them, led by the aged and stubborn Grover Cleveland, had turned thumbs down upon him. He was already in the position of a man who would soon be looking for a job, when one of his admirers, the irrepressible Colonel George B. McL. Harvey, hove upon the scene and offered him the chance for the job of President of the United States.

It was the hand of Harvey that was behind the mission of the New Jersey bosses, Smith and Nugent. Harvey, who was an honorary Colonel of the New Jersey militia, was one of the men of substance who had fallen under the spell of Wilson's public, or oratorical, personality. There was in Dr. Wilson at his best moments an evengelical earnestness, inherited perhaps from his Scotch Presbyterian ancestors, that rang forth powerfully in vigorous and happily turned (though often vague) speech. Now

Wilson's public speeches at club gatherings and banquets during the decade before 1910 had been consistently devoted to preaching political conservatism.

Turning against the popular Mr. Roosevelt, and calling to account Mr. Bryan, the entrenched leader of his own party, the president of Princeton would often strike out in defense of the leaders of great corporations who were nowadays so much maligned. For example, an occasion when he spoke on "The Authors and Signers of the Declaration of Independence," at Jamestown in 1907, was used by him to extol, in the name of Jefferson and the founding fathers, the principles of individual liberty which reformist politicians seemed at times to violate. At the time of the financial panic of 1907, Wilson attributed the disaster to the "hostile" legislation, the experiments in government control, especially of railroads, that had been introduced by the trust-busting President.

It was folly, he said, to regulate or punish corporations as such:

> When we fine them, we merely take that much money out of their business—that is, out of the business of the country—and put it into the public treasury where there is generally a surplus and where it is likely to lie idle. When we dissolve them, we check and hamper legitimate undertakings and embarrass the business of the country much more than we should embarrass it were we to arrest locomotives and impound electric cars, the necessary vehicles of our intercourse. And all the while we know perfectly well that the iniquities we levy the fines for were conceived and executed by particular individuals who go unpunished. . . .[2]

Therefore, Wilson urged, *individuals* guilty of wrongdoing should be found out and punished, not *corporations*. His conservative hearers, who knew full well how much difficulty the government experienced in winning effective convictions under existing laws, were doubtless satisfied with such proposals that Wilson may have offered in all sincerity at the time. He could be equally fervent in attacking socialism; and his vigorous attacks upon labor unions which aspired to the closed shop—to his mind a

[2] *North American Review*, Sept., 1907.

cardinal sin against our constitutional liberties—were no less appreciated.

Even in his last days at Princeton, Wilson seemed chiefly concerned lest it should become impossible to dissociate the Democratic party, the party to which he had been traditionally attached, from its recent "errors and heresies": Bryanism, money inflation, government ownership of railroads, direct election of Senators. To one who proposed to him the formation of a new party of conservatives, he argued that he did not despair, for his part, of seeing the Democratic party drawn back to the "conservative principles which it once represented." [3]

Colonel Harvey, who had been enjoying Wilson's talk ever since 1902, when he had witnessed his inauguration as president of Princeton, was a most curious character who had all his life worshiped "the god in the machine" and longed to be that himself. As a young newspaper reporter for the New York *World* in the 1890's, he had had the good fortune to win the favor of those two precious "robber barons," W. C. Whitney and Thomas Fortune Ryan, for whom he acted as a confidential agent. Living across the river in New Jersey, he served as liaison officer between the New Jersey politicians and the New York financiers in a series of diplomatic negotiations that concerned the franchises of future traction and public-utility companies. It was Harvey, for instance, who had first brought together Whitney and Ryan, the angels of the Democratic party, and Senator "Jim" Smith, leader of the New Jersey Democrats. After ten years of this kind of work, while still a comparatively young man, George Harvey had himself amassed a sizable fortune and was financially independent for life. Through the friendly interest of J. P. Morgan, to whom also he had sometimes been of service, he was made the head of the old publishing concern of Harper and Brothers, then undergoing reorganization; in his own right he later bought and edited the famous old *North American Review;* he was also the publisher

[3] Baker, *Wilson*, Vol. III, p. 185.

of the somewhat declining *Harper's Weekly*.[4] Now, from his high post in the publishing world, Colonel Harvey was able to indulge his active interest in public affairs: he gave select dinner parties, brought men of note together, attended and spoke at public functions himself as often as possible, and strove in every possible way to become an "influence" in his own right.

In those days of financial scandal, trust busting, and muckraking, the vigor and intelligence of the exponents of radical reform provided sore problems for conservative publicists such as Harvey. It is in this light that Harvey's pleasure in Dr. Wilson may be best understood. Harvey was utterly convinced that in the eloquent Princeton scholar he had found, so to speak, an inspirational conservative of rare power. And the conservative interests now realized that they needed effective ideologues; this was in itself a sign of the higher political culture of the times. There was no mere crude talk of the Full Dinner Pail when the head of Princeton spoke. "That man could win the people," Harvey remarked. He followed and cultivated him, obsessed by the notion that Dr. Wilson might be a distinguished Presidential possibility, that he might lead the nation out of the wilderness of radical reform, while Harvey would be his Warwick, nay, his Mark Hanna. Taking the plunge, on February 3, 1906, at a dinner arranged in honor of Wilson at the Lotos Club in New York, Harvey made his surprising speech offering Wilson as the Democratic candidate for the Presidency of the United States in 1908. It was a moment when the Democratic party, after its 1904 fiasco, showed every sign of returning to the control of the Bryanites. Harvey's personal nomination of Woodrow Wilson "of Virginia and New Jersey" as a contrast to the political idols of the day, Roosevelt and Bryan, was intended to catch the public eye, which it did. The people present at the banquet, the sort who gave their money to party chests, were accustomed to investing in a professional politician. But Harvey proposed that our public life now needed a leader of education, a man of culture and personal distinction,

[4] Johnson, *Harvey*, pp. 71-72.

who, though he clung to old traditions, promised to elevate the tone and methods of our politics.

> No one would think for a moment of criticizing the general reformation of the human race by Executive decree, but it is becoming increasingly evident that that great work will soon be accomplished. When that time shall have been reached, the country will need at least *a short breathing spell* for what the physicians term perfect rest. That day, now not far distant, will call for a man combining the activities of the present with the sobering influences of the past.[5]

After the Lotos Club demonstration, to which Wilson responded with modesty and reserve, Harvey continued to pursue his hobby of giving publicity to Wilson as a Presidential possibility. Favorable mention of him and articles upon his achievements appeared in the magazines that Harvey controlled, or in friendly newspapers such as the *World.* So much quiet interest was aroused in high circles that one day in March, 1907, Wilson was actually induced to come to New York for "inspection" by a group of newspaper publishers, corporation lawyers, and financiers.

It was at a private dining room of Delmonico's restaurant that the inspection was held; the notables present who catechized Dr. Wilson including Thomas Fortune Ryan; F. L. Stetson, counsel for J. P. Morgan; and Laffan, editor of the New York *Sun,* which also was said to be closely related to the House of Morgan at that time.

"Mr. Wilson talked freely and alluringly to conservative sentiment as if he were conscious of the inspection he was undergoing."[6] This same group had catechized Judge Alton Parker before he was accepted for the Presidential nomination in 1904. Wilson actually prepared and sent his political credo to be studied by Laffan, the editor of the New York *Sun,* and his friends; in the credo he "expressed vigorously his opposition to the tendency of the times to regulate business by governmental commissions."[7]

[5] *Ibid.*, pp. 111-112.

[6] E. P. Mitchell, *Memoirs of an Editor*, pp. 387-388.

[7] Baker, *op. cit.*, Vol. III, p. 35.

Yet, for the moment, nothing came of these pourparlers. Wilson continued to commend himself to the conservative classes by sallies at the Rooseveltians, sometimes in pointed and witty remarks.

"We have heat enough; what we want is light," he said in one public address early in 1909. ". . . Anybody can cry a nation awake to the necessities of reform, but who shall frame the reform but a man who is cool . . . ?"[8] Conservative intellectuals who had been close to the Wall Street group of Whitney and Ryan, which had dominated the Eastern Democracy in Cleveland's time, continued to think well of Wilson as a latter-day Jeffersonian who might halt the centralizing tendency in government where it affected corporate enterprise. Walter H. Page, the head of Doubleday, Page, and Company, himself a Southerner and an old acquaintance of Wilson's, embodied these views fully when he wrote in a letter at the time that Wilson was

> . . . a rightminded man of a safe and conservative political faith. He would not have the government own the railroads; he would not stir up discontent . . . he does not speak the language either of Utopia or riot. . . . If the Democratic party should come to its senses again and assert its old doctrines and take on its old dignity, and seek real leadership (and pray Heaven it may!), leaving its Bryans and its Hearsts alone, this suggestion of President Wilson is logical, sound, dignified and decent.[9]

But, alas, he was "not a politician." Boss Smith of New Jersey thought of him at first as a "Presbyterian priest." When Harvey engineered a scheme by which Wilson was to be offered the Democratic nomination for the United States Senate—purely honorary, since the Democrats were then a small minority in the New Jersey Legislature—the affair, even as a publicity enterprise, proved to be an abortion.

But early in 1910, when the Ballinger-Pinchot case raged in Washington and the signs of Republican defeat were on every

[8] *Public Papers*, Chicago, Feb. 12, 1909, Vol. II, p. 100.

[9] Hendrick, *Walter H. Page*, Vol. III, pp. 12-13.

hand, the inner-circle Democrats busied themselves with plans for 1912. Terror of Bryan's resurgence gripped the Easterners; while some of them began to labor on behalf of the veterans, Congressmen Champ Clark of Missouri and Oscar Underwood of Alabama, Harvey redoubled his efforts to advance Wilson as a candidate for the party nomination. From January, 1910, he pursued Boss Smith with his scheme. Finally, at another private conference at Delmonico's between Smith and Harvey, the New Jersey boss was brought to see a great light. His own position in the chess game of New Jersey politics was weak at the moment; the Democratic organization in New Jersey was under heavy attack and badly needed a victory. To be sure, the choice of a college president was a most unpleasant innovation. But would he not be suitable for these strange times? Known to be honest and distinguished, Dr. Wilson as candidate for the governorship would deflect the arrows of reformers, and perhaps prevent a liberal uprising threatening in the Democratic organization itself. The Republicans, it was known, planned to run a candidate who would be both liberal and popular. Perhaps Wilson would produce the needed victory? His high Wall Street connections, furthermore, assured an abundance of campaign funds. The old boss, with some misgivings, accepted Wilson as candidate for Governor. He agreed to "go the whole hog"; and to put the best face upon the matter he would even publicly withdraw from the race for the Senatorship, lest it be said that Dr. Wilson was being used as a respectable "front" to cover his scheme to return to the United States Senate.

Then, as Harvey himself related, he went to Wilson and told him that he would handle the matter of the gubernatorial nomination so that it "shall be tendered to you on a silver platter, without you turning a hand to obtain it, and without any requirement or suggestion of any pledge whatsoever. . . ."[10] Would Wilson, then, accept? Wilson, strongly tempted to escape from the truly unstable ground he held at Princeton, yet fearing also the pitfalls of public life, promised his "very serious consideration." That is.

[10] W. O. Inglis in *Collier's Weekly*, Oct. 7, 1916.

he gave a cautious, qualified approval to Harvey's effort, as before.

In the spring of 1910, Wilson was deeply embroiled in his conflict with the Princeton trustees. In April he made speeches in New York and at Pittsburgh before gatherings of Princeton alumni, in which he defended his plan to eliminate the exclusive eating clubs in his college. At the same time he continued to offer himself as a possible new leader in public life, as a more satisfactory alternative than the current political prophets. In a speech at Chicago before the Princeton Club, at this time, he said in a characteristic passage:

When will leaders arise? When will men stop their questionings and recognize a leader when he rises? When will they gather to his standard and say, "We no longer question; we believe you; lead on, for we are behind you."

America needs men of that sort. Will you encourage them? Will you make your universities such places as can produce them?

Then, in a sentence that is very significant, when we take into account the political fears rampant among the class typified by Princeton alumni, he added:

. . . *You are your own saviours, and when you have come to the determination to save yourselves you will know your leader the moment you meet him, for you will know if he is of your sort and of your purpose.*[11]

In these words Wilson breathes his more or less conscious, more or less secret, political aspirations. The inducements he offers are expressed in cryptic terms; but they are there.

Meanwhile Harvey continued to play a lively little Mephistopheles in tortoise-shell glasses who knew how to tempt the hesitant Dr. Wilson. Rumors were circulated of Wilson's candidacy; and a claque organized by Harvey and Smith in April of 1910 saluted Wilson, on one public occasion, as "our next governor." At a number of later conferences between Smith and friends of Wilson, Wilson was prodded into giving his definite

[11] Speech, Chicago, May 12, 1910; italics mine.

consent, and the grounds for an agreement were marked out. In return for the organization support he promised Jim Smith that he would not set about "fighting and breaking down the Democratic organization and replacing it with one of [his] own." These were conditions similar to those the young Theodore Roosevelt had made with boss Platt in New York. Wilson, however, stipulated clearly that the existing Democratic organization machine was to give thorough support of "such policies as would reestablish the reputation of the State and the credit of the Democratic party. . . ." [12] The Big Fellow was now satisfied with this minimal agreement, and ready to work for Wilson's nomination. Time was short; there were other "deserving Democrats," who must be steam-rollered out of the way; and Wilson, who still hesitated before the final plunge, was not surely collared until June 26, 1910, when he was literally hustled off to a dinner and conference at Harvey's country house. Jim Smith and "Marse" Henry Watterson, the Kentucky editor and politician, were present with Harvey when Wilson gave his consent. At a second gathering, soon afterward, in the early days of July, Wilson met a number of New Jersey Democratic leaders, among them Richard V. Lindabury, counsel for the United States Steel Corporation, which as a local concern was an interested party. It was then that Wilson accepted his destiny, and also made his terms, which according to Mr. Lindabury involved no political pledges or obligations.[13]

Smith and his lieutenants now went to work in earnest to win the needed delegates and also to "get the liquor interests behind the Doctor . . . ," as Boss Smith nicely phrased it. What they did, the Doctor was wholly ignorant of, since he believed, as he wrote at the time to one of the Princeton trustees, that other candidates stood ready to withdraw gladly in his favor, and that he was to receive the gubernatorial nomination "by acclamation." [14]

[12] Baker, *op. cit.*, Vol. III, pp. 49-53.

[13] Kerney, *op. cit.*, p. 46.

[14] Baker, *op. cit.*, Vol. III, p. 63; Vol. III, p. 57.

right language and with all possible solemnity that he owed his nomination to them, "the representatives of the people," and not to any leader or combination of leaders. The weary conspirators Harvey and Smith could hardly keep their faces straight; and the applause at the beginning was feeble, half-hearted, as if the delegates were incredulous. Was Wilson ignorant, or audacious?

He spoke with a note of independence that seemed needlessly brusque, in a voice that rang musically through the large Trenton House. "I did not seek this nomination," he cried. It had come to him unsolicited; he would enter upon his duties as Governor, if elected, "with absolutely no pledges of any kind" to prevent him from serving all the people. There was to be no mere playing of politics, and no demagogy, cried the "schoolmaster in politics." "The time when you can . . . fool the people has gone by; now it is a case of put up or shut up. . . ." Now cheers from the progressive wing that had opposed his nomination began to resound; Wilson went on to sketch the "renaissance of public spirit, a reawakening of sober public opinion, a revival of the power of the people. . . . We shall serve justice and candor and all the things that make for right," he wound up in a glowing peroration.[16]

The Doctor in short gave a surprising and bold performance that touched the best impulses of the party men. If he were going to be a mere "stool-pigeon for the Interests," as some had charged, then this was the wrong way to begin the business. The Jersey men began to suspect that by some chance a leader had been found who had a backbone under his coat. They applauded him; they followed him.

"His words ring true" was an impression often conveyed in the newspapers that reported the nomination proceedings.[17]

From the very outset Wilson showed resolution and initiative. He knew that he had been called by interests that kept themselves in the background. He may not have known definitely why he was called, or what ulterior purposes he was expected to serve. But he

[16] Tumulty, *Wilson*, p. 21.

[17] Newark *Evening News*, Sept. 17, 1910.

made it clear that they must take him as he was, for better or worse. He was bound to no secret pledges to anyone; his hands were free. Jumping into his new role, bolder, more extroverted than he had ever before been in his academic offices, Wilson soon showed a force of character, a tenacity in negotiation, that troubled the devoted schemer Harvey and the crafty Jim Smith.

He was an innocent in politics. Yet, as he himself said on several occasions, university politics, with its own devious wire-pulling, with its terrible conspiracies and jealousies, was a hard school; by comparison, the Machiavellis of practical politics seemed easy to read. On the other hand the dialectics of Wilson, in conference or negotiation, were hard for the practical politicians to cope with.

On the occasion of that September day when Smith and Nugent called at Princeton, the agenda for the moment included consideration of the claims of local party leaders representing Wilson's home county of Mercer. Wilson had always kept aloof from local politics; he had scarcely ever voted in a local election, and up to 1910 barely read New Jersey newspapers, since those of New York City were easily available. But now, as related by James Kerney, publisher of the Trenton *Times*, the bosses coached Wilson in the diplomacy required for treating with the local leaders and district captains, informing him of their individual hopes and grievances. With an aptitude for affairs natural to him, Wilson quickly grasped what was required.

> When the Mercer County leaders had in turn been formally presented by Nugent and had taken seats in the library, Wilson proceeded to discuss local political affairs as if they were the one thing in all the world in which he had been taking interest. He called the various leaders by name and . . . made them feel very much at home.[18]

2

Dr. Wilson's "political education" proceeded at tremendous speed and was concentrated within a very brief space of time: less

[18] Kerney, *op. cit.*, pp. 63-64.

than a year after his nomination for the Governorship of New Jersey, he was launched in the race for the Presidential nomination. Within this time his ideas underwent a very rapid change, and this in itself has given rise to much speculation.

What were Wilson's beliefs? What was his faith? In his writings one searches in vain for marks of intellectual originality. He was accustomed to trace his political doctrines to the influence of Jefferson; but his admiration for the British system of parliamentary leadership, his emphasis upon leadership in government rather than upon limitations of it, belie his Jeffersonism. He was to show no inhibitions whatsoever in adapting himself to the most centralized and "Hamiltonian" tactics.

The real mystery of Wilson, as John Chamberlain has said in his *Farewell to Reform*, is when, and where, and why, he became a Democrat. Frederic C. Howe, who studied under him at Johns Hopkins in the 'nineties, thought he believed essentially in "government by *noblesse oblige*." He thought little of economics, and gave his students glimpses of a glorious ruling caste, upholding the tradition of the Magna Charta, while its power politics were concealed from view.[19] He admired the way of life of the upper-class English leaders, the Arthur Balfours or the Gladstones—and Gladstone too had undergone a famous "conversion" to liberalism. A Calvinist at heart, Wilson believed—as Walter Lippmann remarked—that the world could be set right by the force of human conscience.

In short, there is an evangelical strain in the Wilson who "made political office his pulpit," and there is his heritage of Virginia traditions—absorbed at the law school of the University of Virginia. But it is the tradition of the great Virginians who, while preaching democracy, created more effectively than Hamilton a regime of talent and wealth. Yet signs of some definite, logical body of principles—such as we perceive in Lincoln—are wanting in Wilson. He was to show no abiding loyalty to a conservative's faith, no lasting affinity for the Cobdenism he had sometimes

[19] Chamberlain, *Farewell to Reform*, pp. 283-284.

espoused. Ideas, truths, faiths, systems were not ends for him, but materials for an *ideology*. In the last analysis he triumphed as a dialectician in practical politics. His mind absorbed ideas rapidly from others and threw them into action; his quickness of thought strongly impressed men of more original mental powers, such as Louis D. Brandeis. Whatever successes he had enjoyed, he owed to his mental equipment—rather than to family connections or wealth—and he was proudly conscious of his own intelligence, and inclined to be a little intolerant or impatient of others' stupidity.

He had few or in fact no permanent friendships; yet he had great power over men, to whom he knew how to communicate, by his eloquence of language, something of the cold fire in him, his unlimited ambitions, his intense resolution. He seemed to "love man at a distance," as it was said of Rousseau; and his hopes seem to have been largely self-centered. It might have served as a warning that his main troubles at Princeton were traceable to his habitual quest of augmented power, as in the case of the struggle for control of the graduate school—though in this his efforts may have been justifiable. In the end he had been defeated by the heavy battalions of money on the other side.

But upon emerging from Princeton's neo-Gothic walls, hurled suddenly into the unfamiliar arena of partisan politics, Dr. Wilson found that the components of power were different from those of the schoolman's world. Parties and their organizations had existed long, until they had become traditional. Power, as he saw full well, lay first of all in the hands of those who led the machines that gathered in the voters or the nominating delegates, and controlled the offices of the government. Thus Wilson's first task had been to satisfy boss Smith in some manner. Wilson had written formerly of men such as Smith: "They are the political bosses and managers whom the people obey and affect to despise. It is unjust to despise them." But once in office, extremely conscious of the power—especially the patronage power—he wielded, Wilson would grow far less manageable.[20]

[20] Smith in a fairly illiterate and furious letter, which he wrote after his rupture with Wilson, told Senator Bailey of Texas, August 30, 1911, that Wilson

Beyond the boss and his henchmen there lay another power, that of the moneyed interests that subsidized party organizations. Through Harvey, Wilson had indirect access to these people. Also, the rich Princeton trustees who had supported him, Cleveland Dodge, the copper magnate, and the younger Cyrus McCormick, T. D. Jones, and others, came forward to sponsor his political career.

Yet the party bureaucracy and the moneyed patrons were not the whole story (least of all to Wilson), and especially now in a time when popular discontent ran so strong. As a third component of power, public opinion even in darkest New Jersey, the "mother of trusts," had to be studied and mastered. To this task Dr. Wilson gave himself with an unusually open mind; its problems struck him at once as very different from those he had seen as a scholar.

On certain issues he had been even more conservative than the Wall Street wire-puller, Harvey. A few weeks before the nominating convention at Trenton, when the two men discussed the party platform, Harvey showed Wilson a draft of a resolution in favor of the direct or popular election of Senators. "I don't believe in that," said Wilson. "Neither do I," said Harvey, "and I'll strike it out if possible; but I'm very much afraid the convention will insist upon leaving it in." [21] There were times when even the Harveys and Smiths seemed to yield to the popular will.

As he moved slowly into the hurly-burly of a state campaign,

". . . Is one of the most convincing talkers that you ever listened to, and as our mutual friend Mayor MacLellan informed me two days after the election, is the 'king of liars,' as he termed him. That makes a powerful combination. . . . He has beyond question destructed the Democratic party of this State. . . .

"You will no doubt wonder why I ever nominated him, and then financed him. . . . He convinced me that he would be the most loyal man to me and the organization in the State, that I ever had anything to do with in politics, and that he would do nothing but build us up, and that if he was elected governor, he believed he could be nominated for the presidency."

Smith and his colleagues had seen to it in former years that "backward" New Jersey had very little of the merit system. The Governor had 500 offices to fill, and thus could easily have a large following of his own. (S. Acheson, *"Joe" Bailey*, pp. 303-304.)

[21] Johnson, *Harvey*, p. 151.

Wilson felt the force of public opinion agitated, aroused, on many issues such as that of the direct election of Senators. He felt this force in the breath of the crowds he addressed. The old terms and slogans he had used yesterday before the banquets of Princeton alumni fitted poorly. It needed then some mental sleight of hand, no little dialectical skill—which Wilson always possessed—to turn himself overnight from the man who was reported ready to save the Democrats from Bryan, government ownership, and other Populist notions, to one who would proclaim himself a progressive, who was willing and ready to lead the masses toward the promised land of the New Freedom.

Among the retinue provided the candidate by Smith and Nugent were a few progressive, or anti-machine, Democrats, such as the Trenton publisher James Kerney, the ardently liberal journalist William St. John, and Joseph Tumulty, the youthful Jersey City lawyer and assemblyman. These men warned the ignorant Wilson of the intense discontent rampant among the people, a discontent which he, unwittingly, had been chosen to face. Compared with New York, then under the enlightened Hughes, New Jersey and her citizens seemed left in outer darkness under the shadow of the railroads (especially the Pennsylvania) and the power company, which apparently controlled both parties. Though the public was long weary of Republican rule these last seventeen years, the Democratic leaders by recent maneuvers had aroused even greater disgust, and boss Smith especially had been singled out for his sorry record. One of the greatest grievances was the passenger rate for commutation fares, which the Pennsylvania Railroad had lately increased by 20 per cent while the politicians of both parties remained silent. Wilson was warned that he would be received by the people as a kind of respectable "decoy duck" for the old race-track and gambling crowd in politics. Meanwhile, his opponent, Vivian M. Lewis,[22] owing to an overnight conversion in the Republican party, proved to be an uncommonly independent candi-

[22] Kerney, *op. cit.*, p. 70.

date, who made the most forthright pledges of popular relief. Tumulty, the charming young Irishman who soon afterward became Wilson's private secretary, told Wilson frankly that his speeches lacked definiteness, that he was evading the long pent-up issues of the day, such as the regulation of public utilities and the passage of an employers' liability act. Both parties for years had been delaying the enactment of such measures into law, measures that most large states now boasted. Wilson "listened with keen attention," and evidently thought hard. Soon the candidate "struck his gait and astonished me," relates Tumulty, "and all New Jersey with the vigour, frankness and lucidity of his speeches. . . . No campaign in years in New Jersey had roused such universal interest."[23]

By all accounts, Wilson dropped many of his favorite rhetorical devices and employed a plainer, more vivid speaking style suited to the rough and tumble of a state campaign. The results were remarkable. The local audiences could not recall when they had heard more interesting and pertinent political talk. Wilson promised plainly that the Democratic party would be "reorganized"; he insisted that New Jersey was upon "the threshold of a new era." He sang now the praises of the common people, to whom he had given so little attention before.

> When I look back at the processes of history, when I look back at the genesis of America, I see this written over every page, that the nations are renewed from the bottom, not from the top; that the genius which springs up from the ranks of unknown men is the genius which renews the youth and the energy of the people. . . .

Then at times he would close with one of his old-time perorations, which were passable imitations of the manner of Daniel Webster:

> . . . As the tasks multiply, and the days come when all will seem confusion and dismay, we may lift up our eyes to the hills out of these dark valleys where the crags of special privilege overshadow and darken

[23] Tumulty, *Wilson*, pp. 29-31.

our path, to where the sun gleams through the great passage in the broken cliffs, the sun of God, the sun meant to regenerate men, the sun meant to liberate them from their passion and despair and to lift us to those uplands which are the promised land of every man who desires liberty and achievement.[24]

An unexpected crisis arose during the late stages of the campaign. In reply to charges that he was an impractical schoolmaster, Wilson had issued a challenge to any Republican representative to meet him in public debate upon the affairs of New Jersey. He expressed his disapproval of the methods used by both of the old party machines which formed, as he said, "an illegitimate and abominable partnership between business and politics." At one point he exclaimed bluntly that he did not want anyone to vote for him who believed that he would "listen to a political boss." Smith, sitting on the platform near by and hearing such statements, was seen to smile complacently and was heard to remark that it was "wonderful campaign stuff." [25]

Early in October an answer to Wilson's challenge arrived from the Republican side. George L. Record, a lawyer residing in Montclair, sent word that he was eager to debate with Dr. Wilson in order to learn definitely whether or not he meant to be the tool of the Democratic bosses. Wilson was warned that Mr. Record, a member of the Legislature, might prove a most dangerous adversary; he was a radical reformer, brilliant and most widely informed on current public issues; in short, he was scarcely a proper or "regular" Republican spokesman.

There was a delay in hostilities. Record's challenge was widely spoken of as creating a predicament for the Doctor; and Wilson, who heartily disliked being charged with want of fighting spirit, communed with himself for a week. At length he wrote Record suggesting an exchange of public letters discussing all issues in full and explicit detail, to be published in the New Jersey newspapers.

On October 17, 1910, about three weeks before Election Day,

[24] Tumulty, *Wilson*, p. 33.
[25] Kerney, *op. cit.*, p. 71.

Not long afterward, the brilliant young lawyer who was a friend of Lincoln Steffens, Judge Ben Lindsey, Brand Whitlock, and other reformers became a valuable member of Wilson's Kitchen Cabinet at Trenton.

The effect of the debate, conducted upon so high a plane, upon the New Jersey citizens was electric. They felt Wilson's words could not be unsaid. Even in small towns, the people came out in great crowds to see and cheer him during the last two weeks of the campaign. They gave enthusiastic testimonials of their faith in his leadership, in his independence, which did not fail to move his heart. His speeches of his "new phase" assumed a style of simplicity, clarity, and earnestness that his earlier papers had too often lacked; they were easily the most distinguished expressions of their kind. Even the hardened politicians were astonished at the completeness with which the new leader conquered the old Republican stronghold of New Jersey, carrying over to his cause all the "doubtful" voters and the Progressive Republicans. In 1908 a majority of 80,000 had been given to Taft as Presidential candidate; but in 1910 a Democratic majority of nearly 50,000 was won by Wilson and a Democratic Legislature swept into office. Woodrow Wilson's spectacular victory made him nationally famous overnight. The glowing words in which he called the people to join his enterprise of "regeneration" and reform were cited far and wide; they gave to the New Jersey contest a prophetic significance similar to that which attached to the great Lincoln-Douglas debates in Illinois a half century earlier. Wilson too spoke of the "House of Democracy divided against itself." In his final speech he had said:

> We have begun a fight that, it may be, will take many a generation to complete, the fight against privilege; but you know that men are not put into this world to go the path of ease. . . . All through the centuries there has been this slow, painful struggle forward, forward. . . . America has undertaken to lead the way; America has undertaken to be the haven of hope, the opportunity for all men.

3

In tune with the political "revolution" that was sweeping the country, New Jersey in 1910 had adopted for the first time the system of Preferential Primaries to indicate the popular choice for the United States Senator. Instead of having the Legislature name the Senator, as before, in "Room 100" of the Trenton House, its majority party was to abide by the primary vote. Long before it was grasped that Wilson would carry in his wake a majority of the local legislative elections, the nomination for the Senate, without serious resistance on the part of Smith's faction, had gone to a certain James Martine, of Plainfield, who was something of a Bryan follower. But in the late stages of the election campaign rumor held that Jim Smith had reconsidered the Senate primary business, did not regard it as binding, and would seek to return to Washington after all.

Wilson had chosen to ignore the rumors before Election Day. But soon afterward the Big Fellow made his candidacy for the Senate public; the experiment of the Preferential Primary was said to have no serious weight; and Mr. Martine was labeled as "unfit," "inexperienced," and "a silly old man." At once there was a raging controversy, Martine's friends and the younger, progressive element in the Democratic party throwing themselves into the fray with fierce protests at the betrayal of the popular mandate.

The Governor-elect waited silently. The prudent, the "constitutional" course would be to remain neutral, and leave the issue to the Legislature, his conservative advisers at Princeton told him. After Harvey, Wilson was most indebted to Jim Smith for his nomination. He was a "fine fellow," as everyone knew, and longed to return to the Senate, which he had left under a cloud engendered by his former close relations with the exceedingly corrupt sugar trust. If Wilson led the fight against him, it would split the party and endanger the whole ambitious law-making program he had in view.

But the liberals, Kerney, St. John, and Tumulty, besieged Wilson to lead the people in this fight. He had promised that he would act as Governor in the interests of all the people. Many politicians had said that before. But now was the time to see to it that a beginning was made with the popular election of Senators. Here, in fine, was "a clear issue of good faith and observance of party pledges," St. John told him. St. John, who believed that Woodrow Wilson was a great leader in the making and "the most promising figure the genuine progressives ever had," never desisted in his pleas.[28] They were rivaled by those of Tumulty, whom Wilson in his perplexity suddenly visited at his Jersey City law office on November 25, 1910. Tumulty argued that the people were "yearning for leadership" which Wilson had promised to give them. They would turn to another if he faltered at the very beginning. The affair was being widely discussed not only in New Jersey but beyond her borders, in New York and Philadelphia. If Dr. Wilson could make a bold stroke, it would be the first step to the higher calling he sought.

The Governor-elect, however, asked only in a cool, noncommittal voice, and with his usual granite expression, whether Tumulty thought "we could win the fight in case he should decide to enter it." The reply was that the machine was perhaps not more solid than papier-mâché; a hard blow might cause it to fall apart.[29]

In the three weeks that followed the election, Wilson was undecided, though he told George Harvey, his backer, of his belief that the election mandate condemned Smith and his methods. Looking beyond the state boundaries, Wilson perceived the radical tide, and noted that Theodore Roosevelt, now "returned from Elba," also swam upon it. The example and the menace of Roosevelt were ever in back of his mind. Two months before, Roosevelt in his speech at Osawatomie, Kansas, had alarmed the whole country by his announced conversion to a whole series of radical doctrines. Wilson concluded his letter to Harvey with the warning

[28] Kerney, *op. cit.*, p. 80.

[29] Tumulty, *op. cit.*, pp. 54-55.

that if the independent voters who had supported him were disillusioned, they would "surely turn again in desperation to Mr. Roosevelt. . . ."[30]

In December, Wilson's mind was made up. He called upon Smith and in the most courteous terms urged him to withdraw from the Senatorial race. He received only a firm refusal; Smith hoped that the Governor would make only a perfunctory opposition "for the record." Wilson sounded out certain of the powerful city bosses, but found they would not play with him. He then moved energetically, by holding several large conferences, to rally influential members of the Legislature, local leaders, and newspaper editors to his side. He felt his position growing perilous.

On December 9, 1910, he struck hard at the adversary in a manner that Theodore Roosevelt himself could not have bettered, releasing to the press his manifesto in support of Martine and condemnation of Smith's candidacy. Not only New Jersey but the nation heard of "Woodrow Wilson's Challenge to the Bosses." Once more he had written a clear and splendid public paper, stating his position simply and well, and bringing a fresh spirit into New Jersey's sickly political affairs by his whole-hearted action.

The question of who should be chosen to occupy the seat in the Senate was "both a question of political faith and . . . genuine representation . . ." he declared.

> I had hoped that it would not be necessary for me to speak; but it is. I realize the delicacy of taking any part in the discussion of the matter. . . . Legally speaking it is not my duty even to give advice with regard to the choice. But there are other duties besides legal duties. The recent campaign has put me in an unusual position. I offered, if elected, to be the political spokesman and adviser of the people. I even asked those who did not care to make their choice of Governor upon that understanding not to vote for me. . . . I cannot escape the responsibility involved.[31]

[30] Wilson to G. Harvey, Nov. 15, 1910; Baker, *op. cit.*, Vol. III, p. 112.
[31] Newark *Evening News*, Dec. 9, 1910.

The vote cast by the people in the primaries must be heeded by the Legislature; Mr. Martine must be chosen Senator. Once more Wilson exceeded the narrow frame of partisan political struggle and made his appeal in the name of eternal principles of justice and democracy. The response showed that the people of New Jersey, long boss-ridden by a whole chain of Tammany Halls, were not too case-hardened to heed him. Pressing the fight, Wilson called several large public meetings in the machine strongholds of Jersey City and Newark. The "amateur politician" talked to great cheering crowds with a vigor and candor that made the "regular" leaders who were pledged to Smith's cause tremble for their future.

> Do not allow yourself to be dismayed. You see where the machine is entrenched, and it looks like a real fortress. It looks as if real men were inside, as if they had real guns. Go and touch it. It is a house of cards. Those are imitation generals. Those are playthings that look like guns. Go and put your shoulder against the thing and it collapses.[32]

It was plain that old Jim Smith's cause was lost. He made dramatic charges of heartless ingratitude against this erstwhile protégé. But his frightened followers, fearing the Governor's appointive power, began to give way, one by one. They sent word that they would gladly consider terms for a compromise; but these were refused.

As the Legislature gathered in the capital in the third week of January, Smith, whose whole political life was at stake, made a brave show of confidence, and marched upon Trenton with all his retinue of followers, including a brass band which paraded before the Trenton House to serenade the boss. But shortly after the Legislature convened, the Smith following collapsed utterly, and Martine was quickly elected.[33]

Ex-Senator James Smith, Jr., Democratic boss of New Jersey, was thus the first of Woodrow Wilson's political friends to be thrown relentlessly to the sharks.

[32] *Ibid.*, Jan. 5, 1910.
[33] *Ibid.*, Jan. 22, 23, 1910.

Wilson commented upon his victory in a graphic letter to a friend:

> I pitied Smith at the last. It was so plain that he had few real friends,—that he held men by fear and power and the benefits he could bestow, not by love or loyalty or genuine devotion. The minute it was seen that he was defeated his adherents began to desert him like rats leaving a sinking ship. He left Trenton . . . attended, I am told, only by his sons, and looking old and broken. He wept, they say. . . . Such is the end of political power—particularly when selfishly obtained and heartlessly used. It is a pitiless game, in which it would seem, one takes one's life in one's hands,—and for me it has only begun! [34]

Wilson's spectacular victory over the machine not only caught the eye of intelligent citizens throughout the country, but made certain that his legislative program would not be obstructed. He had come, as he realized, in the "fullness of time," when the situation was ripe for change. He had been able to accomplish what Theodore Roosevelt had longed to do with the Platt machine in New York, but dared not, a decade earlier. At once Wilson moved swiftly to seize the helm of the party organization, to fill, himself, the place of the deposed party chieftain.

4

Woodrow Wilson was like a man who all his life carefully avoided vice, but discovering it by chance, in the ripeness of age, pronounced it not too bad, and, in truth, began to enjoy it heartily. He had disapproved of demagogues, and he was far from being one; but he represented himself as "the Governor of all the people," and the masses whom he now flattered in his speeches made his public meetings look like a succession of folk festivals. Other principles and methods than those he once was accustomed to extol before his students he now began to esteem more highly on closer contact. His opinion of the radical agrarian La Follette

[34] Wilson to Mrs. Mary A. Hulbert, Jan. 29, 1911; Baker, *op. cit.*, Vol. III, p. 127.

and his "Wisconsin Idea" changed rapidly, and he began to adopt some of La Follette's measures. Nor did he attack Mr. Bryan in public any longer. Reform, which he had held to be not far removed from vice, lost its terrors; experiments formerly decried as dangerous were now called "new tools of democracy" that permitted the popular will to function through leadership.

He became hospitable to all sorts of new ideas and methods. One day William S. U'Ren, the single taxer and inventor of the so-called "Oregon Plan," dropped into Trenton from the West and held long converse with him. U'Ren, a self-educated son of the frontier, without holding office had become since the early 1890's a most powerful political figure in Oregon, chiefly through his powers of persuasion and organization. He had devised the type of preferential primary which New Jersey, without waiting for a Constitutional amendment, had taken up as a method of bringing about the direct election of Senators; he had generated other measures such as the initiative and referendum as steps toward more "direct" democracy, and they had worked. Wilson's fight against boss Smith had kindled U'Ren's interest in him; and U'Ren in turn made a profound impression upon Wilson, who adopted for his legislative program laws similar to those which U'Ren had brought to Oregon.

Direct popular government under leadership immediately responsible to the people's referendum appealed to Wilson as a great advance over the cumbersome indirection of our political apparatus. To end the tyranny of machines, as it was then hoped, a thoroughgoing direct primary and election bill was made ready for the Legislature.

After U'Ren, the breezy, homespun philosopher, was gone—one met such men so seldom at Princeton!—Dr. Wilson assumed the habit of sitting in his office at the State House with his door open, accessible to all men and women, journalists, labor leaders, social workers and politicians, as if no secrets existed in the Governor's affairs. As late as August 13, 1912, Oswald Villard noted in his diary: "I found [Wilson] in the State House democratically wandering about and talking to the people in the outer office who were waiting to see him. There are no fuss and feathers where he is." [35] He would also go touring the state to the various county seats to report upon his "stewardship" and answer any questions that might be put to him by the citizens face to face, on the spot.

In an intimate letter of this time, he wrote that he felt himself deeply moved at the thought of his "new responsibilities as the representative and champion of the common people." He felt "a sort of solemnity in it all. . . ." [36]

For help in framing his program of reform laws, Wilson on good advice called in George L. Record, with whom he had lately been engaged in debate. Record was something of a "people's attorney" in New Jersey; for years he had fought alone against the bosses of both parties; citing chapter and verse, he could expose, outwit, or confound his opponents with ease. When Record came to Princeton, after the election, Wilson found him a man of idealism and refinement, with a face uncommonly handsome and sensitive. The two men found that party differences could easily be ignored between them—Record was nominally a Republican. At Record's frank counsel that he "cut adrift from the party machine," and seek men he could trust, Wilson gathered a Kitchen Cabinet of his own younger followers, with Record included as the Progressive Republican member. It was Record largely who undertook the tremendous labor of preparing and writing the new reform laws whose passage that year made history in New Jersey.

On January 16, 1911, the day before his inauguration, Wilson took the unusual step of calling a private meeting of prominent New Jersey leaders and legislators at a hotel in New York. Record, according to the editor Kerney, "took command" with Wilson's approval and presented the essentials of a direct primary and

[35] O. G. Villard, *Fighting Years*, pp. 218-219.

[36] Wilson to Mrs. Mary A. Hulbert, Jan. 22, 1911; Baker, *op. cit.*, Vol. III, p. 135.

election law, a corrupt-practices act, a public-utility regulation bill, and an employers' liability act.[37]

Wilson also addressed the gathering and imparted to them his hope of enacting promptly reforms pledged to the voters, as well as his views upon primary and election reforms (much colored by U'Ren's influence). Agreement upon a specific program was achieved; and soon, when reports of the "secret" meeting in New York spread, a storm of attack burst upon the liberals. Principal opposition centered upon the election bill, by which, as the Smith-Nugent men said, Wilson the "dictator" would wreck the organization that nominated him.

At a Democratic caucus held early in March to discuss possible amendments which would have softened the election bill, Wilson broke all precedent by making a personal appearance among the members and debating with them for three hours. He spoke with the fire of an old Scotch covenanter, as in a holy ca[illegible] The Representatives were won over. But "Jim" Nugent, li[illegible]ant to Smith and chairman of the state Democratic party, h[illegible] a bloc of a dozen Senators in opposition. Calling Nugent int[illegible] private office, the Governor attempted to reason with him[illegible]d words followed, Nugent insinuating bitterly that the Gov[illegible]r was using his patronage power to destroy the Old Guard[illegible]y sensitive on this point, Wilson showed the Newark bo[illegible]e door. Thereafter Nugent habitually toasted his Governor as a "liar" and an "ingrate."

In the end it was by the pressure of public opinion, which Wilson knew how to arouse, a judicious use of the patronage whip, and the support of three independent Republicans brought over by Record, that the Old Guard in Trenton were overcome. The drastic election-reform bill, along with its companion measures for utility regulation, employers' liability, and school improvements, were steadily carried through the Legislature, some by narrow margins, and all were made law by April, 1911, when the session adjourned.

[37] Kerney, *op. cit.*, pp. 100-103.

The Governor could hardly forbear to crow a little in private correspondence with a devoted friend:

> I wrote the platform, I had the measures formulated to my mind, I kept the pressure of opinion constantly on the legislature, and the program was carried out to its last detail. This, with the senatorial business, seems to the minds of the people looking on, little less than a miracle, in the light of what has been hitherto the history of reform in this state. As a matter of fact . . . I came to the office in the fullness of time, when opinion was ripe on all these matters, when both parties were committed to these reforms, and by merely standing fast . . . and keeping up all sorts of (legitimate) pressure *all the time*, kept the mighty forces from being diverted or blocked at any point.[38]

After so much "noisome and crooked government by compromise and sordid bargaining behind closed doors . . . it was exhilarating to have another Executive administering public affairs in the broad light of day," Oswald Villard wrote.

Overnight, by a political miracle, New Jersey had been placed in the forefront of the progressive states, and Dr. Wilson, the scholar in politics, was saluted as a *successful* reformer. The great press outside now celebrated Dr. Wilson's courage, administrative ability, and gift for public affairs. His victories over the professionals were acclaimed by liberals, intellectuals, Mugwumps, and reformers of all sorts, who held the New Jersey Governor as a new tribune of the people. In these terms, a strong group of influential journalists, including Oswald Garrison Villard in the New York *Evening Post* and *Nation*, Walter H. Page and William Bayard Hale in *World's Work*, and Harvey in *Harper's Weekly*, sang his praises day by day and spread the Wilson cult. Even Bryan's *Commoner* sent supporting broadsides, which to Wilson's conservative backers were as evil omens. Harvey, the President Maker, with Walter H. Page, Cleveland Dodge, and other men of substance, now worked to raise a war chest for the Wilson Presidential boom. There were already widespread fears of a radical combination led

[38] Apr. 23, 1911, to M. H.; Baker, *op. cit.*, Vol. III, pp. 169-170.

by La Follette or Roosevelt or Bryan, or all three, which might break across party lines. Immediately after the adjournment of the New Jersey legislative session, in the early spring of 1911, it was arranged that Dr. Wilson should go forth upon a long speaking tour of the interior that would introduce him to the people of the West.

XII. COLONEL HOUSE'S VISION

THE TIDAL WAVE of November, 1910, was a good index of the degree in which discontent and anxiety had seized upon the country. A massive Democratic majority now held Congress and conducted an aggressive opposition to the Republican administration which was intended to insure its complete defeat in 1912. Even in Massachusetts a reformer-Democrat, Eugene Foss, was elected Governor, while in New Hampshire, another reformer, Robert P. Bass, overcame the Old Guard in the contest for the Governorship.

In the West the Insurgent Republicans, whom Taft had thought of reading out of the party, were everywhere vindicated—save for Beveridge, defeated in Indiana, who now retired to write his *John Marshall.* George Norris of Nebraska, now entering the Senate, ably replaced Beveridge. Despite the sudden, untimely death of the great-hearted Jonathan Dolliver, in the very prime of life, the Insurgents returned stronger than before, to wield the balance of power in the Senate. In a score of Western and Middle-Western states, men in revolt against the methods of the Republican regular organization named the candidates and wrote the platforms. Wisconsin had been a battlefield, with La Follette standing for reelection; though a supreme effort was made to eliminate him from public life, the leader of Insurgency won an overwhelming popular indorsement.

Immediately after the election, La Follette hurried to Washington and helped to launch the new National Republican Progressive League. Its most prominent office-holding members came from the land west of the Mississippi, and from Wisconsin, Indiana, and Michigan. In its statement of principles the following were advocated: the direct election of United States Senators; direct primaries; direct election of delegates to party conventions; the "initiative, referendum and recall"; a corrupt practices act. It was a program for political democracy, primarily. Senator Jonathan Bourne of Oregon was elected its president, and the brilliant young reformer Frederic C. Howe became its secretary. Louis D. Brandeis, who was one of the founders, declared at the time of the Progressive League's inception: "We are confronted in the twentieth century, as we were in the nineteenth century, with an irreconcilable conflict. Our democracy cannot endure half free and half slave. . . ."[1] The League promised that it would bring about the reformation of the Republican party by a nation-wide campaign of education and publicity. Many suspected that its real intention was to transform the Republican party sufficiently to permit the nomination, in 1912, of Wisconsin's Little Giant in place of Taft.

One of the first steps toward a more extended political democracy was achieved at once by the Sixty-Second Congress when, in April, 1911, it passed a resolution for the popular election of United States Senators, initiating thereby the amendment to the Constitution. Soon the Congress was plunged into debate over President Taft's proposed measure of tariff reciprocity with Canada. Yet no less engrossing during the year that followed were the series of investigations initiated by a radical Congress, dealing with interstate commerce, trusts, railroads, and election frauds. Perhaps the most important of these investigations was that begun by the Senate's Committee on Interstate Commerce, which devoted itself to the new industrial monsters of the age, the trusts.

That spring, on May 14, 1911, a very important decision was handed down by the Supreme Court, dissolving the Standard Oil Company of New Jersey into twenty-nine component parts, but enunciating at the same time the so-called "rule of reason" with

[1] Lief, *op. cit.*, p. 205.

regard to restraint of trade by large corporations. By this rule it was assumed that the Court might determine where undue or "unreasonable" restraint of trade took place, according to its judgment. Partial relief was now felt by the owners of large corporations, yet the working of the law remained as obscure and uncertain to them as before. But from the opposing camp a strong outcry of protest greeted the decision and echoed the dissenting opinion of Associate Justice Harlan, who contended that the Court had opened a breach in the Anti-Trust Act, a breach that would soon be wide enough to allow all the monopolies in the land to pass through unmolested.

To the liberals and progressives who had been leading the anti-monopoly movement it seemed that the inner defenses of the Sherman Act had suddenly fallen. The terms of the Supreme Court decision, though they did not satisfy Perkins and other champions of the trusts, gave no assurance that conditions of fair competition would be restored. Various bills were now introduced in Congress which attempted to redefine the Anti-Trust Act, the most notable of these being the one offered by La Follette and written with the aid of Brandeis.

That summer of 1911, before the Senate committee investigating trusts, George W. Perkins was among the financial magnates who testified in favor of the "good" trusts. He ventilated his favorite theories, which proposed a course of admitting the necessity and inevitability of the great trusts, giving a certain publicity to their affairs, and having them regulated in a sane and friendly spirit.

Brandeis, who also played a leading part at the hearings, expressed now probably the most coherent opinion that existed at the time upon a question which seemed to involve the very fate of the republic. He said that the great trusts were "neither inevitable nor desirable." They were more "inefficient" than small-scale business; they blighted and numbed invention and human enterprise with the "curse of bigness." The remedy was not to accept and institute monopoly, until it grew stronger perhaps than all the force of government, and then attempt to "regulate" it; but to regulate unbridled competition at the wage level, where the strong crushed the weak.

The theory of the "curse of bigness" brought a timely note of criticism in days when mere size rather than quality dazzled too many Americans. Many years later, in the 1930's, such views would be repeated in a new form by a school of economists who studied the rigidities and retarding factors of "monopolistic competition" during a great business depression. But at the earlier period Brandeis, like Veblen, argued that the promoters of the great trusts were less concerned with efficiency, as they claimed, than with the rapid gains to be won through floating enormously overcapitalized combinations. The motives of the investment bankers consisted in disposing of "watered stock" promptly, what Veblen would call "planned mismanagement." The case of the New Haven and other railroad and industrial "empires" which had collapsed lately, or were doomed to failure, were cited at length. Meanwhile solemn warning was given that the multiplication of trusts concentrated all of America's wealth finally in the hands of bankers, in a colossal "money trust."

A disturbing picture of a changing America, a land in which equality of opportunity and individual liberty—which Brandeis sincerely believed in—were being rapidly overwhelmed, was afforded by the testimony of the "people's lawyer." Moreover the great monopolies in steel, oil, and other industries, by coercion, espionage, or violence, relentlessly stamped out labor unions, making no provisions for the growth of democracy in industry. Even while the discussion raged, the story of the terrible bombing outrage which had recently been perpetrated at Los Angeles by the MacNamara brothers spread over the country in the daily reports of a famous labor trail. Thus Brandeis warned the public that the ruthlessness of the trusts, and their anti-labor tactics, prepared the way for a revolution of violence. The trusts, he said, "pointed the way to the Socialists."[2] The concentration of wealth

[2] Senate Committee on Interstate Commerce, 62nd Congress, 2nd Session, *Senate Documents*, 98, Vol. I, p. 1258.

in a few hands made it easier for the expropriators themselves to be expropriated. To avoid this, Brandeis proposed that the monopolies should be dissolved, that the conduct of the great corporations should be controlled according to specific, stipulated competitive conditions of trade, and that the trade unions should be encouraged as "a strong bulwark against the great wave of socialism." He concluded with a parable:

> Just as Emperor Nero is said to have remarked in regard to his people that he wished that the Christians had but one neck that he might cut it off by a single blow of his sword, so they [the Socialists] say here: "Let these men gather these things together; they will soon have them all under one head, and by a single act we will take over the whole industry." So Socialists say in regard to Morgan—Morgan pre-eminently the great organizer and great combiner. They say, "He is our best friend, because he is paving the way for us, and we will have only a slight amount of legislation after Mr. Morgan is through with his work." [3]

At this very time, news of financial "extremism" came from New York, where in July, 1911, the gigantic National City Bank announced the formation of the National City Company as its investment "affiliate." The new company was to be capitalized at $10,000,000 and was so organized that it might "make investments and transact other business which . . . may not be within the express corporate powers of a national bank." It could speculate in stocks or buy other banks.[4]

The fears of a money trust were now seen to be more than fancies. Soon afterward Congress designated a committee that was to be known as the "Pujo Committee," with Samuel Untermyer as its legal counsel, to pursue the trail of the Wall Street money trust.

Even in darkest Africa, Colonel Roosevelt heard the reverberations of the political storms in America. When he returned in

[3] A. T. Mason, *Brandeis and the Modern State*, p. 99.

[4] Sullivan, *op. cit.*, Vol. IV, p. 579.

May, 1910, after a circuslike round of receptions tendered him by the crowned heads of Europe, the opposing Republican factions besought him for his aid and approval. From Pinchot and his friends he heard the tale of the betrayal of the conservation program; from the regular Republicans came requests that he help his party by stumping in the Congressional elections. He behaved with reserve and decorum for a time. He did not at first approve of the rebellious mood of some of his former adherents such as Pinchot, for he wrote, some months after his return:

> Gifford is going in with some of the extremists in Congress with the expectation of trying to form a third party if Taft is nominated. He has become completely identified with the ultra-extremists, and I can only work with him to a very limited extent.[5]

But Roosevelt, too, had been doing some tall thinking, and, an inveterate pulse-taker, had noticed all the signs of fever among the citizens.

In the trunks that went to Africa there had been placed by chance a copy of Herbert Croly's *The Promise of American Life*, published early in 1909. Thus there occurred a wedding of minds. The Colonel was greatly struck by Croly's penetrating and suggestive study of our political government "as it really was," its weaknesses, its problems and its potentialities. Croly's book, as Walter Lippmann said, "made articulate for Roosevelt his aspiration to combine the social and political reforms initiated by Bryan and La Follette with a Hamiltonian affection for a strong national government."[6] While still abroad, the Rough Rider wrote to the learned political philosopher in New York of the intellectual affinity he felt; and upon his return invited Croly to Oyster Bay for lunch and held a whole long afternoon's talk with him.[7]

The Promise of American Life, though written in a rather abstract style, was the most thoughtful work of its kind since Bryce's *American Commonwealth*, of twenty years before. Croly prophe-

[5] *T. R. Papers*, T. R. to Bacon, Jan. 2, 1911.

[6] *The New Republic*, Jul. 16, 1930.

[7] Mrs. H. Croly to author.

sied an era of sweeping change for the country, and examined the nature of our political traditions, our party system, and the relations between professional politics and big business, in the light of their availability for the age of drastic change which he foresaw. In 1909 Herbert Croly still hoped that the existing party apparatus—detached from its ties with corrupt, corporate wealth—might still be converted to the use of a "new national democracy," more centralized, more authoritative, more energetic and responsive to the popular will.

Believing as he did that many of the abuses we suffered from were traceable to our too sacred Constitution, Croly could not approve either the traditional Democrats who still claimed to be followers of Jefferson, or even the Bryanites, with their lip-service to states' rights and "strict construction." True reform would require a centralizing or Hamiltonian tendency in the government authority, a vigorous "New Nationalism" that would overleap the boundaries set by courts and state lines. Thus Croly came to hold up Theodore Roosevelt as his model, "a Hamiltonian with a difference," who would not make the Federal organization a bulwark against the rising tide of democracy, but would instead give to the Hamiltonian tradition and method a "democratic meaning and purpose." [8]

In nearly all respects Herbert Croly and Louis D. Brandeis were antithetical as political thinkers. Concerning the great trusts and the abuses they had brought, Croly, after much thought, believed that we should "recognize the existing corporate economic organization" and attempt to harness it to the general welfare, rather than call it bad names or seek to mutilate or destroy its parts. How to harness the predatory corporation magnates to the nation's welfare was a matter that was still left vague. Croly put hope in the leveling or redistributing agency of direct taxation, and the regulative power of a devoted, high-minded corps of government commissioners and administrators. Such a policy, he hinted, might well lead to the repeal of the Sherman Anti-Trust

[8] Croly, *The Promise of American Life*, pp. 172-175.

Act and a grand merger of monopolistic business organization with political organization. (It would be, in effect, a frank recognition of that which already existed in indirect, loose form.) Croly, in his early period, before he launched *The New Republic* in 1914, thus combined certain ideas of state capitalism with premonitions of the "corporative" guild state. To Roosevelt, who had originally embraced Hamiltonian ideas of rule by talent and wealth, the "Promise of American Life" according to Croly was alluring, and he borrowed from it whole-heartedly for his program of the "New Nationalism."

Brandeis, on the other hand, applying Jeffersonian doctrine in modern form and with brilliant insight to the Age of Big Business, would have perpetuated a society of individuals; "little men" in constant competition with each other, though in peaceful and civilized manner, under restraints of political and social police. Invention, improvement, progress, he held, came through "struggle," and a steady process of education. Democracy depended upon the spread of intelligence, rather than upon government commissions. His program of trust-breaking, "regulated competition," and social laws to encourage collective bargaining and security as he expounded it in public or in magazine polemics, suggested return to the past but made enormous appeal to the mind of his age, and ended by exercising powerful influence upon the mind of Woodrow Wilson, in particular. While Roosevelt popularized Croly's theories under the slogan the "New Nationalism," Brandeis' ideas emerged in the lucid prose of Wilson's campaign speeches of 1912, under the slogan of the "New Freedom."

Theodore Roosevelt could not be long removed from public life. Soon after his return he became a contributing editor of *The Outlook*, a respectable and influential family paper, and wrote weekly of the issues of the day. In the autumn of 1910, he took an active part in the politics of New York, endeavoring to help the liberal Henry L. Stimson in a gubernatorial contest that failed. Here, as in his occasional speech-making journeys to Western centers,

Roosevelt evidently applied pressure against the conservative leaders of his party. Though there was no outward clash with the Taft administration, he suggested plainly his separation from it by the increasing political radicalism of his speech. Invited to speak at Denver, Colorado, on August 28, 1910, before the State Legislature, he gave plain hints of his dissatisfaction with our Federal courts and their power to review and nullify legislation. The courts, he held, in many ways dominated our whole government—something that was true of almost no other land.

Roosevelt's conservative friend Elihu Root expressed to the President the alarm he felt at hearing the Denver speech, and Taft responded that Roosevelt doubtless had the design of appealing to "the bitter sentiments" now rising "throughout the West . . . and especially in the Insurgent ranks."[9]

But two days later, August 30, at Osawatomie, Kansas, the scene of John Brown's early activities, Roosevelt was even more outspoken in sounding the ideas of the obscure prophet Herbert Croly. After denouncing "swollen fortunes" and the "special interests" who purchased political influence or legal talent to protect them in a sort of legislative neutral ground from the jurisdiction of state and Federal governments alike, he continued:

> . . . I ask that we work in a spirit of broad and far-reaching nationalism when we work for what concerns the people as a whole. . . . The betterment which we seek must be accomplished, I believe, mainly through the national government. The American people are right in demanding the New Nationalism without which we cannot hope to deal with new problems. The New Nationalism puts the national need before sectional or personal advantage . . . regards the executive power as the steward of the public welfare. It demands of the judiciary that it shall be interested primarily in human welfare rather than in property. . . .

Roosevelt prophesied that far more governmental interference in business would be seen in the future; and men of all sorts would be compelled to adjust themselves to "new conceptions of the relations of property to human welfare." By these, he asserted, prop-

[9] Jessup, *op. cit.*, Vol. II, pp. 163-164.

erty would be "subject to the general right of the community to regulate its use to whatever degree the public welfare may require it."

Here were bold words. Roosevelt not only asked for the Square Deal and fair play, but suggested that he was willing to see the rules of the game changed, in the name of equality and justice. Here too, in the speech at John Brown's home town, was a passage that borrowed Lincoln's words in praise of labor: property, which man's labor had made, must be "the servant and not the master of the commonwealth." The people "must effectively control the mighty forces which they have themselves called into being."

Roosevelt was now steering into the full current of his time.

2

Dr. Wilson, rolling through the Far West on his long speaking tour, often wondered to himself at the strange fate which had cast him late in life upon a sea of political troubles. The original impetus had come from the inspired George Harvey, who was sometimes called "Morgan's errand boy." Wilson knew that his financial sponsors, Harvey, Dodge, Page, and more lately William F. McCombs, the young lawyer who had once been his pupil at Princeton, all looked to him as a "Grover Cleveland Democrat," who might make head against Bryan's influence. It was hoped also that he might be useful in offsetting any radical leadership, such as La Follette's or Roosevelt's, which might possibly now capture the Republican party.

Yet Wilson, the conservative Democrat, had found himself fighting for his life in New Jersey, against the state boss and his machine from the very start; driven to carrying out a program of long-needed reforms. Thus he had grown strong and found his own legs, while the sponsoring group in downtown New York looked on silently at the upheavals in New Jersey.

Arriving in the West, he had fallen into a land "aflame with the political . . . movements that had descended directly from

Bryanism. . . ."[10] His own convictions had been changing rapidly. The crowds in Kansas City, Denver, San Francisco, and Portland who cheered his liberal messages affected him strongly. En route, a curious incident made a lasting impression upon his mind.

At the small water town of Wymore, Nebraska, the train had stopped to change locomotives. When the Governor descended to take the air upon the platform, a railroad worker in overalls, wiping his hands, came up and introduced himself as Mayor of Wymore. The local worthy, as it developed, had been lately elected upon the Socialist ticket. But why was there so much Socialism in Wymore? "It wasn't Socialism that elected me," the Mayor replied. "Only about 20 per cent Socialism, and 80 per cent protest."

"That typifies a national condition," Wilson observed to his companions as the journey continued. *"There is a tremendous undercurrent of protest, which is bound to find expression. Taft will be renominated by the Republicans; unless the Democrats nominate someone whom the people can accept as expressing this protest there will be a radical third party formed and the result of the election may be little short of a revolution."*[11]

At almost the same period, though he had not come to an open rupture with Taft, Theodore Roosevelt was seized with forebodings similar to those of Wilson. His later, post-Presidential letters show him convinced that the country was faced with tremendously grave *ideological* problems which his erstwhile protégé could not possibly deal with. It was not that he was actually more liberal than Taft in his purpose; his misgivings arose because he felt that Taft could no longer be counted upon to save the country from revolution.

Confidentially, Roosevelt wrote to Elihu Root that he was "bitterly disappointed with Taft, and consider[ed] much of his course inexplicable." While wishing for his own part to be both "sane and progressive," he felt that Taft had "put himself in commission in the hands of Aldrich, Cannon, Ballinger and Wickersham." He

[10] Kerney, *Wilson,* p. 135.

[11] Baker, *op. cit.,* Vol. III, p. 225, after McKee Barclay notes; italics mine.

had begun to eliminate progressives from any share in the party direction or policy "within forty-eight hours of his election, nearly two years ago." Taft appeared to be steering the Republican party toward an imminent disaster.

The choice between the "wild irresponsible folly of the Ultra-Insurgents" and the "sordid" Standpatters presented Roosevelt with "a situation which is very unpleasant," and Taft and his friends were to blame.[12] How to avoid such a dangerous choice was to be his deepest preoccupation. He was to express this thought constantly in his letters and in public speeches for the next two years. If only men would take warning in time from the dread fate of France in 1789-1793, when the folly of splitting into "two camps of unreasonable conservatism and unreasonable radicalism" had brought the old regime to its debacle. Would America too, in a time of discontent and danger, ignore the moderate counsels of her Turgots? [13]

Thus the more lately arrived "amateur in politics" and the veteran leader, Roosevelt, foresaw with the same mind a tremendous political crisis for 1912. As Wilson could feel the sectional-class bitterness rising in the West, so the "sounding-board" in Roosevelt sensed always the monitory reverberations of distant tumbrels. Both men were friends of the existing system, friends of capitalism, patronized and supported by men high in the councils of Wall Street, and not by I.W.W.'s or even the respectable trade unions; the strategy of both the Doctor and the Colonel now turned upon drawing the protest vote to themselves, and thus preventing the formation of a "radical third party," the break-up of the traditional party system, and results "little short of a revolution." Both men, then, accepted for themselves the historic task of modern capitalist statesmen to save society from a revolutionary break-up. (Roosevelt of course prepared himself for his mission secretly up to January, 1912.) Was it surprising that both gave the appearance of running after strange gods for the while, espousing radical

[12] *T. R. Papers,* T. R. to E. Root, Oct. 21, 1910.

[13] Speech of Mar. 29, 1912, Carnegie Hall, N. Y.

heresies, offering more and more generous concessions (ransom) to the people? Their sponsors might fret and complain; but the political captains could cry that there was now no choice; thanks to the follies of the Tafts and Aldriches and Cannons, and the interests standing behind them, the hour had become desperate. Accept reform from us—Rooseveltian or Wilsonian—they seemed to say, or else take something much worse in the end, from a La Follette, a Bryan, perhaps even a Debs!

3

By prior arrangement the strategy of Wilson's boomers during his Western tour in 1911 was to "sell" him to the press as a "sound" liberal. Wilsonism, it was said in the inspired comments reproduced by the newspapers, was "popular leadership with a safety valve," or a "balance wheel." It was "statesmanship without demagogy. . . ."[14]

In his important opening address at Kansas City, May 6, 1911, before an audience of solid business men, Wilson spoke at first with a becoming moderation. A new political era was dawning. But there was no need for fear. It was not to be "a process of revolution, but a process of restoration. . . ." The movement going on was "one of reform . . . rather than that of a revolution. . . ." The American people were "naturally a conservative people," unwilling to overturn the foundations of their life, revering rights of property and contract. But there must be "change" although sober change. Then he himself skillfully injected a thrill of fear into his bourgeois audience when he said meaningfully:

> The man with power, but without conscience, could, with an eloquent tongue, if he cared for nothing but his own power, put this whole country into a flame, because this whole country believes that something is wrong, and is eager to follow those who profess to be able to lead it away from its difficulties.

[14] *Oregon Journal*, May 18, 1911; Baker, *op. cit.*, Vol. III, p. 224.

Wilson would take no such course, it was intimated. He, like all good Americans, felt not "the slightest jealousy of the legitimate accumulation of wealth. . . ." But everyone knew that some of the men who "control the wealth and have built up the industry of the country" sought to control all politics by the iniquitous system of Invisible Government. Our democracy was in danger. What was the solution? A way to "restore and invigorate" representative government had been proposed already. It was the way of the initiative, referendum, and recall, the force of popular plebiscites intervening in courts and legislatures.[15]

Pausing at Lincoln, Nebraska, the capital of the "Bryan Empire," Woodrow Wilson took pains to pay homage to the Great Commoner, who was at the moment on a speaking tour of the East, but whose family and retinue gave the New Jersey reformer a ceremonious reception. And in Wisconsin he paid tribute also to La Follette in moving words:

> I have sometimes thought of Senator La Follette, climbing the mountain of privilege . . . taunted, laughed at, called back, going steadfastly on and not allowing himself to be deflected for a single moment, for fear he also should hearken and lose all his power to serve the great interests to which he had devoted himself. I love these lonely figures climbing this ugly mountain of privilege . . . I am sorry for my own part that I did not come in when they were fewer.[16]

Although Wilson actually directed his speeches to the "unselfish public spirit" of the property-owning class mainly, though he endeavored to conciliate and combine all sorts of clashing groups—capitalists and laborers, farmers and townspeople, Gentiles and Jews—he ended by alarming his own conservative patrons. William F. McCombs, who headed the small Wilson bureau in New York, now "wired him . . . to slow up." The less said about the initiative, referendum, and recall, the better for campaign collections in the East.[17] Yet Wilson's tactics were highly effective in

[15] Speech of May 6, 1911, Kansas City, Mo.

[16] Kerney, *op. cit.*, p. 142.

[17] *Ibid.*, pp. 136, 138.

the political sense. Factions opposing the moribund Democratic machine in important states like Pennsylvania sprang to life and rallied to his cause. In Texas, where Senator "Joe" Bailey was now in disgrace, owing to the recent publication of the stolen Standard Oil letters, the majority of the party with its large delegation swung quickly to Wilson's banner.

To the President Maker, Colonel Harvey, the strange proceedings of his own Pygmalion now brought many heart-burnings. Harvey had been silent, giving neither praise nor blame to Wilson's reform activities in New Jersey; but his Western barnstorming showed a positive tendency to "Bryanize," as the conservative press of New York remarked. Later there appeared rumors that Harvey's old master, T. F. Ryan, feared lest Wilson could not be managed; also that J. Pierpont Morgan had been offended by something Wilson said at a public banquet which seemed a hostile allusion to himself.[18]

What was to be done about their converted college president who went about the land awakening the people in the tones of Bryan and La Follette? In the inner circle, a warm discussion sprang up over the question whether Wilson spoke mere rhetoric or actually meant something as bad as Bryan's or Roosevelt's "line." That other honorary colonel, Henry Watterson, who often engaged in these deep counsels of strategy, assured his troubled friend Harvey that a man of Wilson's stamp must be accepted as a Lesser Evil. The trouble with Wall Street was that it lacked "gumption" and political acumen. Its "*riffraff of rich noodles who think that money will do it all*," that political movements could be managed according to the laws of the counting-house, were not to be trusted for their own good!

Those Wall Street chaps never do know what is good for them. As to Wilson, it is a case of going further to fare worse. They had better take an intelligent Radical, abreast with the times, who knows how and when to discriminate, and is both upright and his own man, than get a

[18] Johnson, *op. cit.*, pp. 181, 187; House, *Intimate Papers*, Vol. I, p. 51; House to Bryan, Dec. 6, 1911.

promissory note for some nondescript, to be repudiated as soon as he is able to feel his oats.[19]

Thus cajoled, Colonel Harvey overcame his misgivings and continued to work for the Wilson cause. Even when rebuffed by a coldness of manner, which could be terrible with Wilson, he continued bravely as ever.

In the local elections of November, 1911, in New Jersey, "Jim" Smith revived his shattered force sufficiently to defeat the Wilson Democrats and help to return a Republican Legislature. The reformist Governor could no longer have his measures passed at will. Yet, despite this hard blow Harvey, after November, 1911, endeavored to capitalize the vengefulness of the boss as giving all the greater credit and glory to his candidate. His local defeats represented a "moral victory." At the top of its editorial page, *Harper's Weekly* now ran the standing head:

FOR PRESIDENT, WOODROW WILSON

But Woodrow Wilson now more and more patently set a distance between himself and the vivacious colonel in tortoise-shell glasses. On two occasions in the late autumn of 1911, he seemed to avoid a meeting with him deliberately. A soft, unfamiliar voice among his counselors whispered to him, late in November, 1911, that he must endeavor to detach himself from Harvey more positively, if he would escape the odium of being "Wall Street's candidate" and win the powerful help of Western Democrats. The younger men in Wilson's entourage had also made the same observations; and he had been thinking hard about it for some months. The journey about the country had opened his eyes to the sentiment of the masses beyond the Appalachian Mountains and the Mississippi; he must win them, and win their leader Bryan, or his cause was hopeless. The time had come, as he sometimes said, "to close his mind and act," cost what it might.

The decision to take a new "line" is well reflected in a letter of this moment, December 6, 1911, written by Colonel Edward

[19] Johnson, *op. cit.*, pp. 179, 181, 182.

House of Texas, still another honorary colonel who now suddenly interested himself in Governor Wilson's career. It was an adroit letter to Mr. Bryan, whom House knew very well, concerning the political situation of the New Jersey Governor. He spoke of a special strain that had arisen between Wilson and his backer Harvey. Only the day before, House had taken lunch with Colonel Harvey and endeavored to learn the man's "real attitude" toward Wilson.

> He told me that everybody south of Canal Street was in a frenzy against Governor Wilson, and said they were bringing all sorts of pressure upon him to oppose him. . . .
>
> He said that Morgan was particularly virulent in his opposition to Governor Wilson. I asked him what this was based on, and he said upon some remark Governor Wilson had made in Morgan's presence concerning the methods of bankers, and which Morgan took as a personal reference.
>
> He told me that he believed any amount of money that was needed to defeat Governor Wilson could be readily obtained. He said he would be surprised if they did not put $250,000 in New Jersey alone in order to defeat delegates favorable to his nomination.
>
> We are going to devise some plan by which we can use this Wall Street opposition to [Governor Wilson's] advantage. If the country knows of their determination to defeat him, I am sure it will do the rest. . . .
>
> If you can make any suggestions regarding the best way to meet the Wall Street attack, I would greatly appreciate it.[20]

The die had been cast; Wall Street must efface itself. The campaign to win over Mr. Bryan to the Wilson banner had been begun in a most skillful manner.

On December 7, 1911, Governor Wilson somewhat reluctantly came to New York for a meeting with Harvey, long avoided. Colonel Watterson was present, and the conference took place at Watterson's rooms in the Manhattan Club.

At the end of the discussion, Harvey asked Wilson if there was

[20] House, *op. cit.*, Vol. I, p. 50.

"anything left of that cheap talk during the gubernatorial campaign about my advocating you on behalf of 'the interests'?"

Wilson replied coolly that there was; that at luncheon, the other day, the young men of his "literary bureau" had volunteered the information that Harvey's public support of himself "was having a serious effect in the West."

Harvey: Is there anything I can do, except, of course, to stop advocating your nomination?

Wilson: I think not. At least I can't think of anything.

Harvey: Then I will simply sing low.

(*Pause. Impressive silence from Woodrow Wilson.*) [21]

Watterson, the third party present, found Wilson's coldness of manner infuriating, and left in a rage to tell all the world at Louisville and Washington of Wilson's base ingratitude and the rupture. Some unbending impulse made Wilson sacrifice personal and political friendships mercilessly, when the hour came, like some modern dictator who orders the assassination of outworn retainers. It was only a few days after the meeting with Harvey, when the latter ostentatiously took down Wilson's name from the *Harper's* masthead, that Private Secretary Tumulty reminded the Governor that he might have wounded the other man. Then only, on December 21, 1911, did Wilson send a letter of lame apology, reproaching himself for having a "single-track" mind, and forgetting the marks of gratitude he owed. But it was too late.[22]

In January, 1912, news of the rupture between Wilson and Harvey had leaked out enough to cause a raging controversy. It was noticeable that Wall Street circles gave renewed consideration to the reputed difficulties of Wilson's ungrateful, quarrelsome character. Could he be trusted? On top of this, gossip of a terrible letter which ex-President Grover Cleveland, a resident and trustee at Princeton, had written to a friend concerning Wilson's "habitual untruthfulness," was suddenly spread. Then, as a final blow, there

[21] Memorandum of Harvey; Johnson, *op. cit.*, p. 186.

[22] Tumulty, *op. cit.*, pp. 85-87.

came on January 6, 1912, the sudden publication by Adrian H. Joline, a Princeton trustee and former friend of Wilson's, of a letter Wilson had written five years before, in the days when he had scarcely dreamt of political ambitions, which assailed Bryan and expressed the wish that he might be knocked "once for all, into a cocked hat." This letter had been taken from the shelf and published with the cruel design of ending Wilson's budding courtship of Mr. Bryan.

The early days and weeks of 1912 marked the lowest ebb of Wilson's political fortunes thus far. An admiring and devoted "literary bureau" directed his boom as vigorously as before. A faction of wealthy capitalists, certainly a minority in their class, still donated funds for his nomination campaign at regular intervals. However, the professional politicians in his party, the heads of great city machines, were but slightly interested in him. He had won cheers in the West; but the cheers gave no certain promise of pledged delegations. Week by week came reports of state delegations captured for the amiable veteran of Congress, Speaker Champ Clark of Missouri; other states turned to Favorite Sons such as Harmon and Underwood. Wilson, from advance indications, would stand but a poor second to Clark; even his home state delegation promised to be divided at the convention, a minority led by the embittered Nugent opposing his candidacy.

4

During the summer of 1911, Woodrow Wilson was made aware of a powerful, unknown friend who, from far-off Texas, worked quietly to further his Presidential plans. As early as March, 1911, Harvey had spoken to him of this "exceptionally able man, well-to-do financially and . . . sound politically."[23] Others such as Representative Burleson of Texas also spoke highly of him as one whom he should know: one who, with a skilled, firm hand, seemed to shape political events in the great state of Texas so that its sup-

[23] Baker, *op. cit.*, Vol. III, p. 298.

port was promised to Wilson's candidacy long in advance of other states, and its progressive leaders called to him to come and speak to them, and to lead them. This he did in October, 1911, at the State Fair in Texas, with valuable effect. Yet the mysterious Colonel House, with whom he corresponded twice that autumn, was still unseen. Wilson's curiosity was piqued until late in November, when his strange benefactor came to New York.

On November 25, 1911, Woodrow Wilson went to New York and proceeded alone to the Hotel Gotham. A small, slight man, bald, keen-eyed, well-groomed, with a gentle voice and sympathetic manner, received him. The two men talked for an hour. Each was delighted with the other.

House conveyed to Wilson his own abiding fears of an oncoming political crisis, a possible revolution. Wilson, who shared these fears, outlined those "certain things" which he fervently wanted to do in time, and do intelligently and well. House expressed fullest accord, and promised to devote all his time, and part of his fortune, to this end.

The first hour they spent together, House recalled, laid the basis for their fast friendship. "We found ourselves in such complete sympathy" that each knew what the other was thinking without need for words. There was something almost feminine about Edward House; he seemed to listen to you with so much eagerness, to solicit your confidence; he was so ready to respond, so quick to attune himself to your mood, yet he asked nothing for himself, nothing but to please.

Wilson had so few friends that he deeply needed a *confidant* and an experienced counselor. House relates in his diary:

> A few weeks after we met and after we had exchanged confidences which men usually do not exchange except after years of friendship, I asked him if he realized that we had only known one another for so short a time. He replied, "My dear friend, we have known one another always." And I think this is true.[24]

[24] House, *op. cit.*, Vol. I, p. 45.

Edward Mandell House was born in Texas in 1858, the son of a pioneer of Dutch-English descent. His father, who had run away from England, fought in the insurrection against Mexican rule, accumulated large wealth as a merchant, and bequeathed this to his son. Educated in the East, well-traveled, widely read, Edward House with his ample means was able to become a man of leisure. He had the experience of various enterprises to be sure: the management of great cotton plantations, banking, the building of a small railroad. Then in the '90's he had removed to the state capital at Austin, built himself a fine home, and, indulging his interest in politics, had become a sort of Talleyrand of Texas.

In this field, House relates, he "began at the top." Texas was swept toward 1892 by the same Populist-agrarian uprising that in Nebraska produced a Bryan. Here political life was intense and colorful, with a Western as well as a Southern flavor. Among the picturesque leaders who came to the surface here, such as Reagan, Bailey, and Culberson, Governor James S. Hogg was the most honest, courageous, and popular, and to him Edward House attached himself closely—because he found that "the railroads and the entire corporate interests of Texas were combining to defeat him." House was always a progressive, one of his friends, T. W. Gregory, recalled. "He wanted to see advanced ideas placed upon the statute book. . . . Although rated as one of the wealthy men of Texas, he was invariably aligned on the side of the plain people and against most of those with whom he was socially intimate."

Soon House learned to foretell with uncanny accuracy the effect of certain measures or tactics; he was taken into the inner circle of politicians who organized party primaries—in that one-party state —and helped create Governors and Senators. Yet he accepted no office for himself, nor title (save that of colonel of militia). He refused usually to assume the chairmanship of campaign organizations which he directed, preferring to work behind the scenes, and "to put someone else nominally at the head, so that I could do the real work undisturbed. . . ."[25] The delicacy of House's

[25] House, *op. cit.*, Vol. I, pp. 28, 34, 31.

health may have contributed to his secretive habits. Moreover, he had no gifts as a public speaker. He effaced himself not because he was wanting in ambition, as some thought. He said once that his ambition was "so great that it has never seemed to me worth while to strive to satisfy it."

At any rate, House was held in high respect, occupied a desk in the office of several successive Governors, and helped to administer the affairs of Texas as an adviser, political manager, and informal prime minister.

At length, toward 1900, he tired of this role. He desired a place in the national councils of his party, to which his power in Texas entitled him. But Bryan was the leading man of the Democratic party, while the Rough Rider held the stage in Washington. Though House was at one time touched with Henry George's doctrines, he had no taste for Bryan's bimetallism as a panacea. At Austin he came to know Bryan well, Bryan having a ranch near by; but he judged that the Great Commoner thought his ideas "God-given," unalterable. At odds with the dominant Western leadership, Edward House bided his time, traveled, studied, even wrote a novel, while his party bore continued defeats.

But in the spring of 1910 our Talleyrand, now in early middle age, bestirred himself to enter national politics, to make a President. He had seen signs in the skies of great change. Coming East to find a brave and truthful leader, he fixed at first upon whimsical old Mayor Gaynor of New York, the foe of Tammany Hall. But wisdom bade this fine official to shun ambition, and he rejected House's advice that he stand for Governor of New York, in 1910, as a step to the Presidency. House then looked across the Hudson River toward Governor Wilson, and soon became persuaded that the former college professor was the only Eastern leader who might win the country at large by his liberalism. House admired Wilson's "political rhetoric."

Meeting Wilson confirmed his highest hopes, as he wrote home the next day. He had feared Wilson would be vain, but saw no evidence of it. ". . . I would rather play with him than any prospective candidate I have seen." Wilson would be "a man one can advise with some degree of satisfaction. This . . . you could never do with Mr. Bryan." [26]

House's essential plan, as he unfolded it, was to build a bridge running from New Jersey to Nebraska. He had therefore added his pleas to others' that Wilson separate himself from Harvey, "Wall Street's errand boy." Harvey would have resisted the plan of an alliance with Bryan to the bitter end. Wilson's loud rupture with Harvey raised his stock immensely in the West, and was providential, since it brought him at once to Bryan's favorable consideration.

At the small "Wilson Headquarters," House, when in New York, came and went softly every day. McCombs, the nervous young man officially in charge there, thought House a secretive, mousy little fellow filled with grandiose visions. He would say to McCombs, in effect: do thus—"and you and I will control the United States!" [27]

House employed himself with policy making. Noticing that Wilson's stump speeches had not stressed the tariff issue, House called on his friend Professor D. F. Houston, former president of the University of Texas, and a lifelong student of tariff questions, for aid. Houston, who was to be Secretary of Agriculture under Wilson, long remembered the ardent discussions of those campaign days. He observed how House loved the game of power, and enjoyed the sense of power, especially when wielded indirectly. He noticed that House was fairly obsessed with the possibilities of Wilson. "He [House] has a *vision*," Houston wrote of him in a private letter, December 11, 1911. "*I should like to make him Dictator for a while. . . .*" [28]

[26] Nov. 25, 1911, to S. E. Mezes; *ibid.*, Vol. I, p. 46.

[27] McCombs, *Making Woodrow Wilson President*, p. 67.

[28] Houston, *Eight Years with Wilson's Cabinet*, Vol. I, p. 21; House, *op. cit.*, Vol. I, p. 48; italics mine.

5

All those who came close to Colonel House thought that he saw visions. What were they?

Fortunately he has left us fullest evidence of his dreams and ambitions in the shape of the utopian or "tendency" novel *Philip Dru, Administrator,* which he was engaged in writing late in 1911, at the time he met Woodrow Wilson, and published anonymously in the autumn of 1912. "Would that mine enemy would write a book," the proverb runs. To House's book, little noticed at the time of its appearance, we may go to study the hopes, fears, and visions of this singular little man.

Philip Dru is the imaginary story of the coming of a great social revolution to America, set many years in the future, and of the national hero who arises to lead his people to peace, equality, and prosperity. It bears some resemblance to the contemporary work of Howells, of H. G. Wells in *The New Machiavelli,* and Jack London, save that it is by the hand of one untrained to write or organize a work of imagination. By all literary standards it is thin and mediocre stuff. Yet its political commentaries upon the Rooseveltian epoch are keen; and many of the prophecies made were to prove startlingly accurate. *Philip Dru,* in short, embodies the innermost preoccupations, the real social thought, of the reformist leaders of 1912.

Colonel House dedicated his book to the unhappy masses "who have lived and died lacking opportunity, because in the starting, the world-wide social structure was wrongly begun." For his epigraph he quotes a passage from Mazzini, in itself most revealing of the temper of House, his "soulmate" Wilson, and other would-be world saviors of the epoch.

> *No war of classes, no hostility to existing wealth, no wanton or unjust violation of the rights of property,* but a constant disposition to ameliorate the condition of the classes least favored by fortune.[29]

[29] Italics mine.

Colonel House's utopia, we perceive at once, has limits set by a bourgeois, a rentier, with real estate and liquid assets to be spared —though this is no serious reflection upon a man who used his wealth and leisure in so many original ways.

"In the year 1920 . . . ," the anonymous author opens, there were "many indications that the social, financial and industrial troubles that had vexed the United States for so long a time were about to culminate in civil war." Corporate wealth had grown too strong, the masses felt themselves "strangled," even farmers, merchants, and professional men grew "sullen and rebellious"; while all save rich capitalists and their satellites foresaw a "gloomy and hopeless future."

The hero of the romance, Philip Dru, native of Kentucky, graduates from West Point at this time and enters upon an army officer's career. Unlike his colleagues, he is a brooding, Hamletic sort of fellow; he reflects day and night upon the evils of the day, and sees the future darkly. Our civil and military institutions, to his mind, have grown debased. When not employed for petty foreign conquests, the army is used for the intimidation of the people under the guise of the "constitutional protection of property." The omens of the period remind him forcibly of those days in France when the "slumbering, chained giant" arose, struck out blindly, and destroyed a whole society. But out of that revelry of blood, one and a half centuries ago, ruminates Philip Dru, there arose hope of a more splendid day for mankind. The feudal rulers were overthrown. Throughout the Western world "one stratum of society after another demanded and obtained the right to acquire wealth and to share in the government." But then the bolder, more forceful individuals pushed on beyond all bounds. "They who had sprung from the people . . . a short life-span ago were now throttling individual effort and shackling the great movement for equal rights and equal opportunities." It was here, then, in the great republic of the West that the next battle for human liberation was to be fought and won. Then would the spirit of love and brotherhood be born and "the Star of Bethlehem . . . shine again."